FIREFOX
HACKS™

Other resources from O'Reilly

Related titles

Don't Click on the Blue E!

Test Driving Linux

Cascading Style Sheets:
   The Definitive Guide

XML Hacks

Flash Out of the Box

Linux Desktop Hacks

Knoppix Hacks

Talk Is Cheap

Windows XP Hacks

Mac OS X Panther Hacks

Hacks Series Home

hacks.oreilly.com is a community site for developers and power users of all stripes. Readers learn from each other as they share their favorite tips and tools for Mac OS X, Linux, Google, Windows XP, and more.

---

oreilly.com

oreilly.com is more than a complete catalog of O'Reilly books. You'll also find links to news, events, articles, weblogs, sample chapters, and code examples.

oreillynet.com is the essential portal for developers interested in open and emerging technologies, including new platforms, programming languages, and operating systems.

Conferences

O'Reilly brings diverse innovators together to nurture the ideas that spark revolutionary industries. We specialize in documenting the latest tools and systems, translating the innovator's knowledge into useful skills for those in the trenches. Visit *conferences.oreilly.com* for our upcoming events.

Safari Bookshelf (*safari.oreilly.com*) is the premier on-line reference library for programmers and IT professionals. Search across thousands of electronic books simultaneously and zero in on the information you need in seconds. Read the books on your Bookshelf from cover to cover or simply flip to the page you need. You can even cut and paste code and download chapters for offline viewing. Try it today with a free trial.

FIREFOX
HACKS™

Tips & Tools for Next-Generation Web Browsing

Nigel McFarlane

O'REILLY®

Beijing · Cambridge · Farnham · Köln · Paris · Sebastopol · Taipei · Tokyo

Firefox Hacks™

by Nigel McFarlane

Copyright © 2005 O'Reilly Media, Inc. All rights reserved.
Printed in the United States of America.

Published by O'Reilly Media, Inc., 1005 Gravenstein Highway North,
Sebastopol, CA 95472.

O'Reilly books may be purchased for educational, business, or sales promotional use. Online editions are also available for most titles (*safari.oreilly.com*). For more information, contact our corporate/institutional sales department: (800) 998-9938 or *corporate@oreilly.com*.

Editor:	Brian Sawyer	**Production Editor:**	Sanders Kleinfeld
Series Editor:	Rael Dornfest	**Cover Designer:**	Hanna Dyer
Executive Editor:	Dale Dougherty	**Interior Designer:**	David Futato

Printing History:

March 2005:	First Edition.

 This book uses RepKover™, a durable and flexible lay-flat binding.

ISBN: 0-596-00928-3
[C]   [5/05]

Contents

Credits ix

Preface xiii

Chapter 1. Firefox Basics 1

    INTRODUCTION *Get Oriented*   1

    1. Ten Ways to Display a Web Page   5

    2. Ten Ways to Navigate to a Web Page   11

    3. Find Stuff   14

    4. Identify and Use Toolbar Icons   19

    5. Use Keyboard Shortcuts   20

    6. Make Firefox Look Different   23

    7. Stop Once-Only Dialogs Safely   24

    8. Flush and Clear Absolutely Everything   28

    9. Make Firefox Go Fast   31

    10. Start Up from the Command Line   35

Chapter 2. Security 39

    11. Drop Miscellaneous Security Blocks   40

    12. Raise Security to Protect Dummies   44

    13. Stop All Secret Network Activity   46

    14. Work with Single Sign-On Servers   49

    15. Work with Web Proxies   54

    16. Fine-Tune Ports and Sockets   60

    17. Manage Digital Certificates   62

18. Digitally Sign Content   65

19. Grant Trust with Master Certificates   69

20. Restrict Script Behavior with Policies   72

21. Make Yourself Anonymous   74

Chapter 3. Installation 76

22. Edit Configuration Files   76

23. Play With the Preference System   80

24. Install Complementary Tools   84

25. Migrate Firefox Profiles   86

26. Dial Up Automatically on Startup   90

27. Fix Web Servers to Support Firefox Content   92

28. Prepare Firefox for Wide Deployment   95

29. Remotely Manage User Configurations   99

30. Install Fonts and Character Support   104

31. Take Firefox with You   108

32. Work with Filtering Systems   111

Chapter 4. Web Surfing Enhancements 113

33. Use Fancy Bookmarks   113

34. Modify Tabbed Browsing   117

35. Govern Image and Ad Display   121

36. Get More Search Tools   125

37. Get More Feeds and News   129

38. Add Stuff to Your Toolbars   134

39. Upgrade Firefox Feature Managers   141

40. Integrate Firefox with Other Tools   142

41. Create Your Own Search Plug-in   146

42. Spider the Web with Firefox   148

43. Waste Time with Toys and Games   153

Chapter 5. Power Tools for Web Developers 157

44. Tweak and Troubleshoot CSS Designs   157

45. Use Gecko CSS Style Magic   161

46. Write Compatible CSS   165

47. Update Browser Detection Scripts   168

48. Submit Background Form Data   171

49. Script Plug-ins   174

50. Quality-Assure Your Web Pages   176

51. Display HTTP Headers   180

52. Stomp on Cookies   182

53. Probe HTML with the DOM Inspector   185

54. Turn Off Absolutely All Caching   188

55. Web Document Debugging Tricks   191

56. Debug JavaScript with Venkman   193

57. Handle Hangs and Other Bad Juju   196

Chapter 6. Power XML for Web Pages 199

58. Pick Display Modes for HTML and XML   200

59. Get Tools for XML Validation   202

60. Mix Content with XML Namespaces   205

61. Make MathML Content   207

62. Make SVG Content   212

63. Use Client-Side XPath   215

64. Use Client-Side XSL   218

65. Work with Mozilla SOAP Services   222

66. Work with Mozilla XML-RPC Services   228

67. Work with Mozilla WSDL Services   232

68. Make Applications and Extensions with XUL   237

69. Make New Tags and Widgets with XBL   241

70. Work with RDF Facts   245

71. Work with RSS Feeds   251

72. Connect SQL to XUL   253

73. Generate XUL Using PHP Libraries   260

74. Get a Taste of E4X Scripting   262

Chapter 7. Hack the Chrome Ugly 267

75. Do Groundwork for Ugly Chrome Hacks   268

76. Spy on Chrome with the DOM Inspector   271

77. Customize Firefox's Interface   274

78. Rebadge Firefox   278

79. Make Firefox Match the Desktop   280

80. Make a Toolbar That Can't Be Hidden   283
81. Content Filter Without Your Smart Friend Noticing   286
82. Add a New XPCOM Component   290
83. Add a New Command-Line Option   294

Chapter 8. Hack the Chrome Cleanly 299
84. Do Groundwork for Extension Development   300
85. Study Packages with the Chrome Manager   303
86. Create a Chrome Package   306
87. Make a Bottom-Up Overlay   312
88. Make, Bundle, and Publish an XPI   317
89. Build an Installable Theme   323
90. Identify Reusable Toolkits   326

Chapter 9. Work More Closely with Firefox 330
91. Handle Cross-Platform Differences   330
92. Get a Custom, Prebuilt Version   333
93. Make Firefox Software   336
94. Run Multiple Mozilla Browsers   340
95. Make Extensions Work Outside Firefox   343
96. Turn on Firefox Diagnostics   346
97. Find the Right Forum for Your Issues   349
98. Survive Bugzilla   352
99. Find Out What Has Been Fixed   358
100. Help with the Future of Firefox   360

Index 365

Credits

About the Author

Nigel McFarlane (*http://www.nigelmcfarlane.com*) is the Mozilla community's regular technical commentator, focused on education, analysis, and a few narrowly scoped bugs. He works full-time on Mozilla matters, except when interrupted by other things. The core Mozilla hackers are slowly getting used to him.

Nigel writes extensively on Mozilla, Firefox, and open source, including the columns *Searching for Substance* at InformIT and *Mozilla Meanderings* for TUX. He contributes to a number of journals, including *Inside Web Development* and *Linux Journal*, numerous online publications, and to the W3C's sXBL specification.

In addition to writing, Nigel messes around with programming and waves his arms about. He sometimes consults to industry and government. He holds science degrees from the University of Melbourne and La Trobe University. He is the author of several JavaScript Web books (WROX Press) and the authoritative *Rapid Application Development with Mozilla* (Prentice Hall)—the Mozilla community's favorite text in print. Other strong points are telecommunications, data systems, and the Web. On the human side, he spends a lot of time studying the forces and processes behind open source, invention, and online communities in general.

When not welded to the computer, Nigel enjoys Melbourne, Australia, his home city. It's often named the world's most livable city, and not without reason. Outdoors there are no computers, so bushwalking, swimming, music, and city rambles are great ways to relax.

Contributors

The following people contributed their hacks, writing, and inspiration to this book:

- John Allsopp and Maxine Sherrin are Western Civilisation Pty Ltd (*http://www.westciv.com*). They are the developers of the leading cross-platform CSS editor *Style Master* and a series of highly influential web development courses. Their web site is one of the longest-standing web developer resources for CSS and web standards. Maxine and John are co-conveners of the annual Web Essentials conference. They are both long-time web standards evangelists.

- Seth Dillingham is president and lead programmer of Macrobyte Resources (*http://www.macrobyte.net*). He and his company specialize in custom development of web applications, such as the popular Conversant (*http://www.free-conversant.com*) groupware and content management system. On those seemingly rare occasions that he steps out of his office, Seth can be found cycling around southern Connecticut or spending time with his lovely wife, Corinne.

- Ben Karel is surprised that you're bothering to read the contributor's bio section. Ben learned the Firefox ropes as a side effect of contributing an improbably large amount of time to the Adblock extension (*http://adblock.mozdev.org/*). He believes that open source software such as Firefox has a wholly unique potential to change the world. Entirely Too Much Information about Ben is available at *http://eschew.org*.

- Brian King has been involved in the Mozilla community since 1999. In that time, he has worked on both free and for-profit software built on top of the Mozilla Application Platform. He is one of the core site admins at *http://www.mozdev.org*, a community site for hosting Mozilla-based projects and for promoting Mozilla technologies. Brian is COO of Mozdev Group, Inc., a Mozilla services and software company.

- Tomáš Marek is a J2EE developer, Mozilla Links Newsletter translator (*http://newsletter.mozdev.org/intro/*), Mozilla evangelist, and an occasional contributor to open source web software. He lives in Beroun in the Czech Republic.

- Roger B. Sidje is mostly known in Mozilla and W3C circles for his work that enabled the display of mathematical documents on the Web through MathML, which is vital for educators, students and researchers. Born in Cameroon, Africa, he moved to France to undertake a PhD on the numerical solution of Markov chains. After that, he headed to

Australia for a position at the University of Queensland in the mathematics department. He works for the Advanced Computational Modelling Centre, where he develops other interests typical of academics.

- Neil Stansbury is the lead engineer for Redback Systems (*http://www.redbacksystems.com*). Living in London, England, he is the principal designer of the cross-platform Mozilla-based client for Novell's GroupWise product.

- Keith M. Swartz is an Enterprise Software Architect at Oracle Corporation, where he has worked for more than 11 years. He has provided support, development, and product management for the E-Business Suite Technology Group and has co-authored and contributed to several books on Oracle products. When not evangelizing the division's future technology directions, he is usually found nagging his senior management to switch to Mozilla and Firefox. He currently resides in Seattle, Washington, with his wonderful wife, Erin, and their cat, Gwen.

- James Vulling (*jrv@rockridge.net.au*), a software engineering graduate, consults in the architecture, development, and maintenance of enterprise scale web applications. The use of XSL in this environment has helped speed up the product development cycle immensely. Away from work, James enjoys home theatre, music and basketball.

Acknowledgments

My thanks to all the contributors to this book, who are a talented bunch and patiently nonjudgmental in the face of ridiculous deadlines. Thank you for your enthusiasm and support. Thanks also to Brian Sawyer, editor extraordinaire, for tolerating me and for deadly precision in email.

Preface

Welcome to *Firefox Hacks*, the book about the browser. Firefox is the web browser that upholds the highest principles of the World Wide Web. It supports and defines the Web as a good place to be—a place where all people can freely and safely participate, without having to tip their hat to anyone. Those are fighting words.

The Firefox product is made by the nonprofit Mozilla Foundation and its legion of helpers. Firefox is *open source* software: software that is free and fully exposed to independent scrutiny. Firefox is a poster-child of the open source trend and the one of the first open source products that average computer users try. If you find yourself liking Firefox, then open source has worked for you.

Firefox is more than just a TV screen for the Web, though. It contains extra technical goodies of all kinds. Whether you're a crusty hacker, a bored web surfer, a contemporary designer, or a frustrated IT professional, Firefox has features to offer you that will make your life easier and more ornamented. Hacking Firefox to meet your needs is what this book is all about.

Why Firefox Hacks?

The term *hacking* has a bad reputation in the press. They use it to refer to someone who breaks into systems or wreaks havoc with computers as their weapon. Among people who write code, though, the term *hack* refers to a "quick-and-dirty" solution to a problem, or a clever way to get something done. And the term *hacker* is taken very much as a compliment, referring to someone as being *creative*, having the technical chops to get things done. The Hacks series is an attempt to reclaim the word, document the good ways people are hacking, and pass the hacker ethic of creative participation on to the uninitiated. Seeing how others approach systems and problems is often the quickest way to learn about a new technology.

The Firefox web browser is built on the extensive and comprehensive engineering effort that is the Mozilla Project. Although the web browser's primary task is to display web pages, it is in fact a remarkably flexible, configurable, and complex environment. It is this broader view of Firefox that leads to many fruitful hacking opportunities. You need not accept Firefox exactly as it is without compromise. There is much you can do to tweak the browser to make working with the Web more pleasant, creative, and time-efficient. Feel free to hack Firefox.

How to Use This Book

You can read this book from cover to cover if you like, but each hack stands on its own, so feel free to browse and jump to the different sections that interest you most. If there's a prerequisite you need to know about, a cross-reference will guide you to the right hack.

Like most books, you can, if you want, start at the front and end at the back. If you know nothing about Firefox at all, the earliest material will ease you into the technology. If you're a hacker *extraordinaire*, then leap to the last few chapters where the hard stuff is. Overall, this book has something for everyone, so start with the chapter that's aimed at your particular needs first.

How This Book Is Organized

Firefox Hacks is divided into nine chapters, organized by subject:

Chapter 1, *Firefox Basics*
> This chapter covers beginner end-user features, without attempting to reproduce the Firefox Help system. It's a brief tour of the browser from a number of different user perspectives.

Chapter 2, *Security*
> This chapter covers the security arrangements that affect how Firefox interacts with the Web. It describes how to raise and lower security in a number of different ways.

Chapter 3, *Installation*
> This chapter explains how to install Firefox your way, rather than the standard way. It provides installation tactics suitable for a number of lifestyles and organizational settings.

Chapter 4, *Web Surfing Enhancements*
> This chapter explains how to make Firefox work harder for you as an information-gathering tool.

Chapter 5, *Power Tools for Web Developers*
This chapter examines Firefox as a testing and development tool for web page design. Web developers love Firefox.

Chapter 6, *Power XML for Web Pages*
This chapter is for more advanced web application projects, where programming or medium-weight XML technology is needed. It describes how to connect content to XML standards and code.

Chapter 7, *Hack the Chrome Ugly*
This chapter looks under the hood of the Firefox installation and finds that with only a drop of programming energy, you can make major changes to the browser.

Chapter 8, *Hack the Chrome Cleanly*
This chapter explains how to properly prepare fancy Firefox enhancements, such as extensions and themes.

Chapter 9, *Work More Closely with Firefox*
Firefox is a complex tool and a building block of the Web. If you hope to modify that building block to suit yourself, then you'll need help getting started. This chapter describes how to connect to the core technology and the people already involved in its development.

Conventions Used in This Book

The following is a list of the typographical conventions used in this book:

Italics
Used to indicate URLs, filenames, filename extensions, and directory/folder names. For example, a path in the filesystem will be written in the form */Developer/Applications*. Italics is also used to introduce new concepts and terms.

`Constant width`
Used to indicate code examples, the contents of files, and console output, as well as the names of variables, commands, and other code excerpts.

`Constant width bold`
Used to show user input in code and to highlight portions of code, typically new additions to old code.

`Constant width italic`
Used in code examples and tables to show sample text to be replaced with your own values.

Color
The second color is used to indicate a cross-reference within the text.

You should pay special attention to notes set apart from the text with the following icons:

 This is a tip, suggestion, or general note. It contains useful supplementary information about the topic at hand.

 This is a warning or note of caution, often indicating that your money or your privacy might be at risk.

The thermometer icons, found next to each hack, indicate the relative complexity of the hack:

 beginner   moderate   expert

Using Code Examples

This book is here to help you get your job done. In general, you may use the code in this book in your programs and documentation. You do not need to contact us for permission unless you're reproducing a significant portion of the code. For example, writing a program that uses several chunks of code from this book does not require permission. Selling or distributing a CD-ROM of examples from O'Reilly books *does* require permission. Answering a question by citing this book and quoting example code does not require permission. Incorporating a significant amount of example code from this book into your product's documentation *does* require permission.

We appreciate, but do not require, attribution. An attribution usually includes the title, author, publisher, and ISBN. For example: "*Firefox Hacks* by Nigel McFarlane. Copyright 2005 O'Reilly Media, Inc., 0-596-00928-3."

If you feel your use of code examples falls outside fair use or the permission given above, feel free to contact us at *permissions@oreilly.com*.

Safari® Enabled

 When you see a Safari® Enabled icon on the cover of your favorite technology book, that means the book is available online through the O'Reilly Network Safari Bookshelf.

Safari offers a solution that's better than e-books. It's a virtual library that lets you easily search thousands of top tech books, cut and paste code samples, download chapters, and find quick answers when you need the most accurate, current information. Try it for free at *http://safari.oreilly.com*.

How to Contact Us

We have tested and verified the information in this book to the best of our ability, but you may find that features have changed (or even that we have made mistakes!). As a reader of this book, you can help us to improve future editions by sending us your feedback. Please let us know about any errors, inaccuracies, bugs, misleading or confusing statements, and typos that you find anywhere in this book.

Please also let us know what we can do to make this book more useful to you. We take your comments seriously and will try to incorporate reasonable suggestions into future editions. You can write to us at:

O'Reilly Media, Inc.
1005 Gravenstein Hwy N.
Sebastopol, CA 95472
(800) 998-9938 (in the U.S. or Canada)
(707) 829-0515 (international/local)
(707) 829-0104 (fax)

To ask technical questions or to comment on the book, send email to:

bookquestions@oreilly.com

The web site for *Firefox Hacks* lists examples, errata, and plans for future editions. You can find this page at:

http://www.oreilly.com/catalog/firefoxhks

For more information about this book and others, see the O'Reilly web site:

http://www.oreilly.com

Got a Hack?

To explore Hacks books online or to contribute a hack for future titles, visit:

http://hacks.oreilly.com

Firefox Basics
Hacks 1–10

Firefox is a software application for interacting with the Web. This chapter gets you up and running with Firefox. You probably know how to surf the Web already. This chapter is a sort of boot camp for the Firefox user interface. You'll learn where all the basic knobs and levers are. You'll also see many interesting nook and crannies. There are no significant programming tasks in this chapter; it's all just learning to fly.

Get Oriented

Before starting our journey, there are a few things you need to know: how to find Firefox files, how to install an extension, and how to set a preference. You don't need this information to read a web page, but it's vital for most of the hacks in this book.

Finding Firefox Files After Installation

After installation, Firefox puts its files in two important directories. The first is the *install area*, also known as the *application area*, which gets the general-purpose bits, such as the Firefox programs themselves. The second is the *profile area*, which gets user-specific information, such as bookmarks. Table 1-1 lists the default locations of these two areas on different operating systems.

Table 1-1. Default locations for Firefox installation and profiles

Operating system	Default install area	Default profile area
Single-user Windows 95/98/Me	C:\Program Files\Mozilla Firefox	C:\Windows\Application Data\Mozilla\Firefox
Multi-user Windows 95/98/Me	C:\Program Files\Mozilla Firefox	C:\Windows\Profiles\%USERNAME%\Application data\Mozilla\Firefox

Table 1-1. Default locations for Firefox installation and profiles (continued)

Operating system	Default install area	Default profile area
Windows NT 4.x	*C:\Winnt\Program Files\Mozilla Firefox*	*C:\Winnt\Profiles\%USERNAME%\ Application Data\Mozilla\Firefox*
Windows 2000 and XP	*C:\Program Files\Mozilla Firefox*	*C:\Documents and Settings\ %USERNAME%\Application Data\ Mozilla\Firefox*
UNIX and Linux	*/usr/bin/firefox, /usr/lib/firefox* (or a custom location)	*~/.mozilla/firefox*
Mac OS X	*~/Desktop/Firefox.app/Con- tents/MacOS/* (if installed on the desktop)	*~/Library/Application Support/ Firefox*

Feel free to have a (careful) look around in these directories.

Installing an Extension

Extensions are small enhancements to Firefox that are added optionally and separately to the main browser install. Just as plug-ins, such as Apple's QuickTime, enhance the display of web pages with special content, extensions enhance the display of Firefox's user interface with extra commands and extra windows. You install an extension when you need an extra feature.

You can install extensions from the official *http://update.mozilla.org* web site or from any web site that offers a *.xpi* file. Such files almost always hold one extension each.

If you choose to install an extension, you are acting like a power user rather than a beginner, so you have to use your judgment to decide what extensions will be useful to you. It's no use complaining that Firefox is too complicated if you have 10 or 20 extensions installed. Just remove them and resimplify your life.

Installing from update.mozilla.org. The Advanced Search Button extension (found in the Search Tools category at *http://update.mozilla.org*) is a harmless extension to experiment with. Here's how to get it.

After browsing to it on the update site, click on the matching install link. Sometimes there's a brief pause, and then Firefox presents an acknowledgement window. After another brief pause, Firefox enables the buttons in that window, asking you whether to proceed. In this case, go ahead.

At this point, most extensions are still *unsigned*, just as the dialog box reports. Although the update site has excellent trust credentials, the extension itself has no signature. Extensions have some credentials, though, because they've been through some checks before the update site makes them available. Ultimately, though, it's up to you to believe whether the update site and the extension provider are persons of goodwill. This is true for any download.

Once the user agrees, Firefox downloads and installs the extension. If you choose Tools → Extensions, you'll see it there in the list, but disabled and unusable (click on it and everything is grayed out). Shut down Firefox completely and start it up again. Again, look under Tools → Extensions. You'll see that the extension is now enabled and ready to use.

The sample extension, Advanced Search Button, doesn't change the Firefox user interface much at all. All it does is offer you a new toolbar icon. Choose View → Toolbars → Customize... to see the list of icons available. Scroll down and you'll see there's a new ASB icon there. Drag it to the navigation toolbar with the mouse. Finally, close the icon window. You can now click on the ASB button or the small triangle next to it. If you put a word in the search box and click the ASB button, the Advanced Search Button extension will search for that word in the currently displayed page.

Installing from elsewhere. By default, the Mozilla Update site (*update.mozilla.org*) is the only trusted web site for extensions. If you attempt to install an extension from another web site, Firefox will complain and ask you to provide extra permission. The complaint appears as a yellow information bar at the top of the page. Figure 1-1 shows this complaint for the version of the EditCSS extension that is available at *http://editcss.mozdev.org*.

If you click the Edit Options... button, a dialog box appears (shown in Figure 1-2), where you can add the web site to a whitelist of trusted sites. That has to be done at your discretion.

If the web site is added and the dialog box acknowledged, you're then sent back to the extension installation page. You have to click the extension's link a second time to restart the installation process, with trust now in place. From here, installation proceeds as explained for the Mozilla Update case.

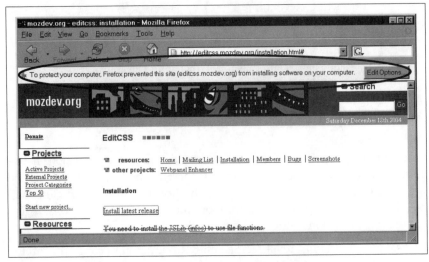

Figure 1-1. Extension warning info bar for untrusted windows

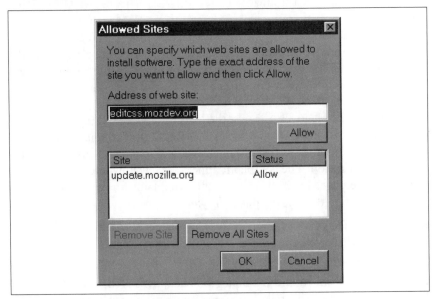

Figure 1-2. Extension web site whitelist dialog box

Setting a Preference with about:config

A *preference* is a user choice that affects how Firefox runs. Firefox has hundreds of preferences. The Firefox Options Dialog box, under Tools → Options (Windows), Edit → Preferences (Unix/Linux), or Firefox → Preferences (Macintosh) is the way to set common preferences. In general, though, the page shown by the special *about:config* URL can be used to set *any* preference. This process is described in detail in "Play With the Preference System" [Hack #23], but you need that information early. Here's a sneak peek.

All you really need to know is that if you right-click (Command-click on a Mac) in the list of preferences, you can change the preference under the mouse or add a new one. To change an existing preference, choose one of the following items from the context menu:

Modify
Enter a new preference value.

Toggle
Change true to false or false to true.

Reset
Remove any change made to the standard value.

To add a new preference, choose the New context menu option and follow these guidelines:

- Choose the type of information the preference must hold. Use Integer for numbers and Boolean for preferences that are true or false. Otherwise, use String.

- Fill in the preference name and value in the small windows that appear. Type carefully, because there is no syntax checking.

After setting the preference, it appears in bold (unless you reset it). The *about:config* list is sorted alphabetically, so you might have to scroll a bit to see what you've added. Preference changes take effect immediately in most cases.

That's all the warm-up you need. Now, let's hack.

HACK #1 Ten Ways to Display a Web Page

Displaying a web page is like painting and hanging a picture: there are plenty of options.

Web pages that display only one way are called *printouts*. Firefox lets you display and view the content of a web page in a number of different ways. You also get to choose decorations for your windows. This hack shows 10 different ways you can display web content in Firefox.

Normal Browser Window

By default, web pages appear inside a frame with a menu bar and toolbars above and a status bar below. Those bars provide user control and feedback.

The whole browser window is a single XML document written in Mozilla's XUL dialect of XML. The web page appears inside an XUL <iframe>. Scripts running inside the web page can't reach out into XUL, so those bars are mostly untouchable. Most bars can be disabled from the View menu. Figure 1-3 shows a normal Firefox window with the sidebar made visible.

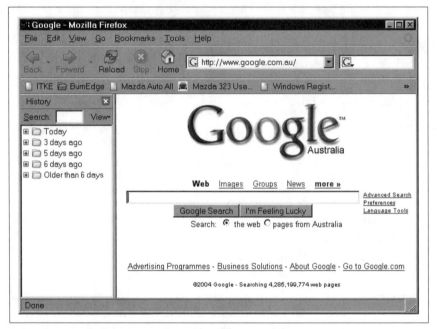

Figure 1-3. Firefox browser window with sidebar

Source Code Window

The source code window is for web developers and hackers only. Choose View → Page Source or press Ctrl-U to display the source code for the current page. If the page is a <frameset> page, you see only the frameset definition. You can change line-wrap and syntax-coloring options from the View menu in the new window.

window.open( )

Web pages can contain logic that opens other windows (usually pop ups). Web designers typically do so with the infamous window.open( ) scripting feature. (Technically, this is a DOM 0 browser feature available from JavaScript only.) These new windows can be opened with specific menu bars and toolbars disabled. Security hobbles prevent some uses of this feature.

If you mitigate security restrictions, then everything is possible. See *Rapid Application Development with Mozilla* by Nigel McFarlane (Prentice Hall PTR) for a more detailed treatment of Mozilla and Firefox's window.open( ) options. See *JavaScript: The Definitive Guide* by David Flanagan (O'Reilly) or any good scripting web site, such as Internet Related Technologies (*http://www.irt.org*), for the features of window.open( ) that are supported by all browsers.

Full Screen or Kiosk Mode

You can expand a web page window to fill your entire screen.

 Viewing the page in Full Screen mode won't help with readability. For that, you also need to increase the text size using the View → Text Size → Increase menu option.

You can take up all the screen real estate several different ways. The simplest is to click the operating system's Maximize button on the titlebar. This method, however, retains all toolbars and the titlebar. To get more space, press F11 (or choose View → Full Screen) for Full Screen mode, which removes nearly all bars. To get rid of the location toolbar as well, hide it using the View → Toolbars menu before pressing F11. Press F11 again to toggle back to normal. Figure 1-4 shows a web page viewed in Firefox's Full Screen mode.

For a robust kiosk mode (full screen with no other display options) that has most Firefox keyboard and mouse commands disabled, you need to *hack the chrome ugly*, as described in Chapter 7. You can't start kiosk mode from the command line. You can start it with a window.open( ) call from a secure web page. The following feature string is suitable for a display that's 1024x768 pixels in size:

```
"chrome,modal,resizable=false,alwaysRaised=true,width=1024,height=768"
```

The alternative to window.open( ) is intermediate scripting of Mozilla's XPCOM components using the chrome system.

Chrome-Free Windows

You can display an HTML or XHTML page free of any browser baggage. To do so, you need access to a command line, such as a DOS Box or cmd box under Windows, or a terminal emulator window (like xterm) under Unix/Linux.

Figure 1-4. A browser window in Full Screen mode

On Windows, you need to follow these preparatory steps. Start a DOS Box from the Start menu, usually via Start → Programs → MS-DOS Prompt. Then move to the Firefox install area with these commands:

```
C:
cd "Program Files"
cd Firefox
```

Next, on all operating systems, just invoke Firefox with the required web page like this:

```
firefox -chrome URL
```

The equivalent window.open( ) feature string is "chrome".

Print Preview

Before printing your page, you can see what it will look like. Firefox prepares pages for printing using Cascading Style Sheets (CSS) styles. To see a preview, choose File → Print Preview and play with the toolbar. Firefox thinks briefly before displaying the preview.

User-Customized

Firefox support for CSS is designed to give the user control of page appearance. If you know CSS, you can exploit the following two files in Firefox:

userContent.css
> For styles that affect the appearance of CSS-styled pages that appear in a normal browser window. These styles work on HTML, XHTML, MathML, and CSS-styled generic XML documents.

userChrome.css
> For styles that affect the appearance of the Firefox chrome. That includes the toolbars, scrollbars, dialog boxes, menu bars, context menus, and other stuff that Firefox drapes around the displayed page. Since these styles are written using Mozilla's XUL tag set, *userChrome.css* provides styling for all Firefox XUL content.

For Microsoft Windows, there are some sample files called *userChrome-example.css* and *userContent-example.css* included in the Firefox install. They're buried deep inside the profile area. For all platforms, it's best to experiment with harmless styling changes (such as color changes) before proceeding to complex modifications of these files.

Once constructed, these files should be put in the *chrome* directory of your Firefox profile. Restart Firefox to see any and all effects. Don't forget to use the CSS imperative !important if you want to guarantee that your styles will override any others at work.

You can make small, generic modifications to suit all of your web browsing, or you can build a custom skin for a web site that you visit frequently. For the latter case, you need Firefox 1.1. You can then write web-site-specific CSS styles using this Firefox-specific syntax:

```
/* one page */
@-moz-document url(http://www.example.com) { color : red; }

/* all sub-pages with this URL as stem */
@-moz-document url-prefix(http://www.irt.org/articles/) { color : red; }

/* all pages at this domain */
@-moz-document domain(mozilla.org) { color : red; }
```

DOM Hierarchy

For HTML and all XML dialects supported by Mozilla, you can deconstruct a given web document into its pieces. These pieces appear as a sideways tree of tags and tag content. The resulting display is much like that of the Windows Explorer or the Macintosh Finder. Technically, the contents of the tree are W3C DOM nodes. That means tags and tag content.

To see this tree, you need to start the DOM Inspector by navigating to Tools → DOM Inspector. The DOM Inspector is an *extension* (an added feature) that comes as a bonus with the standard Firefox install. Initially, the DOM Inspector displays the web page of the window from which you started the Inspector. To view any other page, just type a URL into the top text field and click Inspect at the right. The new page appears below. In all cases, in the main pane on the left, you can drill down through the document, revealing its structure. "Probe HTML with the DOM Inspector" [Hack #53] and "Spy on Chrome with the DOM Inspector" [Hack #76] describe use of that tool.

Debug-Enabled

A web page can be displayed so that it is managed by a script-debugging tool. This is a feature designed for programmers. To use this display, install the JavaScript Debugger extension.

To add the JavaScript Debugger, go to Tools → Extensions. In the resulting dialog box, click Get More Extensions. That opens up a web page at the central Mozilla Update web site (*http://update.mozilla.org*). In that new web page window, you can shop for free extensions. Click the category Developer Tools, scroll down to JavaScript Debugger and click on the install link. Follow the bouncing prompts, and when that is all done, restart Firefox.

If you want the debugger to appear automatically when a given page loads, just put this tiny bit of JavaScript anywhere in the page content:

```
<script type="application/x-javascript">
  debugger;
</script>
```

Chapter 5 provides many techniques for debugging Firefox, including use of this debugger [Hack #56].

Splash Screens

You can display a web page as a *splash screen*, but this is a harder effect to produce than the others and requires intermediate Web programming. A splash screen appears when a program first starts up and usually contains brand information. For example, the Mozilla Application Suite, which preceded Firefox, has a splash screen. Setup of a splash screen requires some hacking of the chrome files [Chapter 7] or of security arrangements [Chapter 2], so explore those subjects first. It also requires scripting. To make such a splash screen appear, use this feature string in a window.open( ) call from JavaScript:

```
"chrome,centerscreen=true,height=200,width=150,titlebar=false"
```

These options are available only if all security is lifted (e.g., from inside the chrome or from a signed and accepted URL). A similar hack for ordinary browser windows is to calculate window size from the `window.screen.x` and `window.screen.y` properties and then use a feature string like this:

```
"toolbar=no,location=no,personalbar=no,status=no,menubar=no,scrollbars=no,
top=225,left=300,height=200,width=150"
```

This alternative does not remove the titlebar or work around the Popup Manager. It is not guaranteed to remove the status bar either. Once you move into the world of Mozilla programming, many other page display options are possible, but that's a more complex matter than quick hacks. Splash screens provide more than enough complexity for an introductory chapter like this.

Ten Ways to Navigate to a Web Page

#2 There are a million ways to move from the current web page to the next one. This hack describes 10 such ways.

Here's how to surf, Firefox style. Chapter 4 covers many ways to use extensions to increase the pleasure and convenience of surfing the Web. This hack explains what Firefox can do without modification.

Click on a Link

It's not rocket science: left-click on a link, and the current page is replaced with the link's page. If you right-click (Command-click on the Mac), you can open that new page in a new window or a new tab, or you can put the link itself into a bookmark or into the copy-and-paste buffer.

Click on a Bookmark Icon

Click any bookmark or bookmark menu item on the Bookmarks toolbar, and you're off to the link that bookmark represents. Bookmarks are complex little beasties, though. See "Find Stuff" [Hack #3] for a way to get through your many bookmarks. See "Use Fancy Bookmarks" [Hack #33] if you want to become a bookmark power user.

Put Something in the Location Bar

You can type all kinds of things into the Location bar where the URL of the current page is displayed. If you start typing a URL, Firefox will autocomplete it, providing you with a drop-down list of candidates. Firefox can even complete an unknown URL for you if you press the right combination of Control, Shift, and Enter keys. Press Enter or click the Location bar icon to start the page fetch.

Pick Something from Your History

There are many history mechanisms beyond the big Forward and Back buttons. See "Find Stuff" [Hack #3] for an introduction to Firefox's history features.

Copy and Paste

The standard Xerox PARC/Apple Macintosh cut, copy, and paste keyboard combinations are available in Firefox. They are Ctrl-X, Ctrl-C, and Ctrl-V, respectively. You can copy a URL from a non-Firefox application and paste it into the Location bar. (You can give that bar's input field the focus by clicking on it.) You can also copy a link's URL by calling up the context menu with the mouse. You can copy and paste that URL within Firefox or into another application.

Under Linux, if you use a multislot copy-and-paste buffer tool, you can stick as many URLs into that set of clipboards as you want. To copy URLs from a terminal emulator window under Linux, such as xterm or gnome-terminal, just highlight the text. There's no need to explicitly choose Copy in this case. Paste into Firefox as you normally would.

Caret Browsing

For people with poor sight and for those that prefer a word-processing interface, a normal Firefox window can be made *caret-enabled*. The caret symbol is the blinking vertical bar that suggests an insertion point: |. Press F7 to turn it on or off. While it's on, you can navigate around the document using the arrow keys or with the assistance of a screen reader that relies on the caret. Just press Enter when the caret is over a link. You can't edit anything at the caret unless it moves into a text field.

Drag and Drop

Firefox allows you to drag URLs around the main window. You can drag bookmarks from the Bookmarks toolbar to the location bar for opening or drag links in a displayed HTML page to the Bookmark or Location toolbars.

You can also drag plain text to the Location bar. To do so, first display a web page that has a URL stated in plain text, not just embedded in a link. The text might literally say http://www.yahoo.com. Highlight the text by left-clicking and dragging across it until it's all selected. Release the mouse button, and then drag the highlighted text onto the input field in the Location toolbar. The highlighted text appears in that text field when you release the mouse, ready to be retrieved from the Web. You can do this trick with non-URL text as well, but that makes sense only if you have keyword bookmarks set up [Hack #33].

Use the Menu Bar

Lots of web pages and web sites are hidden behind Firefox's menu system. The Go and Bookmarks menus provide immediate access to recent pages. The various File → Open options let you type in something useful. The Help menu options all provide locally stored web pages. The Tools menu leads to a set of dialog boxes and windows that let you interact with Mozilla's support sites for themes, extensions, and plug-ins. Finally, there are a few hidden Easter eggs to discover. Technically, they're not Easter eggs, because they're well documented diagnostics that are important for web developers and other technical people. Try typing these URLs, just for starters:

```
about:buildconfig
about:cache
about:plugins
```

Switch Between Windows and Tabs

When you already have many pages displayed, it's easy to toggle between them. You can cycle between whole windows with standard operating system features, such as Alt-Tab on Windows or panels under X11 on Unix. If you have activated tabbed browsing and several tabs appear in the current window, then just press Ctrl-Tab to cycle between them.

Use Accessibility Devices

Firefox's accessibility to disabled people is improving all the time. Part of accessibility depends on web pages being correctly designed. If the correct design is in place, then accessibility depends on the features of the browser. Firefox provides basic accessibility options via the Alt and Tab keys (on Microsoft Windows). Once Alt is pressed, it's possible to navigate the menu system using a simple and limited range of keystrokes (the arrow keys). Once Tab is pressed, it's possible to navigate all the input widgets on the browser and in the currently displayed page. Both provide such simple access to the menu system and web forms that the disabled surfer doesn't need to use a complex device like a mouse or even a keyboard.

Find Stuff

Search both the Web and the browser environment with Firefox.

This hack explains how to find the stuff you've forgotten, left behind, or yet to discover. It starts with local information in the browser and works its way out to searching the furthest corners of the Web.

Search a Displayed Web Page

You can search the content of a displayed web page. To do so, Firefox provides the Find toolbar. It appears at the bottom of the browser window, above the status bar. Figure 1-5 shows most of the features.

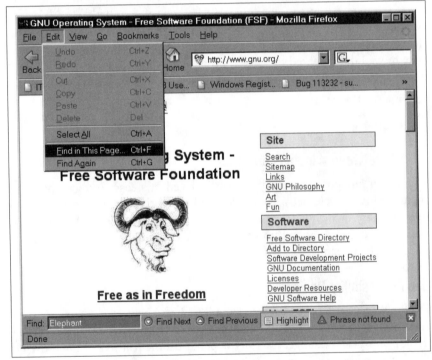

Figure 1-5. The Find toolbar and associated menu items

This toolbar is activated by the Edit → Find or Edit → Find Again menu options or by the Ctrl-F (Command-F on the Mac), Ctrl-G (Command-G on the Mac), or Shift-F3 hotkeys. Here's a rundown of how it works:

1. The Find toolbar starts out disabled but gains the focus and the caret in the toolbar text field when you click on it.

2. Type a string and Firefox automatically begins searching the current page, starting from the page's focused form field, or from the top of the page if no field is selected.

3. Firefox searches all frames but not all tabs. A security feature terminates searching if the page is too big to search in five seconds.

4. If nothing is found, the textbox goes red. "Phrase not found" appears, and a sound is issued.

5. If something is found, you can navigate between items with toolbar arrows or Ctrl-G (Command-G on Mac) and Shift-F3.

6. You can highlight found items with the Highlight toggle button.

7. Press Ctrl-F (Command-F on Mac) again and the current search string is selected for replacement. Dismiss the toolbar by clicking the small cross icon located at its right end.

The Find toolbar contains two searches in one. The default search is the one just described, called *Find As You Type*. It can also be activated with the forward slash (/) key, or if there's nothing focused on the current page and you just start typing. The other kind of search is called *Find Links As You Type*. It can be activated with the single quote key ('). This alternate search scans only hyperlink text on the page. Use it to find specific links on big pages crowded with links.

Search Web Page Source

You can also search the source code of a web page, something that was never possible in old Netscape browsers. View the page's source by choosing View → Page Source or with the Ctrl-U (Command-U) hotkey. A new window appears. That window has an Edit menu with the options Find (Ctrl-F or Command-F), Find Again (Ctrl-G or Command-G) and Go to Line (Ctrl-L or Command-L). Choose any of these and a small dialog box appears to control your search. Figure 1-6 shows most of the available features.

This searching system doesn't use a Find toolbar, but it's similar. It supports full content searching only and doesn't support link searching. It does, however, support case-sensitive searches.

Search Your History

There are several ways to search your surfing history. Figure 1-7 maps out these features.

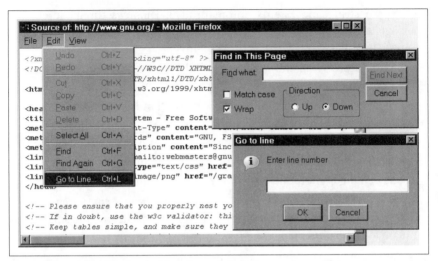

Figure 1-6. Find system for the View Source window

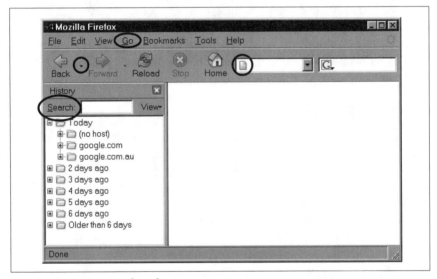

Figure 1-7. History searching features

The most accurate search uses the Back and Forward buttons. Press the small, black down-arrow grippies that sit to the right of these icons. A dropdown list of the *web trail* for the current window appears. If you ever surfed up a blind alley, then reversed, and went forward in a different direction, the set of blind alley pages is lost from the web trail. Full URLs, form data, and scrolled position are all otherwise preserved.

For another way to search, try the Go menu. It shows the most recently viewed URLs across all windows' *session history*. Only remote web pages are shown. Form posts and page scroll positions aren't preserved. As you view more pages, older items are pushed off this menu. To increase the size of the session history, modify this preference [Hack #23]:

```
browser.session_history.max_entries /* 50 is default */
```

The History sidebar, displayed with View → Sidebar → History (Ctrl-H or Command-H), provides the broadest search. It records your *global history* (all the web pages examined in the last nine days). It searches the *titles* of those pages only—no title content, no match. Delete the search string to see the day-wise hierarchy of pages again. Hack these preferences to change the defaults:

```
browser.history_expire_days /* 9 is the default */
browser.history.grouping    /* "none", "day" or "site" */
```

Finally, the Location bar can be used to search recently visited web sites in your global history. Type any string into the location bar and suggested *domain name* matches automatically appear in a drop-down list below the text box. This is called *auto-complete*. You can't search for path-specific bits of a URL until you've got the whole domain name (e.g., *http://www.yahoo. com*) right.

Search Your Bookmarks

Are you overflowing with bookmarks and can't remember any of them? Open the Bookmark Manager using Bookmarks → Manage Bookmarks... and type something into the search window. This search examines the full URLs of all bookmarks and their descriptions. The descriptions usually match web page titles, unless you changed the titles when storing the bookmarks. You can also sort the Bookmark Manager's view of your bookmarks from the View menu, which might be helpful. It's almost a *depth-first tree sort*, though, which is a sophisticated sort. It takes a bit of getting used to. Try it.

Search for Lost Logins

Typed your username and password into a web site and then forgot what they were? Firefox can help. Choose Tools → Options to bring up the Options dialog box. On Unix/Linux, it's under Edit → Preferences. On Macintosh it's under Options in the Application menu. Click the Privacy icon. Note the Saved Form Information and Saved Passwords items. Click each one's *expando* (the small plus icon) in turn. Turn on the various options by clicking their corresponding checkboxes, as shown in Figure 1-8.

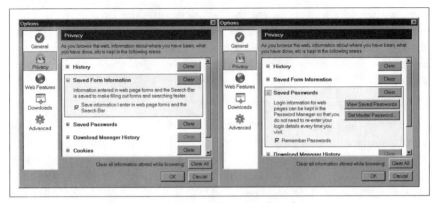

Figure 1-8. Options preferences for form and password tracking

Visit a web page with a form containing at least one text box, fill it in, and submit. Google's home page (*http://www.google.com*) is a good choice. Open a new Firefox window. Visit the page again. Left-click on the textbox twice. A drop-down menu appears, showing you the value you just typed. Pick the one you want.

Alternatively, visit a web page requiring a login. I log in at *http://bugzilla. mozilla.org* a lot (follow the login link). Use Firefox's form completion to enter your username, and Password Manager automatically adds the password. Just click the Login button and you're in.

Later on, you can review what you've saved. Back in the Options dialog box, under Privacy → Saved Passwords, click the View Saved Passwords button. In the resulting dialog box, click Show Passwords and Yes. Your passwords appear in plain text as an additional table column. Found them!

Search the Web

The Navigation toolbar includes a Search field on the extreme right. It uses the Google search engine by default. Type a keyword into the field and press Enter. Google replaces the current page with its search results. Alternatively, click on the small Google icon to see the other search engines installed by default; you can use any of them as well. Empty the Search field again and type a common letter, such as *a*. The Search box drops down a list of keywords starting with *a* that you've typed before.

Search for Firefox Preferences

Firefox has lots of preferences. Type in the URL about:config to see many (but not all) of them. There are too many to understand all at once. Type anything into the textbox labeled Filter: to restrict the list to the ones you care about (try typing go). The set of preferences is marginally different between Linux and Windows, but 99 percent of Firefox preferences apply to all platforms.

HACK #4 Identify and Use Toolbar Icons

This hack explains the mystery icons that sometimes appear on Firefox toolbars.

It's up to you whether you take advice or not. Firefox delivers a number of passive warnings and cautions to you in the various toolbars of the browser window. Here's a rundown of what those things mean.

> If you choose one of the many themes offered by Firefox's Theme Manager, then all the icons will likely appear different. Their locations will be the same, though.

This hack describes only the Firefox-specific icons that are different from standard browser icons:

- This is the standard icon for a Mozilla Extension, Plugin, or Theme. Extensions are small add-on pieces of logic (or whole applications) that can be run or used as part of general web activity. If you have installed one or more extensions into Firefox, then something is going to work differently from the default behavior.

- This icon sometimes appears at the bottom-right edge of the status bar. It tells you that the web page you're looking at has an RSS feed that complements its normal HTML content. You can hover your cursor over the icon to see the status of the feed. Click on the icon to capture the feed as a set of Firefox Live Bookmarks [Hack #33]. See *http://www.mozillazine.org* for an example.

- This icon sometimes appears at the bottom-right edge of the status bar. It tells you that the web page you're looking at has alternate stylesheets. You can apply any of the stylesheets provided by clicking on the icon.

- This icon sometimes appears at the bottom-right edge of the status bar. It tells you that the web page you're looking at has blocked a pop up. Click on the icon to see details of the page blocked, or to alter pop-up-blocking settings.

One of these three icons sometimes appears in the top-right corner of the menu bar. They indicate that there is an update (a patch or new release) for Firefox or for one of the extensions or themes that you've installed. Beware that issues with color and accessibility might mean these icons have been changed by the time you read this. Each icon indicates a different severity. Red means that a security problem with your browser has been detected at the moment, and you should grab the recommended fix by clicking on the icon. The other severities don't require any action, but it's good practice to keep your browser fully up to date. That makes these icons go away.

A subset of these icons appears in the Mozilla Extension Manager and Theme Manager dialog boxes. From left to right, they stand for "uninstall from the local disk," "update from the Web," and "configure options for a given extension or theme." Hover over the icons with the mouse to remind yourself what they're for.

These icons sometimes appear on the Find toolbar at the bottom of the browser window. The first one indicates that your search has been unsuccessful. The second indicates that the search has just wrapped, which means you've just reached the bottom (or the top) of the web page and the find process will continue again from the other end.

These icons sometimes appear at the right end of the Location bar, where the current page's URL is shown. They can also appear at the right edge of the status bar, at the bottom of the window. The uncrossed icon appears when the web page you are viewing is served up securely. That usually means that Secure HTTP (https:) is providing the page. Secure HTTP uses Secure Socket Layer (SSL) technology to ensure that all information between the web server and you is safely encrypted. The other icon appears when you log into a web site using a password, but the password is transmitted unencrypted to the web site. The icon indicates that your login is not as free from prying eyes (network sniffers in particular) as it might otherwise be.

HACK #5   Use Keyboard Shortcuts

Driving Firefox from the keyboard is both the same as and different from other browsers.

This hack shows you which keyboard moves come standard with Firefox. There are many extensions that modify the available set of keystrokes and key chords. You can also hack the keyboard set yourself in a number of ways [Hack #77].

Many Firefox keyboard combinations are the same as those of Internet Explorer. In particular, menu navigation uses the same combination of arrow keys and Alt as most Windows applications, and navigation within text-editing fields supports the same keystrokes as most text editors (Ctrl–left arrow to move one word left, for example). Scrolling keys such as Page Up and Page Down work as you'd expect, too. Table 1-2 shows the major keys used by both browsers.

On the Macintosh, substitute *Command* for *Ctrl* and *Option* for *Alt*.

Table 1-2. Keyboard shortcuts common to Firefox and Internet Explorer

Key combination	Use
Ctrl-A	Select all content
Ctrl-C	Copy current selection
Ctrl-D	Add a bookmark
Ctrl-H	Display the History sidebar
Ctrl-I (and Ctrl-B)	Open Bookmarks sidebar
Ctrl-N	Open a new window
Ctrl-O	Open a file
Ctrl-P	Print current page
Ctrl-R, F5	Reload current page
Ctrl-Shift-R, Ctrl-F5	Reload current page from origin
Ctrl-V	Paste currently copied content
Ctrl-W, Ctrl-F4	Close the current tab
Ctrl-X	Cut the current selection
Ctrl-Y (and Ctrl-Shift-Z)	Redo last operation
Ctrl-Z	Undo last operation
Alt	Begin menu navigation
Alt-D, F6	Focus and highlight the location bar
Alt-F4 (also Ctrl-Shift-W)	Close current window
Alt-Home	Go to home page
Alt–Left Arrow, Backspace	Go back one page
Alt–Right Arrow, Shift-Backspace	Go forward one page
Delete	Delete current item
End	Move to bottom of page
Esc	Stop current operation
F11	Display in full-screen mode
Home	Move to top of page

Firefox also has some unique keyboard combinations. Table 1-3 shows the common ones that don't match Internet Explorer.

Table 1-3. Keyboard shortcuts available in Firefox only

Key combination	Use
Ctrl-hyphen	Decrease text size
Ctrl-+	Increase text size
Ctrl-0 (Ctrl-Zero)	Restore text back to normal size
Ctrl-Down Arrow	Select next search engine in location bar
Ctrl-F, /	Find content by search string
Ctrl-G, F3	Repeat last find operation forward
Ctrl-J (Ctrl-Y on Linux)	Open download manager window
Ctrl-K	Search the Web using the current search engine and keyword
Ctrl-n (where n is a number)	Go to the nth tab
Ctrl-S	Save current page as file
Ctrl-T	Open new tab
Ctrl-Tab, Ctrl-Page Down	Move to the next tab
Ctrl-Shift-Tab, Ctrl-Page Up	Move to the previous tab
Ctrl-U	View page source
'	Find link by search term
Alt-Enter	Open URL in a new tab
F6	Move to next frame
F7	Toggle caret browsing
Shift-F3	Repeat last Find operation backward

Finally, here are some more detailed resources on Firefox keys. There's an up-to-the-minute list in the Firefox Help system, under Help → Help Contents, Keyboard Shortcuts. Otherwise, look here for recent changes:

http://www.mozilla.org/support/firefox/keyboard

More technically, there's some newer discussion about key changes here:

http://www.mozilla.org/access/keyboard/proposal

You might also want to look at this older URL:

http://www.mozilla.org/unix/customizing.html

And finally, this page provides general accessibility information for Mozilla:

http://www.mozilla.org/access/

Make Firefox Look Different

Don't put up with blank walls. You can wallpaper Firefox back into your life.

The menus, toolbars, and dialog boxes that Firefox provides can all be changed. Collectively, they are called the *chrome*. You can change the *content* of the chrome, which includes the set of widgets that are made visible in the window. Alternatively, you can change just the *appearance* of the chrome. In that case, the buttons and other widgets stay the same, but the graphics, text, and colors that decorate them are all different.

To change chrome content, install an *extension* from the Tools → Extensions menu. Extensions are small pieces of programs, not too different from a Java Applet or a Microsoft Excel macro. Some are very sophisticated and are effectively whole applications. This book is full of discussions about which extension does what. Chapter 4, *Web Surfing Enhancements*, is a good starting point. We won't go into detail about extensions here. We'll just cover the install process with the simpler example of adding *themes*, which is done the same way.

To change the wallpaper style of Firefox's chrome, install a new theme. A theme is a bundle of plain content with no program logic. Both extensions and themes are available by default through the trusted *http://update. mozilla.org* content portal, which provides security and safety. Even in the wild, themes are overall much safer than extensions. At most, they make Firefox illegible and unworkable, whereas a truly wild extension can make Firefox curl up and die completely.

A theme is made out of a set of *skins*. A skin is a cluster of files associated with a single application or application subsystem. There's a single skin called the *global* skin that applies to all applications. A sensible theme creator will always provide a global skin in his theme. A creative theme maker will also supply skins for common applications run by Firefox (such as the browser and the DOM Inspector). If applications change, then skins must change to catch up. So, an actively maintained theme is more desirable than one that's been created and left to rot.

To pick up a new theme, connect to the Web and choose Tools → Themes. Figure 1-9 shows the Theme Manager with five themes already installed: that's four, plus one that is the default.

This information is read from datafiles stored in the Firefox user-profile area. Pressing the Update button grabs any updates to your existing, installed themes that have been created since you last checked. If you press the Get More Themes link, a shopping-mall web page is displayed where you can pick the theme that suits you.

Figure 1-9. Theme Manager displaying a sample of the Lure theme

Themes are installed by a bit of Mozilla called XPInstall (Cross(X) Platform Install). A summary of the process goes like this. A theme is delivered as a single archive of small files. The archive is named with a *.xpi* extension, but it's actually in ZIP format. These files are copied into the Firefox profile area. Some registration and housekeeping is done. The theme is detected the next time Firefox starts up. If you know the URL of such an archive, you can simply download it to disk separately from XPInstall and have a look inside.

Figure 1-10 shows Firefox after FireCat PalePinkPaws has been installed and chosen as the current theme.

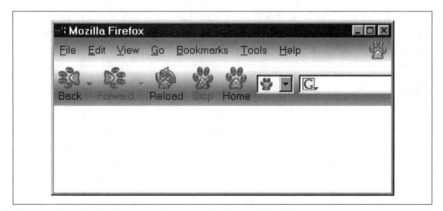

Figure 1-10. Firefox browser window in FireCat PalePinkPaws theme

Just click on the theme name, then on Use Theme, and then restart the browser to make the theme appear.

Stop Once-Only Dialogs Safely

HACK
#7

Don't like to be bothered? Here's how to shut Firefox up and how to deal with the consequences.

After first installation, Firefox intermittently throws up a series of dialog boxes. For a first-time user, these can be confusing. Here's how to shut them up if you don't like them. Also here's how to make them appear, so that you can shut them up if you're installing Firefox for someone else.

Figure 1-11 shows the first dialog presented.

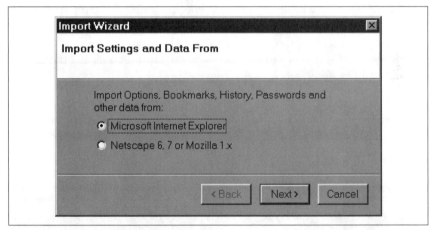

Figure 1-11. Import Settings startup dialog box

By the time you read this, Firefox will be able to import from a number of other browsers, so the Import Wizard might look a bit more detailed than it is shown here, especially if it detects other browsers on your computer. You can cancel this import process safely. It can be repeated at any time after installation from the File → Import... menu.

Importing is a safe process unless you have sophisticated *favelets* or *book-marklets* stored in your other browsers. Web developers are the main users of these small diagnostic helpers. In general, if you choose to import, there are two consequences. First, the bookmarks toolbar might be loaded with old stuff that might confuse Granny. Second, the surfing you did last week with that other browser might be copied into Firefox. That could be awkward if Granny isn't aware of your personal style and spots it.

Once Firefox starts, it confronts you with the dialog shown in Figure 1-12.

Figure 1-12. Default Browser selection dialog box

On Windows, this makes small changes to the Registry. It's harmless to make Firefox the default browser. If you have accidental viruses, spyware, or other nasties on your computer, it might improve security to make Firefox the default. Don't click Yes or leave the checkbox ticked if temporary product evaluation is your goal. If you want Firefox to be the default, but you still want Internet Explorer to work, see "Integrate Firefox with Other Tools" [Hack #40]. Whether Firefox checks at startup time that it's the default browser can be configured with this preference:

```
browser.shell.checkDefaultBrowser /* true or false */
```

The first time you surf to a web site over a secure connection, you get a warning. Then, when you leave that web site, you get warned again. Figure 1-13 shows the two warnings.

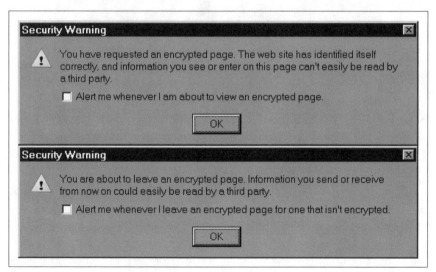

Figure 1-13. First warnings for Secure HTTP border crossings

These messages are border security warnings. When interacting with a web site over plain HTTP (that's the normal case), content sent both ways can possibly be viewed by a spy. If the HTTP connection is performed over Secure Sockets Layer (SSL), then no spying is possible. These warnings tell you that you're either entering or leaving spy-safe territory. If you fail to click the checkboxes, you'll never be warned again. You'll never know if you are surfing "out in the open" or not. But you also won't be driven crazy by dialog boxes. These alerts can be set with these preferences:

```
security.warn_entering_secure            /* true or false */
security.warn_leaving_secure             /* true or false */
security.warn_entering_secure.show_once  /* true or false */
security.warn_leaving_secure.show_once   /* true or false */
```

The kind of spying that SSL prevents is fairly obscure. It requires that someone either wrap equipment around your physical telephone line or cable line, or else get access to one of the computers between yours and the remote web site. An ISP staff member is unlikely to spy like this unless they're assisting some security agency. Your privacy might be an issue if you are surfing from inside a corporate intranet. There, a corporate web server proxy could log any out-in-the-open activities.

If you are out in the open, web page forms you fill in have the same problem. The first time you attempt to submit a form, you'll be greeted with the dialog shown in Figure 1-14.

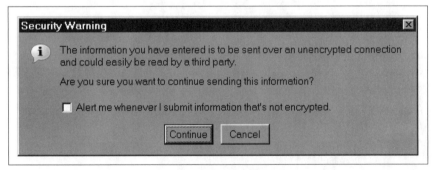

Figure 1-14. First warning for unencrypted form submission

If you click Continue or Cancel, you'll never see this warning again, just like the previous examples. Here are the matching preferences:

```
security.warn_submit_insecure           /* true or false */
security.warn_submit_insecure.show_once  /* true or false */
```

Finally, if the web page form is a login form, Firefox will detect this and ask if you want your login details remembered locally. Figure 1-15 shows the permission request.

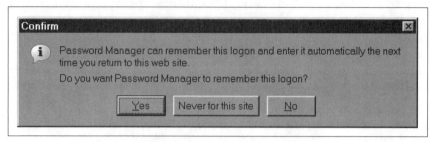

Figure 1-15. Password Manager permission request dialog

If you choose Yes, that password will be held insecurely on your PC. You must have some other password protecting your PC if you don't want that password exposed to office theft. The options are a boot password, a Firefox master password (Tools → Options, Privacy, Saved Passwords, Set Master Password), or a decent operating system login password. Set this preference for the equivalent effect:

```
security.ask_for_password /* 0 = once, 1 = every time, 2 = only on expiry */
```

A password normally expires in 30 days, at which point the user must enter it again. Here is the preference for the expiry horizon:

```
security.password_lifetime /* An integer, default = 30 (days) */
```

Chapter 2 has a lot more to say about security issues in Firefox, but here's a summary of this hack: if you always hit Enter or Return when one of these dialogs comes up, you won't be annoyed by them any more. Your privacy will be only moderately protected afterward, but your online safety will remain high.

HACK #8 Flush and Clear Absolutely Everything

Paranoid about Firefox's tendency to store things about web pages? Reset your browser back to zero.

You might be confident that Firefox can reset itself for you, or you might only be happy if you scrub the decks for yourself. You can do it either way. A further decision you're faced with is this: do you want to clear out just the data that Firefox has stored, or do you also want to clear out all modifications to the browser since it was first installed?

Dispose of Ordinary Web Surfing Information

To clear, flush, and reset everything from inside the browser, proceed as follows:

1. Leave just one Firefox browser window open. Change the URL of the currently viewed page to the URL about:blank and display it.

2. Display the Options dialog box using the Tools → Options or Edit → Preferences menu items. Click on the Privacy icon. Click the Clear All button at the base of the window. That clears just about everything associated with web pages.

For web development activity, that's all you really need to do.

Dispose of Everything Else via the User Interface

If you want to hack further into the state of the browser, you certainly can. To go much, much further, proceed as follows:

1. Click the General icon in the Options dialog box. Then click the Fonts and Colors button. Uncheck all checkboxes except Underline Links and click OK.

2. Back at the previous dialog, click the Languages button. Remove all languages except [en] and possibly [en-us]. Click OK.

3. Back at the main Options dialog box, click the Web Features icon. Three buttons appear at the top right, labeled Allowed Sites, Allowed Sites, and Exceptions. Click each of these buttons and delete any records that are shown.

4. Return back to the main Options panel. Click the Downloads icon. In the box labeled File Types, delete all items by clicking on them in turn and then clicking Remove. Click the Plugins button. Disable all plug-ins by unchecking the column labeled Enabled. Click OK.

You can also flush out all your security records:

1. Click the Advanced icon in the Options Dialog. Under Software Updates, click Check Now and update Firefox to the latest minor releases (this step takes time).

2. When that's done, click the Certificates item to open it up. Click Manage Certificates, and in each of the tabs except Authorities, delete any shown records. Don't remove anything from the Authorities tab. Click OK.

3. Click the Validation item to open it. Click the Manage CRLs button and remove any and all records.

If you're very keen, you can also clear out any user preferences that you've set. Type in the URL about:config. Context-click on any and all preferences that are bold and choose Reset.

Finally, if you want to remove all your bookmarks and customizations, open the Bookmark Manager from the Bookmarks menu. Click on all items—except for the item labeled Bookmarks Toolbar Folder and its immediate parent—and press Delete. Under the Tools menu, choose first Extensions and then Themes. In each resulting window, uninstall everything. Finally, under View → Toolbars → Customize, click Restore Default Set, and then click Done.

Shut down Firefox and make sure no extra Firefox processes are still hanging around. Restart, and everything's as clean as you could hope for by using this method.

Dispose of Everything via the Filesystem

Perhaps you wonder if Firefox is doing everything right for you. The alternative is to clean up Firefox using the operating system only. Here's how.

First, shut down Firefox completely. Then, under Unix/Linux, delete the folder ~/.mozilla. Under Microsoft Windows, delete the Mozilla folder that appears in the path to the Firefox profile; that's the one under *Application Data*. Similarly, under Mac OS X, delete the *Mozilla* folder. That removes nearly everything the user ever created. When you restart Firefox, a new, clean Mozilla folder is created with all the necessary files.

For a less extreme solution, navigate to the profile directory (the one with the weird, jumbled name) and delete these files: everything in the *Cache* folder; *prefs.js; user.js; bookmarks.*; cookies.txt; downloads.rdf; formhistory.dat; history.dat; localstore.rdf; mimeTypes;rdf; search.rdf;* and *XUL.**.

Strip the Firefox Install Area of Extras

While cleaning house, you can also remove a few items from the Firefox install area:

- You can delete the *extensions* folder.
- You can delete everything in the *plugins* folder except the file *libnullplugin.so* (Linux) or *npnul32.dll* (Windows).
- You can remove whatever you want from the *searchplugins* folder.

See Also

There are a few small Registry files that we haven't covered in this hack. To go any further in chopping up the browser is to change its installation rather than just clean up. See Chapters 2 and 3 for deeper surgery on the Firefox installation.

Make Firefox Go Fast

#9 Don't wait for the Web. Firefox can go faster if you just tune it up a bit.

Here are a few steps you can perform to speed up Firefox. Back to performance basics first, though: the user is the slowest thing attached to the computer. Better use of Firefox's features will speed up the user, so be sure to read the rest of the hacks in this chapter.

Fix Dial-Up Modem Bottlenecks

Any dial-up modem you use is the slowest network hardware you have, so tune it wisely. Make sure any modem connection is running as close as possible to the maximum speed for POTS (plain old telephone system) phone lines. That line is usually a 64 Kb service (unless you're stuck on an ancient analog exchange). No one gets every drop of 64 Kb out of it, unless they pay a fortune for ISDN, but you should get 53.3 Kb at least.

If you're on Windows, your modem driver and chipset should support the latest compression standards now available. Update the modem and the modem's Windows driver directly from the chipset manufacturer. Look on the modem card to see who made the chips; don't bother with who made the card. If you buy a cutoff switch that lets you isolate your answering machine, fax, and telephone gear while you're on the Internet, then you won't strain the line voltage as much, and you'll have less noise causing error-correction delays.

If your connection is still slow, ring your telephone provider and complain that their voltages and noise filters are all wrong—they can test and adjust from their end. Ring Microsoft and complain that Windows hasn't tuned your PPP connection correctly. Ring your ISP and complain that their modem bank isn't negotiating the best possible speed. None of that will do you much good, but it's nice to vent sometimes. Move to broadband.

If you're stuck on dial-up, the biggest performance plus you can get from Firefox without using caching is to turn images off [Hack #35]. That's in the Options dialog box under Web Features. Turning off images might reduce your web experience to an unacceptable low, so it's a dramatic step. You can also change the following preference ["Setting a Preference with about:config," in the introduction to this chapter], which ensures that web pages are checked for updates only once per browsing session, instead of every time you look at them:

```
browser.cache.check_doc_frequency /* set it to 0, normally 3 */
```

This preference change shouldn't affect you much if you're just surfing idly. If you spend a lot of time with online message boards or similarly intensive web-based applications, it might cause confusion, though, so avoid it in that case. One possible compromise is to create a separate "I'm not working" profile and turn the preference on in that profile. Use that profile for recreation only. Some of the Firefox ad-blocking extensions prevent advertising images from being downloaded, which is a further performance-saving feature.

Overclock Firefox

Some obscure preferences exist that affect the network performance and display performance of Firefox. They're the equivalent of special hardware tweaks that enthusiasts use to make your CPU run faster. There are security implications to modifying the network performance [Hack #16]. They might make you a hazard as you burn down the street. There are also stability risks in cranking up the display performance. Such tweaks are really meant only as debugging tools. If you can't keep your hands off the engine, here's how to proceed without warranty.

Speed up network access. The following preferences might not make you a good web citizen, but they'll get you as much bandwidth as you can manage. Note, however, that too many simultaneous network connections will just slow you down. The best possible performance occurs when there's one connection only and the remote web server is blindingly fast. If web servers or other hops in the network are comparatively slow, try playing with these many preferences.

Turn the following preferences on for dial-up; they produce little effect for broadband connections. A few web pages that don't support HTTP/1.1 will be confused, but all modern web sites should handle it fine:

```
network.http.pipelining              /* default = false */
network.http.proxy.pipelining        /* default = false */
```

Raise the following for dial-up only. It states how many pipelined requests are possible (has a minor effect only):

```
network.http.pipelining.maxrequests     /* default = 4 */
```

Set the following higher if you want to hammer web servers with many simultaneous requests (suitable for broadband use only):

```
network.http.max-connections-per-server /* default = 8 */
```

Set the following higher if you want to keep an unfair share of web servers that you access a lot. The web server must also be too dumb to deny your request for extra access:

```
network.http.max-persistent-connections-per-server /* default = 2 */
```

Set the following higher if you want an unfair share of web proxies that you access a lot. The web proxy must also be too dumb to deny your request for extra access:

```
network.http.max-persistent-connections-per-proxy /* default = 4 */
```

Set the following higher if you keep millions of tabs and/or windows open (suitable for broadband use only).

```
network.http.max-connections /* default = 24 */
```

Speed up page display. To display pages faster, you first need a fast CPU and memory. Don't try the following things on an ancient Pentium II, unless specifically noted here.

Setting the following preference to false is a brutal performance tweak that tells Firefox to process every byte of Web content as soon as it arrives, rather that buffering it in sensible chunks. This makes Firefox web-page handling work extremely hard but theoretically puts page content on the screen faster (recommended only for burning-hot CPUs with super-fast display cards and dial-up connections):

```
content.notify.ontimer /* default = true */
```

An even more brutal tweak shuts out all interruptions (including user input) while the incoming web page content is analyzed (not recommended at all unless Firefox is being used as an untended monitoring station):

```
content.interrupt.parsing /* default = true */
```

If content.notify.ontimer sensibly remains false, this is the time-out interval for collecting sensible chunks of incoming web page. Lower it for faster incremental page display. Lower it below 10000, and web-page handling will be working extremely hard again (recommended for dial-up):

```
content.notify.interval /* default = 120000 (micro-seconds) */
```

For Granny's slow computer, if nothing's arrived recently, then do extra buffering, which saves more CPU cycles. Set to the number of milliseconds to back off each time the network connection is found to be idle (recommended for ancient PCs on dial-up only):

```
content.notify.backoffcount /* default = -1, meaning never */
```

Make Firefox pay more attention to the mouse and keyboard at the expense of other activities. Making this a larger polling delay slows down recognition of user input but marginally improves page display:

```
content.max.tokenizing.time /* default = 360000 (micro-seconds) */
```

If the user is in the habit of opening 10 web pages (especially 10 tabs) and then sipping coffee while the pages load, making the following parameter's value larger will speed up page display (recommended for slow CPUs):

```
content.switch.threshold /* default = 750000 (micro-seconds) */
```

Make a big memory buffer for big pages. Set to a power of 2 minus 1—e.g., 16385 (recommended for broadband):

```
content.maxtextrun /* default = 8191 */
```

Here are a couple of additional oddments. The following preference tells Firefox to start putting received web pages on the screen right away, even if not much content has been received yet:

```
nglayout.initialpaint.delay /* set to 0, default = 250 (millisecs) */
```

The following preference tells Firefox not to bother putting image placeholders on the screen while the real images are fetched, which will also speed page display up a bit (recommended for broadband):

```
browser.display.show_image_placeholders /* default = true , set to false */
```

Finally, on Linux/Unix, don't run Firefox with X-servers and X-clients on different machines; that can be quite slow. VNC (or PC-Anywhere, or Windows Remote Desktop) does not affect Firefox performance, except for capping the speed at which desktop updates occur. That is not a Firefox-specific effect, though.

Expand Your Caching

Your best defense against a slow network is a big local cache. In the Options panel, make the cache as big as you can manage. It's really the memory part of the cache that provides the performance, so if your computer is low on memory, a big disk cache won't help much. Buy more memory; Firefox will find it and use it. If you want to set the size of the memory cache explicitly, use these preferences:

```
browser.cache.memory.enable     /* default is true */
browser.cache.memory.capacity   /* -1 = size to fit, 123 = 123 Kb */
```

Start Up Faster

You can get a faster startup if you turn on Quick Launch when you first install Firefox. Extensions and fancy themes will encumber performance slightly, so you should avoid those. Windows XP is supposed to be smart enough to optimize disk storage of frequently used applications, but it's doubtful that will help much, even if you can figure out how to control it, and even if you defragment the disk.

On Linux, if you use KDE as the default desktop, you pay a lot when Firefox starts up, because it requires the GNOME Gtk subsystem, and that means extra startup effort. You could use GNOME instead, at least until the KDE project's Qt Mozilla port is fully polished and ready.

Ultimate Speed Improvements

Note also that the standard distributions of Firefox for x86 (Intel) architectures are compiled for the lowest common denominator. They're compiled with dynamic link libraries and support everything back to a 386 (OK, that's an exaggeration). In theory, you can get much better performance if you upgrade your compilers to a recent version and compile a static build of Firefox that's also optimized for (say) Pentium 4 [Hack #92]. There is some evidence that this will speed up your user experience. It has been shown to reduce the runtime size of Firefox, at least on Linux.

 Start Up from the Command Line
#10 You can start Firefox without using the mouse.

How is Firefox started? This hack describes all the command-line options. To see command-line options, most technical people instinctively open a command-line window, such as an xterm (Linux) or an MS-DOS or cmd window (Windows). Then they type *program* /? or *program* --help, depending on the operating system. The latter option works everywhere except in Windows, because Firefox doesn't provide console-based help there. So Windows is a special case: help information isn't automatically spat out there. To see command-line options on Windows, you have to go further with a DOS or cmd box. On Windows, start up a command line (Start → Programs → MS-DOS Prompt) and follow these steps:

```
C:
cd "Program Files"
cd Firefox
firefox --help > help.txt
type help.txt
```

The help options will appear in the newly created file *help.txt*. This advice goes for all options that provide command-line output, such as -version. You don't need to redirect anything on other platforms.

On Windows, you can use / (forward slash) or // (double forward slash) as the command-line switch prefix. On all platforms, Firefox-specific options can be preceded with - (minus) or -- (minus, minus). These two command lines are the same on Windows, but only the first one will work on Linux:

```
firefox -console --jsconsole http://www.example.com
firefox --console /jsconsole http://www.example.com
```

On Unix/Linux, some X11 options are supported. X11 X resources aren't supported, because the Unix/Linux port uses the Gtk configuration system. Table 1-4 describes the user-oriented options.

Table 1-4. User-oriented command-line options

Option	Windows?	Unix/ Linux?	Macintosh?	Description
General options				
-h, -help	Y	Y	Y	State command-line help and exit.
-v, -version	Y	Y	Y	State Firefox version and exit.
Browser options				
URL	Y	Y	Y	Display a browser showing this URL.
-height X	Y	Y	Y	Specify window height in pixels.
-width X	Y	Y	Y	Specify window width in pixels.
-edit	N	N	N	Support for old Composer; does nothing by default.
-inspector	Y	Y	Y	Start the DOM Inspector window.
-jsconsole	Y	Y	Y	Start the JavaScript Console window.
-register	Y	Y	Y	Re-register the set of chrome packages.
-safe-mode	Y	Y	Y	Start without any extensions or plug-ins and stick to the default theme. Use as a last resort.
-install-global-extension "{UUID}"	Y	Y	Y	Move the extension with registration number UUID from the profile area to the install area.
-install-global-theme "{UUID}"	Y	Y	Y	Move the theme with registration number UUID from the profile area to the install area.

Table 1-4. User-oriented command-line options (continued)

Option	Windows?	Unix/ Linux?	Macintosh?	Description
`-list global-items`	Y	Y	Y	List extensions and themes added to the install area.
`-lock-item "{UUID}"`	Y	Y	Y	Lock the extension or theme with this *UUID* so that the user can't delete it via the user interface.
`-unlock-item "{UUID}"`	Y	Y	Y	Unlock the extension or theme with this *UUID* so that the user can delete it via the user interface.
Mozilla options				
`-chrome D`	Y	Y	Y	Start up a plain, chromeless window and display the document at URL *D*.
`-installer`	Y	Y	Y	Migrate data from other browsers on startup.
`-P Foo`	Y	Y	Y	Start up with profile *Foo*, or with the Profile manager if that profile doesn't exist.
`-SelectProfile`	Y	Y	Y	Start up with the profile selection dialog box.
`-CreateProfile "prof dir"`	Y	Y	Y	Auto-create a profile named *prof* in directory *dir* and make it the current profile. *dir* defaults to "."
`-ProfileWizard`	Y	Y	Y	Start up with the Profile Wizard and step the user through profile creation.
`-ProfileManager`	Y	Y	Y	Start up with the Profile Manager. On Mac OS X, Option-double-click Firefox.
`-UILocale L`	Y	Y	Y	Start with language locale *L* string labels for XUL content (toolbars and menus)
`-contentLocale C`	Y	Y	Y	Start with content locale *C* string labels for displayed pages' content.
Windows options				
`-kill`	Y	N	N	Stop any running Firefox instance.
`-console`	Y	N	N	Tie any `stdout` and `stderr` output to a simple text window and display that as well.

Table 1-4. *User-oriented command-line options (continued)*

Option	Windows?	Unix/ Linux?	Macintosh?	Description
Unix/Linux/X11/ Gtk options				
`--g-fatal- warnings`	N	Y	N	All warnings kill Firefox.
`--display=X`	N	Y	N	Choose the X11 display X.
`--sync`	N	Y	N	Synchronize all X11 calls.
`--no-xshm`	N	Y	N	Don't use X shared memory extension.
`--install`	N	Y	N	Give Firefox a private Gtk colormap.

 Windows are opened in the order they appear on the command line.

See Also

For the more detailed programmatic command-line options, search for the DumpHelp( ) function at *http://lxr.mozilla.org*. For Unix/Linux specifically, consider also this URL: *http://www.mozilla.org/unix/remote.html*.

Security

Hacks 11–21

This chapter describes how to change the default security arrangements in Firefox. Security is a big subject, and it has plenty of baggage all of its own. One person's safety is another's prison. One person's privacy is another person's isolation. Changing security options amounts to changing who you are or aren't willing to deal with. It also amounts to deciding how much you're willing to let third parties know when you're browsing the Web.

When you install Firefox, the default security settings give you a safe web browser. It is quite hard to create large holes by accidentally changing options. Firefox has also been closely inspected for internal problems. As a result, the browser and its underlying Mozilla technology have an excellent security track record. Rarely is a new security problem uncovered. When that happens, it is usually fixed within a day. The Firefox Update Manager informs you of new security patches, if any are made available.

If you don't care about security at all, you can simply remove many of the hurdles that Firefox puts in your way. Security is a complex matter, though. Sometimes, doing away with security means just that: leaving the browser's resources open to any exploitation. Some security regimes, however, don't give you that option. In such cases, the best you can do is reply "I don't care" every time you're engaged over security. There are even rare cases in which there's nothing at all that you can do to escape security limitations. It's a case-by-case environment.

Security concerns and installation processes are two related but different things. This chapter discusses security only. Chapter 3 describes gritty modifications to the Firefox install process. Chapters 7 and 8 describe a form of programming that's also a blend of installation and security. See those chapters to go further with the chrome.

Drop Miscellaneous Security Blocks

#11 If your computing environment is secure, then Firefox's own security is of limited use.

To systematically address every single security restriction, you'll have to read all the hacks in this chapter; it's just too complex for one hack. This hack describes many common quick fixes. You might also want to read "Stop Once-Only Dialogs Safely" [Hack #7].

Supply Passwords Automatically

You don't need to constantly reassert your login credentials; you can get Firefox to do it for you. NTLM and dial-up passwords are described in "Work with Single Sign-On Servers" [Hack #14] and "Dial Up Automatically on Startup" [Hack #26] respectively; here, we cover web form passwords and cookies.

The Password Manager is turned on automatically when Firefox starts; all you get is a first-time warning when you use it. Setting a master password serves no purpose if you're trying to defeat security, so the Password Manager saves you that hassle by default. You can stop the remembered passwords from ever expiring by setting this preference:

```
security.password_lifetime /* set to 0 (days), default is 30 (days) */
```

Session IDs are like passwords: they're sent by web sites that want to keep track of you as you move between web pages. Usually they're stored as *cookies*: the correct jargon for web-based session IDs. Cookies are sent between Firefox and the web server as a simple string of plain text in a special HTTP header line. If you have an extension installed that's an HTTP header diagnostic [Hack #51], you can see cookies go to and fro. Firefox has cookie support turned on by default. If you want to configure cookie processing explicitly, use these preferences:

```
network.cookie.alwaysAcceptSessionCookies /* set to true */
network.cookie.cookieBehavior              /* set to 0 = Accept All */
network.cookie.lifetimePolicy              /* set to 0 = until expiry */
```

The following preferences are bits of rubbish left over from attempts to migrate from an old Mozilla or Netscape version to Firefox and should be ignored:

```
network.cookie.lifetime.enabled
network.cookie.lifetime.behavior
```

Allow Foreign Code to Run

One of the great challenges of the Web is the existence of untrusted downloadable code. With the exception of sandboxed Java applets and properly
authenticated code bundles, such things are almost certainly insecure. Firefox won't accept them by default, but you can turn support back on.

Turn on ActiveX. One way to do so is to reignite the native ActiveX support
inside the Microsoft Windows port of Mozilla (and therefore Firefox). To
turn absolutely everything on and make everything scriptable—even those
ActiveX controls flagged as "do not script me"—set these preferences:

```
security.class.allowByDefault                    /* true (default)    */
security.xpconnect.activex.global.hosting_flags /* 31 = bits 00011111 */
```

These affect the behavior of a bit of Mozilla that implements the interface
called nsIActiveXSecurityPolicy. For more on that interface, look for a file
named *nsIActiveXSecurityPolicy.idl* at *http://lxr.mozilla.org*. If the first of
these preferences is set to false, ActiveX objects must be allowed or disallowed on a case-by-case basis with preferences like this:

```
capability.policy.default.ClassID.CIDclassid" /* set to "AllAccess" */
```

In this example, *classid* must be a UUID identifier for the ActiveX object,
written in this format:

```
6BF52A52-394A-11D3-B153-00C04F79FAA6
```

If objects marked "don't script me" aren't wanted, set the same preference
this way:

```
security.xpconnect.activex.global.hosting_flags /* 15 = bits 00001111 */
```

Whatever hijinks Windows goes through to decide whether a COM object
should be scriptable or not, Mozilla also goes through. That includes observ-
ing operating-system-maintained blacklists and so on.

To run such a control, use the HTML <OBJECT> or legacy <EMBED> tag that
specifies the control's URL and class identifier. That's the same as in Internet Explorer.

Turn on more plug-in and helper support. *Plug-ins* are another form of foreign
code. The following two security preferences make plug-in access a bit easier to deal with (the first is set by default):

```
security.xpconnect.plugin.unrestricted    /* true by default */
plugin.expose_full_path                    /* set to true */
```

Having Firefox pass control of a URL directly to the operating system is a dangerous arrangement. For example, URLs prefixed with the shell: scheme can be passed to Windows (which has a poor track record of handling them securely). To turn on that behavior, set this preference:

```
network.protocols.useSystemDefaults        /* set to true */
```

For selective enablement of URL schemes, change the matching preference. All such preferences have this format:

```
network.protocol-handler.external.scheme
```

where *scheme* stands for the particular scheme. So, for the shell: scheme, this is the right setting:

```
network.protocol-handler.external.shell  /* set to true */
```

Of course, another way to activate code in a downloaded object is to associate its file type with a suitable application. That's done at the operating-system level, though, not in Firefox. An example is associating Microsoft Excel files containing Visual Basic macros with the Excel program. Firefox will notice such configuration changes the next time it starts up.

Drop Browser Security Hobbles

When a web page displays, Firefox wraps it up inside some security restrictions. These are designed to prevent the page from taking over the user's computer, which is most commonly attempted with pages that contain JavaScript scripts. Preferences allow you to drop some, but not all, of these restrictions. All of the preferences that begin with the following prefix control access to scriptable features of the DOM 0 web page object model:

```
dom.anything
```

Type dom into the Filter box in the *about:config* window to see them all. Set most of them to true to re-enable the matching feature. These preferences match checkbox features in the Firefox Options dialog box in the Web Features panel.

A few of these preferences rate special mention. This one stops scripts from ever being aborted by Firefox:

```
dom.max_script_run_time /* set to 0 (seconds) or a big number */
```

Set to 0 (zero), no script will ever be aborted. An infinitely running script can tie up the CPU, which can in turn cause a denial-of-service attack, preventing the user from controlling the browser. Better to choose a very big number, just in case.

This next preference turns off limits on pop-up-window generation:

```
dom.popup_maximum   /* set to 0 popups or a big number */
```

Finally, this preference makes all JavaScript events available in modal pop-up windows:

```
user_pref("dom.popup_allowed_events", "mousedown mouseup click dblclick
mouseover mouseout mousemove contextmenu keydown keyup keypress focus blur
load beforeunload unload abort error submit reset change select input paint
text popupshowing popupshown popuphiding popuphidden close command croadcast
commandupdate dragenter dragover dragexit dragdrop draggesture resize scroll
overflow underflow overflowchanged DOMSubtreeModified DOMNodeInserted
DOMNodeRemoved DOMNodeRemovedFromDocument DOMNodeInsertedIntoDocument
DOMAttrModified DOMCharacterDataModified popupBlocked DOMActivate DOMFocusIn
DOMFocusOut");
```

 The example string shown here is excessive—just pick the events you're interested in—but it serves to illustrate all DOM-like events that Firefox knows about.

Of all the security hobbles that Firefox enforces on web pages, there's one that's nearly impossible to remove: the creation of windows smaller than 100×100 pixels in size. The only way to do so is to use a fully trusted script, either one signed with a digital certificate or one installed in the chrome.

Remove Profile Salting

Firefox user profiles are *salted*: the names of profile directories include randomly generated directory names, such as *f8p09nj2.slt*. This is a security measure designed to prevent hostile web sites from guessing the name of your profile and then feeding Firefox data that might have security cracks in it. It also makes administering and moving profiles harder than it might otherwise be. You can remove these salted names by using the -CreateProfile command-line option and this dirty hack. Follow these steps, which create a dummy profile located in *C:\tmp\test*:

```
mkdir C:\tmp
mkdir C:\tmp\test
echo "garbage" > c:\tmp\test\prefs.js
firefox -CreateProfile "test c:\tmp"
```

The echo command just creates a file that Firefox will sense at startup time. That's enough to fool it into using the *C:\tmp\test* directory as an existing profile for the new profile named test.

Update Firefox Automatically

Set these preferences to ensure that Firefox, extensions, and themes are all updated without the user having to do anything:

```
extensions.update.autoUpdate          /* set to true */
extensions.update.severity.threshold  /* set to 0 (lowest severity) */
```

```
app.update.autoUpdateEnabled          /* set to true */
app.update.enabled                    /* set to true */
```

It's also possible to automatically download configuration data [Hack #29], proxy information [Hack #15] and certificate revocation lists [Hack #17]. None of those things require user intervention.

HACK #12 Raise Security to Protect Dummies
Set up Firefox for nontechnical people.

First of all, the Firefox product is designed with nontechnical people in mind. Most of its fancy features are hidden behind unusual key presses or buried in menus. From the beginning, it's pretty safe and secure. For the dazed and disoriented, though, safety doesn't just mean safe from web villains and privacy attacks; it also means being safe from confusion. Struggling users can easily harm themselves accidentally when confused, so that's something to avoid. Here are some of the configuration changes that you can apply to make life safer for struggling users:

- Turn on automated patch updating.
- Turn off password and form auto-complete features.
- Leave on standard caching options, so that pages are always fresh.
- Change the default download directory to the desktop if the operating system is Linux.
- Download language packs and plug-ins when you install, and turn off subsequent plug-in detection.
- Configure the Popup Manager to accept pop-ups from web sites the user trusts, such as banks and finance companies, and then turn off the pop-up blocker alert bar so that it never appears.

To turn on automated patch updates, see "Stop All Secret Network Activity" [Hack #13]. Auto-complete features can be turned off in the Options panel. To change the default download directory on Linux, change the directory preference from something like this:

```
browser.download.defaultFolder /* was /home/nrm */
```

to this:

```
browser.download.defaultFolder    /* to /home/nrm/Desktop */
```

which is the location of the desktop under GNOME 2.x.

If your mother is Italian or Chinese, you might need support for non-English web sites. To prepare any required language packs and plug-ins, the hard way to proceed is to rebundle Firefox with the needed packs included in the install bundle. That's not recommended unless you plan on doing hundreds of installs. It's massive extra preparation for a marginally faster install result.

The easy way is to prepare a set of bookmarks using your own installation of Firefox (or any browser). Surf to a sample web page written in each required language and bookmark it. Do the same thing with demo pages for each required plug-in. Once the bookmark set is collected, export the bookmarks or locate the file that holds them.

Usually, the bookmarks file looks like an HTML file. For Mozilla-based products, it's in the user profile area. Take that file with you to the computer on which you're installing Firefox. Install Firefox normally, and then choose Bookmarks → Bookmarks Manager. In the new window that appears, choose File → Import → From File, and then import your special bookmarks. Now they're part of the bookmark set in Firefox. Surf to each bookmarked page, and you'll be offered the extra files you need as each page appears, or else the yellow information bar will invite you to download missing pieces. Once you've accepted them all (this could be a slow process on a dial-up connection), your install is complete. Afterward, decommission the plug-in manager with these preferences:

```
application.use_ns_plugin_finder    /* false = default */
plugins.scan.4xPluginFolder         /* Set to false. Default = true */
plugins.scan.plid.all               /* Set to false. Default = true */
```

The first preference says, "Don't use an old, backward-compatible plug-in system from the days of Netscape Communicator 4.x." It would be a rare occasion when you would ever want to do that. The second preference says, "Don't check old installations of Netscape Communicator for plug-ins." Normally, Firefox will do that, just in case some old plug-ins are hanging around. The last preference says, "Don't consult the Windows registry for suitable plug-ins."

You can avoid a slow install process if you just note the language packs and plug-ins that are present in the user profile area in your own Firefox install. You can hand-copy them across to the new computer if you want. Just restart Firefox to see the plug-ins recognized.

Firefox knows about four common plug-ins: Adobe Acrobat Reader, Sun's Java Runtime Environment (JRE), Apple QuickTime, and Windows Media Player. You can't stop Firefox from being aware of these things, but by setting the following preferences, you can tell it that your current plug-in versions are so recent that it should never try to upgrade them:

```
plugin.scan.SunJRE                  /* Set to 99.0 */
plugin.scan.Acrobat                 /* Set to 99.0 */
plugin.scan.Quicktime               /* Set to 99.0 */
plugin.scan.WindowsMediaPlayer      /* Set to 99.0 */
```

The value for these preferences is a version string. If necessary, it can be stated in four parts—e.g., 2.1.3.4, which is a specific build of Version 2.1. None of the well-known plug-ins are ever likely to reach Version 99, so 99 is a safe value to use. Each value in the set of four numbers can go up to 255.

Stop All Secret Network Activity

#13 Send packets across the Internet only when they come from user actions.

Firefox has a mind of its own. It sometimes connects to other computers across the Internet without asking you first. Not only is this a privacy issue, but it can also be awkward. For example, the browser might be installed on test equipment that is network-enabled only intermittently. If you are performing network diagnostics, that's another time when you don't want any unexpected chatter on the line. Finally, if you configuration-control all of your installed software, then you probably prefer that Firefox not upgrade itself automatically either. Here's how to stop all of that stuff.

Stop Secret Updates

Firefox periodically (daily) checks the Mozilla Update web site (*http://update.mozilla.org*) to see what's new. If there are critical patches, the home page displayed at startup is replaced with a warning page. If there are any patches at all, an icon appears on the menu bar. To turn off that functionality, set these preferences:

```
app.update.enabled            /* default is false */
app.update.autoUpdateEnabled  /* set to false. default = true */
```

The second preference stops Firefox from polling the web server to see if there's anything new to report to the user.

These two additional preferences do the same job as the previous preferences, but they control update checks for extensions, plug-ins, and themes rather than checks for the core Firefox product:

```
extensions.update.enabled            /* default is false */
extensions.update.autoUpdateEnabled  /* set to false. default = true */
```

Firefox also performs trivial updates of site icons, the small icons that appear next to URLs. Generally, they provide brand marks for web sites. Figure 2-1 shows a browser window with three site icons marked out.

The Google site icon (the rightmost one) is retrieved from a local copy. The other two are drawn from their original web sites. That's fine for the URL that the user typed into the Location bar, but if the Bookmarks toolbar contains a lot of bookmarks that have site icons, Firefox will download them

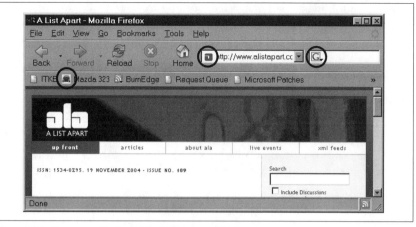

Figure 2-1. Site icons displayed in the browser window

from all over the place in order to make the toolbar look pretty. Site icons can also be downloaded if the sidebar is displayed. To turn off icon retrieval, set these preferences:

```
browser.chrome.site_icons /* set to false. default = true */
browser.chrome.favicons   /* set to false. default = true */
```

Configuration updates are another class of updates that Firefox might perform, if the browser is run under the following conditions. None of these occur in the standard install, but they're all configurable options:

- If web proxies are in place [Hack #15]
- If there are custom configuration files [Hack #29]
- If Certificate Revocation Lists (CRLs) or Online Certificate Status Protocol (OSCP) is configured [Hack #17]

There are also update issues that are separate from the main Firefox installation. You can never be sure what update behavior an extension or plug-in might introduce of its own accord. Extensions are free to contact any web site. If the extension comes from a trusted source, then a consumer review of the extension's intent should suffice. If that's not enough, the extension source code itself must be reviewed for use of any Mozilla XPCOM objects that are network-oriented.

Be particularly careful if an extension adds compiled libraries to the Firefox install. Such code can't be trusted as is; you need to inspect its original source as well. If the compiled source is supplied with the extension, that is still not enough for trust, because the compiled files could have originated from other source. Trust only the provider, not the files.

Finally, the following preference has nothing to do with Firefox. It is used only by the Mozilla Application Suite's Smart Browsing feature. If you see it, ignore it:

```
browser.related.autoload /* 0 = always, 1 = after first use, 2 = never */
```

Stop Secret Submissions

In all quality web browsers, an unsigned web page cannot submit an HTML form to a web site without the user being involved. There are many special cases that need to be avoided if this rule is to be enforced, and there's no way to toggle checking for these cases on or off for an unsigned page.

Firefox, however, also supports submission to web sites using SOAP, WSDL, and XML-RPC. A rule called the *Same Origin policy* allows web pages to "phone home" to their server of origin without asking the user. The only way to stop this activity is to disable JavaScript access to the web page objects that provide these services, and the only way to do that is to use capability-based permissions [Hack #20]. Here's an example that disables the invoke( ) and asyncInvoke( ) methods of the SOAPCall object:

```
capability.policy.default.SOAPCall.invoke      /* set to "NoAccess" */
capability.policy.default.SOAPCall.invokeAsync /* set to "NoAccess" */
```

Such capability settings are required for each object that offers a network-enabled call interface. So, as another example, WebServiceProxyFactory. createProxy( ) and its equivalents also require capability preferences.

A further, trivial example of secret submission is the use of cookies by a web site. If being tracked by a cookie bothers you, you can turn cookie support off this way:

```
network.cookie.cookieBehaviour /* set to 2 (none), default = 0 (all) */
```

Finally, there is the case of Java applets. Applets can "phone home" just as web services can. There's no way to stop this, short of disabling Java entirely. You can disable specific ports [Hack #16] if you want.

As for the update case, you can never be sure what submission behavior an extension or plug-in might introduce.

Stop Not-So-Secret Background Downloads

If you've become addicted to tabbed browsing, you might spend a lot of time looking at one web page, while lots of other web pages are loaded into the tabs that are *behind* the current tab. The most convenient arrangement is to have those tabs load their pages while they're still hidden. When you change tabs, it's likely that the web page in the tab will be ready to view. This convenience is the default arrangement.

The convenience comes at a cost, though. If you maintain, say, five tabs, your demand for web page data is up to five times the demand of a single browser page. If all of those tabs are busy loading, then the front page will get only one-fifth of the share of the connection. So you might have to wait longer to view it. Furthermore, just by opening tabs, you demand more web page data from your ISP—the same amount as if you were opening five separate windows. In the case of tabs, though, people often open tabs *just in case*. That means extra download activity for content that's not actually a high priority for the user. Some call that waste.

There are two preferences that will reduce the tab download burden on your Internet connection at the cost of convenience:

```
browser.tabs.loadInBackground          /* Set to false, default = true */
browser.tabs.loadBookmarksInBackground  /* false = default */
```

The first preference turns off URL loading for tabs that aren't in front. If you change tabs, so that the current one is no longer displayed, the matching page for the new front tab will then start to load. The second preference has to do with bookmark groups. If you store a set of tabs as a bookmark group, you can recall all of those tabs with a single click. By default, those tabs won't start to download, which is what you probably prefer.

There is currently no way to make the Download Manager back off and use only a smaller chunk of your Internet connection. So far, it will always grab all the bandwidth it can get. That means downloads are reasonably fast, but it also means that viewing web pages is always slowed down if downloading is going on.

HACK #14 Work with Single Sign-On Servers

If your web content is hidden behind a security regime, here's how to get through.

This hack explains how to stop Firefox from prompting the user for already supplied login details. In other words, Firefox can be part of a *single sign-on* environment, where several servers, applications, and/or services share login details. Firefox understands several kinds of server requests for user credentials.

Single sign-on servers are usually found in an Intranet environment. They provide a method of controlling who can access remote servers and the services that they provide, and they can reduce user frustration. Such arrangements are not the same as Secure Socket Layer (SSL). Although SSL and Secure HTTP swap credentials with SSL-enabled servers, those kinds of credentials (digital certificates and digital signatures) are mostly organization-based, not user-based.

The good news is that single sign-on is a no-brainer in Firefox for the simple case. The simple case isn't that much fun, though, so let's explore the subject a bit before we come back to it. Note that special server-oriented configuration files [Hack #29] can also be set up to perform server login actions. In that case, the server is an LDAP server.

The Single Sign-On Technology Jungle

In conceptual terms, single sign-on is a constraint enforced by servers. The server demands special information from the client (for example, a web browser) and refuses to process any request until that information is forthcoming. If a weak *security regime* (system of identification) is in place, the client might just send operating system login details as plain text to the server. If a strong security regime is in place, the client and server play complicated information games with each other that keep login details secret from everyone.

 To understand single sign-on technology in detail requires a great deal of study. This section provides a brief overview only.

Locating standards. The first part of sign-on technology involves standards. One technique for sign-on message exchange is to formulate them as HTTP requests and responses. This is the technique that Firefox requires to access secure web servers. Many, many Internet Engineering Task Force Requests For Comment (IETF RFCs) standards cover this subject. They're all available at *http://www.ietf.org/rfc/*. Here are a few of the critical ones:

RFC 822: Standard for the format of ARPA Internet text messages
This is the granddaddy of all messaging standards, and it's a good place to start if you're not familiar with Internet messaging.

RFC 2616: Hypertext Transfer protocol -- HTTP/1.1
This standard shows how the core messaging standard is specialized for web messages. It includes the important 401 and 407 return codes, which are returned by a web server that requires a login but hasn't yet received any login information.

RFC 2617: HTTP Authentication: Basic and Digest Access Authentication
This standard adds header fields to the ordinary HTTP standard so that comparisons of user login data between client and server can occur over HTTP. It adds the critical WWW-Authenticate header item, along with a primitive security regime that can use it.

RFC 2743: Generic Security Service Application Programming Interface, Version 2

This standard specifies GSS-API. It's a programming library that wraps around whatever security regimes are available, providing portability. On a given computer, it might provide access to several separate security regimes, such as operating-system login, database login, and smart-card validation. A client like Firefox can use GSS-API to decide what security regimes are supported.

RFC 2478: The Simple and Protected GSS-API Negotiation Mechanism

This standard describes the forward-looking SPNEGO standard. It describes how a client and server can compare via HTTP the security mechanisms that they have available via a GSS-API implementation. It describes how they can agree on which security regime to use.

IETF draft-brezak-spnego-http-04.txt: SPNEGO over HTTP

This standard offers Microsoft's ideas on how SPNEGO and GSS-API should work together.

Brand names and standards. The second part of sign-on mixes brand names with standards names:

Kerberos

A high-quality security regime that GSS-API can take advantage of. It's a better quality regime than the ones documented in the previous RFCs, and it requires its own server. Although it's available on Microsoft Windows 2000 and later, it's used mostly on Unix/Linux.

LAN Manager

An ancient Microsoft technology from the days of Windows 95 that provided barely secure LAN access in a way that competed in part with Novell's Netware products.

NTLM

Microsoft's upgrade of LAN Manager for New Technology (NT) versions of Windows (i.e., Windows NT 4, 2000, and XP). It was also back-ported to Windows 95 and 98. NTLM is also the name of NTLM's security regime.

NTLMSSP

NTLM with Security Support Provider (SSP) provides enhancements that removed the need to prompt users every time it's used. It was also back-ported to Windows 95 and 98. NTLMSSP has the same purpose as SPNEGO.

Samba

An open source file and print server for Linux that implements several Windows protocols.

Apache

An open source web server.

Squid

An open source caching web proxy.

 Samba, Apache, and Squid all support NTLM and NTLMSSP, so NTLM isn't restricted to Windows.

SSPI

Security Support Provider Interface (SSPI), Microsoft's implementation of a security regime wrapper in the style of GSS-API.

Single Sign-On: The Easy Way

Single sign-on is most commonly used on Windows desktops. Support for this is enabled by default. Using this default setting, Firefox will attempt to silently authenticate the user's Windows domain login against a proxy server. The proxy server used is the default NTLM server for authentication; it can either be a Windows server or Samba, and so on. Firefox's default NLTM behavior is turned on with this preference:

```
network.automatic-ntlm-auth.allow-proxies /* true = default */
```

Provided the current proxy server is set up for authentication, there is automatic support for the NTLM security regime in the local network. That regime has weak security, so it is not automatically supported for connecting to servers over public networks. If that kind of connectivity is required, then all such servers must be explicitly identified as trusted. You can create such a whitelist with this preference:

```
network.automatic-ntlm-auth.trusted-uris   /* default is a null string */
```

The value for this preference is a comma-separated list of URI fragments. This sample string shows the three legal kinds of fragments:

```
"https://, http://www.example.com, test.com"
```

The first fragment says, "Trust all URLs with an http scheme." The second fragment (a full URL) says, "Trust this particular web site." The third fragment is interpreted to mean http://*anything*.test.com, so any web site that is a subdomain of test.com, including test.com itself, will also be trusted.

There are several potholes to avoid when you use single sign-on with NTLM:

- On older Windows boxes running Windows 98 or thereabouts, a Windows patch is required to make everything work. See this Microsoft MSDN knowledge base article for details: "Q266772" (*http://kb. microsoft.com*). This problem is also discussed in Mozilla's Bugzilla (*http://bugzilla.mozilla.org*) bug 212336.

- Depending on the network setup, users must sometimes remember to quote their username as domain\user. This occurs when domains (workgroups) are not defaulted or matched correctly between client and server. Doing so is somewhat nonintuitive for users. Stick to matching, default domains if you can.

- Firefox does not generate Version 2 NTLM responses. It is an implementation that provides *just enough* support. It does not generate LAN Manager 2 (LM2) or NTLMv2 or NTLM2 responses either. The net effect is that the extra information supplied with those later protocols is ignored.

Single Sign-On: The Hard Way

Very briefly, the hard way to use single sign-on is to guarantee a quality security regime for all sign-on activities. That means using Kerberos. Kerberos is available on all Windows versions from Windows 2000 and later, and on Linux and Macintosh.

Support for SPNEGO is required for Kerberos-based single sign-on. In Firefox, this is turned off by default for two reasons. First, a hostile server could negotiate the browser client into using the NTLM security regime, which is too weak for general Internet use. Second, SPNEGO is open to obscure security attacks when the actual security regime also runs over HTTP. It's possible for a hostile web server to pretend that it serves someone else's domain, in which case it can take over negotiations.

Firefox has two preferences that allow SPNEGO to be turned on. They are whitelists of URIs, in the same format as the NTLM whitelist:

```
network.negotiate-auth.trusted-uris     /* defaults to empty string */
network.negotiate-auth.delegation-uris  /* defaults to empty string */
```

The first preference identifies web sites whose SPNEGO messages will be accepted by Firefox. This opens the door to obscure security attacks, so this preference can't be used alone. There are two ways to mitigate that problem. The first is for the browser to ignore requests for HTTP-enabled security regimes, such as NTLM, Basic, and Digest. Currently, that is not implemented, because single sign-on usually occurs in a secure Intranet and those regimes are good enough in that environment. The second mitigation strategy is to use the second preference as well and to carefully control what the web servers send out.

The second preference identifies web sites whose HTTP SPNEGO messages should result in Firefox and the web server delegating the authentication process away from HTTP. This is done using a Kerberos server that acts as a third party. Once SPNEGO starts, Firefox connects, via SSPI or GSS-API, to that Kerberos server. Using the complicated Kerberos protocol, the Kerberos server is told by the Firefox client who the user is. The SPNEGO protocol, which does run over HTTP, then carries some Kerberos information from web client to web server . That is the only time SPNEGO is used. The web server finishes up by checking with the Kerberos server whether authentication was successful. It accepts the reported answer as validation or rejection of the user's identity.

To do all this, set the two whitelists to allow the required web server. That server is then a trusted URI, allowing SPNEGO to go ahead, and it is also identified as Kerberos-enabled. The web server must therefore be a version able to consult a Kerberos server. Then, ensure when configuring the web server that it sends out `WWW-Authenticate` headers that offer only Kerberos as a security regime. That tells Firefox that Kerberos is the only choice.

Finally, ensure that the Kerberos server is set up correctly for the user population. That means configuring it to be aware of the users that require authentication, as well as ensuring it is exposed to enough of the network to cover all users and all white-listed web servers. Note that some web servers may have an integrated Kerberos server, or they might use operating-system-supplied Kerberos service APIs. In these cases, the Kerberos server might be a *virtual server* with no separate existence.

Work with Web Proxies

#15   Make Firefox automatically discover the settings it should use for accessing the Web.

The Web is full of proxy and cache servers. Firefox only has to reach the one nearest to you in order to provide connectivity. If your environment includes web servers hidden behind complex security arrangements, this hack will help you point Firefox at the right proxies.

Overview of Proxy Options

There are four strategies for proxy access: none, static, PAC, and WPAD. Setting up proxies is not the same thing as implementing full server control of Firefox configuration items [Hack #29]. However, it does have some features that are similar to remote configuration.

The Firefox Options dialog box is the starting point for proxy configuration. The General panel holds the Connection configuration item. Depending on your desktop arrangements, such as if your window is slightly too small, you might not see that item. To fix that and expose the Connection Settings... button, just enlarge the window by dragging its bottom right corner outward.

Figure 2-2 shows the Connection Settings subdialog.

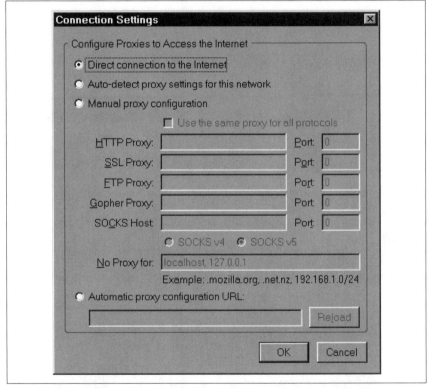

Figure 2-2. Proxy connections dialog box

The four radio buttons in Figure 2-2 are alternative values for a single preference:

```
network.proxy.type  /* an integer, default = 0 */
```

Table 2-1 shows the relationship between the dialog options, preference values, and their associated standards.

Table 2-1. Dialog options, preference values, and associated standards

Radio option	network.proxy.type	Standards used to implement
Direct connection	0	Plain DNS, sockets, and ports
Auto-detect proxy settings	4	Web Proxy Auto-Discovery Protocol (WPAD). IETF draft standard *draft-ietf-wrec-wpad-01.txt plus PAC*
Manual proxy configuration	1	Plain DNS, sockets and ports
Automatic proxy configuration URL	2	HTTP plus nonstandard Proxy Auto-Configuration (PAC) file format.
-	3	For backwards compatibility, same as 0 (zero). Do not use.

The other items in Figure 2-2 also map directly to preferences. Type the URL *about:config* into Firefox and filter on the word proxy to find them.

Setting Up Direct Connects and Static Proxies

Direct connection and static proxies rely only on the underlying TCP/IP network and access to the Domain Name System (DNS). If you avoid domain names and use only TCP/IP v4 addresses, such as 192.168.1.2, then you don't even need DNS.

If you choose *direct connection* in the Connection Settings dialog box, you have immediate access to the Internet and the Web. All that is required is optional access to DNS and a default TCP/IP route. Everything you do is passed through the default route, which presumably has the Internet at the other end. Dial-up connections provide both DNS and routes automatically; corporate PCs usually acquire both at boot time, courtesy of the local network administrator (see him for details). Direct-connected Firefox uses the standard port numbers for all necessary protocols (i.e., 80 for HTTP, 20 for FTP and 110 for POP3; on Linux/Unix, see the */etc/services* file for details). These can be overridden for specific URLs, such as *http://www.example.com:8080*.

If you choose *manual proxy configuration* and fill in some proxy hosts, the situation is the same as a direct connection, except that Firefox will connect to the hosts specified on a per-protocol basis, rather than blindly going through the default route. For many network topologies, this is no different from a direct connection, but it does allow for load sharing if the number of desktops is large. Desktops can alternate in their use of HTTP servers, for example. Any nontrivial LAN switch can be configured to perform per-protocol and per-port redirections, so manual proxy configuration is not widely useful in a fixed setting. Simple-minded, shrink-wrapped, low-end hubs, repeaters, and switches generally aren't powerful enough for this, though. If you access work remotely via a virtual private network (VPN) or a WiFi hotspot, then manual configuration might suit the access requirements dictated by your organization. Make a second Firefox profile with manual proxies and use that for phoning home.

One further use of manual configuration is to reduce load on the web gateway of an organization with a slow link. By blacklisting local networks, requests to hosts on those local networks go direct. That means the local intranet can be served fast and transparently, leaving the web gateway server to be used only for external requests.

Setting Up Scripted PAC Proxies

proxy.pac files were an initiative of the Netscape Navigator 2.0 browser and have been supported by Netscape and Mozilla ever since. Such a file resides at a URL and is downloaded when Firefox starts. This preferences indicates where the file should be accessed:

```
network.proxy.autoconfig_url    /* set to a full URL */
```

Once it is downloaded, the script in the file tells Firefox which proxies to use for which URLs. It is therefore a more powerful mechanism than manual configuration, which knows nothing about specific URLs requested. Since the file resides on the server, it can be configuration-controlled by the server administrator. That's useful if services provided by the server change at short notice. Firefox regularly checks to see if a required *proxy.pac* file has changed. If so, it is downloaded again and rerun.

There is no standard for the file's format, except that it should contain JavaScript. (Internet Explorer supports a similar but not identical format that has the same purpose.) The file should be delivered over the Web with this MIME type:

```
application/x-javascript-config
```

Don't use this other content type, which is old and not supported:

```
application/x-ns-proxy-autoconfig
```

What do you put in the *proxy.pac* file? Implement this JavaScript function:

```
function FindProxyForURL(url, host) { ... }
```

Firefox calls this function each time it attempts to retrieve a URL. The URL argument is the full URL supplied; the host argument is the domain name or TCP/IP address subpart of the URL. The function returns a list of proxy options to the browser as a single, semicolon-separated string. Firefox then goes through the list, trying each option in turn. Here's a simple example of this function:

```
function FindProxyForURL (url, host) {
  if ( url.match("https:")  ) {
    return "SOCKS secure:99";
  }
  else if ( host.match("google") ) {
    return "PROXY gateway:80";
  }
  else {
    return "DIRECT; PROXY gateway:8080";
  }
}
```

In this example, the regular expression methods that are part and parcel of the JavaScript String object are used to analyze the URL. If it's a Secure HTTP URL, a host named secure and port 99 are used. If it happens to be a Google web page, then the proxy host named gateway is used. If it's anything else, Firefox first tries DIRECT (i.e., no proxy), and if that fails, it tries the gateway host, but on a different port. The preceding example illustrates all syntax options for the return string. Note that return values are semicolon separated when more than one option is returned.

Because the *proxy.pac* file is a JavaScript script, you can make the content as complicated as you like. The script runs inside a special, secure sandbox, however, so there is a limited range of features to exploit.

Of the features available, a few are available only within the *proxy.pac* scripting environment. Three special functions are provided; there are also some trivial utility functions that do string processing. Here are the three main function signatures:

```
String tcpip_v4 address myIpAddress()
String tcpip_v4_address dnsResolve(String domain)
void                    proxyAlert(String message)
```

The proxy system is written as an XPCOM component defined in JavaScript. This means you can look at it; see the *nsProxyAutoConfig.js* file in the Firefox install area, in the *components* directory. This file makes advanced use of JavaScript, and it's easy to be confused when reading it: refresh yourself on JavaScript first. To spot the utility functions available in the *proxy.pac* runtime environment, find the variable in that file named pacUtils. It is transformed a bit like this just before the *proxy.pac* file is read:

```
eval(pacUtils)
```

The set of utility functions defined in the big pacUtils string are then available to proxy scripts. No other facilities are, however. Use the proxyAlert() function for debugging.

Setting Up WPAD Proxies

WPAD is an extension to the *proxy.pac* system. Instead of the proxy script being retrieved from a user-specified URL, it's retrieved from a known URL that requires no user data. All the work is done by the server administrator. The user merely chooses "automatic proxy configuration" (WPAD) when Firefox is first installed, or picks that option at a later time. Firefox expects the proxy script to be located at this URL:

http://wpad/wpad.dat

Since this string is fixed, the setup game consists of making sure that this URL points to a real host. You must set up a web server, copy the proxy script to the top of the web site, and then make the right domain name point to the whole thing. The last bit is the only hard part. Here's how to do it for Linux/Unix.

First, you can hack the required configuration files by hand. You need root access.

> Beware that some tools, such as RedHat's bindconf, manage important files for you and might overwrite your changes. If you use bindconf, go via the GUI; don't follow these instructions.

If you don't have DNS configured, then your */etc/resolv.conf* probably doesn't exist, and you must be relying on the */etc/hosts* file or a Network Information Services (NIS) equivalent. In that case, all you need to do is add a line for the new web server:

```
192.168.1.99 wpad
```

Add wpad as a new alternate name if the web server already has a name.

If you do have DNS configured, then it's trickier. In your DNS host's */etc/named.conf* file, you should already have a record for the current domain. It should look something like this (if your domain is called *example.com*):

```
zone "example.com" {
  type master;
  file "named.example.com";
};
```

The file called *named.example.com* probably resides at:

/var/named/named.example.com

You need to edit this file. Add a line at the end like this:

```
wpad IN A 192.168.1.99
```

Save the file and restart named. You've just added the *fully qualified domain name* (FQDN) wpad.example.com. You should be able to ping it and download the WPAD URL normally afterwards.

Firefox has Class 0 (minimally compliant) WPAD support. That means DNS support only, with no DHCP support. There is one exceptional feature. A security hobble prevents failed requests from being passed to higher level (more generic) domains if the first attempt at fetching the proxy script fails. You don't want to accidentally download *http://wpad.com/wpad.dat* instead of *http://wpad.example.com/wpad.dat*.

Ignore this preference if you see it, since it is left over from older Mozilla versions:

```
network.enablePad /* default = false, Pad = Proxy auto-detect */
```

HACK #16   Fine-Tune Ports and Sockets

You can configure Firefox network access down to the last detail if you want.

This hack explains how to chop off pieces of network access at the backend of the Firefox browser. This is done with preferences. Doing so provides strong protection against malicious web attacks, but it offers only weak security against user tampering. That's because, in the normal case, users can undo network-access changes via the *about:config* system. There is a way to serve these preferences up more securely using a server [Hack #29]. You can also configure proxy arrangements [Hack #15].

Disallow Ports

Firefox ports are allowed or disallowed using a multi-tiered system. In highest to lowest priority, these are the rules:

1. Always allow any port that Firefox absolutely must have to get its job done. The primary example is access to DNS via port 53.
2. Always allow some ports for their standard uses. Here's the current list:

   389, 636 (LDAP), 70 (gopher), 21, 22 (FTP), 79 (finger), 13 (datetime)
3. Allow all ports specified in Firefox's override list (a whitelist). You can indicate these ports by setting the following preference to a string containing a comma-separated list of port numbers that should be allowed (do not use spaces):

   ```
   network.security.ports.banned.override /* unset by default */
   ```
4. Disallow all ports specified in Firefox's blacklist. You can indicate these ports by setting the following preference to a string containing a

comma-separated list of port numbers that should not be allowed (do not use spaces):

```
network.security.ports.banned        /* unset by default */
```

5. Allow any port not covered by the other rules.

Set Socket Limits

You can fine-tune the performance and use of sockets, but only for specific protocols. There are many configuration options for HTTP, just one option for FTP, and none for other protocols. For FTP, tweak the following preference for a slow connection, for a heavily loaded server, or for ancient-style point-to-point UUX networks running over serial connections:

```
network.ftp.idleConnectionTimeout   /* 300 (secs) = default */
```

For HTTP, you can control the type, number, and aging behavior of the underlying sockets. You can also control which kind of sockets are used by default.

Here's the preference for secure sockets:

```
network.http.default-socket-type  /* "socks", "socks4", "ssl", "starttls" */
```

The default of nothing specifies ordinary, insecure PF_INET, SOCK_STREAM sockets. That's the sensible value; use socks only if you're on a VPN and don't want your HTTP requests to be visible. The checkboxes in the Advanced panel of the Option dialog box just enable or disable these protocol alternatives; they don't change the default.

Here's the preference for specifying the number of sockets. You can set several hard maximums. To set the limit for the Firefox client, use this preference:

```
network.http.max-connections            /* 24 = default */
```

To set the limit for each server the client connects to, use this preference:

```
network.http.max-connections-per-server   /* 8 = default */
```

That prevents the browser from flooding any particular server with connection requests.

A difficulty for web browsers and other programs that use short-lived TCP/IP connections is that TCP/IP v4 (the common version) is optimized to perform best for connections requiring high data volumes. That's not typical behavior for an HTTP request. The TCP/IP v4 startup phase for a connection, during which the data volume requirements are unknown, is always slow. It's best, therefore, to keep a socket connection open and reuse it to avoid this overhead. These preferences ensure sockets hang around for a while after the browser has finished its first use of them:

```
network.http.keep-alive              /* true = default */
network.http.keep-alive.timeout      /* 300 (secs) = default */
network.http.proxy.keepalive         /* true = default */
```

If sockets can be kept open, then a browser can take up many socket endpoints that a web server has to offer and keep them. That's a denial-of-service attack on a web server, something that no friendly web browser should do. These preferences set high-water limits on how many reusable sockets are allowed, per server:

```
network.http.max-persistent-connections-per-proxy  /* 2 = default */
network.http.max-persistent-connections-per-server /* 4 = default */
```

Finally, this preference does nothing, so ignore it:

```
network.http.connect.timeout             /* socket startup time */
```

Manage Digital Certificates

#17 Who gives Firefox trustworthy advice? You can change that set of advisors.

All content from a web site that advertises itself as secure has to be checked. Secure content must be accompanied by a digital signature and by a certificate that says whom the digital signature belongs to. The certificate must originate from a Certificate Authority (an organization) that Firefox knows. This hack explains how to change the certificates and Certificate Authorities (CAs) that Firefox knows about.

Examining Existing Certificates and Authorities

The Firefox Options dialog box lets you manage digital certificates. Click the Advanced icon to display that panel, expand the Certificates item, and click the Manage Certificates... button. Figure 2-3 shows that window, with the fourth tab in front.

If you click on any of the rows labeled Builtin Object Token, you can then examine the certificate by pressing the View button or limit its use via the Edit button. All of the certificates listed are bundled with the standard Firefox install. There's little reason to delete them, but you can if you want. If you do so, that will restrict the number of secure web sites that Firefox can successfully visit.

You can also list these certificates from outside Firefox. Copy these files from the current Firefox profile to a temporary directory:

```
cert8.db key3.db secmod.db
```

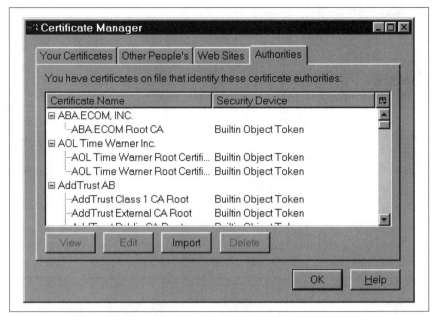

Figure 2-3. Default certificate authority certificates in Firefox

All three files (*cert8.db*, *key2.db*, and *secmod.db*) are required. To see their contents, use signtool [Hack #18], like this:

```
signtool -L -d"."
```

These three files contain, respectively, certificates, public-key encryption keys, and a list of security modules that provide enabling regimes for browser security. An enabling regime is just a starting point for security. The alphabet soup that describes such regimes includes PKCS #11 and PSM standards. Implementations of those standards make up the default (built-in) security regime for Firefox. Other regimes that could be added (via additional software libraries) include systems that support smart cards and dongles.

The other tabs in this dialog box contain these details:

Your certificates
> Certificates you might use to sign email or other outward-bound information. Firefox does not use these certificates, but it might share its profile with another application, such as Thunderbird. They are sourced locally or from a smart card.

Other people's certificates
> Certificates received from inbound information, such as signed email. Firefox does not use these certificates, but it might share its profile with another application, such as Thunderbird.

Web site certificates

Certificates stored by user action. If a web site presents a certificate to the user, and the user both accepts it and tells Firefox to allow that site in future, then the certificate will be copied here.

Adding More CA Certificates

Certificates are defined by a range of standards, collectively called X.509. You can add authoritative CA certificates to Firefox at any time. The first step is to establish the credibility of the CA you're going to add. Don't assume that all CAs are credible. Free software exists that lets anyone set themselves up as a CA. Once the CA has delivered (for free) its root certificate, import it.

To import via the GUI, click the Import button in Figure 2-3 and supply the certificate file. Firefox thinks files with the following extensions are certificates, but you can identify the file by hand (the extension isn't important):

```
.crt .cert .cer .pem .der
```

The file should be in either in DER or (old Netscape) Base-64 encoding. Firefox can handle chained certificates stored together in one file, but it might not display all of them before final import.

To import direct from the Web, make sure the CA certificate is served up with this content type:

```
application/x-x509-ca-cert
```

Use this alternate type for web server certificates:

```
application/x-x509-server-cert
```

To import certificates using the command line, work on copies of the *cert8.db*, *key3.db*, and *secmod.db* security files with the certutil tool that is bundled with signtool. Here's a suitable command-line argument:

```
certutil -A -n "nickname" -t c -d "." [ -a ] -i new_ca.cert
```

Use the -a option for Base-64-encoded certificates only. Note that the -d option requires a space before its argument. Copy the files back to Firefox afterward.

Rejecting Certificates with CRLs and OSCP

If a certificate owner loses his credibility, he shouldn't be allowed to use his certificate anymore. Somehow, the browser user needs to find this out. The browser displays a warning if it detects a trust request that uses a bad certificate. But how does the browser know?

Certificate Rejection Lists (CRLs) are one solution. CRLs are files with formats defined in RFC 2459. Each list is a set of certificates that a particular CA wishes they could revoke. Firefox checks all installed CRLs when signed content requests user trust. None are installed by default. If you have all the CRLs from all of the CAs Firefox knows about, then the number of bad folks you'll accidentally trust is much reduced.

One problem with CRLs is that they get out of date. Every CRL should be brought up to date frequently. Firefox can do that either at set expiry times in the future or at a fixed regular frequency. The default frequency if any CRLs are installed is 30 seconds. Some update information is also stored in the preferences system, but the details are too gory for this hack.

To collect all the CRLs you need, visit the web sites of all CAs known by Firefox. Click on all the links to CRLs at those sites. CRLs are then downloaded and installed. They're detected using this content type:

```
application/x-x509-crl
```

You can also import a CRL from a file if the CA delivers it to you as an email attachment.

A second solution to bad certificates is Online Certificate Status Protocol (OCSP). If it's enabled, Firefox won't check CRLs each time trust is requested by signed content. Instead, Firefox will send a request to the URL specified when OCSP was turned on. The server at the other end (or a proxy server) will report if the trust request includes a safe certificate or not. If it is, the original content will be trusted. That's a lot of extra network overhead for a dial-up connection, though.

HACK #18 Digitally Sign Content

Content delivered to Firefox can request special privileges from the user.

Normal Firefox content, whether it's HTML, XHTML or XUL, runs inside a sandbox that stops it from doing anything risky, such as modifying files stored on the local disk. This hack explains how to ask the user for permission to escape the sandbox. If permission is given, the content (usually scripts) can do whatever it likes. You can also arrange matters so that the user is never asked for permission [Hack #19].

Get Oriented on Security Concepts

The design ideas behind granting permission are *trust* and *identity*. If the web page content is to have full control over the browser, there must be trust between the browser user and the content creator—two real, live people. Access to technical features is secondary to this human principle. In the conservative world of security, trust can be assured only if identity can be properly determined. Here are the identity constraints built into Firefox:

- The browser user always knows whom a content maker requesting trust is.
- The browser user can always physically track down a content maker that requested trust.
- The browser user is always free to reject a request for trust.

The Firefox user can drop these constraints if they so choose. When presented with information about a content maker, the user can tell Firefox to trust that content maker in the future. That puts identity information about the content maker in files in the user profile area. Firefox will always validate signed content, but it can do so silently if the user directs it to do so.

Validating signed content is done automatically by Firefox. Making signed content is a task for a web site content creator.

These identity constraints are supported by technology—digital certificates and digital signing—and by a special sandbox-breaking API that only works when trust is in place. They also demand some old-fashioned paperwork. A real, live person called a Certificate Authority (CA) is required. Little of that infrastructure is obvious or meaningful to an end user confronted by a permission request, though.

Get Signing Tools

Netscape Security Services (NSS) is a technology that is part of the Mozilla source code used to make Firefox. NSS includes a small, separately downloadable program called signtool. Get it here:

> *http://ftp.mozilla.org/pub/mozilla.org/security/nss/releases/*

signtool can combine content (HTML, JavaScript, XUL, CSS, images, anything) with digital signatures by using certificates. signtool is incompatible with similar systems used in Netscape 4.x, Internet Explorer, and Java. It is good only for Mozilla-based browsers and other software systems that support it. signtool has some compatibility with Java, but a second tool called certtool (*http://ftp.mozilla.org/pub/mozilla.org/security/nss/releases/*) is also needed.

Signing content is called *object signing*, which is different than signing a certificate. The result of object signing is a JAR file [Hack #86], which contains both content files and digital signature files.

Signing content is a nuisance for technologists that just want to build something. Mozilla allows signing to occur in two separate ways. You can sign in a test environment, where it is easier to use, or you can sign in a published environment, where it is fully secure.

Sign Content for Test Purposes

In a test environment, two of the three identity requirements can be dropped. The browser user can be kept ignorant of the content maker. The browser user is thus unable to track down that person. That leaves only the requirement that the browser user explicitly grant permission to the content maker. To enable this weaker security arrangement:

- The content maker uses a special certificate instead of a normal one from a CA.

- The browser user ensures it's OK for Firefox to accept content signed with that special certificate.

In a test environment, both of these roles are likely to be taken by one developer. To create the special certificate, first create a certificate database. Then, make the special object-signing certificate and put it into the database:

```
mkdir certs
cd certs
certutil -N -d .
signtool -G 'special' -p 'password' -d .
```

special is the name chosen for the new certificate. The *password* string should be whatever you typed in when certutil ran. Use single quotes on Linux/Unix to prevent shell reinterpretation.

To tell Firefox it's OK to work with this certificate, use the following preference:

```
signed.applets.codebase_principle_support /* set to true. Default = false */
```

Note the security hole: this setting indicates that content signed with *any* special certificate (from any web site) will be accepted. The name of this preference is an historical artifact from Netscape 4.x. There is no Java or Java applets at work.

You are now ready to sign your content. Suppose it's in the directory *content*, which is a sibling of the *certs* directory:

```
cd ..
signtool -d certs -k 'special' -p 'password' -Z result.jar content
```

The file *result.jar* is all the signed content. Put it behind the web server and retrieve it with a URL, or with a jar: URL. jar: URLs are normally used for chrome packages [Hack #75], but you can put ordinary web site content in them, too.

Sign Content for Publication

In a production environment, you must have a genuine digital certificate before you start. Suppose your organization's name is *Acme*, and the certificate comes from the CA Verisign, who gave it this short name: *Acme Cert (Verisign)*. Once that certificate is in a handy certificate database [Hack #17], make your object-signing certificate based on it as follows:

```
cd certs
signtool -G 'objcert' -k 'Acme Cert (Verisign)' -p 'password' -d .
```

Next, sign your content with it. This is the same as in the test environment, except this time we have a real certificate:

```
cd ..
signtool -d certs -k 'objcert' -p 'password' -Z result.jar content
```

Put the *result.jar* file on the web server as before. You're ready to go and don't need the special preference.

Do Something with Trusted Content

If you've asked the browser user for trust, you must need it for some reason. There are two things you can do: you can sign an XPI file, and you can write scripts that break normal web scripting rules.

If you sign an XPI file, that file can be installed into Firefox from any web site, provided that the user gives permission. Since an XPI file and JAR file have the same format, the signing procedure is also the same. The web site that delivers the XPI file does not need to be listed as an authoritative source of extensions or patches in this case.

This sample JavaScript script requests all possible permissions and then runs some code that wouldn't work in a normal web page:

```
function run( ) {
  // normal permissions to start with
  critical_section( )
  // normal permissions again
}

// Might be a trusted function, depending on who calls it.
function do_stuff( )
{
  var list = window.Components.classes; // try to access XPCOM
}
```

```
function critical_section() {
  // ask the user for permissions; should check return value as well

  netscape.security.PrivilegeManager.enablePrivilege(
    "UniversalBrowserRead"       + " " +
    "UniversalXPConnect"         + " " +
    "UniversalPreferencesRead"   + " " +
    "UniversalPreferencesWrite"  + " " +
    "CapabilityPreferencesAccess" + " " +
    "UniversalFileRead"          + " " +
    "myCapability");

  window.resizeTo(20,20);   // make current window tiny - requires trust.
  do_stuff()                // called with trust in place

} // permissions will end when this function returns

run() // do it
```

The myCapability option is a custom capability class [Hack #20]. See *http:// www.mozilla.org/projects/security/components/signed-scripts.html* for details on the meaning of all the options.

HACK #19 Grant Trust with Master Certificates

Control secure uses of Firefox completely with an overriding master certificate.

Web site content can request trusted access to Firefox by presenting content that is digitally signed [Hack #18]. Trusted access lets the content break out of the web page sandbox. The user must manually confirm that they trust the signed content presented before this can happen. This hack explains how to avoid that manual confirmation.

Master Certificate Concepts

Firefox supports the use of a *master certificate*. Such a certificate is different than the *master password* that can be set in the Options dialog box in the following ways:

Master password
Stored in the Firefox user profile area: one piece of data per user profile. Provides an overall security check per profile and privacy for each user.

Master certificate
Stored in the Firefox install area: one JAR file only. Provides an overall security check for one or more remote websites and secure access to the browser for those web sites.

In other words, a master password keeps other users out; a master certificate lets web sites in. Since all this information is stored on the same computer as Firefox, both are subject to change from anyone who can log in to the computer.

A typical use of a master certificate is for a vendor, distributor, or deployer to bundle it with a Mozilla-based product. This gives a distributor a back door through which they can control the browser's security status. This back door can be exploited for different reasons, depending on the web environment:

In a conservative environment

> It allows the distributor to create a community of trusted web sites that all have secure access to the user's browser. Such a community can aggregate value-added services in the user's browser.

In a liberal environment

> It allows a distributor to insist that security restrictions must be dropped by those that read either the vendor's web site or the vendor's friends' web sites. Such an environment ensures that no user can hold back from engaging with the rest of the community.

Master certificates are, therefore, a management tool similar to Firefox's Update Manager, with the following differences:

- The Update Manager requires both dialog boxes and user interaction. Master certificates work automatically.

- The Update Manager provides search, version, download, and install tools. Master certificates must be deployed by hand.

- The master certificate uses fine-grained security. Update Manager is all-or-nothing.

- Scripts trusted via the master-certificate system must still request the secure access they need. Scripts in updated extensions and patches are automatically secure.

In both cases, the user must download a URL before any security checks happen. You can arrange matters so that such checks are automatic. For example, you can set the home page to a URL that points to suitably signed content.

Deploying Master Certificates

A master certificate is deployed as a signature on a JAR file. No other contents are required in the JAR, so it can contain either nothing (an empty directory) or some dummy content. Just store the certificate [Hack #17] and sign the nonexistent content normally [Hack #18]. The JAR file must be named *systemSignature.jar* (the filename is case-sensitive).

Do not keep the master certificate inside any of Firefox's user profiles. That can become very confusing at runtime. Maintain separate copies of the three *.db* files `signtool` requires, and keep them in a secure place. At worst, maintain a separate, dedicated Firefox install or a separate Firefox user profile. Use that separate configuration for nothing other than maintaining the master certificate.

Next, place the JAR file in the Firefox install area. It should go in the same directory as *firefox.exe* (Windows), *firefox-bin* (Linux/Unix), or in the *Essential Files* directory on Mac OS X. Restart Firefox.

To test whether the certificate is working, sign a piece of content with the master certificate. The content should also use the `netscape.security.PrivilegeManager.enablePrivilege()` method [Hack #18]. Put the resulting JAR file behind a URL. Download it and confirm that the privileges are automatically granted.

Master certificates can also be wrapped up inside an Extension and deployed that way.

Delegating Trust to Others

The trust that the master certificate provides can be passed on (inherited, adopted, or added) to other certificates. This means that content signed with those other certificates can gain full access to the browser. To do this, content signed by the master certificate must tell the browser who else should be trusted, using a special web page JavaScript script.

The `netscape.security.PrivilegeManager` API includes two methods that are available only to scripts signed with the master certificate. These JavaScript methods spread trust to other certificates. They look like this:

```
netscape.security.PrivilegeManager.setCanEnablePrivilege(fprint, privs)
netscape.security.PrivilegeManager.invalidate(fprint)
```

`fprint` is the SHA1 fingerprint of the other certificate that is to be trusted—normally, a web site certificate. That other certificate may or may not be installed in the Firefox certificate database. Any certificate can be specified, though. `privs` is a set of space-separated capability privileges [Hack #20]. MD5 fingerprints are not supported.

To find out the fingerprint of a certificate, either view its details in the Firefox Certificate Manager, if it happens to be recorded there, or run these commands, downloaded as part of the Mozilla NSS package:

```
signtool -L -d "."            # list all known certificates
certutil -L -d "." -n"name"   # display details for cert. "name"
```

Scripts delegating trust can also be wrapped up inside an Extension and deployed that way.

Alternatives to Master Certificates

You don't have to use a master certificate. There are several alternatives:

- Provide a page of links to all content to be trusted and ask users to spend Friday afternoon clicking on all of them. Get them to save their choices so that they are never asked again.
- Follow the preceding approach for a single user. When finished, copy the user's updated certificate database to all other Firefox users' profiles.
- Extensions can do anything, and security arrangements are stored in the Firefox preferences file. You can build a custom security system as an Extension that sets up whatever security arrangements are required for normally secure web pages.

HACK #20 Restrict Script Behavior with Policies

Internet Explorer has security zones. Firefox has capability classes instead.

When web pages load into Firefox, they stay inside a sandbox where they can't compromise the user's security. All unsigned web pages are displayed securely. Such pages still have a lot of latitude, though. Scripts in web pages can do all sorts of things. This hack explains how to change what scripts are allowed to do. Use of policies is extreme fine-tuning of Firefox.

Capabilities and Policies

You can control *script access* to features of Firefox by defining *access rules* and collecting those rules together into a named *policy*. You can define more than one policy. If a Firefox feature such as window.open( ) is put together with a particular kind of access, the combination is called a *capability*. Each access rule allows or denies one or more capabilities. Each policy therefore represents a set of capabilities.

Every method and property of every browser or document object exposed to JavaScript by a DOM standard can be controlled with a capability.

Ordinary policies automatically apply to ordinary web pages. Before a script can use a built-in feature of Firefox, it has to get through all the existing policies unscathed. Firefox provides two policies automatically: one default policy, named default, and one wildcard policy, named *. The existing default policy applies everywhere and is the normal state of affairs. The wildcard policy does nothing, but it is a convenient place to override default policies, if that is required. Policies are typically used differently, depending on the kind of web page to which they are applied:

For ordinary web pages
> Policies usually lessen rather than expand capabilities. Such pages don't need to request anything.

For signed web pages
> Policies usually grant extra access. Such pages need to explicitly request the policies that will provide that access **[Hack #17]**.

Firefox policies are stored in the preference system as simple preferences. You can add more default policies, enhance the wildcard policy, or make your own policy.

Make a Policy

First, register the new policy or policies. Set this preference to whatever policy names sound meaningful:

```
capability.policy.policynames        /* eg "nohistory lax imageswap" */
```

Set this preference instead if you want the policies to be default policies:

```
capability.policy.default_policynames /* eg "nohistory lax imageswap" */
```

Once the policies are registered, assign them to web sites or to whole URI schemes. The default policy applies to all web sites. Assign the sample nohistory policy like this:

```
capability.policy.nohistory.origins   /* eg "https: http://www.x.org" */
```

In this example, every https: URL and every URL on the X-Consortium's web site will have the nohistory policy applied to scripts run inside its web pages.

Finally, add the access rules to the policy. In this example, we prevent scripts from calling window.history.back( ) and from looking at or setting the document.location.href property. The following example is incomplete, because there are many features that need to be blocked if scripting of history is to be completely prevented:

```
capability.policy.nohistory.History.back       /* set to "NoAccess" */
capability.policy.nohistory.Location.href.get  /* set to "NoAccess" */
capability.policy.nohistory.Location.href.set  /* set to "NoAccess" */
```

NoAccess is the only practical value for policies aimed at ordinary web pages. The first preference is suitable for a JavaScript host object method. The second and third preferences are for a JavaScript host object property. The object names used in these preferences are Mozilla XPIDL interface names with the prefix nsIDOM ripped away. So, History is really nsIDOMHistory.

To see if this works, just load any web page with a piece of JavaScript like this:

```
alert(window.location.href);
```

Using a Policy from a Signed Script

Capabilities for signed scripts can be set to NoAccess, SameOrigin, or AllAccess. These are combined with an access type, such as the presupplied access type UniversalXPConnect [Hack #18]. Instead of using these standard access types, use the custom policy name.

HACK #21 Make Yourself Anonymous

Don't let anyone know that you're on the Web.

Here are some ways to reduce the amount of information that web sites and other onlookers find out about you.

Basic Web Surfing Strategies

If you want maximum privacy, follow all of these rules:

- Never fill in web forms that request names, addresses, credit card information, or any geographic or demographic information. Never fill in online questionnaires. Never join a singles site. Never buy anything.
- Never download any programs, demos, or novelty animations from the Internet.
- Never provide your email address. Never use your email address in bulletin boards, newsgroups, message boards, IRC, or anywhere else.
- Don't use Windows or Linux/Unix with automatic operating system updates turned on.
- Never use an Internet Service Provider (ISP) that supplies you with a fixed IP address; it should be a DHCP address that's different each time you use it.

If having a known IP address or a known IP subnet bothers you, consider using services such as Anonymizer (*http://www.anonymizer.com*) for maximum anonymity. Before using such services, you must first persuade yourself that they are an organization that will credibly protect your privacy. You are using them as a portal for all your activities, after all.

Firefox Changes to Support Anonymity

In addition to careful web surfing, here are some concrete changes you can make to Firefox:

- Turn off all cookie support by checking the box in the Privacy panel of the Options dialog box.

- Carefully examine the installation for each plug-in you use. Don't let the plug-in send personal information back to those who deliver plug-in content. Ideally, delete all plug-ins, except the default plug-in file, from the Firefox profile and the install areas. The default plug-in file is named *npnul32.dll* (Windows) or *libnullplugin.so* (Linux).

- Examine your configuration of Adobe Acrobat carefully. Don't let it connect to servers or send form data.

- Review the extensions you've chosen to install; uninstall any that might have server connectivity.

- Stop all secret network activity [Hack #13].

Finally, you can fool web sites into thinking you're using another browser. If you do so, the content set by the sites might change and the page display might not be exactly what you expected. This preference changes the User Agent that identifies Firefox:

```
general.useragent.override    /* set to string */
```

A typical string for a Windows version of Firefox reads:

```
Mozilla/5.0 (Windows; U; WinXP; rv:1.7.3) Gecko/20040913 Firefox/0.10.1
```

For best results, leave the words Mozilla and Gecko intact. Here's the string for Internet Explorer 6.0 on Windows XP (you can masquerade as that browser if you have nothing better to do):

```
Mozilla/4.0 (compatible; MSIE 6.0; Windows NT 5.1)
```

Installation

Hacks 22–32

This chapter deconstructs the Firefox installation process. The standard install process is designed for minimum fuss. It is designed so that ordinary users don't have to think. If you don't feel ordinary, or if you have special constraints placed upon you, then you need to mess that standard installation up. This chapter explains how.

Install is just another way of saying *deploy*. To deploy Firefox is to bed down all its numerous files into spots where they can do some good. That might be on a local disk, on a server, wrapped up into an installable bundle, or perhaps more esoteric possibilities. There are also many small configuration changes you can make after the standard install completes. You don't have to build a whole, alternate installation system; you can just modify the current install in place.

In the introduction to Chapter 1, we touched briefly on the profile and installation areas that Firefox maintains. If you skipped that bit, have a quick look at Table 1-1 before reading on here.

 HACK **Edit Configuration Files**
#22 Modify configuration files where it makes sense to do so, and ignore the rest.

Table 1-1 in the introduction to Chapter 1 describes the location of the two important file areas that Firefox uses: the install area and the profile area. This hack runs through the files in those two folders, pointing out which ones can be modified for good effect and which ones are pointless to modify. If changes are made to these files using the Firefox GUI, then a restart is rarely required. If files are changed by hand, as described here, then a full restart of the browser is almost always required and is always a sensible policy.

Note that on Windows, the *%TMP%* directory is also used. The self-extracting Firefox installer temporarily unpacks its files into that directory. On Linux, you must untar non-RPM install bundles by hand to an arbitrary temporary directory before install. On all operating systems, OS files, or at least desktop files, are also touched during install.

Many of the following files can be modified with a simple text editor, although few are designed with that in mind. Of the rest, mostly binary files, small tools exist that can expose their content. To get these tools, either compile Firefox **[Hack #93]** or explore the contents of a nightly build **[Hack #92]**.

The preference system **[Hack #23]** spans the install and profile areas. It is not discussed in detail here.

Files in the Install Area

Here is a breakdown of the install-area subdirectories. A file with a *.xpt* suffix is a binary XPIDL type library, similar in concept to Microsoft ATL type libraries. A *.jar* file is an archive in PK-Zip (*.ZIP*) format:

chrome

This directory holds all the user-interface content that is part of Firefox, including skins, themes, locales, packages, and associated resources. Such content can be present in a JAR file or spread over a further hierarchy of ordinary package folders. The *installed-chrome.txt* file is written by the installer and registers all bundled chrome packages. This file can be added to by hand, if a package is also copied in by hand, but beware of accidental syntax errors. This directory's parent directory exactly matches the top-level of the resource: URL scheme.

chrome/overlayinfo

This directory is a set of generated RDF files derived from and duplicating all of the *contents.rdf* files to be found in the chrome. There is little reason to touch it. It is regenerated on startup if it doesn't already exist. It is also regenerated if the *installed-chrome.txt* file has been modified (touched) since the last startup.

components

This directory contains XPCOM components bundled with the standard install. They're not considered part of the core runtime libraries. *master.ini* and other odd files belong to the third-party Full Circle Talkback system that generates diagnostic information if a critical error occurs.

defaults

> This hierarchy holds configuration items that are applied before any user profile items. The only extension normally contained in here is the default theme. Note that most preferences in here can be overridden via *user.js* in the profile area.

defaults/autoconfig

> This directory contains references and scripts that apply to locked preference files [Hack #29]. Note that the JavaScript functions defined in *prefcalls.js* are the ones available for use in such locked files. The files in this directory can be modified with a text editor.

extensions

> This directory contains extensions bundled with the standard install. The default theme, Firefox (default), is the sole bundled extension. The files in this directory can be hacked.

greprefs

> The Gecko Runtime Engine (GRE) is a semi-independent part of the Mozilla platform inside Firefox. It has its own specific preferences and defaults. These can be overridden normally with *user.js*.

icons

> For Linux/Unix only, this directory contains desktop XPM icons. The files in this directory can be modified [Hack #78].

plugins

> This directory contains installed plug-ins. Files can be copied here by hand. Type the URL about:plugins into the browser Location bar for more details.

res

> This directory contains content required for the proper display of web pages, such as DTD entity definitions like   and placeholder images. The files in this directory can be modified.

searchplugins

> This directory contains specs for bundled search-bar search engines. The files in this directory can be modified.

uninstall

> For Windows only, the files in this directory uninstall Firefox and record install logs. Don't touch the files in here.

On Linux/Unix only, the *registry* file in the install area is the do-nothing top-level registry of Firefox versions installed at this location. There can only ever be one version. This file is present only because there is a similar but more useful file on Windows.

Files in the Profile Area

Here is a breakdown of the profile area subdirectories. Any directory named *Profiles* or *default* that is a sibling of the *Firefox* (or *firefox*) directory is a profile for the Mozilla Application Suite Version 1.x. Also at that top level is the operating-system-wide *registry.dat* (*mozver.dat* and *appreg* on Linux/Unix) file, which records information about all Mozilla-based installations on the current host for the current OS user, and all profiles for that OS user. Inside the *Firefox* directory is the profile area proper. Two generated files for Linux/Unix located here shouldn't be touched.

The profiles proper have random characters in their top-level directory names. New profiles have eight characters of random digits; older profiles migrated to the current version have only three digits. These are *salted* directory names, a term borrowed from cryptography. Since files inside this directory are sometime updated in response to data delivered over the Web, it is safer if this directory's name is not publicly known. That reduces the chance of relatively obscure Trojan horse attacks, although the jury is out on whether such measures are excessive or not. These salted names also pose challenges for profile migration [Hack #25].

The files in the salted directory hold all state (all information changes) derived from the browser session. All files can be hacked, except for *.dat* files in Mozilla Mdb/Mork format—they are in too obscure a format to modify easily—and the *XUL.mfl* file, which is a binary cache of compiled chrome. Modifying the *xpti.dat* file is also useless. All files can be deleted and will be regenerated as empty files the next time the browser starts up. It is unwise to delete the certificate database [Hack #17] because then Firefox cannot visit secure websites. The *localstore.rdf* file contains the last known positions of all windows and any values specified with the XUL persist attribute. *compatibility.ini* is used as a timestamp flag for re-registering extensions [Hack #84]. Here are the other folders:

Cache, Cache.Trash

These folders hold the Firefox disk cache of web page content. It is harmless to delete the cache by hand. Change the location of the cache with this preference:

```
browser.cache.disk.parent_directory /* default = path to Cache parent */
```

chrome, chrome/overlayinfo

These folders duplicate the function of the *chrome* directory in the install area. They're used if packages of any kind are installed in the profile. The sum of the two chrome directories is all the chrome that Firefox understands, unless clever developers add other locations to the chrome registry. These folders are also used by extensions to store content or state information as required.

extensions

This folder contains any extensions installed into the user profile. When the first user-selected extension is installed, the user is asked whether to put it in the profile area, where migration is possible [Hack #10], or in the install area. All subsequent extensions go into the same place.

Any directories named *ImapMail*, *Mail*, or *News* are installed by Mozilla Mail or Thunderbird, not Firefox. Extensions can also write files directly into the topmost profile directory where all the other stateful files are stored. Aggressively written extensions can modify any user-accessible file on the local disk and can modify the Windows Registry on Windows.

HACK #23 Play With the Preference System

Dig underneath Firefox's user interface and hack the preference system directly.

Firefox's preference system holds many of the small configuration items of the Firefox browser. These items are hidden from the user: behind formal user interfaces, unimplemented by user interfaces, or invisible because no default values are recorded anywhere. This hack explains how to work with the preference system directly.

Understanding the Preference Database

The preference system is equivalent to a tiny database. It sits in memory while Firefox runs. The preference database is a thread-safe but single-user database. It consists of a single table of four columns:

Name

Contains a unique string that identifies the preference. This is the primary key.

Value

Contains the data for the preference. It can be a string, number, or true/false (Boolean) value.

Locked Attribute

States whether the preference has been locked. Users cannot change locked preferences.

Default Attribute

Remains true as long as the user does not set (override) the preference.

The last two columns are not set explicitly; they are set indirectly ["Modifying
Preference Files," later in this hack] Here is a typical preference:

```
Name                    Value
----                    -----
browser.chrome.site_icons  true   /* not locked, user set */
```

Any string (within reason) can be used as a preference name. The dots (peri-
ods) are not especially meaningful. They are just a convenience for programmers. Programmers can compose a query that pulls out all the preferences
that start with a given string followed by a dot. Dots also help readers clas-
sify preferences into a simple hierarchy.

Like any database table, you can add whatever rows (preferences) you like.
However, Firefox will look only at preferences that it knows about. All others are excess baggage. An extension or other code can add new preferences. Upgrading from old Mozilla or Netscape versions can also add
preferences. Firefox will ignore all preferences that it doesn't understand. If
extensions need to read the preference database, they do that on their own
initiative.

The preference database is constructed by reading files from disk when Firefox starts up. The database is *not* written out in full before or while Firefox
shuts down. There is nowhere on disk where you can see all the currently set
preferences. However, you can see all the currently set preferences using the
about:config URL, discussed next.

There is also nowhere where you can get a list of all known preferences.
There are, however, several web pages that act as preference birdwatchers.
They provide extensive lists of preferences spotted in the wild. It's not really
as bad as it sounds; the majority of preferences are very well known.

Tweaking Preferences with about:config

The special *about:config* URL provides an XUL page inside the normal
HTML display area. It can be used to query, insert, update, and delete preferences. Preferences changed here are accurately picked up by any configuration dialog boxes in Firefox that also use those preferences. Any changes
made apply immediately.

Figure 3-1 shows this page at work after all preferences have been filtered to
display only those whose names contain the substring browser (You can filter preferences by putting something in the top Filter: field.). One preference has been context-clicked to reveal the set of operations that can be
applied. The options under the New submenu are not specific to the highlighted preference.

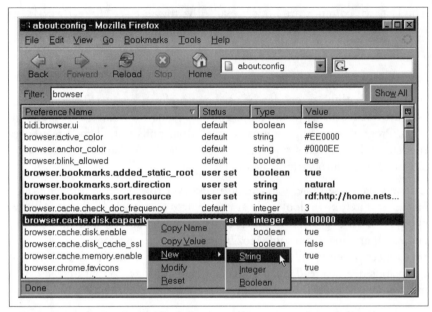

Figure 3-1. Generic preferences interface

The Status column describes whether the preference is user set or not (see the next section for more details). All such preferences are shown in bold. In such cases, it is usually harmless to choose Reset from the context menu to take away changes made by the user of the current Firefox profile. There is no undo functionality; if you change a preference, you must remember to change it back.

Many preferences are meaningful on their own. Some preferences, however, work together in groups. If you use *about:config*, any required coordination between preferences is up to you. Most Firefox dialog boxes do the coordination for you.

Spotting Files that Contribute to Preferences

Preference files exist in both the install area and the profile area. They run in a certain order, and later scripts can override *some* settings that earlier scripts have made.

The install area folder *defaults/pref* contains *.js* preference scripts delivered with the Firefox install. These scripts are executed first when Firefox starts up. All files in that directory are executed. By default, only the standard files *firefox.js* and *firefox-l10n.js* are present.

The install area can also contain a *.cfg* ReadConfig configuration script [Hack #29]. That file, if it exists, is read second on startup.

The profile area can contain a *prefs.js* script, one per profile. It is run third on startup. No such file is provided with the standard install. This file is written to when preferences change, and it's also written to when Firefox shuts down. It contains only those preferences whose values have been changed from the values set by install-area preference scripts. This makes copying the *prefs.js* script between profiles both easy (because it is a small set of changes to manage) and hard (because it is an incomplete picture).

Lastly, the profile area can contain a *user.js* script, one per profile, in the same directory as the *prefs.js* script. This file must be put in place by hand. No such file is supplied at install time. This script is run last on Firefox startup.

Modifying Preference Files

All files that contribute to preferences are JavaScript files (but see also the special case of remote configuration [Hack #29]), which means they must contain JavaScript syntax. If bad syntax is used, the script will fail silently. Although JavaScript 1.5 does not insist on trailing semicolons on each line, future versions will, so put them in. Putting in general-purpose JavaScript code is not at all useful; the only useful thing to do is to call one of these functions:

```
pref(name, value);
user_pref(name, value);
lockPref(name, value);
unlockPref(name, value);
```

Therefore, here's a simple example of setting a preference:

```
user_pref("browser.chrome.site_icons", false);
```

If you're doing remote configuration, double-check the names used. Some names are different in that environment. Here are the standard preference functions:

pref(*name, value*);
> This function sets the named preference, if it is not locked, and turns on the default attribute. It can be called by all preference scripts.

user_pref(*name, value*);
> This function sets the named preference, if it is not locked, and turns off the default attribute. It can be called by all preference scripts. It is the only function that is sensible to put in *user.js*.

```
lockPref(name, value);
```
This function sets the named preference and also sets the locked attribute. It can be used only in remote configuration *.cfg* scripts.

```
unlockPref(name, value);
```
This function sets the named preference and also unsets the locked attribute. It can be used only in remote configuration *.cfg* scripts.

HACK #24 Install Complementary Tools
Get the rest of the standard gear you need for a fully featured Firefox.

This brief hack explains how to add some general-purpose tools that aren't bundled with the standard Firefox install. Such additions are either necessities or lifestyle options. This book is full of options that you can explore, particularly extensions and search engines. This hack focuses on the more critical tools, such as these:

- Plug-ins
- Java JVM
- Fonts [Hack #30]
- Mozilla Application Suite tools
- Helper applications
- Search engines [Hack #36]

The first stop for the most commonly used extras is the Firefox Central page at *http://www.mozilla.org/products/firefox/central.html*. For more detail and more options, read on.

Managing Plug-ins and Java

For popular plug-ins and Java, this URL contains everything you need to know:

> *http://plugindoc.mozdev.org/*

If a plug-in isn't listed on this site, the plug-in likely won't work.

> The default Windows-specific page lists the *most popular* plug-ins; a set of links near the top lists a much larger collection of plug-ins alphabetically.

Mozilla works hard to be backward-, forward-, and sideways-compatible when handling plug-ins. Plug-in files are not merely added to the *plugins* folder inside the install area; they are also recorded in Mozilla registry files.

pluginreg.dat (Windows) in the profile area is an example. Firefox can exploit plug-ins added to its own install area, plug-ins that exist in other installations of Mozilla, plug-ins that are present in Netscape product installations, and even plug-ins that are installed elsewhere in the operating system, such as the Adobe Reader plug-in. The first time Firefox starts up, it scans the operating system (on Windows, this means the Windows Registry) for plug-in IDs (PLIDs). You can read about them and the associated issues here:

> *http://www.mozilla.org/projects/plugins/plugin-identifier.html*

The upshot of all this is that plug-ins can be messy to manage if more than one browser is installed on a given computer. The best advice is to collect together all plug-ins so that they are installed into Firefox, even if there are duplicates elsewhere. That way, if upgrades or cross-grades are ever required, then at most the contents of the Firefox *plugins* folder can be copied over in one action.

The heyday of Java applet technology is now a fading memory, and there is decreasing wisdom in installing the Java JVM. Perhaps the only real remaining use is to support "legacy" Web applications that are still bound to applet technology.

Finding Substitutes for Application Suite Features

The Mozilla Application Suite (MAS) and Netscape Navigator/Communicator products include several features that Firefox does not have by default; Firefox is a leaner, meaner product. Some of those features are available as extensions and can be added via the Extension Manager. Some are available as applications, and some are not available at all. Table 3-1 provides a rundown.

Table 3-1. MAS features and equivalent Firefox extensions

MAS feature name	Equivalent Firefox extension
Composer (HTML editor)	The Composer equivalent is installed as a separate product. Get it here: *http://www.nvu.com*.
What's Related sidebar	None, but see "Get More Search Tools" [Hack #36].
Netscape Buddy List sidebar	None.
AOL Instant Messenger	None.
JavaScript Debugger	JavaScript Debugger (at *http://update.mozilla.org*).
Profile Switcher	None.
Java Console	Open Java Console (at *http://update.mozilla.org*). Java JVM must also be installed.

Table 3-1. MAS features and equivalent Firefox extensions (continued)

MAS feature name	Equivalent Firefox extension
Mail & Newsgroups	Thunderbird (at *http://www.mozilla.org*) is a full application that is installed as a separate product.
IRC Chat	ChatZilla (at *http://update.mozilla.org*).

Top Two Helper Applications

Finally, of all the numerous Helper applications that you might install, two classes of application stand out as noteworthy for the Windows platform:

Download Managers
Firefox and Mozilla do not yet support FTP sessions that can be resumed at a later date or that can be reduced to low network priority. The FireFTP extension also suffers from this limitation. An integrated download manager is therefore a good idea. Tools such as those offered by *http://www.freedownloadmanager.org* are ideal.

Disk Caretakers
Those with tidy minds might want to complement Firefox with a disk cleanup tool, such as Crap Cleaner (*http://www.ccleaner.com*). Firefox is not particularly messy, but such a tool can automate the tidying up that some users might want to do on a regular basis.

HACK
#25

Migrate Firefox Profiles

Move user data between separate Firefox installations or between separate versions.

Welcome to complexity. Every piece of software has an Achilles heel, and Firefox's is the tangle of issues that surround its user profiles. Moving profiles is tricky, and you have to be careful. Fortunately, it's a well-established problem and all that's required is excessive care. There are plans afoot to simplify all of this in a future, minor version. But for now, moving complete Firefox profiles is difficult for numerous reasons:

- Use of absolute pathnames in some configuration files causes problems.
- Some pathnames aren't portable across Windows, Unix, and Macintosh.
- Profiles are constrained to obey operating system conventions on all platforms.
- Some features were completed only recently, after protracted investigation.
- There are numerous deployment variations, all of which have to be catered for.
- Security requirements for salted directory names [Hack #11] make life harder.

- Some information is stored outside profiles in registry files (*registry.dat*, *mozver.dat*, and the Windows Registry on Windows, *registry* on Unix).
- Preferences customized at the platform level can affect profiles [Hack #23].

There are at least three ways to effect a partial escape from these problems:

- The Windows-only solution is to use MozBackup (*http://mozbackup. jasnapaka.com/*), a small backup tool that copies the *web browsing state information only* (history, bookmarks, etc.). It's a simple copy approach that requires new profiles at each target installation before restoring the data.
- The second escape hatch is to experiment with server-oriented profile tools [Hack #28].
- The third option is to simplify matters with desalted profiles [Hack #11].

Before proceeding to the details, here are two things to keep in mind:

- Never share one profile between two separate running instances of Firefox.
- The Mozilla registry (*registry.dat* on Windows) records the locations of all profiles.

Migrating Between Identical Platforms

If two computers have the same operating system version and the same users, and the users' home directories have the same paths, then the whole profile area can simply be copied from one computer to the other. Mozilla registry files must be copied as well. On the target computer, replace the local profile with the copied one. Do the same for the registry files. Since the target computer already has Firefox installed, the Windows Registry should not need updates.

Even if the two versions of the Mozilla or Firefox installs are identical, the profile might behave differently after migration. This can happen if one or both platform installs has been *customized* so that default preferences are not the same on both [Hack #23]. The profile will notice these different defaults at runtime but will not record them anywhere.

Migrating Between Mozilla Versions

Firefox can read all the profile information of any older Mozilla-based versions. Examples are beta versions of Firefox, the Mozilla Application Suite, and Netscape Versions 4.x–7.x. To read that early information, Firefox must either migrate it (a formal, one-time process undertaken at install time), import it (in the case of bookmarks and address books) or read copies of it in place. The Firefox GUI can drive all but the last option.

You can read copies in place only for browsers based on Mozilla 1.x or later. To do so, identify the name of an existing Mozilla profile (default is the default name) and the directory of the same name that is at the top of the profile data. Write down the parent directory of that directory. Hand-delete (ideally move to one side) the Mozilla registries for the old version. Install Firefox, creating new registries. Start Firefox with the Profile Manager [Hack #10] and create a new profile with the same name as the old Mozilla profile. Select Choose Folder and enter the noted folder name. The profile will forever be stored under the older Mozilla folders, but it will be usable by Firefox.

There is no way to stop a new install of Firefox from automatically migrating an existing profile when it first starts up, but forced migration leaves the original profile undamaged. You can choose the destination profile of the migration using these preferences (modifying the migration process), or hand-delete the new profile after migration (undoing the effects of migration), or both:

```
profile.migration_behavior    /* 0 = default = put in "Profiles" */
profile.migration_behavior    /* 1 = leave in Netscape 4.x profile */
profile.migration_behavior    /* 2 = use specified directory  */

profile.migration_directory  /* absolute path to new profile */
```

Since no profile exists that includes these preferences, a special hack is required. Find the *all.js* file in the Firefox install area, and insert the wanted options there. Use the pref( ) function rather than user_pref( ).

Migrating Between Different Operating System Versions

Migration between Unix versions and Unix platforms is trivial. Delete the *~/.mozilla* and registry files on the new OS. Copy the old *~/.mozilla* folder and registry files to the new OS. If $HOME also changes, use a parallel technique to the following procedure recommended for Windows.

Under Windows, the main migration difficulty is crossing the gap from Versions 95/98/98SE/ME/NT3/NT4 to Versions 2000/XP. The former versions use filesystem paths that are different from the ones used by the latter versions, and some hand conversion is required. On the older host, note these strings:

- The full pathname of the salted directory for the profile to be migrated
- The profile name

Now, migrate the preferences. Make a copy of the *prefs.js* file from the old profile and save it. Install Firefox on the new OS and make a profile of the same name as the old one. Close Firefox. Note the full pathname of the salted directory in the new profile. Open the old preference file and change all instances of the old salted full pathname to the new salted full pathname. Change all `mail.` preferences to match those in the new preference file exactly and save. Overwrite the new preference file with the modified old one.

Finally, copy all other files from the old salted directory to the new one. Start Firefox to confirm the profile has migrated correctly.

Recent versions use the shorthand notation [ProfD] to describe the path to the topmost directory. This increases portability in simple cases, but it can yield some bizarre paths on Windows if files outside the current profile's top folder are referenced:

```
[ProfD]../../../../some/other/file.dat
```

It is possible to use the one profile under two versions of Windows on a dual-boot computer (or under VMware). Boot into the Windows version where Firefox already exists. Note the path to the profile required. Reboot into the other Windows version. Install Firefox with the same profile name, and pick Choose Folder when you create the profile. Choose the folder of the profile used under the other Windows version.

Migrating Between Different Operating System Users

This migration operates in the same way as the last one. Care is required to get all hardcoded paths in the preference files correct. Firefox doesn't care much who the current operating system user is, except for the purposes of NTLM on Windows. When copying files from user to user, ensure that the right ownership and protections are granted.

On Windows, if you change your username and then log out and log back in as that new user, Firefox won't recover the profile of the old user and won't start up properly. To fix that, start Firefox with a profile creation option [Hack #10]. After the new profile is created, shut Firefox down and migrate the old profile to the new one ["Migrating Between Identical Platforms," earlier in this hack].

Migrating Between Windows and Linux

There is currently no simple way to achieve this end, other than to copy profile information file-by-file from Windows to Linux. In the case of the preference files, each line of those files must be checked for operating-system-specific paths and modified as required.

Dial Up Automatically on Startup

HACK #26

Save yourself from having to hand-connect to the Internet before surfing with
Firefox.

This hack explains how to automatically dial up your ISP when Firefox
starts. Disconnecting is more problematic. Attack that using timeout configuration items provided by the operating system. If you want Firefox to auto-
dial for you, this preference must be left on:

```
network.autodial-helper.enabled    /* default = true */
```

Windows 95/98/98SE/ME

Dial-up technology under these Windows versions has a top layer called
Dial Up Networking (DUN). To get this working without fail, make a copy
of a Firefox desktop shortcut and change the copy. Change the specified
firefox.exe program to run *firefox.bat* instead. Create that *.bat* file with these
contents:

```
@echo off
start /B /MIN /W rundll32.exe rnaui.dll,RnaDial "connectoid"
firefox.exe
```

The string *connectoid* is the name of the connection icon in the *Dial-Up Networking* folder. It is case-sensitive. Do not use the name of a desktop shortcut that points to the connection icon. Change the name displayed on the
new desktop icon to Firefox Internet or similar.

This fix always works, but there is an alternate way. Firefox has a File →
Work Offline menu option. If Firefox is started in Offline mode, changing it
to Online mode will instruct Firefox to always dial the ISP for you.

It is also possible to make Firefox dial the ISP if the first web page request
(such as the home page) fails. In order for this to happen, extra Windows
setup is required. In the Internet Options Control Panel item, in the Connections tab, choose any radio button other than the one labeled "Never dial a
connection."

Windows NT/2000/XP

Top-level dial-up technology under these Windows versions is called
Remote Access Services (RAS). It should be started automatically when any
program, including Firefox, attempts to access the Internet. If that's not
working for you, check that the RAS Connection Manager and RAS Auto
Connection Manager services are enabled using the Services icon in the Control Panel. The rules are otherwise the same as under 95/98/98SE/Me.

If it still isn't working, make a copy of a Firefox desktop shortcut and change the copy. Change the specified *firefox.exe* program to *firefox.bat*. Create that *.bat* file with these contents:

```
@echo off
start /B /MIN /W rasdial.exe "connectoid"
firefox.exe
```

The string *connectoid* is the name of the connection icon, as described in the previous section. It is case-sensitive. Do not use the name of a desktop shortcut that points to the connection icon. To suppress the dialog that prompts for your ISP login details, try this instead:

```
@echo off
start /B /MIN /W rasdial.exe "connectoid" "username" "password"
firefox.exe
```

 Beware: this saves your password as cleartext.

Mac OS X

Automatic PPP dial-up under OS X is handled through System Preferences—the same as automatic Internet connection of all types. To set it up, choose System Preferences under the Apple menu and follow these steps:

1. Click on the Network icon, in the Internet & Network group.
2. From the Show pop-up menu near the top of the window, select your modem.
3. Make sure the PPP tab is selected and click on the PPP Options... button near the bottom of the panel.
4. Tick the first checkbox labeled "Connect automatically when needed."
5. Click OK, and you're all set up.

Linux/Unix

To dial up before Firefox starts, just wrap the command-line call to Firefox in a shell script. Before you're ready to go, you must have the following things in place:

- Modem hardware that's known (usually present; test with kudzu --probe)
- Serial and PPP drivers in the kernel (usually present; test with modprobe -1)
- Correct serial devices in */dev* (usually present)
- Software for PPP, such as pppd (usually present)
- Software for DHCP, such as dhcpd (usually present)

For example, under Red Hat Fedora Core, much of the work is automated for you. Run this GUI tool and review the information in its help system:

```
/usr/bin/system-config-network
```

If no profile is defined for the modem, use the GUI to create one. In the DNS tab, clear all the DNS entries except for DNS Search Path. Enter the ISP's domain name here, making sure the IP address is also recorded, either in the /etc/hosts file or using the tool:

```
/usr/bin/system-config-bind
```

If dial-up access via DHCP has been started, Linux DHCP will usually overwrite the /etc/resolv.conf file, which can affect or ruin any existing DNS arrangements that you might have in place.

To configure and run dial-up by hand, configure *dhcpd.conf* to contain the ISP's DNS and IP Address information. Identify the tty in /dev that matches the modem, and simply run:

```
pppd /dev/modemtty
dhcpd
```

Those commands can go in the wrapper script that starts Firefox.

 HACK
#27

Fix Web Servers to Support Firefox Content
Provide support for the bonus content types that Mozilla technology supports.

Firefox supports more varied content than just that of web pages. In addition to the big world of XUL-based applications, there are a number of configuration and security content types that can be delivered to the browser. This Hack explains how to set up Apache so that all these types are delivered with the right Content-Type. It also explains what to do about broken versions of Internet Explorer.

Configuring Firefox Content Types in Apache

The following MIME types are the ones most commonly used by Firefox. Update your Apache *httpd.conf* file to include these directives, and then restart httpd or signal it to reread the config files.

Support for HTML content types:

```
AddType application/xhtml+xml       .xhtml
AddType application/http-index-format .hti
AddType text/html                   .html
AddType text/css                    .css
AddType text/xsl                    .xslt
AddType application/x-javascript    .js
```

Support for other presentable XML content:

```
AddType application/xml       .xml /* or .. */
AddType text/xml              .xml
AddType image/svg+xml         .svg
```

Mozilla does not use the MIME type required for pure MathML; such content should be delivered inside a compound document identified as XHTML or XML.

Support for remote XUL and RDF:

```
AddType application/vnd.mozilla.xul+xml .xul
AddType application/rdf+xml             .rdf
```

Support for delivery of extensions, patches and configuration items:

```
AddType application/x-xpinstall         .xpi
AddType application/x-javascript-config .cfg .jsc
```

Support for server delivery of certificates, either for certificate-database install or for immediate use as data:

```
AddType application/x-x509-ca-cert     .x509ca
AddType application/x-x509-server-cert .x509sv
AddType application/x-x509-crl         .x509_crl  # OSCP
AddType application/x-x509-user-cert   .x509ua
AddType application/x-x509-email-cert  .x509em
AddType application/x-pkcs7-crl        .pk7_crl
AddType application/pkix-crl           .pk_crl
AddType application/x-pkcs7-mime       .pk7m_crl
AddType application/pkcs7-signature    .pk7_sig
AddType application/pkix-crl           .pk_crl
AddType application/ocsp-response      .ocsp
```

Filename extensions are merely suggestive in this case; most content of these types will likely be generated by a server program rather than delivered directly from flat files.

Supporting Both Standards and Internet Explorer

All modern browsers, except for all Internet Explorer (IE) versions, can handle XHTML content delivered with the correct application/xhtml+xml MIME type. Generally speaking, IE can't handle this case. Something has to be done to accommodate that. In the past, all XHTML content was delivered as text/html for IE's benefit. Now that many standards-oriented browsers are gaining in market share, it's time to reduce IE to a special case and deliver the correct content types by default.

The XHTML standard *does* allow XHTML 1.0 to be delivered as text/html. This is a stopgap measure that works for all browsers. The XHTML standard does *not* allow this trick for XHTML *1.1* content or higher. That means that there is no standards-based fix available for most IE versions for XHTML 1.1 or higher. The only available solution is to hack the Windows Registry so that content with application/xhtml+xml is treated as text/html. See *http://juicystudio.com/xhtml-registry-hack.asp* for details. To make the server lie when required, try the following code snippets.

PHP content rewriter. These tests pick up all the weird variants of IE, including Pocket PC versions, and replace the true content type with a lie for IE:

```
<?
$agent = $_SERVER['HTTP_USER_AGENT'];
$broken = FALSE;
$broken = $broken || (stristr($agent, "msie") && !stristr($agent, "opera"));
$broken = $broken || stristr($agent, "microsoft internet explorer");
$broken = $broken || stristr($agent, "mspie");
$broken = $broken || stristr($agent, "pocket");

if ( $broken ) {
   header("Content-Type: text/html");
}
else {
   header("Content-Type: application/xhtml+xml");
}
?>
```

For more complete browser-sniffing code, visit *http://www.apptools.com/phptools/browser/source.php*.

Perl CGI content rewriter. Similarly, here's the rewriter in Perl:

```
use CGI;
my ($query,$broken) = (0, false);
$query = new CGI;
$query->use_named_parameters(1);

$broken = $query->http("HTTP_USER_AGENT") =~ /pocket/i;
$broken = ... # as for PHP

print "Content-type: application/xhtml+xml\n\n" if not $broken;
print "Content-type: text/html\n\n" if $broken;
# ... and so on.
```

Native Apache rewriter. For static files, use Apache's mod_rewrite module, which must be configured and enabled before it is usable. The obscure code required for the IE lie is:

```
RewriteEngine on
RewriteBase /
RewriteCond %{HTTP_USER_AGENT} pocket [nocase,ornext]
```

```
RewriteCond %{HTTP_USER_AGENT} mspie [nocase,ornext]
RewriteCond %{HTTP_USER_AGENT} pocket [nocase,ornext]
RewriteCond %{HTTP_USER_AGENT} msie [nocase]
RewriteCond %{HTTP_USER_AGENT} !msie.*opera [nocase]
RewriteCond %{HTTP_USER_AGENT} !opera.*msie [nocase]
RewriteCond %{REQUEST_URI} \.xhtml$
RewriteCond %{THE_REQUEST} HTTP/1\.[^0]
RewriteRule .* - [type=text/html]
```

HACK #28 Prepare Firefox for Wide Deployment

Choose from several strategies for rolling out Firefox across an enterprise.

This hack describes how to deploy Firefox when there's a large community of users to support. It covers changing Firefox from the standard install bundle provided by the Mozilla Foundation to a set of files laid out correctly for the user. These files can be deployed to a workstation, a server, or both.

If profile files are stored on a server, you can improve performance by moving the location of the Firefox disk cache back to the local disk [Hack #22]. It also makes sense to put the profile somewhere separate from any Windows user profile that's also on the server (i.e., any *roaming profile*), because you don't want Windows replicating the Firefox profile information down to the client when it logs on, as it does for everything else in the Windows user profile.

If the base install files (executables) are stored on a server, only the *registry.dat* file (Windows) needs to be on the local client, and even that can be faked by mapping %APPDATA% to a server location via Active Directory.

It is also possible to arrange installation so that Firefox can be centrally managed after it is installed [Hack #29]. It makes sense, however, to leave Firefox's automatic update system on [Hack #13]. It's too much work to hand-manage patches from *http://update.mozilla.org*. You might as well let Firefox do it as though it were a virus checker.

At the time of writing, the Mozilla Client Customization Kit (CCK), Mozilla's equivalent to Microsoft's Internet Explorer Administration Kit (IEAK), is still in development and unusable. Recommended reading for smaller stopgap techniques can be found at *http://www.alain.knaff.lu/ ~aknaff/howto/MozillaCustomization/index.html*.

Alain's small tools make reading and writing Mozilla registry files easier to handle. You can also graphically display the registry with an extension.

Getting Leverage on Windows File Paths

Interchanging file paths and URLs can be confusing. Here are a few note-worthy Firefox items:

- Both UNC pathnames, such as *server**share**subpath*, and drive path-names, such as *c:\tmp*, are supported.

- Environment variables such as %APPDATA% are respected and used, even if mapped to other locations by Active Directory or other mechanisms.

- Paths put in Firefox configuration files *cannot* include %FOO% syntax. The only macro expansion available is [ProfD], which is used only for Thunderbird email.

If a server is described by a UNC, files on that server can be addressed either by a path, a mapped drive, or a URL. This path:

```
\\server\share\dir\dir2\filename
```

when mapped to X: is equivalent to this path:

```
X:\dir\dir2\filename
```

or to this URL:

```
file://localhost///server/share/dir/dir2/filename
```

or, more briefly, to this URL:

```
file://///server/share/dir/dir2/filename
```

 That is five forward slashes in the preceding URL, which is different than in Internet Explorer.

The mapped drive can also be stated as these URLs:

```
file://localhost/X|/dir/dir2/filename
file:///X|/dir/dir2/filename
file:///X:/dir/dir2/filename
```

In general, there is little need for URL versions of UNCs when configuring Firefox. They cannot be put into web pages as links anyway, unless standard security restrictions are overcome. The most reliable format for configuration text is simple drive paths:

```
X:\dir\dir\filename
```

Using the Standard Install

The standard Firefox install might be enough for you. Write up a set of install prompt responses as a documented procedure and publish it. Get users to download Firefox from *http://www.mozilla.org* or from your server staging area, and then follow the bouncing ball. In the case of a normal install, there's little state retained by the browser that's business critical, although use of POP email via Thunderbird can complicate matters. By itself, Firefox can be treated in a more cavalier manner than complex tool installations like Word or Office. Except for bookmarks, there's little that's too precious to lose.

There is an alternative distribution you can use instead of the standard install. A non-self-extracting, simple ZIP file of Firefox install files is available here:

> *http://ftp.mozilla.org/pub/mozilla.org/firefox/releases/1.0/win32/en-US/*
> *Firefox 1.0.zip*

Imaging an Instance of Firefox

If you are building user workstations from scratch, you can build an installed version of Mozilla as part of a standard disk image, perhaps with a tool such as Norton Ghost. This image will work, but it will have a slight weakness.

Each Firefox profile is salted with a random name, even the default profile, to prevent villains from guessing it and using server-based attacks. The name is calculated randomly at profile creation time. If all of your Firefox installations are derived from the one image, that salting will be the same across the organization and will be well known internally. That ruins salting as a defense against internal villains who are collecting user data through a server exploit. It also decreases the security margin against external villains. It is an obscure matter, however, and it is irrelevant if access to local disks is otherwise easy.

Using the registry-editing tools noted earlier, it's possible to remove salted names from the profile's path completely. Just modify *registry.dat* so that the profile paths point somewhere else and copy them to that location. Update any preferences dependent on the salt.

Customizing the Install

This section provides three tactics for customizing the install.

Preinstall: change the install bundle. The *Firefox Setup 1.0.exe* file is a 7-Zip (*http://www.7-zip.com*) self-extracting executable that has been squeezed into a smaller file with UPX (*http://www.upx.org*). You can hack it. The script responsible for constructing it is located here:

> *http://lxr.mozilla.org/mozilla/source/browser/installer/windows/7zip.bat*

At the moment, it looks like this, but beware that it's just part of a larger bundling process:

```
cd 7zstage
7z a -t7z ..\7z\app.7z *.* -mx -mO=BCJ2 -m1=LZMA:d24 -m2=LZMA:d19 -m3=LZMA:
d19 -mbO:1 -mbOs1:2 -mbOs2:3
cd ..\7z
upx -9 7zSD.sfx
copy /b 7zSD.sfx+app.tag+app.7z SetupGeneric.exe
cd ..
```

The + syntax in copy is used to concatenate three files into one final file, in the style of Unix's cat(1). 7z (7za on Linux) can be used to unpack and repack this final self-extractor. You can unpack either a UPX-squeezed or UPX-unsqueezed copy. If you repack, the file content order must be preserved, so do a test repacking before making any modifications.

One simple modification is to change the unpacked *config.ini* file. It's human readable, heavily documented, and easy to follow. More generally, you must change the unpacked *browser.xpi* file. It's in plain ZIP format, so it needs to be unpacked once more. Inside the file, easy changes include:

- Modifying *install.js* (an XPInstall script) to add registry hacks or extra files
- Modifying *bin/defaults/pref/firefox.js* (a preferences file) to add preferences

During install: customize user profile creation. A small Windows program called mozptch can be used to customize the construction of Firefox profiles. Once initial customization is complete, it can be repeated in a fully automated way. The process is involved and takes some study. Read about it at *http://mozptch.mozdev.org/*.

Another in-process alternative is to exploit the preference-locking system [Hack #23], which allows scripts to retrieve details from an LDAP server at startup time and use those details to set preferences. That's a good way to acquire user login details that can be used to construct server pathnames.

Post-install: overwrite files on login. A brute-force approach that ensures Firefox profiles and Mozilla registries are behaving properly is to dump down copies of required files to the client workstation when the user first logs in. This covers all Firefox profile files and the *registry.dat* file, leaving only the Window registry to manage. This command will do that last part:

```
regedit /s file.reg
```

where *file.reg* is an exported Windows registry fragment to be reapplied.

Remotely Manage User Configurations

HACK #29

Make sure all users in an enterprise have a uniform set of configured preferences.

This hack shows how to take configuration control away from the Firefox user. Firefox provides a little support for locking preference files. It provides no support for other parts of the profile. This means that most parts of the profile must be managed with filesystem access controls, such as ownership and read/write permissions. This is something of a problem if you require extensive configuration control.

On the plus side, the two configuration features described later in this hack, *ReadConfig* and *AutoConfig*, apply to Netscape 4.x–7.x and all these Mozilla-based products: Mozilla Application Suite, Firefox, Thunderbird, Camino, and probably a few others as well. They can be used to manage all these products from one central point. The two features are sometimes collectively called *autoconfig*.

Locking Files Using the Operating System

Many of the files in the profile that you would want to lock (for example, *cookies.txt*, *mimeTypes.rdf*, and the *Chrome* subdirectory) are located directly underneath the profile's salted directory name. It is not enough to make these files read-only. The user can remove them if write permission remains on the parent directory (permission models differ in detail between Unix and Windows). Default versions will then be regenerated the next time Firefox starts up, with read/write permissions restored. So making files read-only isn't enough.

If write permission is taken off the salted directory, extensions or other oddities that are installed at a later date will not be able to add their files to that directory. The salted directory is a common place for such oddities. Currently, the only solution to this extension problem is to assess each extension for impact using an unlocked test system before approving it for use.

You might also want to lock files in the install area. If Firefox runs over a network from a central application server, you can lock all the default (or modified) preference files and other default configuration in the install area.

It is also important to lock the *registry.dat* file. Users can change their profile entirely if they can modify or replace this file, so remove that possibility.

Surviving Special Preference Configuration Rules

The rest of this hack describes use of special configuration files. Keep these points in mind. First, *.js*, *.cfg*, and *.jsc* files are all JavaScript scripts; there is no special meaning behind these filename extensions.

There are four special syntax arrangements for *.cfg* scripts:

- The first line of such files should be *invalid* JavaScript, so that the file cannot be run by accident as an ordinary script.

- Such files are very weakly encrypted (*shrouded*), making them unreadable by eye.

- All these files have full support for the core JavaScript language, but only a limited range of functions are available. There are no alert( )or user-friendly error messages.

- The lock_pref( ) and unlock_pref( ) functions—not pref( )—should be used in these scripts. This is also true for *.jsc* files.

The *first line invalid* rule is quite confusing, because it means that Firefox ignores that first line completely. Recommended practice is to make sure files look like this:

```
#Mozilla Example Security Header Line
lock_pref("example.pref.enabled",true);
lock_pref("example.pref2.enabled",true);
...
```

Do not use #!, which can cause a program to run under Unix. If this line uses correct JavaScript comment syntax (either // for whole lines, or /* */ pairs) instead of #, then:

- The file is now valid JavaScript, a minor security hole.

- The special behavior is less obvious and so is easy to forget.

This example shows that ill-advised use:

```
// Mozilla Example Security Header Line
lock_pref("example.pref.enabled",true);
lock_pref("example.pref2.enabled",true);
...
```

If you forget this feature entirely, you could lose the first line of your file accidentally, which might wreck the script if it's no longer a whole JavaScript, or at least cause a statement to be missed:

```
lock_pref("example.pref.enabled",true);  // line 1 - ignored and lost
lock_pref("example.pref2.enabled",true); // line 2 - recognized
...
```

Finally, if there is a JavaScript syntax error anywhere in the file, the remainder of the file's contents is silently ignored. Always make a line like this the last line of your file:

```
lock_pref("check.config.enabled",true);  // my check
```

This preference has no special meaning; it is a made-up flag. If it appears in *about:config*, your file has been read successfully. Don't forget to delete it using *about:config* before testing changes to your files.

Locking Preferences Using ReadConfig

ReadConfig is a small enhancement to the preferences system [Hack #23] designed to lock down preferences using a local file. It doesn't appear anywhere in the Firefox GUI or in the files supplied at install time. Two files must be modified for ReadConfig to work. First, Firefox must be told that ReadConfig is enabled. This is done with normal preferences:

```
lock_pref("general.config.vendor","acme");
lock_pref("general.config.filename","acme.cfg");
```

Those preferences should be set in the install area, either as part of a custom Firefox installation or hacked into place afterward. They are not set by default. acme is an opaque string that names the organization (vendor) providing the custom install of Firefox (you). These preferences must be put in a file called *all.js*, and nowhere else. This file must be put in the install area here:

```
defaults/pref/all.js
```

The other file, *acme.cfg*, is a new file that must be placed at the top of the install area in the same directory as the Firefox binary (e.g., *C:\Program Files\Firefox*). The following preference controls the shrouding (trivial encryption) of this *acme.cfg* file. The normal case is encryption using a simple ROT-13 algorithm:

```
lock_pref("general.config.obscure_value",13);
```

Set this preference to 0 (zero) to ease testing of ReadConfig. It allows an unshrouded *acme.cfg* file to be read.

Summarizing all that, a minimal *all.js* file designed to enable ReadConfig with a standard, shrouded file looks like this:

```
lock_pref("general.config.vendor","acme");
lock_pref("general.config.filename","acme.cfg");
lock_pref("general.config.obscure_value",13);
lock_pref("check.alljs.enabled",true);          // my syntax OK flag
```

On startup, Firefox will see these preferences. It will load, unshroud, and first-line-strip the *acme.cfg* file, and then interpret its contents.

The script inside *acme.cfg* file is not interpreted the same way as a straight-forward JavaScript script. Two extra things happen when it runs:

1. Before it is interpreted, the content of these two other files are exposed to its use:

   ```
   defaults/autoconfig/platform.js
   defaults/autoconfig/prefcalls.js
   ```

2. After it is interpreted, these preferences are reapplied (if they are present) and overwrite any previous values:

   ```
   general.config.vendor
   general.config.filename
   autoadmin.global_config_url
   ```

The first point simply provides the configuration script with some extra functions that it can call. A highly customized Firefox install might extend that set by providing a bigger *prefcalls.js* file. The second point is a security feature. The user should not be able to reset the names of configuration files after they are read.

A sample *acme.cfg* file, without AutoConfig support (see the next section) and without shrouding, looks like this:

```
#Mozilla ReadConfig Security Header Line
lock_pref("general.config.vendor","acme");
lock_pref("general.config.filename","acme.cfg");

lock_pref("browser.chrome.toolbar_tips",false);  // whatever's needed

lock_pref("check.readconfig.enabled",true);       // syntax ok flag
```

To shroud the *acme.cfg* file, use Alain Knaff's script (Perl 5.8 required):

http://www.alain.knaff.lu/howto/MozillaCustomization/moz-byteshift.pl

ReadConfig offers little remote control by itself. The most you get is a customized install and a trivial hurdle for the user. You must use filesystem security to protect the ReadConfig information, but since it's in the install area, not in the profile, this is an easy task, especially if the Firefox install is on a central server. ReadConfig serves as a jumping off point for AutoConfig, discussed next.

Updating Preferences Using AutoConfig

AutoConfig is also a small enhancement to the preference system. It doesn't appear in the Firefox GUI anywhere, or in the default install files. It allows preferences to be set from a file delivered by a web server. It facilitates centralized control; preferences can be modified in one place and automatically reapplied to all users the next time that Firefox starts up. In that respect, it is similar to the AutoProxy feature [Hack #15], but the similarity ends quickly.

AutoConfig preference scripts are specified by a URL. Any http: or ftp: URL is fine, as long as the HTTP Content-Type sent is correct [Hack #27]. If the file is static, the convention is to name it *autoconfig.jsc* (*jsc* stands for JavaScript Configuration). This preference causes the server-based file to be downloaded at Firefox startup time:

```
autoadmin.global_config_url    /* set to a http: or ftp: URL */
```

This preference can be put in any preference file. The only sensible place to put it is inside a ReadConfig *.cfg* file, where the user can't change it. The only place that uses this preference for its fundamental purpose is the internal bit of Mozilla that reads the *.cfg* files.

AutoConfig writes a file to the Firefox profile *failover.jsc.*, which is a copy of the web-delivered configuration script grabbed automatically by Firefox. The configuration script is downloaded each time the profile is switched. Firefox 1.0 doesn't yet support live profile switching (unless you add an extension), so the download occurs only when Firefox starts up. It also occurs if there's no profile at all (but that is an abnormal state of affairs).

No AutoConfig file contains JavaScript-unfriendly header lines. No such file is shrouded with ROT-13. They are plain and correct JavaScript syntax.

Several preferences control the way AutoConfig behaves. They should also be set somewhere that's away from the user's grubby hands.

The following preference indicates whether to tell the server who the user is, using dodgy HTTP GET syntax to send the user's email address to the server:

```
autoadmin.append_emailaddr /* default = false, set to true */
```

Firefox will do its best to find in the preference system a Thunderbird, Mozilla Email & News, or Netscape Email email address to use. The sent URL will look like this:

```
http://www.example.com/example-config.jsc?foo@bar.org
```

A sample server-supplied AutoConfig file looks like this:

```
lock_pref("browser.chrome.toolbar_tips",false);  // whatever's needed

lock_pref("check.autoconfig.enabled",true);      // my syntax OK flag
```

Handling Failover Scenarios

AutoConfig does not rely on or use the general-purpose Firefox Cache. This preference determines what AutoConfig must do if Firefox is set to offline mode by the user:

```
autoadmin.offline_failover /* default = false, set to true */
```

If this preference is set to true, Firefox will read the locally stored *failover.jsc* file instead of reaching out over the network.

This further preference indicates what AutoConfig must do if Firefox fails to retrieve the configuration script from a web server:

```
autoadmin.failover_to_cached   /* default = false, set to true */
```

If this preference is set to true, Firefox will read the *failover.jsc* file if retrieval or parsing of the *autoconfig.jsc* file fails for any reason. If that happens, Firefox will also lock this preference, which prevents any online activity until the browser restarts.

Finally, this preference is a security measure designed to stop clients from being flooded with bad configuration data:

```
network.online    /* set to true or false */
```

Set to false, Firefox will not seek out the AutoConfig file. Firefox will set this preference to false if it detects problems retrieving the config file.

HACK #30 Install Fonts and Character Support

Protect your tired eyes from ugly fonts when staring at web pages.

Firefox can display web pages in a variety of languages, but whether Firefox picks great-looking fonts depends on three different factors:

- Fonts available in your OS
- Fonts specified for the language in use
- CSS fonts specified on the web page

Installing Good Fonts

This is the take-off point. At the end of the day, Firefox can use only fonts that your OS provides to applications. Platforms such as Windows come preinstalled with beautiful TrueType fonts. If you are a Linux user and have a Windows license, you can migrate its TrueType fonts to your Linux partition and enable them in your Linux desktop for Firefox to use. Otherwise, you can get Microsoft's free TrueType core fonts for the Web at *http://corefonts.sourceforge.net/*.

Anti-aliasing may or may not be enabled on your particular Linux distribution. Some users like it and others don't. You can disable it in Firefox (if you have an XFT-enabled build) by simply setting an environment variable:

```
export GDK_USE_XFT=1 /* Linux only: set to 0 to disable anti-aliasing */
```

This applies to all GTK2/XFT applications. Because there are many distributions and configurations, each with its own syntax and documentation, we assume that you can refer to them to install nice fonts. The rest of this hack will concentrate on Firefox tricks.

Forget about *downloadable fonts*. They have been abused in the past to work around browser limitations. Documents were using them through bogus Latin letters posing as glyph indices. Firefox is Unicode-based and in the recent years much effort has gone into supporting international languages through Unicode. Remember that when Firefox can't find any font in your system for a particular character, it will display a question mark to get your attention. In particular, MathML documents need special fonts [Hack #61].

Selecting Good Language Fonts

Later, when we cover the font-selection algorithm, we'll see that what you select for language fonts is equally important for web pages that mix different languages. Firefox comes with a good selection of default fonts for the main language groups (Western, Japanese, Arabic, etc.). You can make other choices by visiting Tools → Options → General → Fonts & Colors.

Beauty is in the eye of the beholder, and while you are there, consider also setting a *minimum font size* if your eyes are weak. You can also temporarily magnify the text when you encounter badly designed pages (View → Text Size → Decrease/Increase).

Overriding Web Page Fonts

Web page authors can specify fonts that they prefer. By default, these take precedence over your settings in the preference dialog. Sometimes, however, you might not like what authors specify, or their fonts might not be available on your system. In the latter case, if authors set a lang attribute (xml:lang for XHTML), Firefox will immediately fall back to your own preferences. The lang attribute is inherited and, if put in the root <html>, it will apply to all elements until it is overwritten by an inner descendant.

When a page does not state its language, Firefox will attempt to automatically detect it based on the document's *charset*, the user language, or the OS language (in that order of importance).

Disabled users, even those as able as older people with poor sight, might want to override page authors altogether. To do that, choose Tools → Options → General → Fonts & Colors → Always Use My Fonts.

Another way to override fonts is through *userContent.css*. You can create this file in your profile and put overriding style rules in there:

```
* {
    font-family: serif !important;      /* set to your favorite fonts */
}
listing, xmp, pre, tt, code, kbd, samp, textarea {
    font-family: monospace !important; /* set to your favorite fonts */
}
```

Always end your CSS font-family lists with a generic CSS type (e.g., serif, sans-serif, etc). That ensures that Firefox will favor the specified class of fonts for the elements under consideration but that Firefox will also have a guaranteed fallback font if required.

> Firefox's chrome fonts are fetched through your system-wide desktop preferences. But you can further tune Firefox appearance by setting chrome fonts in *userChrome.css*:
>
> ```
> * {
>     font-size: 10px      !important;
>     /* your preferred size */
>
>     font-family: serif !important;
>     /* your favorite fonts */
> }
> input, textarea, select, button {
>     font-size: 10px          !important;
>     /* your preferred size */
>
>     font-family: monospace !important;
>     /* your favorite fonts */
> }
> ```

Knowing How Firefox Selects Fonts

Because a document can mix different languages, Firefox uses sophisticated algorithms to select the most suitable fonts. Of course, this won't be apparent to you if you predominantly visit pages in just one language, such as English. It is more apparent to readers who visit multilingual pages.

Consider a page whose main language is Hebrew. We saw earlier how to specify fonts for this language in the font preference dialog. But what about English words that might be intermingled on the page? Well, use this preference (which works on Windows but might not work on all platforms):

```
font.name-list.serif.he /* set to a CSS list of alternative fonts */
```

If Firefox encounters words that involve characters not in the primary font specified for the Hebrew language, it will fall back to this alternative list in order of preference. Change .serif to another generic type or change .he to another language code to cover other cases.

Here is a quick, somewhat oversimplified rundown of how the hack works. To render a character, Firefox's Gecko engine looks for a suitable match in the CSS font-family list specified by the web author. If no fonts are specified or no match is found, it moves on to the default font for the language of the character. If it still can't find a match, it then looks at the fallback list. In case you missed where the trick is, Gecko automatically detects the language of a character inside an <html> tag that might have a different lang attribute for its main language.

Using Character References and Entities

It might happen that you want to include Greek letters, the Euro symbol, or the British pound sign in a page. The *numeric character reference* (NRC) is a notation that suits this situation well. It can be in decimal form as *&#number;* or in hexadecimal form as *&#xnumber;*. Thus, the NRC for α (officially called GREEK SMALL LETTER ALPHA in Unicode) is α or α.

All Unicode characters can be referenced this way, so it is an interoperable way to combine all characters. It is a versatile notation, especially useful when the character cannot easily be entered on a keyboard. But again, whether the character is ultimately displayed on the user's side is subject to the availability of a font that holds a glyph (a picture) of that character.

Another problem is that the NCR notation is not user-friendly. It is hard to remember that many numbers! A friendlier alternative is to use a *character entity reference*, or entity for short. This is a *case-sensitive* mnemonic name that takes the form &name;. Examples include © for the copyright symbol and Λ for the Greek capital letter lambda. But there does not exist a universal list that covers all of Unicode's millions of potential characters. The number of standardized entity names is limited. Which set of entities Firefox uses depends on the document and its DOCTYPE.

A plain XML document (one that is not pretending to be a specific application of XML) supports only five predefined entities: amp, gt, lt, apos, and quot. An HTML or XHTML document supports entities for accented Latin letters, Greek letters, and other special markup symbols, as defined in HTML 4.01. A document with a MathML DOCTYPE **[Hack #61]** supports over 2000 predefined mathematical entities to ensure the interoperability of scientific documents. Note that for XML, XHTML, and MathML at least, you can define more entities in a set held internally in the document, which is ideal if a given entity is used a lot.

Figure 3-2 shows the result of the following example :

```
<?xml version="1.0"?>
<!DOCTYPE html
   PUBLIC "-//W3C//DTD XHTML 1.0 Strict//EN"
   "http://www.w3.org/TR/xhtml1/DTD/xhtml1-strict.dtd"
[
   <!ENTITY diamondsuit '&#x2666;'>
   <!ENTITY smiley "data:image/gif;base64,
   R0lGOD1hDwAPAIAAAAAAAP///yH5BAAAAAAALAAAAAAPAA8AAAImjA2
   Zx7H8DmhQOjYdyi5PHoXcJY1kdOLeta6VBneKhZxmtJEKHhQAOw==">
]>
<html xmlns="http://www.w3.org/1999/xhtml">
<head>
  <title>Entities</title>
</head>
<body>
  A self-contained document with entities for an
  embedded smiley in a data: URL and a diamond suit:
  <img src="&smiley;"/> &diamondsuit;
</body>
</html>
```

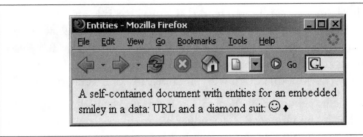

Figure 3-2. Defining entities in a document

—*Roger Sidje*

HACK #31   Take Firefox with You

Install a portable version of Firefox so that you can move from computer to computer.

This hack explains how to take Firefox with you wherever you go. You can install Firefox on a number of mobile devices. Whether it can run directly on the device, write data there, or merely be stored conveniently depends on the device. We'll consider these devices:

- A laptop
- A server-based virtual private network (VPN)
- A roaming VPN

- A mobile consumer device, such as a digital camera, mobile phone, or PDA
- A USB drive
- A RAM drive

It's the so-called removable media (USB and RAM drives) that are the interesting cases. Let's briefly dispose of the other possibilities first.

Laptop

If you install Firefox on a *laptop*, you can surf the Web using that laptop from anywhere that TCP/IP connectivity is in place—a WiFi hotspot, for example. It's up to you to ensure that the laptop acts as its own firewall, or else that it correctly establishes a VPN with the organization that you're using as an Internet gateway. If that's done, Firefox typically just needs to be set up *direct connect* with no proxy.

Server-Based VPN

A *server-based* VPN runs Firefox on your computer after the install area is loaded from the server disk. All you need is file-sharing access and perhaps server login [Hack #14].

Roaming VPN

A *roaming* VPN runs Firefox from a local or remote installation, but it also replicates your profile area from a central server to local disk. At the moment, this has to be set up using special network admin steps [Hack #28]. Automatic roaming is not supported in Firefox 1.0, but at the time of this writing, this functionality is close to being finished. Perhaps it will be available in Version 1.1.

Mobile Consumer Devices

Memory-rich consumer devices such as digital cameras can sometimes be recognized as USB or Bluetooth drives by a host computer. In this case, they operate just like a USB key drive and can perform the same way, as discussed in the following section.

> The press has reported that a version of Mozilla is slated to run directly inside Nokia mobile phones, and possibly in another vendor's mobile phones as well. Such versions aren't strictly Firefox but do display pages using the same Gecko technology as Firefox.

USB Drive

Here's where things start to get interesting. If you can carry Firefox on a USB drive, you can plug it in and run it wherever you go.

There are several options for USB-based Firefox installs. The simplest is to put the standard Firefox installer on the key drive and install it everywhere you go, like Johnny Appleseed planting apples. That puts both the install area and the profile area on the local hard disk, and none of your profile files move with you.

Get PortableFirefox. John Haller has repackaged and reconfigured the official Firefox 1.0 install into PortableFirefox, which can run entirely from USB. This means the install area and the profile area are both retained on the USB drive while Firefox runs. See his work and get his package at *http:// portablefirefox.mozdev.org/*

This package is too large to fit on a floppy disk, but it will fit on a Zip drive. Zip drives, however, are slow to access. PortableFirefox contains official Firefox software.

Use a USB launcher. If you don't want to be tied to a custom distribution, you can use the Firefox Launcher tools, available at *http://people.emich.edu/ mkinnunen/tblaunch/* (Windows only).

The Firefox Launcher is a small Windows program that starts up Firefox once you've installed the profile and install areas on the USB key. Install it on the USB key as well. A trivial launcher can also be made using a simple *.bat* file. It need only contain the following lines:

```
cd U:\
start \install\Firefox\Firefox.exe -profile \profiles\ProfileName
```

Here, the install and profile areas are preloaded to the equivalent directories on the USB drive.

Build a USB-aware Firefox. Finally, another alternative is to smarten Firefox up so that it scans for profiles on any USB drives that are plugged in. This leaves the install area on the local computer, and the profile data (your important data) follows you wherever you go. This link describes a customization that provides this feature, but at the time of writing, you have to be able to compile Firefox with these changes in place yourself:

http://www.cs.sjsu.edu/faculty/pollett/masters/Semesters/Spring04/Yun/ index.shtml

The Mozilla Thunderbird email product has formally planned support for USB drives. The benefits of that work will probably also benefit Firefox, but most likely not until a minor version later than 1.0. Read the release notes for Firefox 1.1 and later versions to see if that feature has arrived yet.

RAM Drive

If you can make Firefox run from a RAM drive, you're one step closer to running it from any drive, anywhere. This URL describes how to put Portable Firefox on a RAM drive on Windows:

http://www.patik.com/guides/mozilla/ffram

RAM drives are somewhat overkill on Linux/Unix. To put Firefox in RAM on Unix, simply execute these commands, which load all Firefox files into the disk buffer cache, where they are subsequently accessed at RAM speed:

```
find /path/to/firefox/install ! -type d | xargs cat > /dev/null
find /path/to/firefox/profile ! -type d | xargs cat > /dev/null
```

This will not, however, remove the need for a disk drive, and neither will it keep Firefox in memory if the system has heavy disk access.

At the time of writing, there is not yet a Knoppix-like CD distribution of Firefox alone, although Knoppix distributions exist that include Firefox. For a real, memory-locked Firefox on Linux or Solaris, create a `tmpfs` filesystem and install, copy, or load standard Firefox there each time you need to use it. Knoppix distributions automate that process but allow bookmarks to be stored only until the PC is rebooted.

HACK #32   Work with Filtering Systems
Keep your web experience neat and tidy by integrating properly with other Net watchers.

Security programs can interpose themselves between Firefox and the network; this is especially common in organizational environments. There are few such tools on Linux/Unix—where tools do exist, they are generally called *firewalls* or *daemons*—but they are common on Windows. This hack reports briefly on what works and what doesn't.

In general, Firefox works with such tools well. There are many reports in the Mozilla community **[Hack #97]** about particular tools' successes or failure, but here's a summary: best practice requires that you have the latest minor version of your filtering tool installed if you want to interoperate with Firefox successfully.

You'll find a list of common filtering tools at *http://yaggy.web1000.com/webads.htm*. Here are some brief comments about such tools:

Ad blockers

At least the following Windows tools have been reported interoperable: AdSubtract, atGuard, and adKiller. The popular Firefox extension AdBlock prevents advertorial content from being downloaded, and once that feature is enabled, no other ad-blocking tools should be required.

Security monitors

Tools like ZoneAlarm may complain about Firefox when it is first installed. Firefox occasionally communicates with itself via sockets, and this is what ZoneAlarm picks up. Configure ZoneAlarm to permit this, or tell the users to allow it when prompted. I know people who believe in Norton Internet Security and other Norton tools, but I personally have never had any success with them.

Download tools

Heavyweight download tools take care of big downloads, such as movie clips and game demos, for you. Most of these tools are well integrated with Firefox. I recommend Free Download Manager (*http://www.freedownloadmanager.org*).

In addition to these tools, Firefox proxies [Hack #15] can be used to redirect web requests to filtering proxy servers as required.

## CHAPTER FOUR

Web Surfing Enhancements

Hacks 33–43

The problem with software is that there's never enough choice. There are only a few really good word processors, only a few really good graphic design tools, and only a few really good web browsers. Among those few choices, it's just not possible for one browser, not even Firefox, to satisfy all of the people all of the time. This chapter explains how to change the Firefox user interface so that it behaves the way you want it to.

They say dog owners tend to look like their dogs, and maybe the same is true of web surfers and their web browsers. How Firefox looks to you depends on which parts of it you spend the most time with. A classic example is bookmarks [Hack #33]. The Firefox bookmark system is quite a rich little thing, as you'll see. If you happen to be a heavy user of bookmarks, there are many powerful and less well-known bookmark tricks to try out.

Most of the power features of Firefox are not bundled with the browser. They're available as extensions, both from Mozilla's official update web site (*update.mozilla.org*) and from miscellaneous places around the Web. Most of this chapter is a tour of the very best user extensions currently available. Finding an extension that matches your activity profile—one that blesses you with faster workflow and less frustration—is like finding a gold nugget in your own backyard. So start digging. There are new extensions being published all the time.

 Use Fancy Bookmarks

#33 Bookmarks can do more than record web pages. See how they've grown.

Hidden inside Firefox's bookmark system are a number of advanced features. This hack explains how to use them.

The Firefox bookmarks user interface is different from that of the Mozilla Application Suite or Netscape. In particular, the Check for Updates and

Notify functionality is missing in Firefox 1.0. That feature causes the browser to optionally poll bookmarked web pages to see whether they have changed recently. Firefox supports the same bookmark format as other Mozilla browsers, but Version 1.0 just doesn't do any polling. Check the release notes for later, minor versions to see if that feature has been added back in recently. In these modern times, RSS is probably the new way forward for polled web content. See "Live Bookmarks" later in this hack for more on RSS.

In addition to the features described in this hack, there are several extensions that extend the bookmark system. Feed readers [Hack #37] are just one example. Have a look at the Bookmarks category at *http://update.mozilla.org*.

Use Tab Group Bookmarks

If you have multiple tabs open at once, you can bookmark them all in one go. Choose Bookmarks → Bookmark this Page and tick the "Bookmark all tabs in a folder" checkbox, as shown in Figure 4-1.

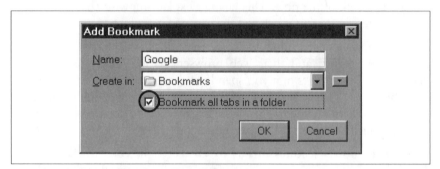

Figure 4-1. Adding all open tabs to a bookmark

The folder will be named with the title of the leftmost tab. To reopen that set of bookmarks as tabs, drill down through the Bookmarks menu and submenus to the folder you want to see and then choose the bottom menu item (the one labeled Open in Tabs).

It's also possible to start up Firefox so that multiple tabs are displayed. This functionality is *not* available in bookmarks. Use a URL in this format to make it happen:

```
http://www.example.com/page1.html|http://www.example.com/page2.html
```

The vertical bar character (|) separates the URLs for each tab. This syntax can be used on the command line when starting Firefox, or it can be specified as the default home page in the Tools → Options → General dialog box. Because the pipe character has other historic uses, this syntax is not locked in stone yet, but it is available and working in Firefox 1.0.

Use Sidebar Bookmarks

A bookmark can be opened in the Firefox sidebar rather than in the main page. To do so, first create the bookmark. Next, open the Bookmark Manager using Bookmarks → Manage Bookmarks.... Drill down to the bookmark, right-click on it, and choose Properties. In the dialog box, tick the "Load this bookmark in the sidebar" checkbox, as shown in Figure 4-2.

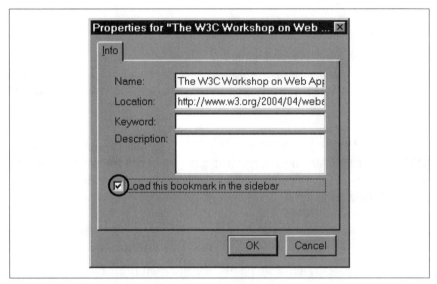

Figure 4-2. Making a bookmark display in the sidebar

Once the bookmark is saved, recalling it opens the sidebar and loads the page into it.

Use Keyword Bookmarks

A *keyword bookmark* matches more than one web page. Usually, the page you want is *parameterized*, which means that it represents an HTTP GET request and includes special query values. Keyword bookmarks allow one parameter of the bookmark's URL to be left unspecified. When that is done, the bookmark can't (usually) be loaded by clicking on any bookmark icon. Instead, you use the bookmark by typing a keyword and parameter into the Location bar.

Here are two examples. The first URL identifies a Mozilla Bugzilla bug report by bug number. The second identifies an Amazon.com book by its Amazon ASIN, which for a book is typically its ISBN number:

```
https://bugzilla.mozilla.org/show_bug.cgi?id=273050
http://www.amazon.com/exec/obidos/ASIN/0131423436/
```

After the special bookmarks are created, you can recall any bug or any book just by typing short keywords into the Location bar:

```
bug 273050
book 0131423436
```

In short versions, the second term can be varied without changing the bookmark, so all of these are supported as well:

```
bug 12345
bug 13
book 0131313131
```

To create such a keyword bookmark, construct a bookmark for each original URL and open the Properties dialog box for each one. Then, make the URL for the bookmark more generic by changing the Location: field as follows:

```
https://bugzilla.mozilla.org/show_bug.cgi?id=%s
http://www.amazon.com/exec/obidos/ASIN/%s/
```

The %s characters (stolen from the syntax of printf( ) format masks) will be replaced with the single parameter supplied. %s can appear only once. In the Keyword: field, type in the new keyword for the bookmark, in this case one of these two:

```
bug
book
```

Save these changes. Figure 4-3 shows the final setup for the Amazon.com example.

The SmartSearch extension adds some user-interface niceties to keyword bookmark functionality. Find it at *http://update.mozilla.org*.

Live Bookmarks

Firefox's major bookmark innovation is to integrate RSS feeds into the bookmark system. In this case, one bookmark stands for a whole RSS feed and appears as a bookmark folder. When the folder is opened (usually after being placed on the Bookmarks Toolbar), the feed is downloaded and a bookmark is created in the folder for each feed item found. The simplest way to create a Live Bookmark is to click on the RSS feed icon [Hack #4] that appears on the status bar when a web page advertises that a feed is available.

To create a live bookmark manually, just open the Bookmark Manager window (Bookmarks → Manage Bookmarks), click on the folder that will hold the live bookmark, and choose File → New Live Bookmark. Fill in the RSS XML- or RDF-based URL, and you're finished.

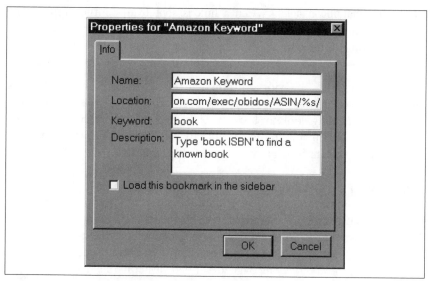

Figure 4-3. Keyword bookmark for Amazon.com books

 ## Modify Tabbed Browsing
#34 Customize the look and behavior of tabs to any degree.

Tabbed browsing is often touted as one of Firefox's killer features. Indeed, it's very useful, but the default preferences aren't perfect for everyone. That's OK, because Firefox offers plenty of preferences for customizing your tabbed-browsing experience. If you can't find what you want in the preferences, you can go a step further by installing one of the many Firefox extensions that can make minor alterations to your tabs.

Still not satisfied? The most aggressive of all the tab-related extensions, discussed at the end of this hack, completely replaces Firefox's tabs with its own.

Tabbed-Browsing Preferences

Firefox preferences allow you to control how tabs respond to certain types of events. Some of the preferences are easily set in the Preferences window, while others require you to use the special *about:config* page in the browser.

 To find tabbed-browsing preferences in *about:config*, type tabs in the Search box at the top of the list.

Links from other applications. When a link is sent from another application, such as when you click on a URL in an email, what should the browser do? There are three options: open the page in a new window, open the page in a new tab in the front window, or replace the current page in the front window.

The options for this behavior are shown at the top of the Tabbed Browsing panel in the Preferences window. If you ever feel the need to set this preference via *about:config*, look for `browser.link.open_external`. Setting this preference to 1 opens the link in the current tab and window, 2 opens it in a new window, and 3 opens it in a new tab in the front window.

Loading tabs in the foreground or background. There are three preferences that control whether new tabs load in front of the current tab or behind it. These preferences correspond to the three types of events that can open a new tab. Two can be set in the Preferences window (checked or `true` means "load in foreground"; unchecked or `false` means "load in background"), while the third requires the *about:config* page, described earlier in this hack:

Control (Command)-clicking a link in the browser to open a new tab
> Set this in the Preferences window with the checkbox labeled "Select new tabs opened from links" or in *about:config* by changing `browser. tabs.loadInBackground`.

Opening a tab from a bookmark or the browser history panel
> In the Preferences window, this event is called "Select new tabs opened from bookmarks or history." In *about:config*, it's `browser.tabs. opentabfor.bookmarks`.

Opening a tab from a link sent by another application
> There is no checkbox in the Preferences window for this setting. In *about:config*, this preference is `browser.tabs.loadDivertedInBackground`.

Getting rid of tabs when there's only one. This preference hides the tab bar at the top of the set of tabs when only one tab exists:

```
browser.tabs.autoHide  /* set to true to enable hiding */
```

Single Window mode. Do you hate it when links on web pages open new windows (because they set a `target` attribute on the link)? You can force Firefox to open those links in a new tab instead of a new window. This is called Single Window mode. It doesn't prevent all new windows, but it catches most of them. The radio buttons for setting this preference are in the Preferences window, but only if Firefox knows you want to see them. Go to *about:config* and set `browser.tabs.showSingleWindowModePrefs` to `true`. Figure 4-4 shows the items that are added to the Preferences window's Tabbed Browsing panel after making this change.

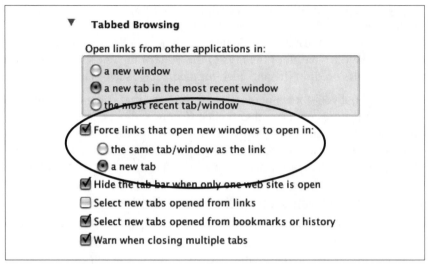

Figure 4-4. Single Window mode preferences for tabbed browsing

Extensions that Alter Tabbed Browsing

There are a number of Firefox extensions that interact with tabbed browsing. Two are designed to make it easier to set the preferences exactly how you like, and one adds some useful new features via the creative use of tabs and keystrokes. New extensions are being written all the time, so check the Mozilla Updates web site (*http://updates.mozilla.org/*) for the latest additions.

Tabbrowser Preferences. The Tabbrowser Preferences (TBP) extension (*http://www.pryan.org/mozilla/site/TheOneKEA/tabprefs/*), by Bradley Chapman, organizes all of the preferences related to tabbed browsing into a single pane in the Preferences window. You can set all of the same preferences via the special *about:config* page, but by using TBP, you don't have to remember what the different preference names mean or what value to set in order to get the behavior you want.

Quick Tab Pref Toggle. The Quick Tab Pref Toggle (QTPT) extension (*http://jedbrown.net/mozilla/extensions/#QuickTabPrefToggle*), by Jed Brown, allows you to maintain two sets of tabbed-browsing preferences. The idea is that you'll usually want to divert all new windows into new tabs, but occasionally you'll work with a page that really should pop up a separate window. This extension lets you put a small button (a *toggle*) in the toolbar to flip back and forth between two sets of preferences with a single click.

Magpie. Magpie (*http://www.bengoodger.com/software/tabloader/*), by lead Firefox developer Ben Goodger, is not a tabbed-browsing extension per se, but it has a related feature that demonstrates a completely different use for tabs. Magpie can save all of the tabs to the right of the one you're currently viewing to files on disk. (It's intended for media files, such as pictures.)

For example, if you open a photo album web page that contains thumbnails of a dozen pictures, you could Ctrl-click (Command-click) each of them to open the full size photos in separate tabs. Then, a single use of Magpie's Ctrl-Shift-S would save all of those images to disk in a single folder and close the tabs. This is much faster than saving each image to disk one at a time.

Tabbrowser Extension: A Complete Tabbing Overhaul

The Tabbrowser Extension (TBE, *http://piro.sakura.ne.jp/xul/_tabextensions. html.en*), by Shimoda "Piro" Hiroshi, is a power user's tool. It's the super-ultra-deluxe tabbing system, with every feature you can imagine and a few you probably can't. TBE completely replaces the built-in browser tabs with TBE's own. Review the install notes and latest status, as TBE is still being polished and debugged as this goes to print.

TBE's tabs look just like the regular tabs in Firefox (by default, anyway) but offer lots of features you simply can't get any other way. In fact, TBE is so flexible that the Preferences window for tweaking its behavior has almost as many options as Firefox's own Preferences window! TBE allows you to do the following things:

- Rearrange tabs by dragging them to the left or right
- Duplicate tabs in the same window or into a new window
- Color your tabs
- Display tabs on any side of the browser window (not just the top)
- Automatically load the same group of tabs you were using when you last quit Firefox
- Undo a closed tab (reopen it to the same page)
- Lock a tab so that all links within it automatically open in a new tab
- Block the page in a specific tab from being listed in the Referer: header when you click a link
- Automatically reload a tab every *n* seconds, minutes, or days
- Add a Close button to every tab
- Loads more...

TBE also supports plug-in modules of its own. You'll find these plug-ins and more listed at *http://piro.sakura.ne.jp/xul/_tabextensions_modules.html.en*:

ContextMenu Rearrangement Module
Adds another preference panel to change the order of menu items in the tab bar's context menu (the menu shown when you right-click or Ctrl-click anywhere on the browser's tab bar).

Tab Numbering Module
Even Firefox's regular tabs allow you to switch to a specific tab by Ctrl-#, where # is the number of the tab (1 to 9) you want to switch to. With TBE and the Tab Numbering Module installed, holding down the Control key causes the tab numbers to pop up over the tabs, so you immediately know which number you need.

Highlight Unread Tab Module
When a new tab is opened in the background (behind the tab you're currently viewing), TBE marks it as *unread*. This module allows you to change how the unread tabs are displayed, making it easy for you to see which tabs you haven't looked at yet.

Smooth Resizing Patch
When your browser window has lots of tabs open, you might find that resizing the browser window is slower or *jerkier* than expected, especially if your computer is not the latest and greatest model. This module lets you resize the windows much more smoothly, but it causes a slight delay when switching tabs.

Focus Previously Selected Tab Module
Keeps track of which tabs you visit and in which order and allows you to step backward and forward through that *history*, which is useful when you have many, many tabs open and accidentally switch to another tab before finishing with the current one. One quick keystroke, and you're back where you started.

The Tabbrowser Extension is far too feature-rich to cover everything here. If you take your tabbed browsing seriously and want full control over every aspect, then TBE is worth a look.

—*Seth Dillingham*

HACK #35 Govern Image and Ad Display

A picture is worth a thousand words; here's how to make the most out of web page pictures.

Images are a big fraction of web content. They consume most of your Internet bandwidth and most of the energy your brain devotes to comprehension. There are many tricks you can apply to poke and tweak images to suit your taste. This hack describes a few.

Block Images and Advertising Content

Firefox provides simple image-blocking options under Tools → Options → Web Features. You can also turn to extensions or your own custom styles. Attempting to block advertising is a technology war. Web browsers can now block pop-ups, straightforward advertising banners, and Flash ads, so if you don't want such things, you're currently enjoying a well-earned respite. In the near future, though, commercial web sites will discover ways around these blocking techniques.

Using standard features. If you uncheck Tools → Options → Web Features → Load Images, no images at all will be downloaded for display and web pages will load faster. Locally cached copies of images will not be used. Images drawn in via CSS stylesheets will not be used. If the page displayed comes from local disk, then local images will be displayed. In all cases, blocks of color on the web page added with CSS color styles might still appear.

If Load Images is enabled but "for the originating web site only" is also checked, web pages that try to load images from other web sites for display in their own pages will not be able to do so. This option can be used to check a web site for image copyright violations.

Here's the preference for these two checkboxes:

```
network.image.imageBehavior /* 0 = default, 1 = origin only, 2 = none */
```

The Exceptions button next to these options implements a combined blacklist and whitelist for web sites, which overrides the other two options. If you enter *http://www.example.com*, then all pages on that web site will be either allowed or denied, according to the button pressed. You can add an image's web site to the blacklist by context-clicking on it and choosing "Block image from [url]."

If images aren't displayed, this preference controls whether a placeholder icon is shown where the image would otherwise have been:

```
browser.display.show_image_placeholders  /* true = default */
```

The ultimate image roadblock is the user's *userContent.css* stylesheet. This file placed in the profile area can override, via the CSS !important directive, any layout of any web page. For example, this fancy new CSS3 selector can be used to block all ads from the imaginary *www.adspam.com* ad-placement web site:

```
img[src*="adspam.com"] { display : none !important; }
```

Using the Adblock extension. The Adblock extension (*http://update.mozilla.org*) is a well-maintained filtering system for advertising banners and spots that are embedded in web pages. It has a Hide option that downloads but doesn't display ad content, and a Remove option that prevents that content from being downloaded in the first place. It can also block Flash ads.

After installation, Adblock must be trained before it will do anything. You must context-click on a web page image and choose Adblock Image to prevent that image from being displayed again.

A more systematic approach is to build a set of filters that apply to all web sites loaded. These can be added from the Tools → Adblock → Preferences dialog box. Filters can be added by hand or imported as a group from a file by clicking on the Adblock Options text in the dialog box. You can find a recommended set of filters at *http://www.geocities.com/pierceive/adblock/*. Choose the most recent file and follow the instructions in the *-instructions.txt* file. To delete that file on Unix/Linux after use, type the following command:

```
rm ./-instructions.txt
```

Each filter in such a file is a string pattern that is matched against the URL of every image reference on every loaded page. Those image URLs that match are never loaded/displayed, so the set of filter lines in a filter file form a blacklist. A URL need only fail one filter to be rejected entirely.

The two kinds of filter content are plain-text substring matches, which can be typed directly and can contain * wildcards:

```
*.adsource.com
```

and JavaScript regular expression literals, which must be surrounded by forward slashes:

```
/advert[a-z]{,4}.com/
```

Forward and backward slashes don't need to be escaped in these regular expressions because they're fed to the AdBlock processor as a string. You can find popular resources for image-quashing rules at *http://www.floppymoose.com* and *http://krath.dk/writing/flash_blocking/*.

Manage the Way Images Are Displayed

Firefox supports all the image-resizing features implied by HTML 4.01. If an image is displayed alone in a window, rather than as part of a web page, then simple resizing is available. To see this in action, go to a web site that shows big images, such as *http://antwrp.gsfc.nasa.gov/apod/astropix.html*, and context-click to view an image in its own window. Shrink the window to see the image resize, and then click on the image to make it toggle between full size and "fit to window" size. This feature is enabled by the preference:

```
browser.enable_automatic_image_resizing /* default = true */
```

Extensions that modify or enhance image display behavior are common; browse the Page Display category at *http://update.mozilla.org* for the latest list. There is not yet an extension as popular or as useful as the freeware Windows image viewer IrfanView, although there is an image-viewer extension called mozImage. Here are a few of the more useful extension offerings:

AniDisable
    Stops animated GIFs from running via a context menu option.

Image Zoom
    Provides context-menu support for image zooming using step-wise magnification. Expands on the features of the default click-to-resize functionality.

Nuke Anything
    Allows you to temporarily remove images from pages. Similar to DOM Inspector and Web Developer Toolbar functionality, but lighter and simpler.

Show Image
    Makes failed image downloads retry without reloading the whole page. If you're on a slow dial-up connection, this context-menu enhancement can be helpful.

ImageShowHide
    Makes an easy-to-reach toolbar copy of the Load Images configuration option. This tool allows toggling of page images like that available for the Web Developer Toolbar.

Image Toolbar
    Makes a floating image toolbar appear over images, providing file and print features. This tool works just like the irritating image toolbar provided by Internet Explorer.

Magpie
    Functions mostly as a spidering tool [Hack #42]. Magpie includes Digit Flipper functionality that resembles the Site Navigation Bar of the Mozilla Application Suite. It allows pages in a photo-album-like (or otherwise numbered) web site to be stepped through using special Next and Previous keys. It's also useful for HTML-based slideware presentations.

Get More Search Tools

Update the Search bar with more search engines, and add some other search tools as well.

Searching the Web has never been easier in Firefox. All you need to do is enter one or more terms into the search box in the upper-right corner, press Return, and you're on your way. But the searching capabilities of Firefox are far more than a single field.

Adding Search Engines

By default, the Search box queries the Google search engine. You can tell this from the small *G* icon that appears on the left side of the box. If you click on that icon, however, you'll see a list of several other available engines, such as Yahoo!, Dictionary.com, and Amazon.com. You can change which search engine is used. Just select a different engine from this list before hitting Return to launch your query.

If the site you want to query isn't listed, you'll want to visit the Mycroft extension site at *http://mycroft.mozdev.org*.

You can also get there by selecting Add Engines from the bottom of the search engine list and following the last link in the Add New Search Engines section.

Mycroft is a project dedicated to collecting a wide variety of search plug-ins for Mozilla-based browsers. You can find plug-ins for hundreds of sites, from *A9.com* to *Zoek.nl*. If you're looking to add a specific site to your Search bar, you can query the site name using the search option on the main page, or you can browse the list of submitted engines by category. Once you find the site you want, just click on the name and Firefox will add it to your list automatically.

The search plug-ins are installed in the directory where Firefox was installed, *not* in your profile directory. If you do not have permission to write to this directory, Firefox will silently fail in its attempt to install the plug-in.

If there is a web site you want to search using the Search box that is not listed in Mycroft, don't despair: it's easy to create your own. We'll see how to do that shortly.

Searching Without the Search Box

There are various extensions you can explore that add more searching flexibility to Firefox. For example, the Dict extension (available at *http://dict. mozdev.org/*) allows you to select a word on a page and query a Dict server with the selected word by right-clicking the selected word and choosing "Define...." The results appear in a pop-up window.

One of the most useful search extensions is one called Conquery (*http:// conquery.mozdev.org/*). This tool adds a context menu that allows you to select an area of text from the page you are viewing and send that directly to *any* of the search engines you have installed, as shown in Figure 4-5. The effect is almost the same as if every piece of text on a web page were instantly linked to the search engine of your choice!

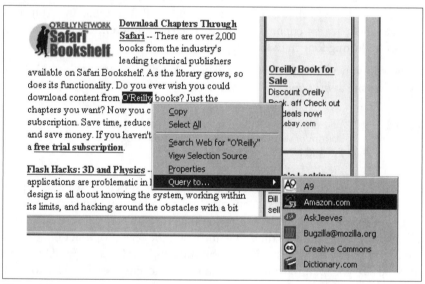

Figure 4-5. Using Conquery's context menu to search with any engine you have installed

Anatomy of a Search Plug-in

Under the covers, the Search box is simple. By selecting an engine from the drop-down list, you choose a search plug-in. Each plug-in consists of two files, located in the *searchplugins* subdirectory where Firefox is installed: a *.src* file, and an image file (either GIF, JPG, or PNG format).

The *.src* file contains the real meat of the plug-in. It contains information about the site itself, how the site builds the URL for a search query, and how it displays its results. Its syntax is based on Apple's Sherlock specification, with a few extensions. (The project name *Mycroft*, a character from Sherlock Holmes stories, is a play on that name.)

The image file must have the same base name as the source file, and it is displayed as the small icon displayed next to each site name on the search box and the drop-down list.

The easiest way to create your own plug-in is to copy an existing plug-in and modify it to suit your needs. Many of the parameters expose functionality for Mozilla's Search sidebar, which is not available in Firefox by default but is still easy to provide.

Let's start by looking at a sample plug-in—the one for Creative Commons—and go through it line by line to see how it works.

Nearly all plug-ins have four major sections: the search tag, one or more input tags, the interpret tag, and the browser tag.

The <search> tag. The search tag defines what the plug-in is and what site it will query. Looking at our sample Creative Commons plug-in, we see the following:

```
#
# Mozilla/Netscape 6+ MyCroft Plugin for search.creativecommons.org ...
# Created by Ben Snider on April 1, 2004.
# E-Mail: stupergenius@columbus.rr.com.
#
# Updated by Matt Haughey on August 26, 2004.
# E-Mail: matt@creativecommons.org
#
<search
  version="7.1"
  name="Creative Commons"
  description="Find photos, movies, music, and text to rip, sample, mash, and
share"
  action="http://search.creativecommons.org/"
  searchForm="http://search.creativecommons.org/"
  method="GET"
```

The version, name, and description parameters identify this particular search plug-in. name is what is displayed in the search box drop-down list.

The action and method parameters indicate how the query is submitted and the base part of the URL to be queried. At the time of writing, only GET methods are supported, so if you are building a plug-in for a site that works using POST forms only, you might be out of luck.

Actually, you can try using a *bookmarklet* (a special book-marked URL starting with javascript:) to change the form from POST to GET and use that information to construct your plug-in. However, if the site explicitly checks for POSTed values or includes user-specific cookies, you're definitely stuck.

The searchForm parameter denotes the main search page for the site, and is not strictly necessary.

The <input> tags. Next, the input values define the query parameters for the URL:

```
<input name="q" user>
<input name="sourceid" value="Mozilla-search">
```

There is only one argument passed to the plug-in, which is the search term. The term user in the first input tag is replaced with this value. For example, this plug-in will add &q=searchterm to the query URL. This parameter is URL-encoded automatically by the browser, so "firefox browser" will become &q=firefox+browser.

The sourceid value is included in all plug-ins, to help webmasters identify how many users are conducting searches from a Gecko-based browser. If any other parameters need to be sent to the search engine, you should include them here as well.

The <interpret> tag. The interpret tag tells us how the search results are displayed, so the browser can parse the results into individual items in the sidebar:

```
<interpret
  browserResultType="result"
  resultListStart="<!-- start results -->"
  resultListEnd="<!-- end results -->"
  resultItemStart='<p class="resultitem">'
  resultItemEnd="</p>"
>
```

The browserResultType parameter indicates whether the page being returned lists actual search results or a list of categories for browse-oriented searches. You can typically omit this parameter from most searches.

The remaining parameters indicate the HTML code that denotes the beginning and end of the list of items and the beginning and end of each individual item. You can usually figure this out by examining the HTML source of the page returned by the search engine. If the HTML is essentially tag soup and there is no easily definable way to delineate individual results, don't worry about this tag. This isn't real XML, by the way; don't encode your quotes or angle brackets, unless they appear that way on the results page.

The <browser> tag. Last is the browser tag, which provides information about this plug-in:

```
<browser
    update="http://mycroft.mozdev.org/plugins/creativecommons.src"
    updateIcon="http://mycroft.mozdev.org/plugins/creativecommons.png"
    updateCheckDays="3"
>
</search>
```

The update and updateIcon parameters indicate where the browser should check for updates of this plug-in, while the updateCheckDays parameter says how many days it should wait in between checks. This tag is strictly optional if you aren't planning to make your search plug-in available to others.

Finally, don't forget to close the search tag we used to open the file.

—Keith M. Swartz

HACK #37 Get More Feeds and News

Not getting enough information? You have several different ways to get more in Firefox.

This hack introduces you to the *push* content that a couple of extensions—Sage and ForecastFox (previously named WeatherFox)—make possible. Push content comes to you without you asking, or at least without you asking much.

Get Feeds with Sage

Long before Live Bookmarks came out in Firefox 1.0, Sage, a sidebar extension (shown in Figure 4-6), provided RSS and Atom feed aggregation in the Firefox sidebar. It's still a very useful extension.

Sage provides full-service feed aggregation. It includes a feed preview rendered in the contents area; a tooltip description of each item in the feed, usually containing a brief excerpt of the article; the ability to mark items as read or unread; and many other features.

To begin using Sage, you first need to install it from the Mozilla Update web page (*http://update.mozilla.org*). Don't forget to place the Sage icon in your toolbar (context-click on a toolbar, select Customize, and drag and drop the icon onto the toolbar). Once Sage is installed, you can start setting up some feeds.

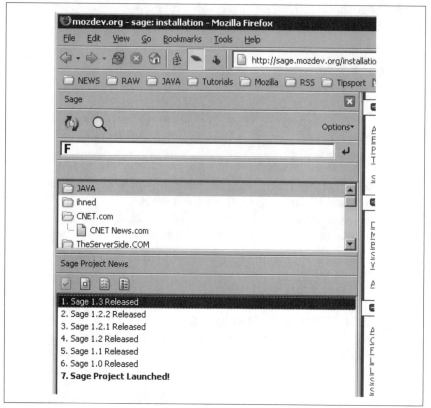

Figure 4-6. The Sage sidebar

Setting up the feed system. First, you must create a folder in your Bookmarks hierarchy. That's where you will place either bookmarks pointing to the feed URLs or live bookmarks that directly implement the feed (live bookmarks use Firefox's autodiscovery service). When such a folder is created and you've placed some bookmarks into it, you can open Sage in the sidebar. This can be done several ways:

- Sage's toolbar button
- Keyboard shortcut Alt-S
- Tools → Sage
- View → Sidebar → Sage

Once that's done, click the Options drop-down menu in the Sage sidebar and select Settings. Here, you can find and select the folder into which you have put the feed bookmarks. That should be all that's required to begin with.

In the Sage Settings window, you can also choose automatic update of the feeds and switch between 12- and 24-hour time display mode. You can also select the sorting method: chronological order or source order. The latter uses the order from the feed source.

Adding feeds. There are several ways to add feeds in the Sage sidebar:

- Display a web page that has a feed link. Right-click the link and select Bookmark This Link.

- If the orange RSS feed icon appears on the status bar, just click the icon and follow the instructions.

- Use the discovery service of Sage to put the feeds in. It's available via the Sage icon on the sidebar.

Just make sure that all the bookmarks and live bookmarks to be shown in Sage are placed in the common bookmark folder that you set as Feed Folder in the Sage configuration.

Show the content. Now, when you select a feed in the Sage sidebar, the last 10 feed items will load, provided that you selected automatic feed update. If not, you must press the Refresh button.

Hovering over the feed items might show Description Tooltips, if you have enabled them in the Options menu. When you click an item, the content will load in the content area, unless you configured Sage to render feeds in the sidebar. When shown in the sidebar, you can customize the matching CSS file to change the look of rendered feeds. As a starting point, just modify Sage's default CSS file at *chrome://sage/content/res/sage.css* and save it in any convenient location. Then, open Sage settings and choose Using Custom Stylesheet and browse to your modified file.

Get Weather News with ForecastFox

Another example of a news-retrieving extension is ForecastFox, which allows you to have the weather forecast at your fingertips. The first step is to download the ForecastFox extension, available through the Mozilla Update web site (*update.mozilla.org*). Figure 4-7 shows its About dialog box.

> The figures in this hack display the original name of the extension (WeatherFox), which has since been renamed ForecastFox.

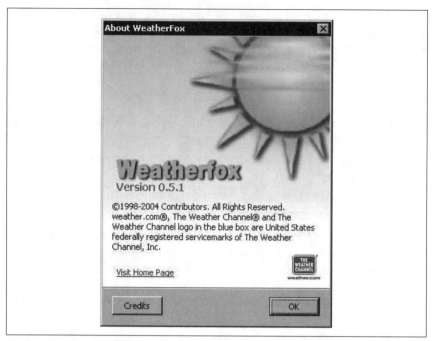

Figure 4-7. The About ForecastFox dialog box

Setting a location. Once the installation process has been completed, you need to set up a location for the forecast you want:

1. Open the extension's Options window. Start it from either the Extension Manager or from the pop-up menu that appears when you click the ForecastFox extension icon on the Status bar.

2. In the Options window, select the Profiles tab.

3. Create a new profile by pressing the Create Profile button and providing a profile name. These profiles are geographic profiles specific to ForecastFox. They've got nothing to do with Firefox profiles.

4. Once the profile has been created, set it as the current profile by highlighting it in the list and pressing the Select Profile button. The name of the profile will then displayed in the Current Profile field. Figure 4-8 shows the completed dialog box.

5. A profile is just a name. Next you need to choose the location for the forecast you want to obtain. Just select the General tab and, assuming you don't know the location code, press the Find Code button.

6. In the opened Location Search window, type the name of the city you want to watch and then press Search. In the returned list of found

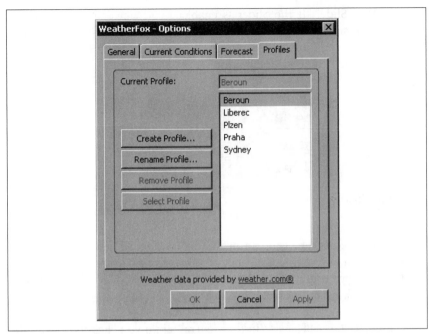

Figure 4-8. Geographic Profiles defined in ForecastFox

locations, choose the one you've been looking for. Close the Location Search window.

7. Lastly, just press Apply or OK to refresh the data on your status bar and close the Options box.

Tweaking the display. On the General tab of the ForecastFox Options window, you can adjust several attributes that specify how the data is displayed:

- In the Unit of Measure section, choose between displaying Metric (Celsius) or American (Fahrenheit) units.

- In the Location section, choose the location where you want Forecast-Fox to be placed. If you have some toolbars installed, your list of options will also include those.

You can also define display options for both the current conditions and the forecast. The two tabs for these purposes are again located in the Options window:

Current Conditions
  In this tab, you can enable or disable whether the current conditions show up at all, and enable or disable showing images on the toolbar and labels when the mouse is hovering. You can also enable popping up of

the Alert Slider. If the Slider is enabled, you can define in what frequency it shows up. The highest frequency is 1, which tells ForecastFox
to show the pop-up at every refresh. Figure 4-9 shows the pop up hovering over the Windows dashboard.

Figure 4-9. ForecastFox pop up

Forecast
   In the Forecast tab, you can define the number of days for which you
   want to show the forecast. Nine days is the maximum. In the Display
   Options area of the tab, you can choose to show days and/or nights, as
   well as images and/or labels for each day.

Customizing tooltips and labels. In the General tab, if you click the Customize
Tooltips and Labels button, a new window will appear, allowing you to
change the look of labels and tooltips, as shown in Figure 4-10.

Here, you can define tooltip and label text using predefined variables and
choose whether to show images in tooltips for both the current conditions
and the forecast. Descriptions of the variables used can be found at the bottom area of the window. This window acts like a very simple report of ForecastFox's template system.

                                                      —Tomáš Marek

HACK Add Stuff to Your Toolbars
#38 Install extra stuff on the Firefox toolbars and use it to browse in new ways.

This hack shows how to upgrade Firefox toolbars and use the new features
added. There are many extensions that can be usefully put on toolbars, but
currently few extensions do this automatically. This hack focuses on two
example extensions that benefit from toolbar icons: InfoLister and Gmail
Notifier.

Adding toolbar icons, whether they're standard Firefox ones or special
extension ones, is simplicity itself. Make sure the toolbar you're interested in
modifying is already displayed; then, choose View → Toolbars → Customize
to see the list of available icons. Merely drag an icon to the desired spot on

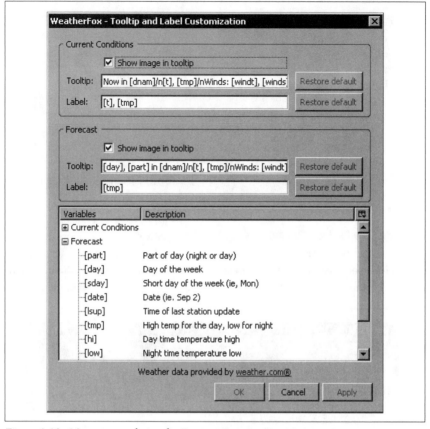

Figure 4-10. Message templating for ForecastFox pop ups

the desired toolbar and release the mouse button. Some extensions do this set up for you when they install; others don't. If nothing seemed to happen after you installed an extension and restarted, check the set of available icons in case more have been added.

Try InfoLister

Let's generate an HTML list of all the stuff you currently have installed in your implementation of Firefox. All you need to achieve this is InfoLister, a Firefox/Thunderbird extension (*http://mozilla.klimontovich.ru/infolister/*) by Nickolay Ponomarev.

Once you have installed the extension and placed its icon in the Location toolbar, it looks something like Figure 4-11. You can see lots of extra tool-bar icons in this screenshot.

Figure 4-11. Firefox toolbar with InfoLister icon highlighted

Displaying the InfoLister window. Clicking the InfoLister toolbar icon brings up the InfoLister window, shown in Figure 4-12. In the main area of the window, an HTML page lists all your extensions, themes, and plug-ins. All the extension and themes names in the list are linked to their respective home pages.

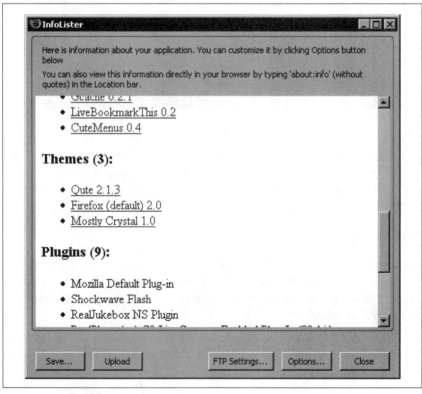

Figure 4-12. The InfoLister window

Customizing the page. If you want to tweak the info page a bit, just press the Options... button. A new InfoLister Options window will pop up. In the Customize section of this window, you can choose whether to display the page in HTML or plain text. Then, if you choose HTML formatting, you can provide content details of the <head> tag. In the next part of the form, also available for plain text, you can put some stuff at the head of the page. Then you can define the appearance of extensions and themes on the page, using several variables:

%homepageURL%
> Replaced by the actual extension's homepage URL

%name%
> Holds the extension's real name

%version%
> Holds the extension's version number

You can also compose footnotes at the base of the page. There are three checkboxes that, if selected, generate their respective information just under the page's headline:

Last Update Time
> Specifies whether to write a timestamp when the InfoLister report is saved to disk

User Agent
> Gives you an exact description of your implementation of Firefox (i.e., agent name, platform, locale, build, and browser name), including its version

Plugins List
> Allows you to switch the plug-ins list on or off

Some extensions might be disabled. To list them separately on the page, just choose the last option: "Make a separate list for disabled extensions."

Saving the page. There are two ways to save the generated page: in a local file or on a remote server. To save it locally, just fill in the file location in the "Autosave to file" section. Once you provide the file location, you can write to it immediately by clicking the "Write now" button, or have it rewritten each time you restart the browser. To upload the page to a remote server, you need to provide some information to set up a connection and log to the server. Press the "FTP settings..." button to display a form in which you can include these details, as shown in Figure 4-13.

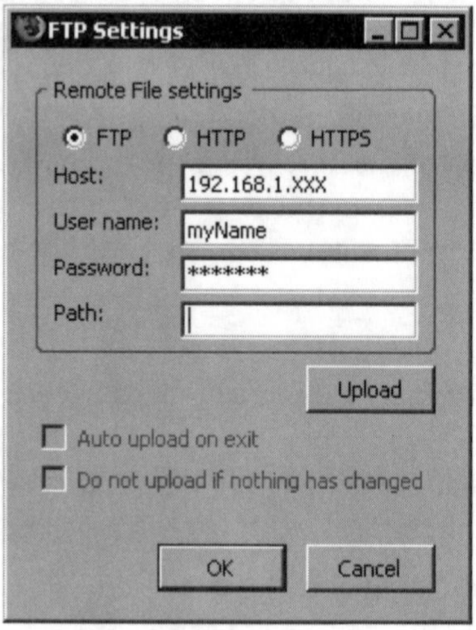

Figure 4-13. InfoLister FTP Settings dialog

Try Gmail Notifier

Another example of a useful extension that provides a toolbar icon is Gmail Notifier by Doron Rosenberg. This extension checks your Gmail (Google Mail) inbox and alerts you when new mail arrives.

Installing Gmail Notifier. To start using Gmail Notifier, you first need to install it. It's available from the Mozilla Update web site (*http://update. mozilla.org*). As with InfoLister, when the install is complete, place Gmail Notifier's icon on your Firefox toolbar using View → Toolbars → Customize. Figure 4-14 shows the installed extension's toolbar icon, status bar icon, and its initial login window.

Getting to your inbox. To get access to your inbox, you need to set up Gmail Notifier with your username and password. If you hate remembering passwords, you can select the "Remember password" option on the login form. Firefox will then skip this prompt the next time it gets online, and you'll log on automatically. Once you are logged on, simply click the toolbar or status bar icon and you'll display your Gmail inbox. You can open this page in the current tab, a new tab, or even a new window, depending on what you have configured in Notifier's Preferences pane.

Gmail Notifier preferences. You can use Gmail Notifier's Preferences pane to specify where your inbox page will open, how often Gmail Notifier will

Figure 4-14. Gmail Notifier toolbar icon and login screen

check for new email, and other options. To change your settings, just context-click (Right-click or Command-click) on the Gmail Notifier icon on the
status bar and choose Preferences. Figure 4-15 shows the context-menu
options.

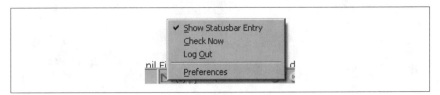

Figure 4-15. Gmail Notifier context menu

In the User Interface section of the Preferences pane, you can choose to also
show the icon on the status bar, select where to open your inbox page (current tab, new tab, or new window) when you click the icon, and choose to
be alerted when new mail arrives. The last setting is currently available for
Windows only. Figure 4-16 shows that standard alert.

Figure 4-16. New Gmail alert

In the Connection section, you can define how many minutes the Gmail Notifier should wait between periodic checks for new email and whether you want to log in automatically. Enabling this last feature is much appreciated when you don't share the computer with others.

Gmail tips. When Gmail Notifier spots a number of new email messages in your inbox, the Gmail icon is marked with that number, but unfortunately you don't have a clue what kind of emails they are, unless you open the inbox page. This might be cumbersome in some circumstances. To gain a list of arrived emails subjects, you will need to create a Live Bookmark [Hack #33] with the following URL:

```
https://yourUserName:yourPassword@gmail.google.com/gmail/feed/atom
```

Note that this stores your Gmail username and password in cleartext in the bookmarks file. A Live Bookmark with this URL will check the content of your Gmail inbox with the frequency set in Firefox for Live Bookmarks. When you open the Live Bookmark folder, any new emails appear just as if the email were part of a news feed (which it effectively is), as shown in Figure 4-17.

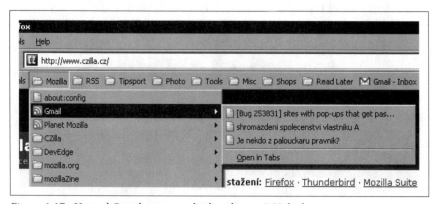

Figure 4-17. Unread Gmail messages displayed as an RSS feed

Be aware that sometimes the number of new email messages shown by this Live Bookmark might be out of step with the number of new email messages shown in the Gmail Notifier icon. In such a case, just choose Refresh Live Bookmark from the context menu of the Live Bookmark.

Finally, this Live Bookmark works only when there is new email in your inbox. If there isn't, Firefox fails to download the Live Bookmark feed. Hopefully, this functionality will be nicely embedded into the Gmail Notifier icon by the time you read this. Gmail Notifier is an extension with a bright future.

—Tomáš Marek

Upgrade Firefox Feature Managers

#39
Turn Firefox into Firefox Deluxe with extensions that upgrade standard features.

The standard Firefox browser has a standard set of dialog boxes. If you want to do more than those dialog boxes offer, you need to install extensions. This hack describes extensions that provide more functionality than the existing dialog boxes. Expand your horizons!

Extensions rarely *replace* Firefox's existing dialog boxes; they usually provide *additional* menu options instead. If you want full replacement of existing dialog boxes, you'll have to unbundle, hack, and rebundle the extensions one at a time. The required hack necessitates making each extension's browser overlay [Hack #87] match the spot where the existing dialog box is normally called from and also disabling that normal call. A complete solution is to bundle the hacked extensions with a new Firefox installer, effectively creating Firefox Deluxe.

If you don't want to go to all that trouble, just pick your least favorite Firefox feature and go extension shopping. You can also erase the feature you don't like [Hack #77], if you want.

Table 4-1 provides a shopping list of alternatives for you to explore. With more extensions being created every week, this list is likely to be a taste of the full range of options, at best. Table 4-1 includes only well-established extensions.

Table 4-1. User interface items and related extensions

User interface item	Related extensions
File → Open File	Filer Extension
	Open Long Url
File → Save Page As ...	Down Them All
	Mozilla Archive Format
File → Print Preview	Print Preview
View → Toolbars → Navigation	Magpie, AutoMarks
View → Sidebar	Optimoz Tweaks
	OutSidebar
View → Text Size	TextZoom
View → Character Encoding	Right Encoding
View → Page Source	ViewSourceWith
Bookmarks → Manage Bookmarks → File → New Bookmark	Pagebookmarks
	OpenBook

Table 4-1. User interface items and related extensions (continued)

User interface item	Related extensions
Bookmarks → Manage Bookmarks → File → Live Bookmark	Sage
	Live Bookmark This
	LiveLines
Bookmarks → Manage Bookmarks → File → Export ...	Bookmarks Synchronizer
	Favorites Converter
	SyncMarks
Tools → Web Search	Mycroft
	Advanced Highlighter Button
	Advanced Search Button
	All-In-One Search Button
Tools → Read Mail ...	Launchy
Tools → New Message ...	Launchy
Tools → Downloads	Download Manager Tweak
	Download Statusbar
	Disable Targets for Downloads
Tools → JavaScript Console	JS Console
Tools → DOM Inspector	Web Developer Toolbar
Tools → Page Info	View Cookies
Tools → Options	Prefbar
Tools → Options → General → Fonts & Colors	ColorZilla
	Web Color Names
Tools → Options → General → Connection Settings	SwitchProxy Tool
	Tweak Network Settings
Tools → Options → Privacy → Saved Passwords → Set Master Password ...	Secure Password Generator
Tools → Options → Privacy → Cookies → Exceptions	Add & Edit Cookies
	Cookie Culler
Tools → Options → Privacy → Cookies → View Cookies	CookieBar

HACK #40 Integrate Firefox with Other Tools

Juggle all your info tools from Firefox with cross-application integration features.

If you're moving over to Firefox from Mozilla, you've surely noticed how Firefox is built to be a sleeker, faster browsing engine. It accomplishes this in part by shedding all of its counterparts from the Mozilla Suite, including an email/news client, composer, and chat client. But that doesn't mean this functionality is no longer available. With a few extensions—or with no work at all—you can make Firefox integrate with your email client as though it were still part of a suite. You don't have to stop there, either; at least one valuable extension gives you the power to connect Firefox with virtually any program on your system.

Integrate Email and News

Firefox does not include a mail client: this functionality has been outsourced to its cousin, Thunderbird. However, a quick glance at some of the menu options might make you think the Firefox developers didn't get that memo:

File → Send Link
  For emailing the current URL

Tools → New Message
  For composing a new email message (Windows only)

Tools → Read Mail
  For opening your mail client to read new messages (Windows only)

In addition to these menu items, there are frequent *mailto:* or *news:* links on the Web that should allow you to send an email message or read a newsgroup. Firefox contains just enough glue to pass all these potential actions on to another program.

The good news is that if you have a default mail program set up on your operating system, all of these functions will integrate seamlessly with that program without any additional work. (The process for defining a default mail program varies according to operating system.)

If you are running Firefox on Unix/Linux and you don't have a default mail program set up on Linux, or if you want Firefox to use a different program, you can integrate Firefox with your mail program by setting the following preferences:

```
network.protocol-handler.external.mailto /* set to true, no default */
network.protocol-handler.app.mailto      /* set to filepath, no default */
```

For example, if you want Linux Firefox to launch Thunderbird when you click on a *mailto:* link, set the network.protocol-handler.app.mailto preference to the following filepath, if that happens to be where Thunderbird's startup program is located:

```
/usr/local/bin/thunderbird/thunderbird
```

To do the same thing for links that use the news:, snews:, or nntp: protocols, verify that the following preferences are set to true:

```
network.protocol-handler.external.news
network.protocol-handler.external.snews
network.protocol-handler.external.nntp
```

Then, set one or more of these matching preferences to the name of your newsreader:

```
network.protocol-handler.app.news
network.protocol-handler.app.snews
network.protocol-handler.app.nntp
```

Another option for handling mailto: links is to use the Launchy extension, as discussed in "Integrate Everything Else with Launchy," later in this hack.

If you prefer to use a web mailer, such as Gmail or Hotmail, there's a solution for that, too. The Webmailcompose extension (*http://jedbrown.net/ mozilla/*) allows you to override the behavior of mailto: links by directing you to a web mail provider of your choice. It also replaces the various mail-related menu options with a list of supported services from which you can choose.

Integrate Email Message Counts

On Windows operating systems, there are two additional items under the Tools menu: Read Mail and New Message. The New Message button will start a new message in your default mail client (or whatever client you have chosen to override the default), just as though you had clicked on a mailto: link with no recipient. The Read Mail option does the same thing, except that it also displays how many new unread messages you have. That might seem curious, given that Firefox has no mail functionality of its own. Figure 4-18 shows these options.

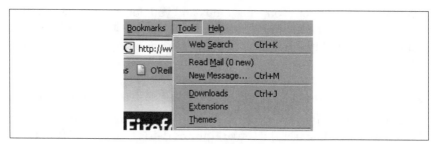

Figure 4-18. Unread messages reported by Firefox for Windows

In fact, you might find that it indicates you have 125 new messages, but you've already checked and are sure you don't. Or maybe it reads "(0 new)," even when you know you have unread mail waiting for you.

The problem here is that Firefox is not actually checking to see if you have new mail but rather is relying on Windows to provide this information. More specifically, Firefox is looking in the Windows Registry for the key `HKEY_CURRENT_USER\Software\Microsoft\Windows\CurrentVersion\UnreadMail`. If the key exists, it queries the `MessageCount` registry property for the default mail account (or the first one that is listed if there is no default). This property is updated by mail utilities such as Outlook Express. It is not used by Thunderbird or other third-party mail clients. Therefore, the text in the Tools menu will be accurate only if your mail client tells Windows this information on a regular basis.

Integrate IRC

If you're a fan of Chatzilla, the native IRC client for Mozilla, you'll be happy to know it's only a click away. The Chatzilla extension for Firefox (*http://update.mozilla.org*, under the Chat category) will provide you with the same functionality, sidebar and all.

Integrate Everything Else with Launchy

The Launchy extension (*http://gemal.dk/mozilla/launchy.html*), shown in Figure 4-19, is a veritable Swiss Army knife when it comes to integrating Firefox with other programs. It provides you with a new context menu for pages, links, and images, giving you the ability to open these items in any of dozens of recognized external programs. On Windows, these programs are all discovered automatically, but you can customize the list and even add your own on any operating system.

Launchy is an ideal way to handle all kinds of integration points that are otherwise unavailable in Firefox. For instance, if you want to edit the current web page, you can use the Launchy context menu to send the page source to Mozilla Composer or NVu. If you're on a page with an extremely large image, you can send it to Photoshop for better viewing or editing with a single click.

If you're forced to use a web site that has the audacity to only work in Internet Explorer, perhaps the best feature of Launchy is its ability to send the page straight to Internet Explorer—but hopefully, this won't ever happen to you!

—*Keith M. Swartz*

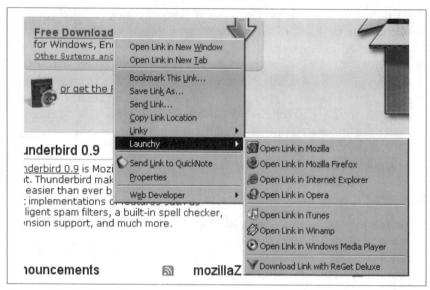

Figure 4-19. The Launchy extension

Create Your Own Search Plug-in

HACK #41

Found a search engine that suits you? Put it up front on the Search bar.

Now that we've looked at a sample plug-in [Hack #36], let's make our own. We'll query for articles in the CNET News.com archive.

The first step is to visit the web site and conduct a sample query, to see how the query URL is formed. Go to *http://www.news.com*, enter firefox in the Search box, and click on "See all matching results." This submits the following query:

```
http://news.search.com/search?q=firefox&cat=230&int.1278=1
```

From this we can deduce the following items for our plug-in:

- The action parameter in the search tag is http://news.search.com/search.
- The input parameter q is set to our user-specified input.
- The input parameters cat and int.1278 should also be specified.

Building the Plug-in

With the information in the previous section in hand, we have enough details to build most of our plug-in:

```
<search
    version="1.0"
```

```
    name="CNET News.com"
    description="Search CNET News.com"
    method="GET"
    action="http://news.search.com/search"
>

<input name="q" user>
<input name="cat" value="230">
<input name="int.1278" value="1">
<input name="sourceid" value="Mozilla-search">
```

If we look at the HTML source, we can see that the results are neatly captured as an enumerated list, with each news story as a list item. We can use
this information to build the interpret tag in the following code. We'll also
add a browser tag, so we can make our plug-in available to other users and
enable them to retrieve updates automatically when the site changes and we
change our plug-in to accommodate it:

```
<interpret
    resultListStart="<ol start="
    resultListEnd="</ol>"
    resultItemStart="<li>"
    resultItemEnd="<br>"
>
<browser
    update="http://www.kswartz.com/kswartz/projects/mycroft/cnetnews.src"
    updateIcon="http://www.kswartz.com/kswartz/projects/mycroft/cnetnews.png"
    updateCheckDays=3
/>
</search>
```

There's a lot more that can be done with Mycroft plug-ins than just tabulat-
ing simple results. For a complete definition of the plug-in syntax, read the
Mycroft Developer's Guide at *http://mycroft.mozdev.org/deepdocs.html.*

All that's left now is to create a 16×16 icon for the site, which is left as an
exercise for the reader. Remember to save it with the same basename as your
search plug-in.

> One easy trick is to capture the site's *favicon.ico* file, if it has
> one. Just type its URL to get it: *http://www.example.com/*
> *favicon.ico.* Such files are conveniently 16×16 pixels in size.
> Just use a freeware tool such as Icon2Png or the GIMP to
> convert it to a *.png, .jpg,* or *.gif* file.

Installing the Plug-in

Before we install the plug-in, it's usually a good idea to run it through a validator, such as the one available at *http://www.mindzilla.com/auditform.php.*

You can use this page to verify your plug-in syntax, as well as to verify your list and item start/end identifiers.

If the validation page reports no errors in your plug-in, it's time to install it. There are two ways you can install your plug-in. If you are only developing the plug-in for yourself, you can manually install it by copying the file to the *searchplugins* directory where Firefox is installed and restarting your browser to have it reread that directory.

Alternatively, you can post the files to a web site, and use this JavaScript code to download the files to the *searchplugins* directory and dynamically update the list of known plug-ins:

```
<script type="text/javascript">
function addEngine(name,ext) {
  if ((typeof window.sidebar == "object") &&
      (typeof window.sidebar.addSearchEngine == "function")) {
    window.sidebar.addSearchEngine(
      "http://mycroft.mozdev.org/plugins/"+name+".src",
      "http://mycroft.mozdev.org/plugins/"+name+"."+ext,
      name, '');
  }
}
</script>
```

Include the preceding code on an HTML page, and then link to your search plug-in with the following line:

```
<a href="javascript:addEngine('myplugin','png')">Install myplugin</a>
```

At this point, you should see the icon and name of your plug-in in the drop-down list of the Search box, as shown in Figure 4-20.

Your new search plug-in is ready to use!

—*Keith M. Swartz*

Spider the Web with Firefox
#42

Save lots and lots of web pages to your local disk without hassle.

If a web page is precious, a simple bookmark might not be enough. You might want to keep a copy of the page locally. This hack explains how to save lots of things at once with Firefox. Usually this kind of thing is done by a *web spider*. A *web spider* is any program that poses as a user and navigates through pages, following links.

For heavy-duty web site spidering done separately from Firefox, Free Download Manager (*http://www.freedownloadmanager.org*) for Windows and wget(1) for Unix/Linux (usually preinstalled) are recommended.

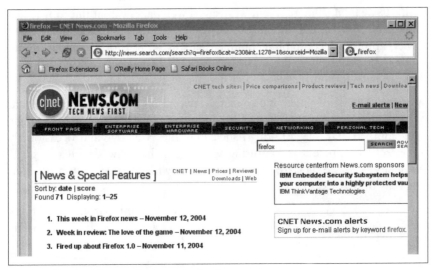

Figure 4-20. Searching with your new plug-in

Save One Complete Page

The days of HTML-only page capture are long gone. It's easy to capture a whole web page now.

Saving using Web Page Complete. To save a whole web page, choose File → Save Page As... and make sure that "Save as type:" is set to Web Page Complete. If you change this option, that change will become the future default only if you complete the save action while you're there. If you back out without saving, the change will be lost. When the page is saved, an HTML document and a folder are created in the target directory. The folder contains all the ancillary information about the page, and the page's content is adjusted so that image, frame, and stylesheet URLs are relative to that folder. So, the saved page is not a perfect copy of the original HTML. There are two small oddities to watch out for:

- On Windows, Windows Explorer has special smarts that sometimes treat the HTML page and folder as one unit when file manipulation is done. If you move the HTML page between windows, you might see the matching folder move as well. This is normal Windows behavior.
- If the page refers to stylesheets on another web site using a `<link>` tag, these stylesheets will not be saved. As a result, Firefox will attempt to download these stylesheets each time the saved HTML copy is displayed. This will take forever if no Internet connection is present. The only way to stop this delay is to choose File → Work Offline when viewing such files.

Saving using Print. One problem with saved web pages is that the copy is just a snapshot in time. It's difficult to tell from a plain HTML document when it was captured. A common technique that solves this problem and keeps all the HTML content together is to use Acrobat Distiller, which comes with the commercial (nonfree) version of Acrobat Reader.

When Distiller is installed, it also installs two printer drivers. The important one is called Acrobat PDFWriter. It can convert an HTML page to a single date-stamped PDF file. Although such PDF files are large and occasionally imperfect, the process of capturing web pages this way is addictive in its simplicity, and the files are easy to view later with the free (or full) Reader. The only drawback is that PDF files can be quite large compared to HTML.

To save web pages as PDF files, choose File → Print... from the Firefox menu, choose Adobe PDFWriter as the device, and select the Print to File checkbox. Then, go ahead and print; you'll be asked where to save the PDF results.

Save Lots of Pages

To save lots of Web pages, use an extension. The Download Tools category at *http://update.mozilla.org* lists a number of likely candidates. Here are a few of them.

Down Them All. The Down Them All extension (*http://downthemall.mozdev. org*), invoked from the context menu, skims the current page for foreign information and saves everything it finds to local disk. It effectively acts as a two-tier spider. It saves all images linked from the current page, as well as all pages linked to from the current page. It doesn't save stylesheets or images embedded in linked-to pages.

Two of the advantages of Down Them All are that it can be stopped part-way through, and download progress is obvious while it is underway.

Magpie. The Magpie extension (*http://www.bengoodger.com/software/ tabloader/*) provides a minimal interface that takes a little getting used to. For spidering purposes, the context menu items that Magpie adds are not so useful. The special keystroke Ctrl-Shift-S, special URLs, and the Magpie configuration dialog box are the key spidering features.

To find the Magpie configuration system, choose Tools → Extensions, select the Magpie extension, and then click Options. Figure 4-21 shows the resulting dialog box.

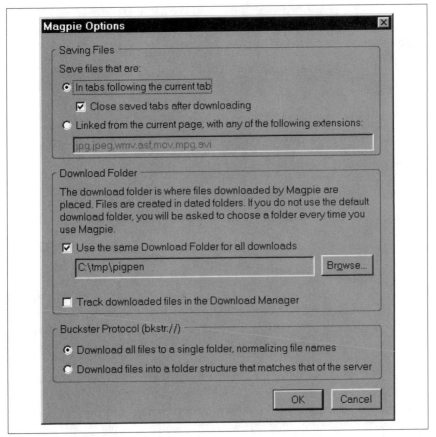

Figure 4-21. Magpie configuration window

Using this dialog box, you can set one of two options for Ctrl-Shift-S (detailed in the radio group at the top). Everything else in this window has to do with folder names to be used on local disk.

The first time you press Ctrl-Shift-S, Firefox asks you for the name of an *existing* folder in which to put all the Magpie downloads. After that, it never asks again.

By default, Ctrl-Shift-S saves all tabs to the right of the current one and then closes those tabs. That is one-tier spidering of one or more web pages, plus two-tier spidering for any linked images in the displayed pages.

If the "Linked from the current page..." option is selected instead, then Magpie acts like Down Them All, scraping all images (or other specified content) linked from the current page.

In both cases, Magpie generates a file with the name *YYYY-MM-DD HH-MM-SS* (a datestamp) in the target directory and stuffs all the spidered content in there.

The other use of Magpie is to download collections of URLs that have similar names. This is like specifying a keyword bookmark, except that only numbers can be used as parameters and they must be hand specified as ranges. For example, suppose these URLs are required:

```
http://www.example.com/section1/page3.html
http://www.example.com/section1/page4.html
http://www.example.com/section2/page3.html
http://www.example.com/section2/page4.html
```

Using the special `bkstr:` URL scheme (an unofficial convenience implemented by Magpie), these four URLs can be condensed down to a single URL that indicates the ranges required:

```
bkstr://ww.example.com/section{1-2}/page{3-4}.html
```

Retrieving this URL retrieves the four pages listed directly to disk, with no display. This process is also a one-tier spidering technology, so retrieved pages will not be filled with any images to which they might refer. This technique is most useful for retrieving a set of images from a photo album or a set of documents (chapters, minutes, diary entries) from an index page.

Slogger. Rather than saving page content on demand, the Slogger extension (*http://www.kenschutte.com/firefoxext/*) saves every page you ever display. After the initial install, the extension does nothing immediately. It's only when you highlight it in the Extensions Manager, click the Options box, and choose a default folder for the logged content that it starts to fill the disk. The configuration options are numerous, and Perl-like syntax options make both the names of the logged files and the content of the log audit trail highly customizable.

Since Slogger saves only what you see, how well it spiders depends on how deeply you navigate through a web site's hierarchy. Note that Mozilla's history mechanism works the same way as Slogger, except that it stores downloaded web pages unreadably in the disk cache (if that's turned on), and that disk cache can be flushed or overwritten if it fills up.

Learning from the Master

Bob Clary's CSpider JavaScript library and XUL Spider application are the best free tools available for automating web page navigation from inside web pages. You can read about them here: *http://www.bclary.com/2004/07/10/mozilla-spiders.*

These tools are aimed at web programmers with a systematic mindset. They are the basis of a suite of web page compatibility and correctness tests. These tools won't let you save anything to disk; instead, they represent a useful starting point for any spidering code that you might want to create yourself.

HACK #43   Waste Time with Toys and Games

Amuse and inspire yourself with these decorative inventions made by bored minds.

Not everything's about substance. Sometimes, you just want to be entertained. This hack describes a few such things. Calling them *fluff* would be unkind, though; there's a fair bit of talent, imagination and effort at work here. Most of them won't get you a pay raise, though.

Messing Around with Games

Any computing environment worth its salt will eventually be able to play Tetris, or at least adventur. Firefox is no different. With lots of scripting and display technology, it's no surprise that simple games are knocking on the door. Of course, the biggest game you can play with Firefox is called "Where's that web page I forgot about?"

Text adventures. You can play Zork and other retro text adventures of days gone by. The Gnusto Firefox extension uses JavaScript to implement a virtual Z-machine required for all such games. Some games are listed at *http://gnusto.mozdev.org*. Zork, shown in Figure 4-22, can be found at *http://www.batmantis.com/zorks/*. It's best to download the *.z5* games to local disk and then open them from the Gnusto window. Don't try to load them directly from web links.

Card games. The Card Games extension provides dozens of single-person card games if you happen to be snowed in over winter. Figure 4-23 shows an example of a game in progress.

Console games. It's also possible to play simple 2 ½ D console games from the 80s and 90s. Dynamic HTML (and Dynamic XUL) provide a fast enough basis for the required sprites. To play these games, you don't even need an extension. Just visit the MozDev Games web page (*http://games.mozdev.org*). You can run the games online by clicking their links, or you can download the games pages to your laptop and open them whenever you want. Figure 4-24 shows Xultris, a Tetris-like game.

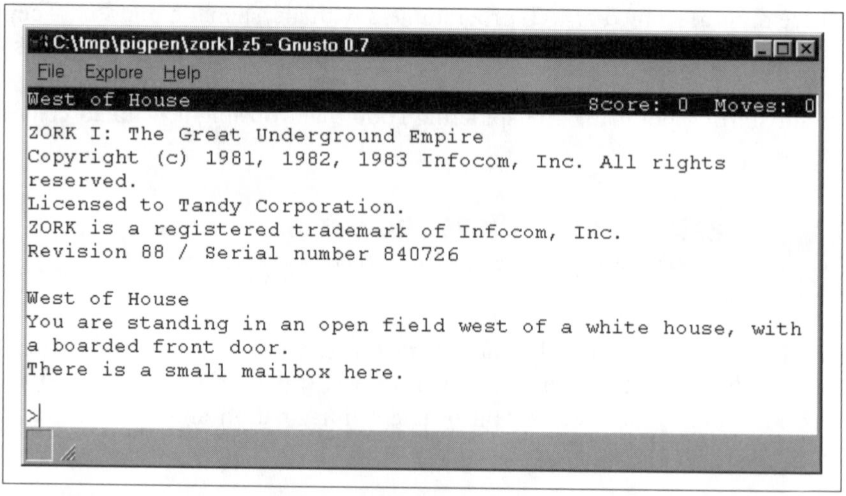

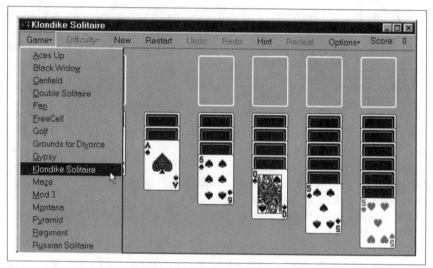

Figure 4-22. Zork I running inside the Gnusto extension

Figure 4-23. Card Games extension showing game options

Stretching Your Wings with Gestures and Pie Menus

Pie menus aren't seen much in desktop applications, but they're common in games, ever since they were made popular in fantasy console games (change from sword to potion!). Pie menus link a mouse movement to a context menu in a way that offers fast selection. Such things are innovative enough to get you a job at Microsoft.

The easyGestures extension presents a fully customizable pie menu for your enjoyment. Figure 4-25 illustrates the default set of options.

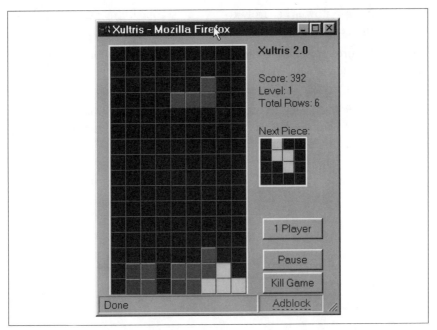

Figure 4-24. Xultris block management game

Figure 4-25. easyGestures extension at work

Move the mouse upward sharply to see the secondary menu, press Alt for the alternate menu, or do both to amaze and confuse yourself.

The easyGestures extension is highly configurable; just double-click it in the Extensions Manager window.

Of all the Firefox extensions, gesture extensions probably sit least well with each other. By all means, try out the many excellent alternatives, such as Mouse Gestures and Radial Context, but it's probably better to have only one installed at any given time.

## CHAPTER FIVE

Power Tools for Web Developers

Hacks 44–57

If traditional, non-GUI programmers had any idea what web developers have to go through to get their sites working, they'd be more than just scared; they'd be running for their lives. The number of technologies that a web developer has to master is legion, and that's a big number. This chapter describes the Firefox features that make that balancing act a more graceful affair. You can spin up your web sites faster if you have a bit of Firefox at hand.

At the time of writing, there's also plenty of news about Firefox's successful launch. The portion of the total web audience that's using Mozilla-derived products (Firefox, Mozilla, Epiphany, Netscape, Compuserve, Camino, and so on) is likely to pass 10 percent without much trouble. That's an audience larger in size than the whole Macintosh audience. Industry commentators are now saying that corporate web sites can't afford to miss out on that big an audience, so the demand for standards-compliant, or at least standards-friendly, web sites is rising. Firefox and Mozilla are no longer a fad or a fashion; they're a trend.

There are many ways to exploit Firefox for development. This chapter covers the basic ones. Advanced Firefox-specific content and scripting techniques are covered in Chapter 6.

Tweak and Troubleshoot CSS Designs

#44 Get to the bottom of your CSS difficulties with smart Firefox extensions.

Since its debut, CSS browser compatibility issues have given web developers headaches. Support for CSS in contemporary browsers such as Firefox is very good, but there are still inconsistencies between different browsers, at least until the whole world wakes up to how good Firefox is. You'll have to deal with that.

Firefox's extensible design has encouraged the development of a number of indispensable extensions to help you troubleshoot and tweak your CSS. In this hack, we'll look at how two of these, Web Developer and EditCSS, can help you quickly track down exactly which CSS statements are causing problems.

Install Must-Have Extensions

The Web Developer extension, by Chris Pederick, is available at *update. mozilla.org* or here, and includes some EditCSS functionality:

> *http://www.chrispederick.com/work/firefox/webdeveloper/*

The EditCSS extension, by Pascal Guimier and others, is available at *update. mozilla.org* and also here (beware version differences):

> *http://editcss.mozdev.org/installation.html*

Install them as you would any other Firefox extension [**"Get Oriented," at the beginning of Chapter 1**]. The EditCSS will perhaps be bundled inside the Web Developer extension eventually, but for now it is still available separately. Check the home pages for both extensions.

Use the Web Developer Toolbar to Locate Style Rules

The Web Developer extension places a number of menus in a new toolbar. There are far too many features to go into all of them here, so we'll stick to those relevant to this hack. However, do make sure you look at all of them.

One of the most time-consuming aspects of debugging and tweaking CSS is working out which CSS statements are causing the problem. More than one CSS statement can affect the same HTML element, and elements inherit CSS properties from their ancestors. The Web Developer toolbar helps isolate the relationship between a style sheet and an HTML document.

Open any page in Firefox. Once you have the Web Developer toolbar installed, it should look like Figure 5-1.

Particularly when you've used lots of classes and IDs, as any nontrivial layout requires, it's difficult to work out exactly which elements you are looking at on the page. And working this out is the first step in tracking down a troublesome statement.

Under the CSS toolbar menu, choose View Style Information. Then move the cursor over the page; it changes to a crosshair. The containment hierarchy for the element currently under the crosshair is displayed in the status bar of the window.

For instance, on O'Reilly's home page you might see the status bar shown in Figure 5-2.

Figure 5-1. Web Development toolbar installed on Macintosh Firefox

Figure 5-2. Revealing tables in an O'Reilly web page

In a flash, the status bar at the bottom tells you that O'Reilly needs to update their page-layout techniques from old-fashioned tables to modern CSS.

So, in an instant, you can see exactly which element is at a given location on the page without having to View Source, remember the content you're looking for, find it, and other laborious processes. On top of this, you get a great snapshot of the inheritance structure of that element, which is essential to working out which CSS statements might be affecting it.

However, that's not all. You can also find out exactly which CSS rules are affecting any element on the page. While in View Style Information mode, click an element. A new tab opens, displaying all the CSS rules in all the relevant stylesheets that affect this element.

Going back to the O'Reilly example, I clicked the content near the top of the page that says "News and Articles," which I know from the status bar is a `<span>` of class `hdr4-w`. Here's the first set of information I saw:

```
chrome://webdeveloper/content/stylesheets/view_style_information.css
*    (line 2)
{
    cursor: crosshair;
}
```

Ignore this first style: it is simply the Web Developer Toolbar's own CSS for showing the crosshair. In CSS, the asterisk (*) is a universal selector that selects any element in a document. After this first rule, we have the more relevant information:

```
http://oreillynet.com/styles/main.css
.hdr4-w    (line 190)
{
    font-family: Verdana,Arial,Helvetica,sans-serif;
    font-size: 8.5pt;
    font-weight: bold;
    text-decoration: none;
    color: rgb(255, 255, 255);
}
```

First, you can see the URI for the stylesheet. Most importantly, you then get a rule in this stylesheet, which selects the specific element of class hdr4-w.

Working down this tab, you can see all the statements that explicitly select and style the element. If a property you are interested in is explicitly set for this element, you'll find it here. Sometimes, this will identify the problem, and you can review and modify the CSS.

Use the DOM Inspector to Find Inherited Values

Because of inheritance, not all rendered property values (called *computed values*) are explicitly set. These values are often affected by inheritance, and their source can take the longest to track down.

To find out where an element is inheriting a property from, you can turn to a built-in part of Firefox, the DOM Inspector [Hack #53], which is discussed here in the context of CSS.

Open the DOM Inspector from the Tools menu. In the left pane, you'll see the document's DOM tree; you can select any element (or node in XML/XHTML-speak) in the document here. Sometimes it can be hard to find the element you're looking for if all you can see is the DOM tree. Click Inspect at the top right and make sure Blink Selected Element is chosen in the View menu. Then, as you click nodes in the DOM tree, they will flash in the Preview pane at the bottom.

In the right pane, use the drop-down menu to choose different property panes for a selected element. Initially, this shows DOM Node. Change it to Computed Style. Note that Computed Style won't be available until you select the <html> element or something below it in the DOM tree.

You'll see all of the computed values, explicit or inherited, for all of the CSS properties of the selected element.

To find out where a value is being inherited from, move up the DOM tree, watching the property in question. In the left pane, click the parent nodes, and their computed values will be displayed in the right pane. When the property you are watching changes in value, the culprit is the node directly below this in the hierarchy. The value is explicitly set at this node and then inherited all the way down to the element causing you trouble.

From here, you can quickly find the statement in question by switching in the right pane from Computed Style to CSS Style Rules. This, like the Web Developer Toolbar, shows all the statements that explicitly select this element.

Edit CSS in Firefox

Now that you've found the exact statement you need to tweak, you can actually *edit* it in Firefox and see the effects *live*. Go back to the page itself. In the Web Developer toolbar, turn off View Style Information by selecting it again under the CSS toolbar menu. Then, still under the CSS toolbar menu, choose Edit CSS. A panel opens on the left side, showing each of the stylesheets affecting this page. This is the EditCSS extension at work. If it's installed separately, start it from the Tools menu.

Not only can you view the stylesheets with this sidebar, but you can also edit their text directly, and the page is updated as you make changes. Note that you are not making changes to the actual stylesheet that is linked to the page when you do this. However, you can save what you have created at any time. This is a real bonus, because it makes it easy to do numerous edits and quickly create numerous versions to return to if necessary as you work.

With the EditCSS panel, you can modify properties in your stylesheet in real time and see the results instantly, which is invaluable when tweaking and debugging. To use just one aspect of CSS coding as an example, many page layouts these days rely on the complex interaction of positioning and box model properties such as margin and padding. It can be difficult to get these layouts to work right. With the EditCSS panel, you can change property values and instantly see the effect on a layout.

—*John Allsop and Maxine Sherrin*

HACK #45 Use Gecko CSS Style Magic

Give your web pages extra style using fancy Gecko CSS extensions.

The Gecko display engine inside Firefox can do marvelous things to your web page with its standard, forward-looking, and custom CSS style properties. This hack looks at a few of its custom features. The most marvelous thing Gecko and Firefox can do together is, of course, XUL [Hack #68]. But that's a separate subject.

Firefox and Mozilla identify most of their CSS enhancement keywords with the prefix -moz. These keywords may appear as style properties, property values, or pseudoselectors. Examples include:

```
/* Three style rules with Gecko Magic */
p { -moz-float-edge : border-box; }
p { background-color : -moz-dialog; }
p:-moz-drag-over { color : red; }
```

Use of these style extensions is fairly harmless, because outside of Mozilla browsers, they do nothing. There are too many custom properties to list here; in fact, it's a bit of a treasure hunt to find them all. We'll cover just a few of the most useful ones.

Add Fancy Borders

Firefox can go further than the simple dotted and dashed border styles defined by CSS2. Once a border exists, it can be given rounded corners:

```
p {
    border : solid thick;
    border-width : 20px;
    padding : 20px;
    -moz-border-radius : 20px;  /* Gecko Magic  */
}
```

Gecko also defines -moz-border-radius-topleft, -moz-border-radius-topright, and so on for individual corners.

Alternatively, such a border can be given a color gradient:

```
p {
    border : solid thick;
    border-width : 20px;
    padding : 20px;
    -moz-border-right-colors : /* Gecko Magic */
      red orange yellow green blue purple transparent brown pink;
    -moz-border-left-colors :
      red orange yellow green blue purple transparent brown pink;
    -moz-border-top-colors :
      red orange yellow green blue purple transparent brown pink;
    -moz-border-bottom-colors :
      red orange yellow green blue purple transparent brown pink;
}
```

Unfortunately, there's no all borders style property yet. Each color is one pixel wide, and the last color fills any remaining pixels.

If both techniques are used at once, then gem corners result. Figure 5-3 shows a page illustrating all three effects. With a little design, soft gradients and other eye candy are possible.

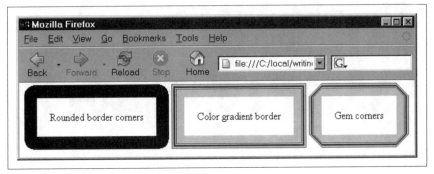

Figure 5-3. Gecko custom CSS border styles

Add Fancy Colors

Firefox also supports *fancy colors*, which take the form of CSS2 placeholder colors. These next two examples show a paragraph colored like a dialog box and a paragraph colored like an operating system's hyperlink:

```
/* all Gecko magic */
p.dialog { background-color : -moz-dialog;
                  color : -mox-dialog-text; }
p.href   { color : -moz-hyperlinktext; }
```

Figure 5-4 shows the result (the link is purple when viewed live on Windows).

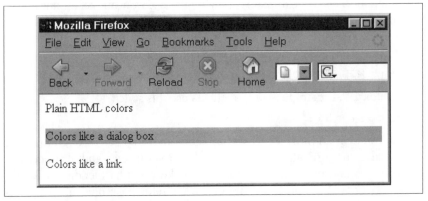

Figure 5-4. Gecko custom colors from the operating system

Add Unbreakable Fonts

Firefox fonts are a large matter [Hack #30]. Gecko CSS supports this special, unbreakable font:

```
p { font : -moz-fixed; } /* Gecko Magic Font */
```

This is a fixed-width system font that is available at every single pixel size (and part pixel size), as shown in Figure 5-5.

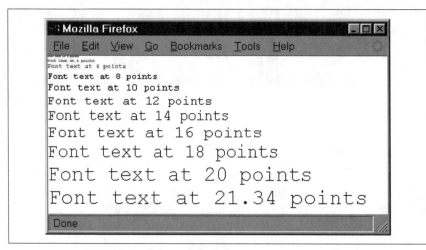

Figure 5-5. Gecko's unbreakable fixed font

Add Fancy Blending

Firefox supports all the following effects: *translucency*, *transparency*, *alpha blending*, and *opacity*. Ultimately, they're all based on one technology: see-through content support. On an increasing number of operating systems, Firefox is very close to supporting translucency against the surrounding desktop environment. That's done (for example) with this style:

```
html { background-color : transparent; } /* Gecko Magic */
```

For Firefox 1.0, the simpler content effects use this style:

```
p { -moz-opacity :  0.3; }  /* Gecko Magic */
```

This allows text and images to overlay each other in a see-through manner. Firefox also supports alpha blending within PNG images and also between PNG images and other content. Figure 5-6 shows alpha blending at work. The two words Over and Under are <span> contents positioned absolutely—one with 0.3 opacity, the other with 0.5. Note how the text is darker where the two words overlap. This can't be done in Internet Explorer.

Figure 5-6. Gecko's opacity support illustrated with text

Opacity is another tool that allows gentle and subtle shading effects. Such effects make web sites appear visually pleasing and very professional.

HACK #46 Write Compatible CSS

Style a web page that benefits from Firefox but that also works in all browsers.

The messy days of all Netscape Version 4.x web browsers are falling into the past, and the days of reasonable CSS support in all browsers are upon us. This hack explains what you can do to ensure that a web page looks good in all browsers.

Remove Older Browsers from the Problem Space

If there were no older browsers in use, cross-browser compatibility would be far easier. Since all modern browsers have some CSS support, there is a large subset of tools to find a solution with. This is far easier than attempting compatibility with a narrow set of tools. You can remove old browsers from the problem space, making the remaining compatibility problems easier to handle. The cost is that little CSS is used for pages designed for those older browsers.

That compromise is not such a bad thing. After all, web pages should be easily viewable with CSS support turned off. This is a litmus test for good design, based on the principle of *semantic markup*: the sparing and meaningful use of tags. It is also a requirement for web site accessibility. So, we lose little by reducing the use of CSS in older browsers that are barely used anyway.

To extract older browsers, we deny them access to CSS information.

Deny style access to Netscape 4.x and earlier. These web browsers don't support the @import CSS directive. Use it like this in a stylesheet to exclude Netscape 4.x:

```
<style type="text/css">
/* styles for Netscape 4.x go here */
@import "modern.css"; /* styles used everywhere else */
</style>
```

Deny style access to Internet Explorer 5.x on Windows. Internet Explorer (IE) 5.x doesn't support escaped quotes in CSS files. That means that a string like this:

```
"foo\"bar"
```

is understood like this:

```
"foo" bar"
```

This can be leveraged to ensure that some styles in a style rule are ignored by Internet Explorer 5.x:

```
p {
    /* styles for Internet Explorer 5.x go here */
    width : 50%;
    any-unused-property : "\"}\"";      /* 'voice-family' is a common choice
*/
    any-unused-property : inherit;      /* reset it for modern browsers */
    /* styles used everywhere else go here */
    width : 60%;
};
```

In the third line, IE 5.x terminates the style rule when it sees the closed brace and treats the remaining content as garbage, ignoring it. All modern browsers choose the second definition of the property *any-unused-property* (or any one you elect to use), so this hack has no effect.

Deny style access to Internet Explorer 5 on the Mac. This browser has a bug with escaped CSS comments. A string like this:

```
/* a comment \*/
/* another comment */
```

does not have the end-of-comment mark recognized in the first line. It is read this way:

```
/* a comment &#x2A;/
&#x2F;* another comment */
```

The result is that the first comment extends into the second comment, for one comment in total. This can be used to exclude styles from IE 5 for Mac:

```
/* styles for Internet Explorer 5 on Mac go here */
p { width : 50%; }
/* stop IE 5 mac from reading anything below this point \*/
/* styles used everywhere else go here - don't include any comments ! */
p { width : 60%; }
/* a comment to finish the styles excluded from IE 5 Mac */
```

Make CSS Work Across All Modern Browsers

Here are the CSS styling features that are not well supported across browsers. This list is fairly rough, because CSS property support is a minefield of special cases:

- Complex table styles, especially tabular values for display
- Fancy border-style values, such as groove
- Applying and then removing display : none
- Expecting font-family values to display identically across browsers
- Expecting list-style-type icons to display identically across browsers
- outline styles
- padding styles (see the "Box model" section later in this hack)
- Properties in CSS2 that aren't in CSS2.1
- Complex style rule selectors that depend on two or more identifiers
- Mozilla-specific style selectors, properties, and values prefixed with -moz.

In addition to these specific properties worth avoiding, there are three issues that affect stylesheets, layout, scripting, or a combination of all three.

Display contracts. In all cases, it is better for a web page to force the browser into *Standards mode* than to leave it in *Quirks mode*. The full range of modes is a complex issue even for Firefox alone [Hack #58]. This DOCTYPE is generally recommended:

```
<!DOCTYPE HTML PUBLIC
  "-//W3C//DTD HTML 4.01 Strict//EN"
  "http://www.w3.org/TR/html4/strict.dtd">
```

For a tortuously near-complete discussion of display contracts, see the articles written for *Inside Web Development* (*http://www.elementkjournals.com*) by Nigel McFarlane. These articles predate Internet Explorer 6.0 Service Pack 2, which now supports the following content type, but they are otherwise accurate:

```
Content-Type: application/xhtml+xml
```

Viewport. Internet Explorer and other browsers don't agree on the reference point for the x- and y-coordinates of styled elements on a page. Peter-Paul Koch explains scripting solutions at *http://www.quirksmode.org/viewport/compatibility.html*

Box model. If your web page does not establish a *strict mode* display contract with the browser, Internet Explorer 6 will use an older, nonstandard box model that doesn't combine padding, margins, and borders properly. Use a strict mode, or read more about Tantek Çelik's original use of the exclusion technique that excludes older browsers at *http://www.tantek.com/CSS/Examples/boxmodelhack.html*

HACK #47 Update Browser Detection Scripts

Work out whether your web page is loaded into Firefox.

There are all kinds of Mozilla browsers and even different variants of Firefox [Hack #92], although the standard distribution of Firefox is by far the most popular distribution. This hack explains how to detect Firefox. Your web page can also make a display contract with Firefox [Hack #46].

Detect Firefox by UserAgent

Either behind the web server or in the web page, the foremost identifier of Firefox is the browser user agent (UA) string. The UA string is defined in RFC 1945 and RFC 2068. It is sent over the wire from web browser to web server in this header line:

```
User-Agent: string
```

It appears in the Apache server environment as this environment variable:

```
HTTP_USER_AGENT=string
```

It appears in JavaScript as this host object property:

```
window.navigator.userAgent
```

For quick sanity checks, the user agent for Firefox can also be displayed using the Help → About Mozilla Firefox menu item. That page can be displayed separately using this URL:

```
chrome://browser/content/aboutDialog.xul
```

Select the text of the user-agent string with the mouse and drag up or down if it looks odd when it first appears.

To detect Firefox, chop up the UA string. Useful JavaScript functions include these:

```
userAgent.substring(start, length); // returns a fixed substring
userAgent.split(" ");               // returns array of whitespace-separated
pieces
userAgent.match(/.*fox/i);          // returns case-insensitive regexp match
```

Here are the meaningful substrings of the user agent:

Mozilla

The user agent is probably a web browser.

Gecko

The user agent contains Mozilla Gecko display technology, a big part of Firefox. Gecko guarantees that web pages will look the same across all Mozilla browsers and that quality web standards support is present. Browsers such as Galeon and Camino also fall into this category; however, they don't support Firefox extensions.

Firefox

The user agent is a Firefox browser, with full extension support and other niceties that are implied by Firefox.

Firebird, Phoenix

The user agent is a very old version of Firefox. It is best to treat it as a non-Firefox browser, because the version is too early to support some modern Firefox features.

en-US *(or other strings in the same spot)*

The menus, status bar messages, and other browser text appear to the user in U.S. English. Don't write alerts or other messages in the wrong language.

Detect Firefox via the DOM

The user agent string is exposed to the Document Object Model (DOM) of a given web page as described earlier in this hack. Other detection methods also exist in the DOM.

document.all. Testing this DOM property like this is a common way of detecting Internet Explorer (IE):

```
if (document.all ) { ... }
```

Some web pages are built in ignorance of the constraints of the global Web. Such pages use document.all without first checking to see if it exists. These cases, such as the following example, cause pages displayed in non-IE web browsers to fail:

```
if ( document.all("id") == null ) { ... }
```

Firefox has special support for document.all, as follows:

- If the all property is stated in a Boolean (true/false) context, as in the first example, then Firefox (and all recent Mozilla-based browsers) will report that the method doesn't exist. This is the same as matters have always been.

- If the all property is invoked as a method, as in the second example, then Firefox (and all recent Mozilla-based browsers) will behave the same way as IE. This preserves the display of some old, ignorant web pages.

This support only exists when a web page is displayed in *Quirks mode*. Quirks mode is for old, legacy HTML documents. One easy way to ensure that Quirks mode is operating is to leave out an HTML document's <!DOCTYPE> declaration. You can see if a page uses Quirks mode or not using Tools → Page Info → General. Look at the Render Mode line item for the current mode.

document.implementation.hasFeature(type,version). This method is defined in the W3C's DOM 2 Core standard. It allows a script to test for UA support for specific standards. For example, this test can be used to test for CSS2 support:

```
document.implementation.hasFeature("CSS2","2.0");
```

In particular, this method can be used to test whether the Firefox UA is built so that it includes SVG:

```
document.implementation.hasFeature("org.w3c.svg","dummy string");
```

It can also be used to report whether specific *SVG features* (a term specific to SVG) are implemented. To do so, provide an SVG 1.1 feature URL as the first argument, like this:

```
"http://www.w3.org/TR/SVG11/feature#Structure"
```

document.layers. This DOM 0 collection, present in Netscape 4.x, is not present in Firefox at all. It's unusable as a positive test of Firefox, so it no longer stands for "Netscape 4.x or higher." Now it stands for "Netscape 4.x only."

Detect JavaScript Version Support

All Firefox browsers support at least JavaScript Version 1.5. That version fully supports ECMAScript Version 1, Edition 3. Firefox also supports earlier versions of JavaScript, but you should never use them. Include external scripts within HTML and XHTML with this tag:

```
<script type="text/javascript" src="..."></script>
```

Similarly, include embedded scripts with this tag:

```
<script type="text/javascript">
... content ...
</script>
```

Support all scripts used strictly in XUL with this tag:

```
<script type="application/x-javascript" src="..." />
```

See also "Get a Taste of E4X Scripting" [Hack #74] for some fancy new features.

Submit Background Form Data

#48 Submit form data without using a Submit button and without replacing the current page.

Web pages have a variety of security restrictions designed to protect the end user. When it comes to fill-in forms, HTML pages can't ordinarily submit form data without direct action from the user.

There is one exception. In the days of Java Applets, an applet could "phone home" to the server it came from, without user intervention. Web pages can now do that too. The XMLHttpRequest object makes it possible. The XML prefix is meaningless; any kind of data can be sent over HTTP using this object.

Getting Oriented

The syntax for Firefox's XMLHttpRequest object is slightly different than for Internet Explorer's version (a browser incompatibility). A jumping-off point for this technology is *http://www.mozilla.org/xmlextras/*. You can hear about issues with cross-browser syntax from the front line here:

http://www.scss.com.au/family/andrew/webdesign/xmlhttprequest/

The XMLHttpRequest object can make a *synchronous* or *asynchronous* request. In the synchronous case, the page will freeze until the web server sends back the response. In the asynchronous case, other activity can happen while the request is in progress, but the programmer has to remember to set up a script to listen for the results.

In all the examples shown here, assume that the current page is HTML and that it includes this fragment of content:

```
<form name="form1">
  <input type="text" name="field1" value="test1">
  <textarea name="field2">test2</textarea>
</form>
```

The XMLHttpRequest object can equally be used in XUL pages, provided that the different tags used for user-input elements are taken into account.

In the following examples, the server-supplied Content-Type header sets the type of any content returned. The overrideMimeType(*string*) method can be used to force that returned content to be treated as another type, but if so, that method must be called before the request is started with send( ). Overriding types flies in the face of Internet standards and is usually the mark of a poor programmer. The only good reason for doing so is if you're sure that the server-supplied content is delivered wrongly in the first place.

Sending a Synchronous GET Request

This script queries the web server for data based on the current form. It examines results sent back in the HTTP headers and in the HTTP response body content and puts those results into the form:

```
var form    = document.form1;
var request  = new XMLHttpRequest();
var params = encodeURI("field1="+form.field1.value+";field2="+form.field2.
value);

request.open("GET", "query.cgi" + "?" + params);
request.send("");                        // no POST data in a GET request.

if ( request.status == 200 )
{
   form.field1.value = request.getResponseHeader("Content-Length");
   form.field2.value = request.responseText;
}
```

Sending a Synchronous POST Request

This script packs up the form data and submits to the server. It checks the results to make sure everything went OK. POSTed data doesn't usually return a document, only repsonse headers, so this is a natural use of the XMLHttpRequest object:

```
var form    = document.form1;
var request  = new XMLHttpRequest();
var params = encodeURI("field1="+form.field1.value+";field2="+form.field2.
value);

request.open("POST", "submit.cgi");
request.send(params);

if ( request.status == 200 )
{
   form.field1.value = request.getResponseHeader("Content-Length");
   form.field2.value = "Form data has been successfully sent";
}
```

Sending an Asynchronous GET Request

In this GET variant, an event handler is lodged on the request. The handler fires when the response is received. The script continues immediately after send( ) is called:

```
function response_handler( )
{
  if ( request.status == 200 ) {
    form.field1.value = request.getResponseHeader("Content-Length");
    form.field2.value = request.responseText;
  }
  else {
    form.field1.value = "Query Failed";
  }
}


var form    = document.form1;
var request = new XMLHttpRequest( );
var params = encodeURI("field1="+form.field1.value+";field2="+form.field2.
value);


request.onload = response_handler;
request.open("GET", "query.cgi" + "?" + params, true);   // true = async
request.send("");
form.field1.value = "Waiting for Response";              // runs straight away
```

To see this at work, put a sleep statement (or other delay) in the server *.cgi*, *.jsp*, or *.php* form handler code. You can still interact with the web page while the server's asleep.

Sending an Asynchronous POST Request

In this POST variant, an event handler is also lodged on the request. The handler again fires when the response is received. The script continues immediately after send( ) is called:

```
function response_handler( )
{
  if ( request.status == 200 ) {
    form.field1.value = request.getResponseHeader("Content-Length");
    form.field2.value = "Form data has been successfully sent";
  }
  else {
    form.field1.value = "Submission Failed";
  }
}


var form    = document.form1;
var request = new XMLHttpRequest( );
var params = encodeURI("field1="+form.field1.value+";field2="+form.field2.
value);
```

```
request.onload = response_handler;
request.open("POST", "submit.cgi", true);              // true = async
request.send(params);
form.field1.value = "Waiting for Confirmation";        // runs straight away
```

Again, to see this at work, put a sleep statement (or other delay) in the server *.cgi* form processing code to see that the browser isn't suspended waiting.

HACK #49 Script Plug-ins

Drive your plug-ins from JavaScript using the new NPAPI features.

Once upon a time, you could script plug-in content from a web page. The web page surrounding the plug-in content could supply HTML user-interface elements (such as form controls) that could be used to drive the behavior of the plug-in content. A common example was a button that stopped an audio track from playing. That functionality was partially lost to Mozilla products when dependency on Java was reduced. This hack describes recent enhancements that have brought back this functionality.

Requirements for Scriptability

To script a plug-in such as Flash or Adobe Acrobat, there are many hurdles to overcome.

The plug-in to be scripted must be built to support two vendor standards: the original *NPAPI* (Netscape Plug-in API) and the *NPAPI Extensions*. These are both C programming API specifications of little interest to web developers, except that it is a requirement for scripting that plug-ins implement them. The original NPAPI standard is unreliably located here:

http://devedge.netscape.com/library/manuals/2002/plugin/1.0/

If it's offline as you read this, you can use the WayBackMachine (*http://www.waybackmachine.org*) to get a copy. The NPAPI Extensions are documented here:

http://www.mozilla.org/projects/plugins/npruntime.html

Once you're sure the plug-in is built correctly, it must be installed and recognized by Firefox [Hack #24]. Web developers also need to know the MIME type of content that is managed by the plug-in.

When constructing a web page that seamlessly supports plug-ins, a web developer should follows these recommendations:

- Detect plug-in availability with scripts. A page should gracefully degrade if the `window.navigator.plugins` array indicates the specific plug-in is not available and if the `window.navigator.mimeTypes` array indicates that no third-party tool exists for the required content.

- Specify plug-in content with the `<object>` tag or, at worst, with the legacy `<embed>` tag. Attributes of this tag are passed to the plug-in and are plug-in-specific.

- The URL of the plug-in content must come from the same web site as the surrounding page content; otherwise, security hobbles will prevent access.

- Initial scripting of the plug-in should only be done from an onload event handler or from a callback function if the plug-in provides a mechanism for registering one.

Finally, if the plug-in is implemented as an ActiveX control, you must drop additional security restrictions [Hack #11].

Scripting Away

To script a plug-in, access the DOM object for each plug-in instance, either with the `document.embeds` array or by using `document.getElementById( )`. Any good book on scripting web browsers will provide a basic introduction on doing this. The specific properties and methods available per plug-in instance vary according to each plug-in manufacturer. You'll need to consult their documentation for the detail.

The new NPAPI extensions let you do these things from the web page—all possible long ago but only recently replanned and resupported by browser makers:

```
var plugin = document.embeds[0];
var temp = "something";
function handler = function () { return true; }

plugin.exampleProp = temp;
temp = plugin.exampleProp;
plugin.exampleFunction( );
plugin.exampleHandlerRegistration(handler)
```

The names used here are illustrative only. All of this code runs in the context of the web page. Actions performed on the plug-in instance are driven from the web page, even when they're performed as separately invoked handlers, as in the last line. Mozilla's JavaScript interpreter is single-threaded, so all browser scripting stops while any of this code runs. That also means that only one attempt to access the plug-in instance can be in progress at any time. If the plug-in is multithreaded, any streaming content will continue to be loaded and played, and will be unaffected by the single-mindedness of the Mozilla JavaScript interpreter thread.

Some plug-ins, particularly the Adobe SVG Viewer and Adobe PDF Reader, contain a full JavaScript interpreter of their own and have the potential to use NPAPI in reverse:

```
<?xml version="1.0" encoding="iso-8859-1"?>
<!DOCTYPE svg PUBLIC "-//W3C//DTD SVG 20000303 Stylable//EN"
  "http://www.w3.org/TR/2000/03/WD-SVG-20000303/DTD/
  svg-20000303-stylable.dtd">
<svg width="500" height="400">
  <script>[!CDATA[
    var text;
    text = svgDocument.getElementById("example");
    text = text.firstChild.nodeValue;
    svgDocument.browser.window.document.title(text);     // example syntax.
  ]]>
  </script>
  <g>
    <rect x="35" y="145" width="110" height="85" rx="10"/>
    <rect x="40" y="150" width="100" height="75" rx="10"/>
    <text id="example" x="50" y="180">
      Example
    </text>
  </g>
</svg>
```

In this illustrative code (at the time of this writing, Adobe hasn't said what NPAPI callbacks they'll make available), the SVG plug-in's implementation of JavaScript runs scripts downloaded as part of the plug-in-specific content. By exploiting NPAPI, such script content can also access a browser object, as shown in the emphasized line. The browser object is called in the SVG interpreter's context, not in the browser interpreter's context, but it can still manipulate objects created by the browser.

HACK #50   Quality-Assure Your Web Pages

Make sure your web development work is polished and professional.

Quality assurance (QA) is a vital part of any professional process, and today this must extend to web design. Using Firefox and the Web Developer extension, you can do some basic QA on code validity and page accessibility.

Ensure Code is Valid

Validating markup and CSS isn't an optional extra; it's an integral part of the development process. Only valid HTML and CSS can be guaranteed to work, now and in the future. Once you've installed the Web Developer extension [Hack #44], validation is also straightforward.

Load the page you would like to validate in Firefox and then validate both the HTML and CSS using the Validation → Validate HTML and Validation → Validate CSS menu items on the Web Development Toolbar. Note that these two menu items can only be used to validate documents that are online. Far handier are two items further down the menu: Validate Local CSS and Validate Local HTML. Use these to validate pages and stylesheets on your local hard drive.

Another handy item in this menu is Validate Links. Use this to check for broken links, but note that you can't do this with local files; they must be online pages.

Check Accessibility

Code validation is a black-and-white process: either something is valid or it isn't. Accessibility, on the other hand, has numerous aspects, some of which have implications for how pages appear in the regular browsers we are accustomed to developing for. Before you do anything, you need to decide which aspects of accessibility you are prepared to commit to. Once you've done this, Firefox and the Web Developer Toolbar have a number of features to help you make checking the accessibility of your pages a simple part of day-to-day coding.

S.508 and WAI accessibility. Links to validators that check compliance with the U.S. national S.508 legislation and the W3C's international Web Accessibility Initiative (WAI) Guidelines can be found in the Validation menu. See *http://www.w3.org/WAI/* for supporting documentation. Both these links use the Cynthia Says web content accessibility checker.

If you're new to accessibility, these validators can come back to you with a report that seems pretty daunting. A simpler approach to accessibility is to start by looking specifically at some of the more basic accessibility problems.

Check those images. Plenty of people, for a whole host of reasons, browse with images turned off. Your pages need not look as stylish and attractive to these people as they are intended to be. You should, however, ensure that the content and functionality of the site is available to them. Go to the Images menu and check Hide Images. Then, go through and make sure you can do everything a user would expect to do on your page. At the most basic level, this means reading the content. Beyond that, make sure to check your navigation, confirm that any forms are still reachable, and make sure any glitches in the layout aren't actually hiding content.

Simply removing images from problematic pages isn't a fair test of what most users who aren't seeing your images will get. By and large, they'll be able to take advantage of the alt attribute, if you've provided it. Judicious use of the alt attribute on images is an easy way to improve accessibility not just for people with images turned off, but also for those visiting your site using devices like screen readers. Most browsers display the content of the alt attribute when images are turned off, and screen readers read it out. There is simply no good reason to ignore it.

To check for use of the alt attribute, go to the Images menu and check the Outline Images Without Alt Attributes item. You need to get rid of all of the problems that show up, because people browsing with images off might miss something vital, and people using screen readers will hear the name of the image itself, which can be both useless and irritating. Choose the content of the alt attribute carefully. Leave it empty if the image is purely for decorative or layout purposes:

```
<img src="decorative_panel.gif" alt="" />
```

This zero-length string will be ignored by screen readers and won't be distracting for users browsing with images off. For other images, you should always add an alt attribute that is meaningful and descriptive. The Web Developer toolbar can help you test this as well. From the Images menu, check Replace Images with Alt Attributes. Go through and see how usable the page is. Better yet, get someone else to do it.

Check those links. The Web Developer Toolbar also lets you check that title attributes have been used on links. Choose Outline Links Without Title Attributes from the Outline menu. The title attribute can be used to give further information about the destination of links, because its content is shown by contemporary browsers as a tooltip. This is especially handy for providing more information on navigation bars. However, in terms of accessibility for screen readers, you should not see this as a solution to the problems created by uninformative link text such as this:

```
<a href="news/story_01.html">Read more</a>
```

While many screen readers do have a setting that will make them read out the content of the title attribute, by and large, this is not turned on by default, so most users will still be stuck with the uninformative "Read more." The only real solution to this problem, according to the WAI, is to make sure that linked text is meaningful enough to make sense when read out of context.

Slow downloads are still a big issue. Accessibility is not just about making your pages accessible to people with disabilities; it's about making them accessible to the widest possible audience. It's easy to lose sight of visitors who are still on low-speed dial-up connections, but showing some consideration for them is what makes the Web *worldwide*.

Load a page in the browser and go to View Speed Report in the Information menu. Again, your page needs to be uploaded before you can do this. The standout information on this page is the table of Download Times. Before you dismiss the displayed report as irrelevant, consider that as of December 2004, almost 50 percent of home Internet users in the United States are on 56K modems or less. And that's just one well-provisioned country. The site that gives you the speed report information (*http://www.websiteoptimization. com*) has excellent advice on improving the performance of your pages.

Not all screens are the same. Developers still need to design pages where all the content is visible if the page is viewed at 800×600, but the page also looks attractive at 1024×768. So you'll need to change between these two sizes all the time. The Resize menu comes with a default item, 800×600. Choose Options → Options... → Resize to set up any other sizes that you might use frequently.

How will a nonhuman see your page? Using CSS for page layout gives you much greater control over the order in which content appears in the HTML. Because the document's structure is separate from its presentation, content can be ordered logically. This has benefits not just for screen readers but for all sorts of devices—search engine robots, for example.

Assuming you have done the right thing and put all your appearance information where it belongs, in the stylesheet, if you turn that stylesheet off, you get an idea of the order these devices will find. Do this by going to the Disable menu and checking Disable Styles.

This view is good for seeing how the top-level elements, headers, various navigation bars, main text blocks, footers, and so on will be approached. Firefox also has a handy tool for checking what will happen at a lower level. People who use screen readers often navigate through the text on a page by jumping through the headings. You can easily improve accessibility by making sure these headings are used correctly. From the Tools menu, choose DOM Inspector [Hack #53] and find your main body of text in the panel on the left. Without the distraction of content, it's easy to see if any errors have crept into what should be a logical hierarchy.

—Maxine Sherrin

Display HTTP Headers

#51 See the raw information exchanged between Firefox and web servers.

This hack explains how to inspect the HTTP information that goes back and forth between Firefox and web servers. The simplest way to see web requests is, of course, to examine the server's logs. That strategy doesn't yield every byte of information, though, so here are some alternatives. There are also many tools that can help with cookies [Hack #52]. You might also want Firefox diagnostics [Hack #96].

Get the Live HTTP Headers Extension

The Live HTTP Headers extension is available at *http://livehttpheaders. mozdev.org/*. After installation, HTTP requests and response headers are logged to a separate window. Figure 5-7 shows sample output after a single request. Requests are captured to this window only when the window is open.

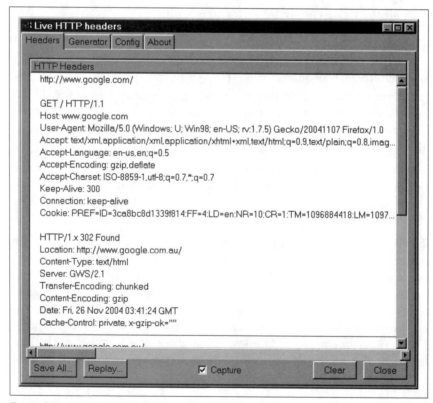

Figure 5-7. Live HTTP Headers at work on the Google home page

Click any line in the display to select that request. Click the Replay... button to bring up the Live HTTP Replay window. From there, you can send the same request over and over again, with original dates intact. Click the content in the Replay window to place the cursor in the headers. You can modify the headers to include whatever text you require. If the request is a POST (form submission) request, you can modify the form values sent in the POST Content pane at the bottom. All in all, it's a very useful tool.

This Replay functionality reminds us of the difference between GET and POST HTTP requests. GET requests are supposed to be *idempotent*, meaning that repeating the request has no effect on the server. POST requests, on the other hand, are expected to change the server's state, so repetition is a trickier matter. For example, you can't easily repeat a POST request that adds a unique key to a database table; such a key can be added only once. Comment out the SQL commit statement in the server code to make this easier.

Analyze Headers in the Raw

If you don't like client-side diagnostics **[Hack #96]**, then to see what Firefox sends to the server on Linux/Unix, you can use nc(1) to act as a fake HTTP listener. To do so, make requests as needed to a real HTTP server, and then on the server side (as root), shut down the web server and run nc as a listener for the next request. Then, make another web page request with Firefox. Here's a suitable command line:

```
nc -l -v -v -p 80
```

This small script will keep nc running across repeated request attempts, but all requests will be aborted without response because nc is not a web server and closes its opened socket without sending a single byte:

```
while true; do
  nc -l -v -v -p 80 |
  while read line; do
    echo "$line"
    if [ "$line" = "^M" ]; then   # ^M is a Control-M character
      pkill -x nc
    fi
  done
done
```

An interesting use of nc is to install it in place of your web proxy server and watch the requests that Firefox makes on startup. Of course, those can also be seen from the proxy server logs. An alternative to nc is to run a full proxy such as squid (*http://www.squid-cache.org*) in diagnostic mode. Here's a suitable command line:

```
squid -d 9 -X -N -a 80
```

Because squid implements HTTP caching policies, its use is not as transparently simple as nc. It also requires a bit of configuration.

For a more transparent solution that shows traffic in both directions, use a packet sniffer or protocol analyzer such as Ethereal (whose output is quite cryptic, however) or else write a tiny HTTP proxy logger using Perl.

HACK #52 Stomp on Cookies
Track, trap, configure, kill, create, and otherwise diddle with HTTP cookies.

HTTP is a *stateless* protocol, meaning that each web request made by the browser is independent of all other requests. This greatly preserves the user's privacy. *Cookies* are an enhancement to the HTTP standard that introduces tracking information that web browsers and servers can share. That tracking information consists of (usually) a single HTTP header line that goes back and forth between the User Agent (browser) and the server. They include a small amount of access-control information based on URLs and expiry dates. This hack explains how to manipulate cookies from the browser side, once they're generated.

Cookies are based on a vendor specification written by Netscape Corporation (you can view that specification at *http://wp.netscape.com/newsref/std/ cookie_spec.html*). Since then, cookies have been more formally defined in RFC 2109. The name *cookie* derives from the intended use of the header data: the supply of an opaque token useful only for session identification (from *magic cookie*).

Particularly in Netscape 4.x and earlier, the number of cookies that browsers would maintain per site was limited to 20. That limit no longer applies, even though one cookie per site is usually enough.

Cookies offer no security at all. Never put any user details in a cookie; never expose any server information in a cookie; never use cookies to *preserve* important data across HTTP requests. Quality browsers go to great lengths to prevent cookies sent from one web server from being viewed by web pages from other servers.

Using the Cookie Manager
To Open Firefox's Cookie Manager, start with the Options Dialog Box, click Privacy and expand the Cookies item that appears in the right pane. Click on Exceptions to view a blacklist of sites that you don't want to create cookies for you. Alternatively, select View Cookies to manage the currently stored cookies. The Cookie Manager won't let you modify cookies in place; you can only delete them or ban sites from using them.

The options variously reported as "Keep Cookies until I close Firefox" or "Allow for Session" mean the same thing: the cookies will not be written to a file on disk. When they are written, cookies appear in the human-readable file *cookies.txt*, stored in the user profile.

To delete lots of cookies at once, open the View Cookies dialog box and use Windows-style mouse-selection techniques. Left-click to highlight one cookie, and then Shift–left-click to highlight another cookie that marks the end of a set to be deleted. The resulting block of highlighted cookies can then all be deleted by clicking the Delete button. Similarly, you can select noncontiguous cookies with Control–left-click (Command–left-click on Macintosh).

Using Cookie Extensions

There are at least two extensions available for manipulating cookies.

View Cookies extension. To locate the View Cookies extension, open the Extension Manager and go to the end of the All list of extensions. It's also available at *http://www.bitstorm.org/extensions/*. This extension discreetly adds an additional tab to the Tools → Page Info dialog box that allows you to view details of the current web page. Figure 5-8 shows this tab after it's been selected and after the sole existing cookie has also been clicked.

Add & Edit Cookies extension. You can find the Add & Edit Cookies extension at *http://addeditcookies.mozdev.org/*. At the time of writing, it's brand new to Firefox, and where View Cookies is discreetly minimal, Add & Edit Cookies does everything you could ever want. In particular, you can change cookies live while the browser is running, and you're not restricted to changing cookies relevant to the currently displayed web page. You can also filter cookies by site.

Once installed, choose Tools → Cookie Editor to start up this extension. The windows can be poorly sized when they first appear; to fix that, just drag the bottom-right corner with the mouse until they're big enough. They'll stay resized while the current profile exists.

Figure 5-9 shows the editing delights that Add & Edit Cookies provides.

Scripting Cookies

The oldest interface to the cookie system is via JavaScript. The document. cookie property allows you to set, alter, or remove any cookies local to the

Figure 5-8. The Cookies tab added by the View Cookies extension

current URL or domain. The days are nearly gone where this property needs to be touched:

- Servers should generally be the source of all cookies if security is to be as robust as possible.
- Data from the user should be delivered in HTTP GET or POST requests, or by other formal means, such as SOAP or XMLHttpRequest, not in cookies.
- The cookie property is confusing to use.

This last point bears brief description. In ECMAScript terms, the [[Get]] and [[Put]] operations on the cookie property are both unusual. If you assign anything to the property, the [[Get]] operation treats it as a single cookie and adds it to the cookie database. If you use the property's value in an expression, the [[Put]] operation provides a report (as a string) of all cookies relevant to the current page.

In short, just don't do it. Note that a secure web page or a secure extension has access to all the cookies in the browser. A hostile extension could share that information between conspiring web sites. This is a form of identity trading, although you are guaranteed anonymity at all web sites, provided that you never supply personal details.

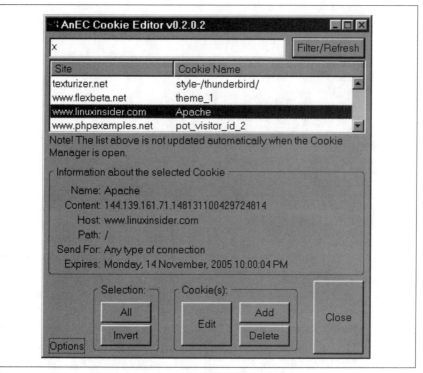

Figure 5-9. The main window of the Add & Edit Cookies extension

 ## HACK #53 Probe HTML with the DOM Inspector

Mozilla's powerful DOM Inspector tool deconstructs web pages for your benefit.

The standard Firefox install comes complete with the optional DOM Inspector tool. This tool gives web developers and Mozilla programmers a microscope that can be used to examine HTML and XML documents after they're displayed. This hack shows how to analyze an HTML page with it. You can also use it to analyze XUL pages [Hack #76]. In this hack, we'll work with the following web page content:

```
<html>
  <head>
    <style>
      .header { font-family : Arial; }
    </style>
    <script>
      function click_handler() {
        alert("Click");
      }
    </script>
```

```
      </head>
      <body>
        <h3 class="header">Test Page</h3>
        <script>
          document.write("<p>Hello, World!</p>");
        </script>
        <p id="link-para">
          <a href="about:blank" onclick="click_handler()">A Link</a>
        </p>
      </body>
    </html>
```

Inspecting a Page

The DOM Inspector can be a tricky little tool to coordinate with your web
page. There are several ways to start it up:

- Display the target web page normally. Choose the menu item Tools
  → DOM Inspector, or press Ctrl-Shift-I. The DOM Inspector window
  appears with the target page loaded.

- Start the DOM Inspector. Type a URL into the top text field and press
  the Inspect button at the right (pressing Enter is not sufficient). The
  Inspector displays the page in a new panel at the bottom, and the existing top portion loads that target page.

- Start the DOM Inspector. Choose menu items File → Inspect a URL...
  and matters proceed as detailed in the previous item.

The formatting and indenting of our sample page results in lots of extra
W3C DOM 1 Core Text Nodes being added to the document when it's displayed. In most cases, and to match the screenshots in this hack, you should
filter out that separator content for convenience. To do so, just pick View →
Show Whitespace Nodes, unticking that item. That reduces the output so
that it matches this single-line version of the document:

```
<html><head><style> .header { font-family : Arial; } </style><script>
function click_handler() { alert("Click"); } </script></head><body><h3
class="header">Test Page</h3><script> document.write("<p>Hello, World!</p>
"); </script><p id="link-para"><a href="about:blank" onclick="click_handler(
)">A Link</a></p></body></html>
```

You can open several DOM Inspector windows if you want. If the window
or pane that displays the target web page ever goes away, the DOM Inspector will stop working. If that happens, close down the DOM Inspector and
restart it. The File → Inspect a Window menu option is not used for HTML
documents; it's for XUL documents.

Deconstructing a Page

Figure 5-10 shows the page as the DOM Inspector sees it, with the tree of DOM 1 Core Nodes in the left pane fully expanded to show detail. The highlighted items are things that are safe to click once the page is displayed.

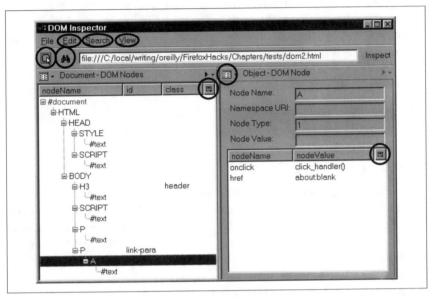

Figure 5-10. DOM Inspector view of a target web page

Let's first look at the left pane. Notice how the <script> element in the body appears in its original form; such elements are usually static content of the page. Notice also how the content *generated* by document.write( ) (the first <p> element) also appears in the tag hierarchy. The DOM Inspector displays the living state of the page, not just the content of the source HTML document.

The right pane displays the tag attributes for the selected <a> element. In this case, the pane displays tag attributes, but that can be changed with the drop-down menu in the top-right corner of the page. The two most useful options in that menu are CSS Style Rules and Computed Style. Unlike other tools, such as the Web Developer Toolbar, the DOM Inspector display can be used to report the state of every CSS and Mozilla property that might apply to a given element.

If the HTML document is big, use the Search → Select Element By Click menu option (or the equivalent icon on the toolbar) to pick out a piece of

HTML in the target document. Click in the target document to reveal and highlight the equivalent element in the DOM Inspector.

Hacking a Page to Bits

The DOM Inspector is a read/write tool. You can cut, copy, paste, insert, delete, or update nodes in the target page in a permanent way. That's more powerful than just applying display: none styles to existing content. To do so, just display a target page as in the previous section, select an item in the tree of nodes in the left pane, and then click in any of these places to see the set of operations you can apply:

- Pick from options in the Edit menu.
- Right-click on the selected tree item to expose a context menu.
- Right-click on any tree or list item in the right-hand panels to expose a context menu.

Make any such change and the window displaying your target HTML document changes to match. Any changes that you make like this will survive until the target page is reloaded. Cut, copy, and paste operations cannot deliver content to other applications via the desktop clipboard. Only the Copy XML operation can do that.

Turn Off Absolutely All Caching

HACK #54

Be sure that the web page you're viewing is freshly retrieved from across the network.

You can clean up Firefox so that no old data is hanging around [Hack #8], but sometimes you might be looking for a more permanent solution. This brief hack explains how to achieve that.

Disable Browser Caching

To turn off the memory and disk browser caches completely, set these preferences:

```
browser.cache.memory.enable /* set to false, default = true */
browser.cache.disk.enable   /* set to false, default = true */
```

Turning these preferences off guarantees that Firefox will make an HTTP request for every URL it is asked to display.

Firefox does not use HTTP HEAD requests, at least not for the retrieval of web pages; it uses GET requests. Every URL can therefore be made to return a full copy of the resource (the web page) in question. Embedded images and other URLs are, of course, retrieved in separate GET requests. It is possible that web pages or Firefox extensions might issue their own `HEAD` requests, though.

`GET` requests never add any HTTP `If-Modified-Since` headers if local caching is turned off. Such headers are only sent when local caching is enabled (the default) *and* if a currently cached copy of the requested page was originally delivered with a `Last-Modified` header.

The golden rule of standard Firefox URL loading is this:

> Everything is always refreshed from the Web if local caching is disabled or if the *Reload (bypass cache)* command is run.

Reload (bypass cache) is run with Shift-F5 (Shift and click Reload on the Macintosh). Just left-clicking the Reload button is not enough, because Reload obeys HTTP caching protocols (see the next section). Clicking Reload is enough if local caching is turned off.

Even less reliable is pressing Enter or Return in the Location bar. In that case, if local caching is still on, Firefox might not issue an HTTP request of any kind. Change this preference to 1 (one) to fix that:

```
browser.cache.check_doc_frequency /* 1 = everytime. default = 3 = as needed */
```

There is, however, an exception to the golden rule. The exception applies to uses of datasources, an advanced XUL programming topic:

> The content of datasources persists until they are destroyed or until Firefox shuts down.

Datasources are an internal feature commonly exploited in XUL applications. Datasources are also used deep inside bookmarks and elsewhere.

Switching Firefox into Offline mode also affects page caching. If Firefox is in offline mode, it will attempt to use cached copies of web pages, even if the network connection is still available and it is only Firefox that is offline, not the network.

Disable HTTP Caching

Even when Firefox is trying to do the right thing, web pages might still be cached by HTTP caching mechanisms. In that case, web server proxies (such as `squid`) between Firefox and the ultimate web server can hold temporary copies of a cached file, and Firefox is denied a taste of the absolutely latest thing. For best results, make sure web pages are sent with all these HTTP headers intact:

```
Expires: Thu, 01 Jan 1970 00:00:00 GMT
Last-Modified: Thu, 01 Jan 1970 00:00:00 GMT
Pragma: no-cache
Cache-Control: max-age=0, no-cache, must-revalidate
```

Don't set these headers in <META> tags; intervening proxies
will not notice them. Instead, set them as part of the HTTP
message itself.

To see the cache-related information that Firefox sends to a web server
when it makes requests, just examine the HTTP headers in the browser
request [Hack #51].

If intermediate web caches and local caches are a concern, then web servers
should be instructed to *never* return an HTTP 304 response code. The 304
code tells the browser that the server has nothing new to offer. The browser
will conclude that any cached copy it has is therefore good enough.

If 304 responses can't be stopped, then ensure that no Last-Modified header
line is ever sent by the server. It's that header that stimulates the browser to
add If-Modified-Since headers to future requests for that page, if it's
allowed to cache the page. The same argument applies to server-generated
Etag headers. The existence of such headers can prompt the browser to add
If-None-Match headers, which again can generate a 304 response.

Disable XUL Caching

By default, Firefox includes a copy of the *XUL.mfl* (Windows), *XUL.mfasl*
(Unix), or *XUL FastLoad File* (Macintosh) file. This is the Mozilla FastLoad
cache that resides in the profile area. You can set the following preference to
prevent it from being used:

```
nglayout.debug.disable_xul_fastload /* default = false, set to true */
```

When *FastLoad* is at work, Firefox reads files directly from the chrome only
if it needs to, which saves disk access time.

The general-purpose web cache is used to cache XUL files whether *Fast-
Load* is at work or not. To turn that other caching off as well, either disable
caching generally as in the previous example, or else set this preference:

```
nglayout.debug.disable_xul_cache /* default = false, set to true */
```

A further hack described by some pundits is to delete the *XUL.mfl* file while
Firefox is shut down and replace it with a directory of the same name. That
makes Firefox think the *FastLoad* cache is corrupt or missing, and XUL files
in the chrome are thus always reloaded from cache or directly. This kind of
trickery is necessary only if preferences can't be set for some obscure reason.

Web Document Debugging Tricks
#55 Firefox has a potpourri of small tricks you can use to debug your web page.

This hack describes some small features and tricks that can ease the page creation process. It's all bits and pieces here. For more systematic techniques, try web page validation [Hack #50], the DOM Inspector [Hack #53], or the JavaScript Debugger [Hack #56], just for starters.

Portable Debugging Tricks

These old saws have been supported by most web browsers for a long time. Here they are again, for completeness. First, some common tripping points:

- JavaScript variables are declared differently in PHP, Perl, and JSP. Use var in JavaScript, nothing in PHP, my in Perl, and int or another type in JSP. Don't punctuate JavaScript variable names unless they deserve a leading underscore.
- It's document.forms, not window.forms.

Use alert(). From any JavaScript script—except for proxy, ReadConfig, AutoConfig, and preference files—the mighty alert( ) spits out a string of text in a small window, just as MessageBox does under Win32 for Visual Basic and related languages. It also suspends all script processing. alert( ) is a property of the window DOM 0 object in both HTML and XUL scripts. Here's that trivial tool at work:

```
var result = 5;
alert("Result times 100: " + (result *100));  // or use window.alert( )
```

Probe page contents with javascript: URLs. The javascript: URL scheme allows a line of code to run interactively. That can also be done in the JavaScript Console (in Firefox), but there the currently displayed page is not in context. For a contextual example, try loading the page *http://www.altavista.com*. Then, type this in the Location bar:

```
javascript:document.forms[0].elements[0].tagName
```

This should be the response (an HTML <input> tag):

```
INPUT
```

To report on a web page's content without destroying the display of the page, do this:

```
javascript:alert(document.forms[0].elements[0].tagName)
```

To perform more complex calculations, just ensure that the last statement executed returns void. This example sets the web page script variable total:

```
javascript: var len = document.forms.length; window.total = len; void;
```

Add diagnostic styles. Place extra styles in your user-defined CSS stylesheets if you want to highlight specific features of your web page. For Firefox, that file is called *userContent.css* and is located in the user profile folder. You must restart Firefox after each change made to this file.

A simple experiment is to add border styles to all HTML elements so that the blocks and line boxes show up immediately. This is useful when you are doing table-free web page design and need to know where chunks of content end. One shortcoming of using borders is that they contribute to the size of blocks and therefore slightly distort the normal page layout. Use outline styles (where they are available) to avoid this effect:

```
* { border : solid thin; }
* {      outline : dotted thin;       /* CSS 2 syntax */
   -moz-outline-style : dotted thin;  /* for Mozilla and Firefox */
   }
```

These kinds of styles can also be applied to XUL via the *userChrome.css* files. For XUL specifically, there is a preference that has a similar but more complicated outlining effect:

```
xul.debug.box /* default = false, set to true */
```

Because a restart is required for hand edits, these changes are hard to apply for one-time diagnosis. Try the Web Developer extension's CSS → Add User Stylesheets toolbar option or, more directly, the ChromEdit extension.

Firefox-Specific Debugging Tricks

Firefox has a few unique debugging techniques. For more extensive custom support, try a debug build [Hack #92].

Use watch points. This code calls a function every time the variable test is set:

```
// thing we're going to watch
var test = "foo";

// watcher
function watcher(id, oldval, newval) { alert(oldval + "->" + newval); }

// initialization
watch("test", watcher);
```

```
// ordinary processing
test = "bar";                        // produces alert("foo -> bar");

// decommission the watcher.
unwatch("test");
```

This logic can be applied to any property of any object. It's a handy way to see when a property is modified.

Tweak preferences. There are a few preferences to fiddle with. Here's the first:

```
browser.dom.window.dump.enabled /* default = false, set to true */
```

Turning this on makes the dump( ) host property available. Call it with a single string argument. On Unix/Linux, the result goes to stdout. On Windows, you need to start Firefox with -console to see anything. On Mac OS X, run the system Console application.

This preference complains about various sloppy techniques that might appear in JavaScript code:

```
javascript.options.strict /* default = false; set to true */
```

It also doesn't like to see any occurrences of the with statement.

Log to the JavaScript console. If your page is running securely (either signed or in the chrome), you can write directly to the JavaScript Console. Here's some script setup that makes logging messages simple:

```
var Cc = Components.classes;
var Ci = Components.interfaces;
var cons = Cc["@mozilla.org/consoleservice;1"].getService(Ci.
nsIConsoleService);

function log(str) {
  cons && cons.logStringMessage(str);
}

log("a test message");
```

HACK #56 Debug JavaScript with Venkman

Sick of alert()? Trade up to Venkman, Mozilla's GUI-oriented script-debugging tool

Before Firefox, there was the Mozilla Application Suite (MAS), and that suite supported a script-debugging tool for complex web pages that contain lots of scripts. That tool is called the *JavaScript Debugger*, or *Venkman* (a project name) for short. Venkman is also available for Firefox.

Finding and Installing Venkman

Beware, there's a lot of older and less relevant information on the Web that describes Venkman. To use the debugger in Firefox, you need a Venkman XPI bundle that behaves like an extension. Here's the best way to find it:

1. Check the Mozilla Update web site (*http://update.mozilla.org*) for Venkman or for the JavaScript Debugger under the Developer Tools category. Install that and ignore the rest of this advice.

2. There might have been some last minute problems in completing the work required to make the debugger work perfectly with Firefox. It's a large and complex tool. You can check bug 247507 at Bugzilla (*http://bugzilla.mozilla.org*) to see the latest status.

3. If you still have no success, then check these URLs for a bleeding-edge version:

    http://silver.warwickcompsoc.co.uk/temp/
    http://silver.warwickcompsoc.co.uk/temp/venkman-0.9.84.xpi

After installation, as for all extensions, you must restart Firefox. When restarting, if a complaint is issued that Venkman and Firefox are incompatible in versions, then just proceed anyway. When Firefox is fully started up, open the Extension Manager and locate JavaScript Debugger in the list. Right-click on it and choose Enable from the resulting context menu. After a further restart, the debugger should now appear in the Tools menu and be ready to use.

Experimenting with Venkman

In this hack we'll reuse the HTML code used to test the DOM Inspector [Hack #53]. Let's call that page *debug.html*.

View web page scripts. Let's view the web page through the Venkman lens. After fully installing Venkman, follow these steps:

1. Start it from the Tools → JavaScript Debugger menu item.

2. Check that the Loaded Scripts pane is visible in the top left. It should be selected under View → Show/Hide → Loaded Scripts.

3. Note that in the Loaded Scripts pane, there are lots of scripts already listed. Venkman tries a little too hard to find scripts to debug. Ignore these items.

4. You've now completed the initial sanity checks. Close the debugger window, which shuts down Venkman.

5. Open a new browser window and display the sample page *debug.html* in it. From that window, start Venkman with Tools → JavaScript Debugger.

6. In the new Venkman window, the Loaded Scripts pane should show an extra line, debug.html, with an H icon next to it. That's the loaded page successfully detected by Venkman.

7. Expand the debug.html line item; it shows one script function named click_handler. Double-click that name to see the source code appear in the debugger's Source Code pane, with the function highlighted.

If many functions were defined in this sample page, the Loaded Script pane could be used to navigate all around the document by clicking on the breakdown of functions. This is very useful for pages with complex scripts or for analyzing the cryptic code used by big sites like Google.

Run web page scripts. These steps continue directly from where the last steps left off. Let's execute the click_handler( ) event handler twice, once from the web page and once from the debugger. To do either, first tell Venkman which web page is under scrutiny:

1. Reveal the Open Window pane. By default, it's stacked underneath the Local Scripts pane. If that's where it is, click the tab labeled Open Windows to bring it back to the front. Otherwise, reveal it with View → Show/Hide → Open Windows.

2. In that pane, drill down into the browser pages listed until you find the line for debug.html. Right-click (Command-click) on that debug.html line item and choose Set as Evaluation Object from the context menu. Don't accidentally pick the item named Browser Window. That will add debug to the scripts in the browser window's chrome, not to the scripts in the displayed page.

Now run click_handler( ) by hand:

1. Check that the Interactive Session pane is open, using View → Show/ Hide → Interactive Session. It's the large pane normally at the bottom right with the one-line text box underneath.

2. In the Interactive Session pane, type click_handler( ) into the text box. The window displaying the *debug.html* page should come to the front showing the alert that the click_handler( ) code creates. Success!

Finally, run the debugger as a full interactive debugger:

1. Bring the Venkman window to the front again.

2. Click the big red X icon in the top left, so that three dots appear on it. Venkman is now primed to intercept any scripting activity in the page under study.

3. Bring the browser window showing *debug.html* to the front again.

4. Click on the sole link on the page. Venkman intercepts the start of scripting and puts itself to the front. The first line of the click_handler( ) function has been highlighted as the *current statement* in the Source Code pane, but it hasn't executed yet. The debugger has taken control of JavaScript processing.

5. Type /step into the text box in the Interactive Session pane. The click_ handler( ) function goes forward one statement, which cases the alert to appear again. You have controlled script execution from the debugger. Success!

Because there's only one statement in the handler and because alert( ) is a more complex operation to handle than a simple JavaScript if statement or variable assignment, no further /step commands are possible in this example. Try adding some simple multi-statement logic to the handler instead of an alert( ) call and rerunning this procedure.

See Also

Svend Tofte has written an excellent, but slightly aged, online tutorial introduction to Venkman. It takes the brief exploration in this hack much further. Read it here:

> *http://www.svendtofte.com/code/learning_venkman/*

In the tutorial screenshots, if Navigator Window appears, read instead Browser Window. Those shots are taken with the Mozilla Application Suite, not Firefox, but otherwise everything's much the same. Also be cautious of keyboard shortcuts recommended in the text.

HACK #57   Handle Hangs and Other Bad Juju

Firefox is only nearly perfect. Here's how to manage when it's not.

All software has defects. Firefox benefits from five years of poking and tweaking aimed at making it as robust as possible. It probably has fewer defects than Windows, although that's hard to say, since the Windows bug database isn't available to public scrutiny. This hack describes what to do if you happen to get stuck with a problem. If you do manage to make Firefox hang, then that's a significant achievement. You should be proud of yourself for pushing the limits and thus proving your skills.

Separate Out Performance Problems from Hangs

A few things slow Firefox down, rather than causing it to die completely:

- If the download manager has a very, very long list of downloaded (or downloading) files, that can slow down the saving of web pages to local disk. Press the Clean Up button in the Download Manager to fix this.
- If the DNS system used to turn domain names into IP addresses is performing poorly or, worse, is offline, then Firefox can't complete any web page retrieval actions.
- Poorly written JavaScript scripts can consume large amounts of memory and CPU and bog down processing in a general way.
- Badly written JavaScript scripts in proxy and configuration files can mess up the browser state.

Things You Can Do to Bust Firefox

There are plenty of things you can do to ruin Firefox's day:

Syntax errors

If you hack the chrome [Hack #77] and you put syntax errors into XUL or JavaScript files in the chrome, the browser window might not start up at all. It's up to you to unwind your changes until you've removed the error in your code. You did make a backup, didn't you? As a last resort, use the -safe-mode startup option.

Command-line combinations

If you make heavy use of the Firefox command line, perhaps in a DOS box on Windows or from the shell, sooner or later you might find a URL string and command-line switch combination that upsets the browser. Take care to quote URLs with the right quotation marks, and use legal URLs only. The file: scheme requires three forward slashes (file:///) when referring to a file on local disk.

A zero-by-zero window

Under Linux, you can't yet create an XUL window (in fact, any window) that's zero-by-zero (0×0) pixels in size. Each window must be at least one pixel in each direction.

Mixing builds on Windows

The debug and nightly build of Firefox sometimes stress out Windows's little mind. Take care to clean up completely (shutdown and reboot in the worst case) if strange things occur when you're experimenting with an unofficial build. The oddities you see in test-only builds can sometimes confuse the running Windows instance, and afterward, even official Firefox releases can have a hard time getting Windows to cooperate. If in doubt, reboot cleanly.

Things You Can Do to Recover

Most importantly, understand the hidden window issue. In order to deco-rate the application menu bar on Mac OS X, Mozilla must maintain a sepa-rate window structure in addition to those that are normally visible as browser windows or as dialog boxes. If Firefox hangs or has other prob-lems, this hidden window can remain when other windows are dismissed. This is true on all platforms. The upshot is that Firefox is still running, even though it looks like it's gone. In this case, it's important to kill all Firefox tasks before restarting it:

- On Windows, search and destroy Firefox processes using the Task Manager (Ctrl-Alt-Del), or start Firefox again with the -kill option.
- On Unix/Linux, just use kill(1) or Ctrl-C.
- On the Mac OS X 10.3 and higher, use the Activity Monitor. It's found on the application toolbar under Applications → Utilities, or you can select Force Quit (Command-Option-Escape) from the Apple menu.

Another obscure issue is corruption of files in the profile area. This has been extensively discussed in the past, but the number of incidents seems to have subsided in recent times. In theory, such corruption could badly affect Fire-fox. If you suspect profile file corruption, then create a fresh new profile, prove that that much works, and then test any suspect files in there.

If you are running a Talkback-enabled build, a crashing or hanging Firefox may invite you to deliver a crash report. You should do so, as well as log a bug with Bugzilla, for these reasons:

- If you don't bother to deliver it, the problem you've had might never be identified by anyone able to fix it. It will keep happening.
- If you do submit a Talkback report but take no other action, it will just sit anonymously on a server, where it theoretically might get attention. In practical terms, it will just become another crash incident in a vast field of test data.
- If you also log a bug with Bugzilla (*http://bugzilla.mozilla.org*) describ-ing the conditions under which the crash occurred [Hack #96], then at least the problem is exposed to view. If you add reproducibility information and help the bug owner narrow down the problem, it will get fixed more quickly. The chances of it inconveniencing you again are then very low.

There are lots of places where you can collaborate with others [Hack #97]. In summary, when it comes to unexpected crashes and other vexatious behav-ior, the more you participate, the better off you are.

## CHAPTER SIX

Power XML for Web Pages
Hacks 58–74

This chapter describes how to jump up and down on Firefox using XML content. Sometimes that content starts out with an HTML page, and sometimes it doesn't. You have the option of a pure XML environment or an HTML-driven one.

One of the big problems with XML support in web browsers is *feature creep*. Once you have XML, you want XML namespaces. Once you have namespaces, you want XLink. The next thing you know, you're buried under an onslaught of XML standards. Feature creep makes cross-browser content more challenging than usual, because every browser has a different idea of which direction it should creep in.

Nevertheless, there are plenty of places where quality XML content is needed and where cross-browser compatibility isn't a problem. Intranets are one such place; help systems, bundled content solutions such as CD distributions, and kiosks are others. Finally, there's the growing area of user interfaces, which are supported by a class of XML standards called XUILs (XML User Interface Languages); in this case, that means XUL. Firefox is a suitable platform for all of these uses.

In fact, Firefox is particularly rich in XML standards support. Whether it's web services, knowledge management, data transforms, dictionaries, or feeds, Firefox does it's best to find a standard to implement. There's no room in this chapter for extensive standards nit-picking; this is just a tour of the major features Firefox supports.

Pick Display Modes for HTML and XML
#58   Firefox has several display options for web content. Here's how to pick between them.

This hack explains how to specify a *display contract* between a web page and Firefox. A display contract is an agreement between the content author and Firefox that guarantees that the content will be displayed as the author intended, right down to the tiniest detail. That means no more guesswork about browser behavior. This hack applies to all Mozilla-based browsers, including Compuserve Version 8 and later, Netscape Versions 6 and later, the Mozilla Application Suite Versions 1.x, Camino, and so on.

To make a display contract, put hints and standards references in or near the content. Provided the content author puts these in, Firefox will fall into line with absolute predictability. You'll need to add several types of hints.

Tell Firefox What the Content Is

If content is delivered across the Internet, everything depends on the HTTP Content-Type header, which advertises a MIME type for the content document. Firefox *always* follows the MIME type, *no matter what*. Here are the correct headers to use for HTML, XML, and XHTML:

```
Content-Type: text/html
Content-Type: text/xml
Content-Type: application/xhtml+xml
```

It's the third line that Internet Explorer (IE) can't always understand. To support IE, you have to fudge a separate type for IE at the server [Hack #27]. For complex XML cases [Hack #60] and for Firefox-specific XML such as XUL [Hack #68], use this content type:

```
Content-Type: application/vnd.mozilla.xul+xml
```

Images used in HTML documents or CSS documents should not be sent over the Web as text/html. They should be sent with the MIME type that is correct for their file format, so use something like this:

```
Content-Type: image/gif
```

If the file resides on the local disk, Firefox will do its best to get a MIME type from the operating system or, failing that, derive one from the filename. Neither is an infallible source of accurate content types.

Tell Firefox Which Parser to Use

Firefox contains two web page parsers: the *strict XML parser* and the *flexible HTML parser*. They're used to break the web page up into pieces in preparation for display. Pick the one you want.

If your content matches the Content-Type you advertised it to be, the choice of parser is automatic. The strict XML parser will be used for everything except content advertised as text/html. If your content is ill formed, the parser will halt with an error.

If you put the strict parser in action and the document contains this namespace declaration in the <html> tag or in the <?xml?> processing directive, the strict parser will go into Smart mode:

```
<html xmlns="http://www.w3.org/1999/xhtml">
```

In Smart mode, the strict XML parser recognizes that a <button> tag has special meaning, because it is an XHTML tag. It will not be treated as an anonymous piece of content; it will be treated as a form element that you can click.

On a bad day, your web pages might be poorly conceived, older than standards, or merely sloppy. All content, good or bad, that is advertised as text/ html is dumped into the flexible HTML parser. That parser can handle ill-formed HTML, ill-formed XML and XHTML, well-formed XML, and well-formed standard HTML—the whole lot.

Tell Firefox How to Render the Content

Firefox contains a single presentation system called Gecko that is based on and extends the CSS2 presentation standard. Gecko's responsibilities include composition, layout, and rendering. Rendering puts pages on the screen. Gecko can operate in one of several modes: Standards mode, Almost Standards mode, Quirks mode, and other modes. Set normal behavior for correctly advertised content this way:

- For XML, Standards mode is triggered by a stylesheet directive like this one:
  ```
  <?xml-stylesheet href="styles.css" ... ?>
  ```
- For XHTML, Standards mode always applies.
- For HTML 4.01, Standards mode is triggered by this DOCTYPE:
  ```
  <!DOCTYPE HTML PUBLIC
      "-//W3C//DTD HTML 4.01 Strict//EN"
      "http://www.w3.org/TR/html4/strict.dtd">
  ```

If Standards mode is not specified, or if badly advertised content is sent to the browser, or if the content is badly formed, then Gecko will operate in Quirks mode. In Quirks mode, Firefox applies a grab bag of *fix-up styles* and special cases to the content. These extra styles are an attempt to make the best sense possible of content that is of unknown intent. Such content is also called *tag soup*. Quirks mode can be enforced by omitting a `<!DOCTYPE>`, or by supplying this one:

```
<!DOCTYPE HTML PUBLIC "-//W3C//DTD HTML 4.01 Transitional//EN">
```

Finally, there is another mode called Almost Standards mode. Standards mode (and the HTML 4.01 standard) differs from ancient and widespread HTML practices in one important way. It silently applies this style to images held in table cells:

```
td > img { vertical-align : baseline; }
```

The result is a gap underneath the image in the table cell. This is undesirable for older pages that use tiled-image in tables instead of CSS for page layout. If Almost Standards mode is applied instead, an alternate style is silently used and the gap goes away:

```
td > img { vertical-align : bottom; }
```

To use Almost Standards mode in Firefox, use this `<!DOCTYPE>`:

```
<!DOCTYPE HTML PUBLIC
  "-//W3C//DTD HTML 4.01 Transitional//EN">
```

Any DTD may be optionally specified in this case.

The other rendering modes that Gecko provides are for XUL [Hack #68], MathML [Hack #61], and SVG [Hack #62]. They're all part of Gecko, but they are used to display non-hypertext documents. The MathML rendering is the one closest to HTML. For more detail on the HTML modes, see this URL:

http://www.mozilla.org/docs/web-developer/quirks/doctypes.html

 ## Get Tools for XML Validation
#59   Complement your XML content development processes with life-saving tools.

XML content is interpreted rather than compiled by Firefox. If XML is interpreted by a nonvalidating parser, only basic syntax errors are reported. This hack shows how to check your XML content more thoroughly.

 There is no DTD or XML schema for either Mozilla's XUL or Mozilla's XBL dialects of XML.

Built-In XML-Checking Tools

Firefox's strict XML parser [Hack #58] checks all XML content for well-formedness. If the content is to be displayed as a document and it contains a simple syntax error, Firefox will display an error. This sample code has incorrectly nested tags:

```
<?xml version="1.0"?>
<foo>
  <bar>
  </foo>
</bar>
```

Figure 6-1 shows the error message that Firefox reports.

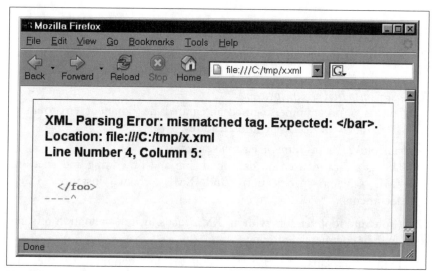

Figure 6-1. A standard XML error message

The problem is that Firefox reports these messages only if the XML content is destined for display. There's no handy feedback if the content is delivered *into* an existing document. Examples of content delivered into an existing, displayed document include RSS feeds, RDF datasources, XBL bindings, and SOAP messages. A simple test strategy is to manually load such XML directly into the browser using a URL or filename and see what happens.

Firefox's strict XML parser is not a validating parser. It doesn't check content against DTDs or schemas. This means that well-formed XML (or HTML) isn't checked for valid tags (*entities*). You have to use a separate tool for such a check. The forthcoming E4X support in JavaScript supports only the five standard entities defined by the base XML standard.

Web-Based Validation Tools

To validate your XML code, you can send it to a web site that provides a validation service. There are several styles of content submission. The following page-based service provides checking based on a tool called RXP. You can cut and paste your own URL into the displayed HTML form, and it will be checked for you:

http://www.cogsci.ed.ac.uk/~richard/xml-check.html

This alternate service lets you upload a local file, use a URL, or paste an XML content fragment into its submission form:

http://www.stg.brown.edu/service/xmlvalid/

Third-Party Validation Tools

You can pay a fortune for a GUI tool that does XML validation for you. Here are two products for Windows, both of which offer free trial versions:

XML Spy (http://www.xmlspy.com)
    This is a programmer-focused integrated development environment (IDE) tool with XML-validation features.

Schematron Validator (http://www.topologi.com)
    This is a tool focused on data modeling and on editing and checking XML schema specifications and XML schema instances (XML documents).

Most software tool vendors with an XML focus include validation of some kind in their commercial offerings.

On Linux/Unix, quality GUI-based tools are less common. Of the GUI options available, the two main editors, Emacs and vi (vim is a modern vi offering) are both troublesome. Expect lots of web research and configuration time. Both editors support simple syntax-highlighting out of the box, but that is not validation.

Things are better at the command line, where libraries like libxml and expat have been built on to provide useful tools. I recommend these:

XMLStarlet (http://xmlstar.sourceforge.net)
    This is a set of XML validation tools with a syntax environment similar to cvs, except all commands are kicked off via the xml command. XML-Starlet is quick on the command line and can be easily integrated with makefiles, scripts, and other simple automations.

Raptor (http://www.librdf.org/raptor/)
    RDF overlays plain XML and XML schema content with an additional data model designed to represent arbitrary relationships between data. A simple validator is not always enough for RDF; Raptor requires compilation from source. A useful command-line tool called rapper analyzes RDF XML content from an RDF point of view.

Mix Content with XML Namespaces

#60 An XML document can combine content of several different types.

The W3C (*http://www.w3.org*) XML Namespaces specification allows document syntax from several different types of XML documents to exist in one file. Firefox's Gecko rendering engine can display some documents that are of mixed type, but not all. This hack shows combinations that are both feasible and useful.

Play with XML Namespace Syntax

Here is the syntax for namespaces. An XML document has a default namespace, which is specified by a URL. The namespace URL is different than the document definition. This XHTML 1.0 fragment shows both:

```
<?xml version="1.0"?>
<!DOCTYPE html PUBLIC
  "-//W3C//DTD XHTML 1.0 Strict//EN"
  "http://www.w3.org/TR/xhtml1/DTD/xhtml1-strict.dtd"
>
<html xmlns="http://www.w3.org/1999/xhtml">
...
```

The URL in the DOCTYPE declaration says where the definition of this document is located. That's a hint to Firefox that explains what resources to use when displaying the document. The URL in the <html> tag says which URL belongs to the default namespace. That's a hint to Firefox that explains how to allocate tags found in the file to the right standard.

Here are the only namespaces that Firefox has special display support for:

```
http://www.w3.org/1999/xhtml
http://www.w3.org/1998/Math/MathML
http://www.w3.org/2000/svg
http://www.mozilla.org/keymaster/gatekeeper/there.is.only.xul
```

These namespaces are XHTML 1.0, MathML 1.0, SVG 1.0, and Mozilla's XUL, respectively. Namespace-less XML is also supported. Of these four URLs, the only sensible choices are to pick either XHTML or XUL as the default namespace. Beware that mixing all these content types is a potent cocktail. No group, not the Mozilla project or even the W3C, has determined in fine detail how various combination should work.

Mozilla supports many XML standards beyond this short list. None of the others have direct display support, however. RDF can provide display elements, but only indirectly via XUL templates. Indirect display is also possible for XSLT and Mozilla's XBL.

For completeness, here are the nondisplay namespaces that Firefox recognizes:

```
http://www.w3.org/XML/1998/namespace
http://www.w3.org/2000/xmlns/
http://www.w3.org/1999/xlink
http://www.w3.org/1999/XSL/Transform
http://www.mozilla.org/xbl
http://www.w3.org/1999/02/22-rdf-syntax-ns#
http://www.w3.org/2001/xml-events
```

Write Reports in XHTML, MathML, and SVG

High standard reports, papers, and presentations have text, mathematical formulas, diagrams, and illustrations as content. The combination of XHTML, MathML, and SVG provides a suitable descriptive environment in which no content needs to be captured as a rendered image. This is a bleeding-edge approach, though, because the standard Firefox release doesn't include SVG. That means the vast majority of Firefox users (those with the standard release) can't read such reports.

Here's a fragment of a document that holds both XHTML and MathML content:

```
<html xmlns="http://www.w3.org/1999/xhtml"
      xmlns:m="http://www.w3.org/1998/Math/MathML">
  <em>An equation
    <m:msup>
      <m:mi>x</m:mi>
      <m:mn>2</m:mn>
    </m:msup>
  </em>
  ...
```

Firefox displays the result like this:

> An equation: x^2

Notice how the emphasized styling from the XHTML <em> tag is also used by the MathML content. Notice also that, although the MathML namespace is used, there's no proper <math> tag surround the math content. If you use MathML properly by including the <math> tag, styling is done more formally [Hack #61]. Nesting other content inside SVG content won't work; write the SVG pieces so that they're pure SVG [Hack #62].

Create Content Browsers with XHTML and XUL

You can mix Mozilla's Graphical User Interface XML dialect XUL [Hack #68] with XHTML (or HTML) in two ways.

The simple way is to use <iframe> tags. XUL, HTML, and XHTML all support <iframe>. If you are describing a user interface in XUL, a portion of the window should contain an XUL <iframe>. That frame in turn displays an HTML or XHTML document. This is useful in situations where the window must display both navigation controls and content, such as these:

- Software installers that show a scrollable view of the license agreement text
- Help windows
- Content management systems
- Web browsers, such as Firefox itself

To see an example of an XUL-XHTML blend, just look at the Firefox browser's interface. It's a set of XUL widgets (toolbars and menus) and a big <iframe> pane that displays HTML (the currently loaded page).

A more complicated twist is to put XUL and XHTML tags together in the same file. If you do this, XUL must be the default namespace and the document must be delivered from the server with the XUL MIME type [Hack #27]. Since XUL tags are all controlled by CSS styles, even the ones backed by XBL bindings, you can mash together XHTML and XUL styles in one CSS stylesheet. Mix up your XUL tags and HTML tags as much as you like, but expect some disconcerting layout results from interactions between these style property values:

```
display : block
display : inline
display : -moz-box
```

Keep everything either inside a set of XUL boxes or inside a set CSS blocks. Inside that chosen framework, use whatever special cases make sense.

This complicated arrangement might be useful for a content-management system. There, you can put sophisticated widgets next to content pieces, without having to go through the torture of extensive Dynamic HTML programming.

 ## HACK #61 Make MathML Content

MathML (Mathematical Markup Language) provides the set of tags with which to express mathematical equations on web pages.

Before MathML there was TeX (pronounced "Tek"), a typesetting system developed prior to the Web by Donald Knuth in the 70s and 80s. TeX has set the standard for professional-looking math on digital devices, especially for print media. TEX and an extension called LATEX have traditionally been what math people use for mathematical documents.

MathML is meant to play a similar role on the Web. Firefox's Gecko layout system has built-in TEX-quality support for mathematics that can be styled and scripted to achieve exciting dynamic effects visually and computationally. MathML is another of those things that really set Firefox apart from other web browsers. Figure 6-2 shows an example of MathML content.

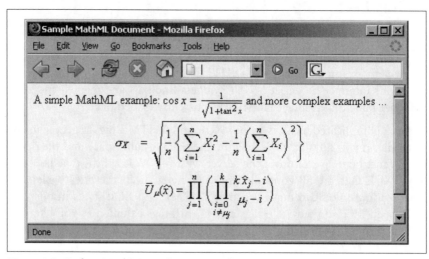

Figure 6-2. Built-in MathML rendering in Firefox

No, the screenshot shown in Figure 6-2 is not made up of images produced by LATEX2HTML (or some such) and included in the page with <img> tags. Nor is the page displayed using plug-ins. What you see is Firefox mastering mathematics with as much dexterity as any mathematician. Firefox does the formatting natively. Now, you too can harness this TEX-quality math power by using MathML.

The example in this hack zooms into a basic template typeset according to W3C standards. It shows how the screenshot in Figure 6-2 was developed and how to experiment with your own examples. But first, some setup.

Deal with MathML Fonts

When experiencing MathML for the first time, chances are you will have problems with fonts. If you don't have the fonts that Firefox needs, it will warn you if they're necessary (that is, when you first stumble on a page with MathML content). Refer to the Mozilla MathML project page (*http://www.mozilla.org/projects/mathml/fonts*) for needed fonts.

For consistent and better-looking stretchy characters (such as parentheses, integrals, etc.), configure Firefox to use either the TeX fonts or the Mathematica 4.1 fonts (but not both):

```
font.mathfont-family /* for a TeX look, set to: "CMSY10, CMEX10"  */
font.mathfont-family /* for Mathematica 4.1, set to: "Math1, Math2, Math4"
*/
```

Consult "Install Fonts and Character Support" [Hack #30] for other useful information about fonts in Firefox.

Make a MathML Example

MathML is an XML application. It generally appears mixed with other content [Hack #60], typically XHTML documents:

```
<?xml version="1.0" encoding="UTF-8"?>
<!DOCTYPE html PUBLIC
  "-//W3C//DTD XHTML 1.1 plus MathML 2.0//EN"
  "http://www.w3.org/TR/MathML2/dtd/xhtml-math11-f.dtd">
<html xmlns="http://www.w3.org/1999/xhtml">
<head>
  <title>Sample MathML Document</title>
</head>
  <body>
    A simple MathML example:
```

Such documents must have a DOCTYPE declaration with a Formal Public Identifier (FPI) that clearly indicates that the document embeds mathematical content. The following are legal FPIs for this purpose:

```
"-//W3C//DTD XHTML 1.1 plus MathML 2.0//EN"
"-//W3C//DTD XHTML 1.1 plus MathML 2.0 plus SVG 1.1//EN"
"-//W3C//DTD MathML 2.0//EN"
```

The last line is only for *standalone* MathML fragments (not composite documents) that are used in special circumstances. The given URL in the DOCTYPE is specific to compound XHTML documents with mixed content. Then come the headers and body parts that you are accustomed to in XHTML:

```
<math xmlns="http://www.w3.org/1998/Math/MathML">
```

To switch from all hypertext rendering modes [Hack #58] and XML to the *mathml rendering mode*, you must enclose your equation in a $...$ fragment and bind the <math> tag to the MathML namespace. (Alternatively, you can use a prefix, such as math: or m:, bound to the MathML namespace at the root <html>). The <math> tag is the top-level tag that encloses other MathML tags. It plays a role similar to the role played by $...$ or $$...$$ in TeX. The <math> tag accepts a number of tag attributes, as do other MathML tags. Some attributes are common, while others are specific to certain tags.

A mathematical expression that is interspersed with the text is called an *inline expression*, as opposed to a *block* expression (usually known in the terminology of TEX as *displaystyle*), which appears alone (and centered) on its own line. You make your choice with either `<math display="inline">` (the default when the attribute is not there) or `<math display="block">` (this was used in the second and third equations in Figure 6-2). Here's the continuation of the web page started previously, showing an inline expression:

```
<mrow>
  <mrow>
    <mi>cos</mi>
    <mo>&ApplyFunction;</mo>
    <mi>x</mi>
  </mrow>
  <mo>=</mo>
  <mfrac>
    <mn>1</mn>
    <msqrt>
      <mn>1</mn>
      <mo>+</mo>
      <mrow>
        <msup>
          <mi>tan</mi>
          <mn>2</mn>
        </msup>
        <mo>&ApplyFunction;</mo>
        <mi>x</mi>
      </mrow>
    </msqrt>
  </mfrac>
</mrow>
```

Figure 6-3 shows the rendered output of this sample expression, with each rendering block highlighted with a dashed outline. You can see the nested structure closely matches the nested elements in the MathML content.

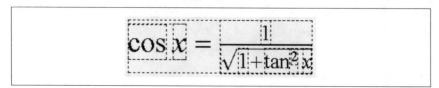

Figure 6-3. Box model of the equation

Inside the `<math>` container, you can use a variety of math-related tags and elements to describe your equation. In the preceding example, you can see such tags in this order:

`<mrow>`
   Horizontally group subexpressions

`<mi>`

　Identifier

`<mo>`

　Operator, fence, separator, or accent

`<mfrac>`

　Fraction

`<mn>`

　Number

`<msqrt>`

　Radical

`<msup>`

　A superscript to attach to a base

Figure 6-3 illustrates the way these tags build the equation's display piece-by-piece. MathML consists of two sets of tags: presentation markup (about 30 tags with about 50 attributes) and content markup (about 120 tags with about a dozen attributes). At present, Firefox has built-in support for presentation markup. But content markup can be rendered as well by turning it into presentation markup via XSLT [Hack #64] and the Universal MathML StyleSheet (UMSS) available at the W3C's web site *http://www.w3.org*. Beware that styling MathML requires a different mindset than styling HTML, as some *content* information is communicated directly by font choices. Finally, here are the end tags for the sample web page, just to make everything tidy:

```
    </math>
    and more complex examples
    ...
  </body>
</html>
```

When you are done with the equation, you close it with `</math>`. In general, you switch back and forth between the *hypertext rendering mode* and the *math rendering mode* as often as necessary. Save the document with a *.xhtml* extension, and let Firefox do the rest.

Mathematical expressions can be accessed and changed programmatically using scripts that manipulate the DOM. This goes for all XML dialects, and in this case allows you to build advanced features, such as a MathML editor. Stylistic effects can be applied as well. For example, Figure 6-3 was obtained rather speedily with these CSS rules:

```
math * { border: dashed 1px; }
math { font-size: 50px; border: none; }
```

View MathML Source

Have you seen View Selection Source? When you select a piece of web page text displayed in a normal browser window, and then bring forth the context menu by right-clicking (command-clicking on the Mac), that option appears in the context menu. It allows you to see just the markup of the selected text with the unique feature of remapping the selection to the markup.

There is a similar function specifically for MathML. When you right-click on any MathML expression (no selection this time), the context menu gives you an option to view just the MathML source under consideration. It then highlights the element on which you right-clicked. This is great for learning, copy/paste operations, and such.

—Roger Sidje

Make SVG Content

#62

Create dynamically changing diagrams based on vector graphics instead of static images.

Scalable Vector Graphics (SVG) is a W3C XML standard for defining two-dimensional images that are composed of vector graphics. SVG is useful for maps, illustrations, diagrams, and numerous other uses. SVG support is being added to Firefox and Mozilla, but at the time of writing, that support is still being finished. Many SVG features are complete, but there are still rough edges and gaps. This hack explains how to do *something*, in preparation for the day when you'll be able to do *anything*. To work with SVG, you need the right build of Firefox [Hack #92] and the right fonts in place [Hack #30]. If you're using an older operating system, this URL describes other files that you might also need:

http://www.mozilla.org/projects/svg/build.html

Understand Versions and Features

Mozilla SVG 1.1 support is being built in a project separate from the Firefox project. This means that Firefox does not always include the latest SVG changes. Here are the levels of SVG support provided by different versions of Firefox and Mozilla (as of the time of writing):

* The standard installations of Mozilla and Firefox don't yet include SVG support.

* Custom versions of Firefox 1.0 have SVG support at least as good as Mozilla 1.6.

- Custom versions of Firefox 1.1 will have SVG support at least equal to that of Mozilla 1.8 (an estimate).

- Mozilla 1.9 and Firefox 1.5 will have extensive cross-platform SVG support (an estimate).

- Standard installations of Mozilla 1.9, and perhaps Firefox 1.5, releases will include SVG support (an estimate).

The following URL describes SVG project progress *in the latest trunk builds*, and therefore goes beyond the SVG support in custom Firefox 1.0 versions:

http://www.mozilla.org/projects/svg/status.html

Basic SVG features such as <rect> have been supported in custom builds of Firefox for a long time. Use the basic features without fear, and expect them in all versions of Mozilla that support SVG.

For such versions, one major restriction on use remains. SVG content and other XML content cannot be deeply intermixed. SVG content and other XML content, such as XHTML, can be present in the same document, but if <svg> tags are present, only SVG tags can appear inside them. This means that SVG diagrams can be inset in other content, but SVG shapes cannot be freely mixed with hypertext. Since SVG has its own <text> tag anyway, this is less of a problem that it might seem. Eventually, this problem will go away. In the interim, the alternative to all these "under construction" matters is to install the Adobe SVG Viewer Plugin.

Make an Interactive Diagram

Once you add JavaScript and SVG styles resembling CSS to an SVG document, the world becomes your oyster. Figure 6-4 shows the end result.

Here's the XML for this page (note the emphasized text where the hooks are located):

```
<?xml version="1.0"?>
<html xmlns="http://www.w3.org/1999/xhtml"
      xmlns:svg="http://www.w3.org/2000/svg">
  <head>
  </head>
    <body onload="init( )">
      <h1>SVG Example</h1>
      <p>Click on the rectangle to rotate it.</p>

      <svg:svg width="300" height="300">
        <svg:g id="shim" transform="rotate(-15,60,100)">
          <svg:rect class="box" x="40" y="50" width="100" height="75" rx="5"/>
          <svg:text x="50" y="80">SVG text</svg:text>
        </svg:g>
```

Figure 6-4. SVG Firefox build showing user-rotated content

```
    </svg:svg>

  </body>
</html>
```

At the moment, it's safer to use inline `<style>` tags than to include external stylesheets. Here's the style and scripting content:

```
<style>
  rect        {stroke:green; stroke-width:5; fill:green; }
  rect:hover {stroke:red;}
</style>
<script>
  var shim, angle;
  function init( ) {
    shim = document.getElementById("shim")
    shim.addEventListener("click",twist,false);
    angle = -15;
  }
  function twist( ) {
    angle -= 30;
    var att = "rotate(" + angle + ",60,100)";
    shim.setAttribute("transform",att);
  }
</script>
```

Here's a brief summary of the code. A *shim* is a thin piece of anything; we've just used it as a name for the rotating rectangle; the `<rect>` shape is certainly thin in the z-direction! The init( ) function installs an event listener as though onclick="twist( )" had been stated. It also initializes two variables. When the user clicks, the transform attribute of the <svg:g> tag is updated by the script, causing the content to be modified. Firefox reflow/redraw automatically brings the display up to date. In many similar ways, content can be added, moved, or deleted in response to user actions.

HACK #63 Use Client-Side XPath

Use XPath to enhance your XSL transformations.

XPath defines a syntax for selecting parts of an XML document. It consists of syntax to select direct elements and their attributes, as well as a set of standard functions. XPath was released as a W3C recommendation in 1999 and is such a major element of XSL that without it, you will not be able to make XSL documents. This hack serves to dirty your hands with basic XPath syntax.

XPath syntax is a superset of the standard patterns that are used to apply templates to XML elements using the match attribute of the xsl:template element. Patterns allow you to say which nodes you do and do not wish to match for a transformation. Basic patterns allow you to match nodes by element name, child elements, descendants, and attributes. The XPath superset allows matching on much more powerful expressions. These expressions can be used in any XSL element that allows a select attribute. Currently, that means these tags: xsl:apply-templates, xsl:value-of, xsl:for-each, xsl:copy-of, xsl:variable, xsl:param, and xsl:sort.

In addition to being able to select a list of element nodes, XPath is able to produce Booleans, numbers, and strings.

The power of XPath lies in its ability to match on all the basic match pattern tests, as well as on ancestor, parent, sibling, preceding, and following nodes. Without the XPath capabilities of XSL, performing anything other than simple operations on XML would be impossible.

Use Criteria to Select an XML Nodeset

To demonstrate XPath, we'll use the following XML:

```
<?xml version="1.0"?>
<?xml-stylesheet type="text/xsl" href="projects.xsl"?>
<mozilla-projects>
  <project version="1.0" downloads="5305002">Firefox</project>
  <project version="0.9" downloads="176083">Thunderbird</project>
  <project version="0.8">Camino</project>
  <project version="2.16" downloads="2731227">Bugzilla</project>
  <project version="0.2">Sunbird</project>
</mozilla-projects>
```

These templates could also be used in the stylesheet document created in "Use Client-Side XSL" [Hack #64].

When performing XSL transformations, it is common to want to select only a certain set of nodes from those available. To restrict the node set, we need to apply a condition to limit the nodes returned. We can apply an expression in a select attribute between two square brackets after the node name is specified.

To display all projects with a version number higher than one, we can use the following template:

```
<?xml version="1.0"?>
<xsl:stylesheet version="1.0" xmlns:xsl="http://www.w3.org/1999/XSL/
Transform">

  <xsl:template match="/">
    <html>
      <head><title>Mozilla Projects</title></head>
      <body>
        <h1>Mozilla Projects</h1>
        <ol>
          <xsl:apply-templates
                  select="mozilla-projects/project[@version &gt;= 1]">
            <xsl:sort select="." />
          </xsl:apply-templates>
        </ol>
      </body>
    </html>
  </xsl:template>

  <xsl:template match="project">
    <li><xsl:value-of select="." /></li>
  </xsl:template>

</xsl:stylesheet>
```

As you can see, we are selecting all project elements that are children of the mozilla-projects node. In addition to this, we are applying the condition to this set of elements that they must have an attribute (represented by the @ symbol) that is greater than (represented by > because the standard greater-than sign is the same as a closing element symbol) or equal to 1. Figure 6-5 shows the output.

Use XPath to Expose Expression Axes

Sometimes, you need to reference other parts of an XML document than the current node and its attributes. Using node axes, you are able to select

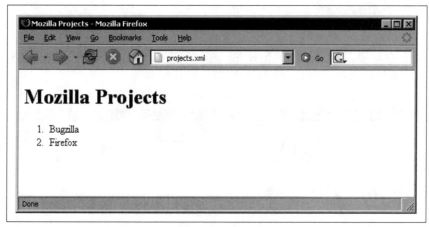

Figure 6-5. HTML elements matched by a simple XPath

different parts of the tree relative to the context node (i.e., to the current node). Some of the axes you can experiment with include ancestor, attribute, child, descendant, following, parent, and self.

To demonstrate this, we will apply templates when we find a particular attribute. Once the template is applied to the attribute, we would still like to reference the element value. We can access this value using the parent axes. Note that we have also maintained alphabetical sorting on the project names by using the extended syntax for parent in the xsl:sort element.

If we want to see all those projects that have a download count attribute, we can change the template document to read:

```
<?xml version="1.0"?>
<xsl:stylesheet version="1.0" xmlns:xsl="http://www.w3.org/1999/XSL/
Transform">

  <xsl:template match="/">
    <html>
      <head><title>Mozilla Projects</title></head>
      <body>
        <h1>Mozilla Projects</h1>
        <ol>
          <xsl:apply-templates select="mozilla-projects/project/@downloads">
            <xsl:sort select="parent::project" />
          </xsl:apply-templates>
        </ol>
      </body>
    </html>
  </xsl:template>

  <xsl:template match="@downloads">
    <li><xsl:value-of select="parent::project" /></li>
```

```
    </xsl:template>

  </xsl:stylesheet>
```

Figure 6-6 shows that this alternate set of transformations changes the output without changing the original XML-based content.

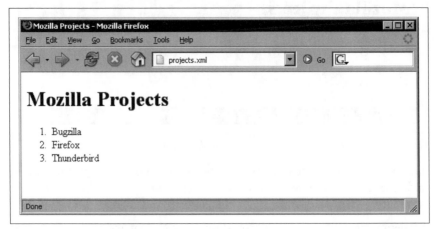

Figure 6-6. Alternate HTML output made with XPath syntax

Although this hack covers only a small amount of the XPath expression syntax, you can already see the powerful results it can produce. You can view the full XPath standard at *http://www.w3.org/TR/xpath*.

—*James Vulling*

HACK #64 Use Client-Side XSL

Apply XSL stylesheets to XML without using a standalone XSL processor.

As someone who is obviously interested in the Web and all it has to offer, you might have heard about wonderful technologies such as XML (eXtensible Markup Language, *http://www.w3.org/XML/*) and XSL (eXtensible Stylesheet Language, *http://www.w3.org/Style/XSL/*). When you throw phrases like "separating presentation from content" into the mix, you have every right to be curious.

Using XML, you can create your very own vocabulary for storing data. Using your very own elements and attributes, data can be stored hierarchically however you like. Obviously, there are certain restrictions on how this is done, but overall, it is quite flexible. An XML document must contain an XML declaration and only one instance of the root node. A *well-formed* XML vocabulary is one in which each piece of data is tagged with meaningful names and that is clear, concise, and, equally important, can be understood at a later stage.

Why Use XSL Instead of CSS?

The main idea behind the XML/XSL combination is to be able to structure information into a meaningful language and then transform it into the required output format, without storing any of the presentation or structural information with the data. While XML allows you to structure the information, we are still, conceptually, one step short of useful output. XSL allows us to restructure the non-output information for output. CSS doesn't have this structural-processing kind of approach.

Although XML and XSL are both still emerging into mainstream software development projects, they show a great deal of promise to help pave the way for the Web to come. They both serve separate and distinct purposes. XML allows information to be structured according to a given vocabulary in a purely textual form. XSL, on the other hand, allows an XML document to be transformed into one of many different formats. These might include another XML document, XHTML (for web pages), Scalable Vector Graphics (SVG, *http://www.w3.org/TR/SVG/*), or PDF (with a little help from XSL Formatting Objects).

Define Firefox and XSL

Where does Firefox come into all this, you may ask? Firefox has the ability not only to display XML documents in its *viewport* (page display area), but also to transform them using XSL. This does not require additional extensions and can be done with a standard install of Firefox.

When Firefox performs an XSL transformation, it's a *client-side* transformation. If a dynamic web page is requested from a web server, the server code used to generate this page might generate XML and then further transform the page using XSL. It then sends plain HTML/XHTML to be displayed in the user's browser. This is called *server-side* XSL, which is not covered here, though the principle is the same.

Client-side XSL is useful if you want to view many XML documents that have a similar structure—for example, an iTunes library listing, MSN Messenger conversations, or other information exported from certain programs.

Write Your First Transform

First, we need some sample XML to transform. Let's use the following list of projects from the Mozilla Foundation:

```
<?xml version="1.0"?>
<mozilla-projects>
  <project>Firefox</project>
  <project>Thunderbird</project>
```

```
    <project>Camino</project>
    <project>Bugzilla</project>
    <project>Sunbird</project>
  </mozilla-projects>
```

In this listing, we can see the XML declaration on the first line, followed by a mozilla-projects root node. This contains several project elements. Using the defined XSL vocabulary, an XSL stylesheet can now process this XML tree and return the data in any one of a number of formats. Viewing the preceding listing in Firefox, as shown in Figure 6-7, we can see that it has no style information attached, so the full document tree is displayed in the viewport.

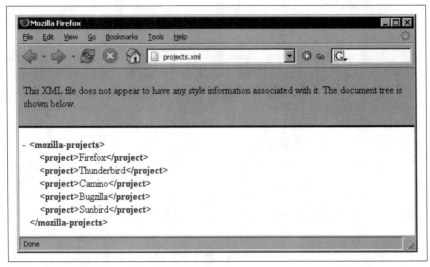

Figure 6-7. Completely unstyled XML content

We can now create a simple XSL stylesheet to apply some formatting to it and immediately view the output in Firefox. A possible stylesheet for this document, which gives it a header and an unordered list of projects, looks like this:

```
<?xml version="1.0"?>
<xsl:stylesheet version="1.0" xmlns:xsl="http://www.w3.org/1999/XSL/
Transform">

  <xsl:template match="/">
    <html>
      <head><title>Mozilla Projects</title></head>
      <body>
        <h1>Mozilla Projects</h1>
        <ol>
          <xsl:apply-templates select="mozilla-projects/project" />
```

```
    </ol>
  </body>
</html>
</xsl:template>

<xsl:template match="project">
  <li><xsl:value-of select="." /></li>
</xsl:template>

</xsl:stylesheet>
```

In this listing, we can see the standard XML definition; after all, XSL is valid XML. The top-level element defines an XSL stylesheet. Inside the stylesheet are two templates. The first will match on the root element in the XML, which is represented by "/". This template will output some standard HTML, including a title, heading, and the outline of an ordered list. The second template will match on project elements and will output a list item for each of the project elements.

When this XSL is processed, it will match the root element first and output the HTML until it reaches the xsl:apply-templates element. At this point, it will apply all the templates it is aware of that match the select statement. This select statement decides which nodes should be considered when the templates are applied. It will match on any project element that is a child of the root mozilla-projects element.

Tell Firefox About Your XSL

Before we can view the transformed XML in Firefox, we need to attach the stylesheet to the XML document. We might name the XML file *projects.xml* and the XSL file *projects.xsl*. To ask Firefox to transform the XML using our XSL file, we need to add another line between the XML definition and the mozilla-projects node so that the start of *projects.xml* file reads:

```
<?xml version="1.0"?>
<?xml-stylesheet type="text/xsl" href="projects.xsl"?>
<mozilla-projects>
...
```

There are many useful and interesting features of XSL that could be added to this simple transform. For example, if we want to order the projects alphabetically, we simply need to change the following line:

```
<xsl:apply-templates select="mozilla-projects/project" />
```

We will instead ask Firefox to sort on the current node, defined using select="." (the period represents the node in context):

```
<xsl:apply-templates select="mozilla-projects/project">
  <xsl:sort select="." />
</xsl:apply-templates>
```

Viewing the result in Firefox reveals the heading and complete list of projects. Because of the sorting option, these projects appear in alphabetical order, as shown in Figure 6-8.

Figure 6-8. Styled output showing basic XSL sort processing

See Also

- For further information on the XSL standard, refer to W3C's documentation at *http://www.w3.org/TR/xslt*.
- See *XSLT* (O'Reilly) for a more exhaustive introduction to XSL and XSLT.

 Mozilla and Firefox don't yet implement every detail of the XSL recommendation.

—James Vulling

 ## HACK #65 Work with Mozilla SOAP Services

Your web pages and XUL apps can speak the native language of web services.

Simple Object Access Protocol (SOAP) is a way for you to run methods (effectively function calls) on a remote server. Commands are formatted as XML documents on the client and sent to the server, which processes the commands and returns an XML-formatted response. This hack introduces SOAP with a simple temperature converter that converts between Fahrenheit and Celsius units.

SOAP is intended for remote servers running a web service, but it can be used on a local server (i.e., your workstation) for debugging purposes. SOAP is a form of object-oriented network programming. Clients connect to objects on the server, send commands, and receive responses in the form of messages.

Parameters in both the command and response are nested in XML elements that specify the name, data type, value, and various other attributes. This makes it relatively simple for both client and server to understand the context of what is being requested. Parameters are no longer just strings to be interpreted on the server, as they are in CGI, because SOAP has the vocabulary necessary to specify parameter types such as numbers, strings, URLs, and even complex types such as structs (tables of names and values, each with their own type).

There are many well-written SOAP tutorials on the Web and in print. A good, quick introduction to server-side SOAP can be found at O'Reilly's Perl.com:

http://www.perl.com/pub/a/2001/01/soap.html

Locate SOAP in Firefox

Firefox has a full set of SOAP client APIs that allow you to write all of the logic in JavaScript. These APIs make it quite simple to convert data held in Firefox (in form fields, variables, cookies, and elsewhere) into XML, package it up into a SOAP envelope, send the message to the SOAP server, and extract the values or errors from the response.

While it can be argued that anything you can do with SOAP can also be done with the Common Gateway Interface (CGI), and often with less overhead, SOAP in the browser has one real benefit: its use does not cause the web page to reload. So, your web application can communicate with the server, sending and receiving data, without ever having to redraw the page. There are other benefits too, not the least of which is the typing of data.

This is not the place for a full treatment of SOAP in Firefox. XUL Planet has full reference material for all components of Firefox's SOAP API:

http://www.xulplanet.com/references/xpcomref/group_WebServices.html

See also Ray Whitmer's "SOAP Scripts in Mozilla" for a basic introduction to scripting Firefox's SOAP services with JavaScript:

http://lxr.mozilla.org/mozilla/source/extensions/webservices/docs/Soap_Scripts_in_Mozilla.html

Start with XML Schema. XML Schema is a standardized way to describe a class of XML documents. Essentially, it dictates which elements can appear in a conforming XML document, and the type of each element. XML Schema allows for the treatment of XML documents as object instances, with the schema as the class definition. See the W3C's XML Schema Primer for a thorough introduction:

http://www.w3.org/TR/xmlschema-0/

Firefox has some built-in support for XML Schema, but at the time of writing, it is only used internally by the SOAP services. Work is ongoing to allow validation of any XML document against a schema, but this code has not yet been checked in to the source.

Review synchronous versus asynchronous messaging. Firefox supports both *synchronous* and *asynchronous* messaging with a SOAP server; the rules are the same as for the XMLHttpRequest object **[Hack #48]**. Synchronous messaging allows only one call to the server at a time, and all processing in the client stops until the response arrives. Asynchronous messaging allows any number of calls to be sent without waiting for a response, but you must also provide a receiver function that will be called for each response as it comes back.

Review security. Firefox can use SOAP in web pages and in the chrome. The only real difference between the two is security. From the chrome, SOAP calls can be sent to any server, because the chrome is a trusted source. Web pages can send SOAP requests only to servers in the same domain as the server from which the page was loaded.

If you load the HTML file into the browser from an untrusted URL, or from your own computer, the page's scripts can break this rule and communicate with any server by asking the user for extra privileges. Any untrusted page so loaded must include this security clearance request:

```
netscape.security.PrivilegeManager.enablePrivilege("UniversalBrowserRead");
```

If the user agrees, SOAP can be used to send a SOAP request to any server on the planet.

Understand the Server

To run SOAP scripts in Firefox, you need a web server with a SOAP endpoint. If you have access to a server with Perl installed, then install the CPAN module *SOAP::Lite* (*http://search.cpan.org/dist/SOAP-Lite/*), which you'll need installed for the following example.

Create a new file in your server's *cgi* directory called *soap-temperatures.cgi*, with the following contents:

```
#!/usr/bin/perl -w

use SOAP::Transport::HTTP;

SOAP::Transport::HTTP::CGI
  -> dispatch_to('Temperatures')
  -> handle;

package Temperatures;

sub f2c {
  my ( $class, $f ) = @_;

  return ( 5.0 / 9.0 ) * ( $f - 32 );
}

sub c2f {
  my ( $class, $c ) = @_;

  return 32 + ( $c * ( 9.0 / 5.0 ) );
}
```

This SOAP endpoint converts temperatures between Fahrenheit and Celsius. It's not the most useful web service ever provided, but it's good enough for our purposes.

This Perl script, run by the web server, does the following:

- Imports and activates the SOAP server routines, via the *SOAP::Transport::HTTP* bundle.

- Dispatches the incoming call to the appropriate endpoint (the *Temperatures* package), automatically calling the right function (f2c or c2f) depending on the message that was passed from the client.

- Converts the input parameter to Fahrenheit or Celsius and returns the result, which is then automatically encoded into a SOAP response and sent back to the client.

For more information on *SOAP::Lite* and setting up your own SOAP server, see *http://www.perl.com/pub/a/2001/01/soap.html* and *http://www.soaplite.com/*.

It's also possible to connect to any of hundreds of publicly available SOAP endpoints, such as those listed at XMethods (*http://www.xmethods.net*). We're not using those here, because many of them are more complex than is appropriate for your first SOAP hack and because they all use WSDL [Hack #67].

Make a Web Page with SOAP

Your JavaScript will typically set up a proxy object to represent the end-point on the server with which your script will communicate. Create methods in your proxy that mirror those on the endpoint. The rest of your scripts will then treat the proxy as if it were the object on the server. The proxy receives the commands and forwards them to the SOAP endpoint and then returns the results back to the caller.

The following JavaScript script uses a minor proxy implementation to handle the communication between the page's scripts (functions convertFtoC and convertCtoF) and the SOAP endpoint on the server:

```
<html><body>
<script type="text/javascript">
var tempsProxy = {
  invoke: function( call, param ) {
    var s = new SOAPCall( );
    s.transportURI = "http://localhost/cgi-bin/soapdemo.cgi";

    var params = new Array( );
    var p = new SOAPParameter( param );
    params.push( p );

    s.encode( 0, call, "urn:Temperatures", 0, null, 1, params );

    var r = s.invoke( );

    if ( r.fault == null ) {  // success
      r = r.getParameters(false, {})[0].value;
      return r;
    }
    else {  // fault
      var f = r.fault;
      var detail = f.detail;
      var ds = new XMLSerializer( );
      var detailStr = detail ? ds.serializeToString(detail) : "";

      alert( "Fault namespace: " + f.faultNamespaceURI
        + "\nFault code: "   + f.faultCode
        + "\nFault string: " + f.faultString
        + "\nFault actor: "  + f.faultActor
        + "\nDetail: "       + detailStr );

      return "#Err#";
    }
  },

  f2c: function( f ) {
    return this.invoke( "f2c", f );
  },
```

```
  c2f: function( c ) {
    return this.invoke( "c2f", c );
  }
};

function convertFtoC() {
  var f = document.getElementById( "F" ).value - 0;
  var c = tempsProxy.f2c( f );

  document.getElementById( "C" ).value = c;
}

function convertCtoF() {
  var c = document.getElementById( "C" ).value - 0;
  var f = tempsProxy.c2f( c );

  document.getElementById( "F" ).value = f;
}
</script>

<label>F: <input type="text" name="F" id="F" /></label>
<button onclick="convertFtoC()">F to C</button>
<br>
<label>C: <input type="text" name="C" ID="C" /></label>
<button onclick="convertCtoF()">C to F</button>
</body></html>
```

> If you're not running this on your workstation, you'll proba-
> bly have to change the bolded line of code to point to the
> right server.

You can find a more robust implementation of proxies, including a base
class you can use to build your own proxies, in Mozilla's source code:

http://lxr.mozilla.org/seamonkey/source/extensions/webservices/soap/tests/

The preceding HTML produces a web page similar to Figure 6-9.

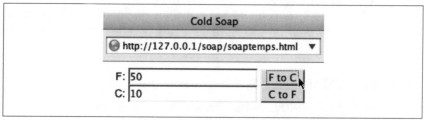

Figure 6-9. Sample web page that uses SOAP to convert temperatures

Put it into an HTML file, and load it into the browser through the same web server where you installed the Perl CGI.

After loading the page in your browser, enter a number in one of the fields and then click the conversion button to its right. The JavaScript sends the SOAP request to the server, receives the response, and puts the converted value into the other field, all without reloading the web page.

—Seth Dillingham

HACK #66 Work with Mozilla XML-RPC Services

Want web service scripting, but don't need SOAP's complexity? Use XML-RPC.

XML-RPC is a way for you to run methods on a server from a remote client. All commands and responses are formatted as XML. It's similar to SOAP [Hack #65], and both are intended to solve the same sorts of problems. However, XML-RPC is a much simpler protocol.

> XML-RPC was developed by UserLand Software. The specification is at *http://www.xmlrpc.com/spec*.

There are two major differences between XML-RPC and SOAP. First, XML-RPC has only eight data types: int, boolean, string, double, dateTime.iso8601, base64, array, and struct, whereas SOAP has many more data types and more can be added via XML Schema. Second, XML-RPC has no standardized discovery mechanisms, such as SOAP's WSDL or UDDI.

You might find that XML-RPC's "limitations" make it easier to learn than SOAP. With fewer requirements, it's easier to make your code work, and there are fewer things that can go wrong.

XML-RPC is widely deployed on web services across the Internet. Most weblog publishing software, for example, includes support for at least one of the major *external editor* protocols: Blogger API, MetaWeblog API, or Movable Type (mt) API.

Locate XML-RPC in Firefox

Firefox supports XML-RPC in the chrome. Your extensions can use XML-RPC to pass commands and data back and forth between Firefox and any web service with a published XML-RPC specification.

Review security arrangements. XML-RPC *used in the chrome* has no security restrictions. Scripts can talk to any server. At the time of writing, Firefox's native XML-RPC service is not yet available to ordinary web pages.

This limitation is bound to change eventually, because of XML-RPC's similarity to SOAP, which is available to scripts in web pages. If you need to use XML-RPC in a web page, there are some free, cross-platform XML-RPC libraries on the Web, written in JavaScript. One oft-used example is Scott Andrew's XML-RPC JavaScript Message Builder, available at *http://www. scottandrew.com/xml-rpc/*.

Start out on the right foot. The XML-RPC component that comes with Firefox is slightly imperfect. It's easy to fix, but until the official component has been fixed, its bug will have implications for any chrome extension you create (for distribution) that uses XML-RPC. You will either have to provide your own implementation of XML-RPC or include the *fixed* version we're about to describe. The latter option might require that your extension's license be compatible with the Mozilla Public License. You don't have to worry about this for hacking your own copy of Firefox.

To fix the bug:

1. Download *http://mozblog.mozdev.org/nsXmlRpcClient.js* to a file on disk.
2. Exit Firefox.
3. Open the *Components* folder in the Firefox installation area and move the existing *nsXmlRpcClient.js* file to a safe place.
4. Move the new file you downloaded in Step one to the *Components* folder.
5. Restart Firefox.

Without this fix, most XML-RPC calls will generate errors.

Create an XUL Test File

Since we need to work from within the security of the chrome, we'll create a small XUL extension that uses a testing service provided by XML-RPC.com (*http://www.xmlrpc.com*). Their server has a function called examples. getStateList. It expects a list of numbers between 1 and 50 and returns a string that contains a comma-separated list of the names of the U.S. states that were specified. States are numbered by their date of acceptance to the Union—oldest first.

Build the frontend XUL file. Our interface needs are minor: a text field to enter some state numbers, a text field to display the results, and a button to run the XML-RPC call. Create an XUL file named *xml-rpc.xul* with the following contents:

```
<?xml version="1.0"?>
<?xml-stylesheet href="chrome://global/skin/" type="text/css"?>
<!DOCTYPE window>
<window title="XML-RPC States"
  xmlns="http://www.mozilla.org/keymaster/gatekeeper/there.is.only.xul"
  style="width: 4in; height: 1.5in;">

  <script type="application/x-javascript" src="xml-rpc.js" />

  <vbox flex="1" style="margin: 8px;">
    <text value="Enter a state code:"/>
    <hbox>
      <textbox flex="1" rows="1" id="statecodes"/>
      <button label="List States" onclick="listStates()"/>
    </hbox>
    <text value="States:"/>
    <hbox flex="1">
      <textbox flex="1" id="states" multiline="true"/>
    </hbox>
  </vbox>
</window>
```

Script XMP-RPC with JavaScript. Just as with SOAP and WSDL, your best bet when scripting with XML-RPC is to create a proxy object to hide the communication details from the rest of your script.

> This will also make it much easier to switch from XML-RPC to SOAP or some other protocol, should you ever choose to do so.

Create a file named *xml-rpc.js* with the following contents:

```
const Cc = Components.classes;
const Ci = Components.interfaces;

var statesProxy = {
  _xmlRpcClient: null,

  get xmlrpc() {
    if ( ! this._xmlRpcClient ) {
      this._xmlRpcClient = Cc["@mozilla.org/xml-rpc/client;1"]
        .createInstance( Ci.nsIXmlRpcClient );
    }
    return this._xmlRpcClient;
  },
```

```
invoke: function( call, aParams, cb ) {
  this.xmlrpc.init( "http://www.xmlrpc.com/RPC2" );

  var Listener = {
    onResult: function( client, ctxt, result ) {
      // assumes result is string
      window[ cb ]( result.QueryInterface( Ci.nsISupportsCString ).data );
    },

    onFault: function( client, ctxt, fault ) { },
    onError: function( client, ctxt, status, errorMsg ) { }
  };

  this.xmlrpc.asyncCall( Listener, null, call, aParams, aParams.length );
},

listStates: function( aStateNums ) {
  var xmlrpc = this.xmlrpc;
  var stateList = xmlrpc.createType( xmlrpc.ARRAY, {} );
  var stateCode;

  for ( var i = 0; i < aStateNums.length; i++ ) {
    stateCode = xmlrpc.createType( xmlrpc.INT, {} );
    stateCode.data = aStateNums[ i ] - 0;
    stateList.AppendElement( stateCode );
  }

  var params = new Array( stateList );

  this.invoke( "examples.getStateList", params, "listStatesCallback" );
  }
};

function listStates() {
  var sList = document.getElementById( "statecodes" ).value;
  var aStateNums = sList.split( /[, ]+/ );

  statesProxy.listStates( aStateNums );
}

function listStatesCallback( result ) {
  document.getElementById( "states" ).value = result;
}
```

Create the Firefox extension. Create an extension [Hack #88] and move the XUL
and JavaScript file into its content folder. Assuming that the name of your
extension is *xmlrpc*, you can then run your test with the URL *chrome://
xmlrpc/content/xml-rpc.xul*. You can also launch Firefox from the command
line with the -chrome switch to open only the XML-RPC window, as follows:

```
firefox --chrome chrome://xmlrpc/content/xml-rpc.xul
```

With the XUL open in Firefox, enter some numbers in the first field, separated by commas or spaces. Press the List States button. If all is well, the names of the matching states will appear in the second field, separated by commas, as shown in Figure 6-10.

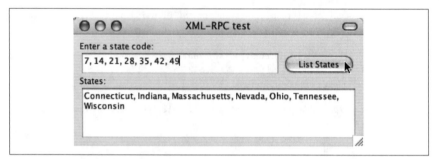

Figure 6-10. *The final, working version of the XML-RPC test file*

—*Seth Dillingham*

 ## HACK #67   Work with Mozilla WSDL Services

Want an easy way to use SOAP web services? WSDL might be the answer.

When scripting a web service with SOAP [Hack #65], you create a proxy object in the browser to represent the object or service you're controlling on the server. Other scripts in the browser can use that proxy as if it were the actual server resource. This is an intuitive approach to web service scripting.

Creating your own proxies can be tedious, however. You must write methods to mirror all of the endpoint's methods that you plan to use. These methods will all do basically the same thing: stuff the input into SOAP parameters, invoke the SOAPCall, and extract the results. Some of this process can be abstracted, but for a web service with more than a couple of methods, you're going to spend a lot of time writing and testing your proxy.

Locate WSDL in Firefox

WSDL (Web Services Description Language) is an XML grammar to describe all of the methods, parameters, and faults (errors) of a web service. A WSDL file lists everything, including the endpoints that can be accessed, the methods available on those endpoints, the parameters and types expected by the methods, and the parameters and faults returned by the methods.

Given the URL to a WSDL file, Firefox can solve many of the tedious aspects of scripting web services for you. With just a few lines of JavaScript, it can create a complete proxy of the web service. Your scripts can then call the methods on that proxy as if they were working with a local, native object. All of the SOAP and XML aspects of the communication remain out of view.

Some of the best documentation on using WSDL in Firefox (or Mozilla) is found at *http://devedge.netscape.com*. In particular, see:

> *http://devedge.netscape.com/viewsource/2003/wsdl/01/*

This site went offline without warning in late 2004; if that happens again, then find it in the Wayback Machine: *http://www.waybackmachine.org*.

Create a WSDL File

We'll create our own WSDL to work with the SOAP endpoint created in "Work with Mozilla SOAP Services" [Hack #65]. This is not the place for a full tutorial on WSDL. There are numerous WSDL tutorials and reference documents on the Web. Instead, just save the following code as *soapdemo.wsdl* in your web site:

```
<?xml version="1.0" ?>
<definitions name="TempConvertService"
  targetNamespace="http://localhost/soapdemo.wsdl"
  xmlns="http://schemas.xmlsoap.org/wsdl/"
  xmlns:tns="http://localhost/soapdemo.wsdl"
  xmlns:xsd="http://www.w3.org/1999/XMLSchema"
  xmlns:soap="http://schemas.xmlsoap.org/wsdl/soap/">

  <message name="F2CInput">
    <part name="inputInteger" type="xsd:integer"/>
  </message>

  <message name="F2COutput">
    <part name="return" type="xsd:integer"/>
  </message>

  <portType name="TempConvertPortType">
    <operation name="f2c">
      <input message="tns:F2CInput"/>
      <output message="tns:F2COutput"/>
    </operation>
  </portType>

  <binding name="TempConvertSoapBinding" type="tns:TempConvertPortType">
    <soap:binding style="rpc" transport="http://schemas.xmlsoap.org/soap/
http"/>
    <operation name="f2c">
      <soap:operation soapAction="http://localhost/Temperatures#f2c"/>
      <input>
        <soap:body use="encoded" namespace="http://example.com/Temperatures"
          encodingStyle="http://schemas.xmlsoap.org/soap/encoding/"/>
```

```
      </input>
      <output>
        <soap:body use="encoded" namespace="http://example.com/Temperatures"
          encodingStyle="http://schemas.xmlsoap.org/soap/encoding/"/>
      </output>
    </operation>
  </binding>

  <service name="TempConvertService">
    <documentation>
      Convert temperatures between Fahrenheit and Celsius
    </documentation>
    <port name="TempConvertPort" binding="tns:TempConvertSoapBinding">
      <soap:address location="http://localhost/cgi-bin/soapdemo.cgi"/>
    </port>
  </service>
</definitions>
```

 Take note of the URL, wherever you put it, because you'll
need it in the next step.

This WSDL file provides all of the information that Firefox needs to create a
proxy with a single method named F2C. Let's put it to use.

Create the Proxy in JavaScript

Before we start, make a copy of the HTML file from "Work with Mozilla
SOAP Services" [Hack #65]. Open that file in your text editor and strip out the
JavaScript; we're going to replace it with all-new code for using an automati-
cally generated, asynchronous proxy.

Add two variables to the top of your (now empty) script:

```
var wsdl_uri = "http://localhost/soapdemo.wsdl";  // adjust as necessary
var gProxy = null;
```

Now, we can create our proxy with two lines of JavaScript: the first creates a
WebServiceProxyFactory, and the second asks the factory for a new proxy.
Wrapping it up in a function with some error trapping results in the follow-
ing code:

```
function createProxy( aCreationListener ){
  try {
    var factory = new WebServiceProxyFactory();
    factory.createProxyAsync( wsdl_uri, "TempConvertPort",
      "", true, aCreationListener );
  } catch ( ex ) {
    alert("Failed to create the proxy: "+ ex);
  }
}
```

The bolded line is the key. It provides five parameters:

- The URL of the WSDL file
- The name of the port from the service element of the WSDL file
- An ignored parameter
- A Boolean that states if the calls we'll make through the proxy will be asynchronous
- A listener object to receive notifications from the proxy when a call is completed

The documentation for WebServiceProxyFactory describes a synchronous version of the same call, called createProxy(). At the time of writing, createProxy() throws an exception that indicates that it hasn't yet been implemented. For more information, see *http://www.xulplanet.com/ references/objref/WebServiceProxyFactory.html*.

Create an Asynchronous Listener

JavaScript is single threaded, but Firefox is not. Since our proxy handles all calls asynchronously, every method run on the proxy kicks off another communications thread with the server but returns control to our script immediately. When the server returns a result, the proxy notifies whatever listener we provide. The following is a simple approach to a listener. It's not robust enough for all applications, but it is fine for this hack:

```
function Convert( value, actionToTake ){
  if ( !gProxy ) {
    // create listener as a local so that a different
    // listener is created each time
    var listener = {
      // called when the proxy is ready
      onLoad: function( aProxy ) {
        gProxy = aProxy;
        gProxy.setListener( listener );
        gProxy[ actionToTake ]( value );
      },

      onError: function( aError ) {
        alert( "An error has occured: " + aError.message );
      },

      // callback function names are hardcoded
      // in Firefox to {methodname}Callback
      F2CCallback: function( aResult ) {
        document.getElementById( "C" ).value = aResult;
      }
    };
```

```
  createProxy( listener );
} else {
  gProxy[ actionToTake ]( value );
}
}
```

Convert( ) takes two parameters: the value to be converted and the name of the operation to call on the proxy (which is the same as the name of the operation defined in the WSDL file). Our WSDL file defines only a single operation, f2c, but we've left room here to expand it to include the c2f function found in "Work with Mozilla SOAP Services" [Hack #65].

> The name of the operation called on the proxy defines the name of the method called on the listener object. It's always {actionToTake}Callback.

The only remaining piece is the convertFtoC( ) function called by the button in the HTML. As we've seen, it just needs to pass the value for conversion and the name of the method to call on the proxy.

```
function convertFtoC( ){
  Convert( document.getElementById( "F" ).value, 'f2c' );
}
```

> Again, this is just a convention for this hack. There are many other ways to do this.

Note Security Issues

If you've completed both "Work with Mozilla SOAP Services" [Hack #65] and this hack, you'd expect that you could just open the HTML file in your browser and start converting temperatures from Fahrenheit to Celsius. You'd almost be right. Firefox (and all Gecko browsers) have a unique security restriction that applies only to web services. Before sending the first SOAP call, they first try to load a file from the root of the web service's server called *web-scripts-access.xml*. If the file cannot be found, if it is not well formed, or if it does not permit loading of scripts from your web server, all calls to the proxy object will fail. This restriction applies to remote servers.

To permit all web remote service calls (which is good enough for testing this hack across the Web), create a file at the root of the remote web server with just one line:

```
<wsa:webScriptAccess xmlns:wsa="http://www.mozilla.org/2002/soap/security"/>
```

The intent of this file is to allow a web service to control which other services and domains they are willing to allow access to their service. For more information about this security issue and configuring the access control file, see:

http://lxr.mozilla.org/mozilla/source/extensions/webservices/docs/New_Security_Model.html.

After saving this file at the root of your web server (the same server that's hosting the SOAP endpoint), your mini WSDL-based web application should run properly.

—Seth Dillingham

HACK #68 Make Applications and Extensions with XUL

Make an application rather than a web page by filling a Firefox window with XUL.

Many books have been written on the craft of making web pages with HTML, and this hack won't cover that broad category. Crafting whole XUL applications (or *extensions*, which are application pieces) is a similar process. XUL can run standalone (as discussed in this hack) or mixed with HTML [Hack #60]. There is extensive source material on XUL development. Chapters 7 and 8 in this book explain how to deploy or install XUL content once it's created. This hack offers a first taste of the XUL tags that can go into such content.

XUL describes user interface elements such as menu bars and scrollbars, just as XHTML describes links and paragraphs of text. It addresses a problem space that HTML is not ideally designed for. It allows record management, content management, control systems, and other nontextual applications to run over the Web without having to bend hypertext content into shape to do it.

Make and Display an XUL Demo

The following document is the start of an XUL-based application. It should be stored in a file with a *.xul* extension, such as *test.xul*:

```
<?xml version="1.0"?>
<?xml-stylesheet href="chrome://global/skin/"?>
<?xul-overlay    href="chrome://example/content/extras.xul"?>
<window
    xmlns="http://www.mozilla.org/keymaster/gatekeeper/there.is.only.xul"
    title="Example App"
>
```

```
<script src="chrome://example/content/example.js"/>
<stringbundle id="str-example"
  src="chrome://example/locale/example.properties"/>

<command id="cmd_start" oncommand="doStart();"/>
<command id="cmd_stop" oncommand="doStop();"/>

<keyset id="hotkeys">
  <key id="key_start" key="A" command="cmd_start"/>
  <key id="key_stop"  key="Z" command="cmd_stop"/>
</keyset>

<toolbox id="top-controls">
  <menubar id="top-menubar">

    <menu label="File" accesskey="F">
      <menupopup id="menu1">
        <menuitem id="menu_start" label="Start" accesskey="A"
          command="cmd_start"/>
        <menuitem id="menu_stop"  label="Stop" accesskey="Z"
          command="cmd_stop"/>
      </menupopup>
    </menu>

    <box flex="1"/>

    <menu label="Help" accesskey="H">
      <menupopup>
        <menuitem id="menu_help" label="Get help" accesskey="H"
          command="cmd_help"/>
      </menupopup>
    </menu>
  </menubar>
</toolbox>

<hbox flex="1">
  <vbox flex="1">
    <description>Left</description>
  </vbox>
  <scrollbar orient="vertical"/>
  <vbox flex="1">
    <description>Right</description>
    <tabbox>
      <tabs>
        <tab label="First"/>
        <tab label="Second"/>
      </tabs>
      <tabpanels>
        <tabpanel>
          <description>First Content</description>
        </tabpanel>
        <tabpanel>
          <description>Second Content</description>
```

```
        </tabpanel>
      </tabpanels>
    </tabbox>
  </vbox>
</hbox>

<stack style="font-family: Arial" flex="1">
  <description style="color:red; font-size:48px;">Red</description>
  <description style="color:green; font-size:24px;"> Green
  </description>
</stack>
</window>
```

Notice in this listing how keystroke and menu items are tied to commands; the commands' ID values are put in those items' command attributes. Similarly <command> tag oncommand attributes specify specific JavaScript functions. That's how you get an XUL window to do any processing—by hooking commands up to keystrokes and GUI features. The other tags show some typical XUL widgets that you can't easily create with plain HTML: a menu bar with two menus, a standalone scrollbar that isn't attached to anything, a tab box, and stacked text.

The bolded lines should be omitted or commented out with XML comments (<!-- and -->) if this file is created for ad hoc testing purposes. These lines, which include chrome: URLs, can only be used if the XUL document is bundled up into a chrome package [Hack #86]. You can put back the <script> tags if you use locally stored scripts, for example:

```
<script src="test.js"/>
```

To test the reduced file, just load its URL into a normal browser window, or start Firefox from the command line as follows. For Windows:

```
firefox -chrome file:///C:/tmp/test.xul
```

For Unix/Linux and the Mac OS X BSD command line:

```
firefox -chrome file:///tmp/test.xul
```

Figure 6-11 shows the resulting window halfway through a mouse menu-selection gesture.

Send XUL Application Data to a Server

XUL doesn't have the HTML concept of a form; the whole XUL window effectively is a form. To send data to the server that the *.xul* page came from, change the previous example as follows.

You must also have the server set up properly [Hack #27].

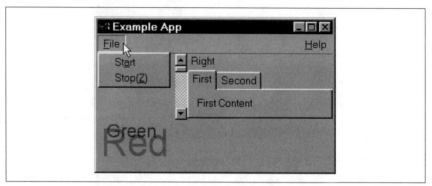

Figure 6-11. Sample XUL window

Replace this line:

```
<script src="chrome://example/content/example.js"/>
```

with this line:

```
<script src="example.js"/>
```

Create the *example.js* file in the same directory as the *.xul* file. It contains this script:

```
function doStart( ) {
  var req = new XMLHttpRequest( );
  req.open("GET", "test.cgi?action=start", false);
  try {
    req.send("");
    if (req.status / 100 != 2 )
      alert("Server Failed! HTTP status: " + req.status);
  }
  catch (e) {
    alert("Request Failed! Error: " + e);
  }
}
```

The try wrapper block is required only if you are too lazy to look in the JavaScript Console for errors. Since the doStart( ) function is hooked up to the cmd_start command, you can run it by choosing Start from the File menu. Security restrictions prevent you from submitting data to servers other than to the one the .XUL file originated from. If you load the *.xul* file from an ad hoc local file, such form submissions have nowhere to go, and an error will result. To get around this, the file must be placed in the chrome [Hack #86] and a full chrome: URL must be used.

See Also

- See Chapters 7 and 8 of this book for more on managing XUL content once it is created. For the theory and detail of XUL programming, see the remaining references in this list.

- *Rapid Application Development with Mozilla* (Prentice Hall Professional Technical References) by Nigel McFarlane is a comprehensive description of and tutorial on XUL and many related Mozilla technologies. On the subject of XUL, it is the most systematic and popular work in print.

- *Creating Applications With Mozilla* (O'Reilly) by Brian King et al is a shorter treatment that provides a speedy tour through the world of XUL.

- XULPlanet *(http://www.xulplanet.com)* by Neil Deakin et al is a dictionary-like reference to XUL tags that also contains a paced but narrowly focused tutorial for beginner programmers.

- Several older books also exist on Mozilla topics. In general, they are of little use when learning XUL, either due to age, incompleteness, or chosen approach.

 HACK
#69

Make New Tags and Widgets with XBL

Don't like the set of HTML or XUL tags that browsers provide? Make new ones.

The HTML and XHTML standards allow a content author to extend the set of composition elements on a web page by applying special styles to the <div> and <span> tags and their content. A styled <div> block might appear to be a navigation bar, an advertisement, or some other specialized content that HTML does not explicitly define. XML Binding Language (XBL) is an alternate strategy for naming features of web pages. This hack shows how you might use it.

XBL is a Mozilla technology that's slowly being adopted by the W3C. It first appeared at the W3C as a technical note at *http://www.w3.org/TR/2001/NOTE-xbl-20010223/*. More recently, it has entered the formal standardization track via the sXBL standard (the *s* indicates that XBL's initial standard use is in SVG). That standard is here: *http://www.w3.org/TR/sXBL*. Mozilla XBL syntax is not yet the same as the W3C syntax, but the concepts are all the same. It will match the standard one day.

In Firefox, XBL is used to create a new tag for any XML or HTML dialect, but most frequently for XUL. Public or strictly conforming HTML and XHTML documents should not be hacked with XBL. Use it for custom, private documents only. An XBL binding written in XML is *attached* to a tag using a Mozilla-specific CSS style:

```
tagname { -moz-binding : url("binding-definition.xml"); }
```

It's also possible to say *the binding is bound to the tag*, but the idea of attachment will get you into far less trouble.

Make a <sidebar> element for HTML

HTML and XHTML can achieve a lot when combined with CSS, but they don't contain any direct support for *sidebars*. Sidebars are blocks of text, usually floating on the right side of the screen, that contain information that's an aside to the main flow of the text. Let's make a <sidebar> tag using XBL. Here's an HTML equivalent, to begin with:

```
<div style="float : right; background-color : lightyellow;">
  <hr />
  <div style="font-weight : bold;">Sidebar Title</div>
  <p>This is the content of the sidebar</p>
  <p>The content could be long</p>
  <div style="text-align : right; font-style : italic;">Anon.</div>
  <hr />
</div>
```

Using XBL, we extract the structural content into a file named *sidebar.xml*:

```
<?xml version="1.0"?>
<bindings xmlns="http://www.mozilla.org/xbl"
          xmlns:xbl="http://www.mozilla.org/xbl"
          xmlns:xht="http://www.w3.org/1999/xhtml">
  <binding id="sidebar">

    <resources>
      <stylesheet src="sidebar.css"/>
    </resources>

    <content>
      <xht:hr />
      <xht:div class="sidebar-title" xbl:inherits="xbl:text=title" />
      <children />
      <xht:div class="sidebar-author" xbl:inherits="xbl:text=author" />
      <xht:hr />
    </content>

  </binding>
</bindings>
```

The <content> part matches the XHTML content, with a few namespaces thrown in. Note the use of XBL's special inherits attribute and <children> tag mixed into the XHTML. The <resources> section is optional. In this case, *sidebar.css* might contain the following styles:

```
.sidebar-title { font-weight : bold; }
.sidebar-author { text-align : right; font-style: italic; }
```

These styles affect the tags *inside* the content part of the binding. These tags can't be styled from HTML. To attach this binding, HTML pages must include extra styles. These styles affect the *whole* binding. The following file, *bind-sidebar.css*, is an example of such a style:

```
sidebar {
  -moz-binding     : url("sidebar.xml#sidebar");
  background-color : lightyellow;
  float            : right;
}
```

The HTML or XHTML page must include this stylesheet with a <link> tag. Once the binding is created, a web page can reuse the structural content freely:

```
<html>
  <head>
    <link rel="stylesheet" href="bind-sidebar.css" type="text/css">
  </head>
  <body>
    <p>

    <sidebar title="First Sidebar" author="Anon.">
      Foo Content
      <br>
      Bar Content
    </sidebar>

    Lorem ipsum dolor sit amet ...

    <sidebar title="Second Sidebar" author="- me.">
      Short Content
    </sidebar>

    Lorem ipsum dolor sit amet ...
  </body>
</html>
```

Figure 6-12 shows this HTML page after the bound <sidebar> tags are rendered.

Make a Custom XUL Widget

A more typical use of XBL is to increase the set of widgets that XUL offers. XUL's default widget set is defined in a file called *xul.css* in the chrome. You can increase the set of widgets by using any stylesheet, or you can hack that file directly [Hack #75]. Figure 6-13 shows an example of a simple new widget called checkbutton.

Each time you click the button, the small checkbox is toggled on or off. The checkbutton widget is hooked up to the <checkbutton> tag using CSS, the same as in the HTML case:

```
checkbutton { -moz-binding : url("checkbutton.xml#checkbutton"); }
```

There are no extra styles in this case. XUL relies on the <?xml-stylesheet?> processing instruction to load CSS. The widget has the focus (the dotted

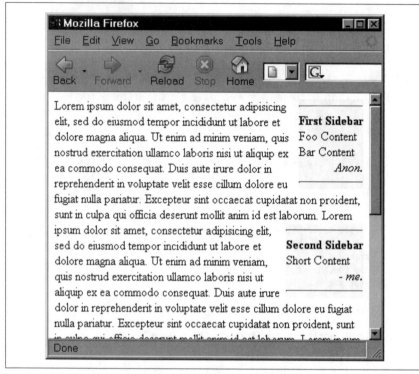

Figure 6-12. HTML page with <sidebar> tags derived from XBL

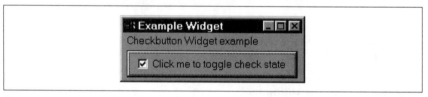

Figure 6-13. XUL window showing XBL checkbutton widget

line), because it's already been clicked a few times. The tag used to create this example is simply this:

```
<checkbutton label="Click me to toggle check state" checked="true"/>
```

Unlike text, widgets are active and responsive, so the checkbutton XBL binding has more object-like features than the sidebar example. Here's the binding definition:

```
<?xml version="1.0"?>
<bindings xmlns="http://www.mozilla.org/xbl"
        xmlns:xbl="http://www.mozilla.org/xbl"  <!-- for xbl:inherits -->
    xmlns:xul="http://www.mozilla.org/keymaster/gatekeeper/there.is.only.xul">
    <binding id="checkbutton">
```

```
<content>
  <xul:button>
    <xul:checkbox xbl:inherits="checked,label"/>
  </xul:button>
</content>

<implementation implements="nsIDOMXULCheckboxElement">
  <property name="checked"
    onget="return this.getAttribute('checked') == 'true';"
    onset="return this.setAttribute('checked', val);" />
</implementation>

<handlers>
  <handler event="click"><![CDATA[
    var state = this.getAttribute("checked") == "true" ? 1 : 0;
    this.setAttribute("checked", state ? "false" : "true");
  ]]></handler>
</handlers>

    </binding>
  </bindings>
```

The <implementation> section can define fields, properties, and methods, mostly not illustrated in this example. The <handlers> section defines handlers, in this case, a single handler for the click DOM 2 event. This handler will fire if no handler is explicitly placed on the <checkbutton> tag.

Here's a sample XUL document that benefits from this binding:

```
<?xml version="1.0"?>
<?xml-stylesheet href="chrome://global/skin/"?>
<?xml-stylesheet href="bind-check.css"?>

<window
  xmlns="http://www.mozilla.org/keymaster/gatekeeper/there.is.only.xul"
  title="Example Widget">

  <description>Test widget for the checkbutton binding</description>
  <checkbutton label="Click me to toggle check state" checked="true"/>
</window>
```

HACK #70   Work with RDF Facts

Make Firefox act like a small database server that is smart about RDF data.

The W3C's Resource Description Framework (RDF) standard is one of the more complex XML standards. RDF is an application of XML, but it makes little use of the XML tag hierarchy. Instead, it turns any specified tags into *facts*. Facts are stored in memory separate from the DOM tree of the RDF content. This hack shows how to use facts. Firefox has both scripting and direct XML support for facts.

What is Firefox RDF good for? It's a very general mechanism for managing any kind of data, whether that data fits in an XML hierarchy or not. The output of an SQL query is an obvious example.

Learn RDF

If you are new to RDF, be selective about the material you lean on. Much RDF literature is not suited for beginners. The book *Rapid Application Development with Mozilla* (Prentice Hall PTR) is one source of a digestible tutorial. An alternate approach is to learn a little Prolog. RDF and Prolog are both examples of *propositional calculus* (a field of mathematical logic). On top of these ideas, you also need a bit of experience scripting Mozilla XPCOM components.

Very briefly, RDF is a more general way of representing data than relational tables. RDF is concerned with making statements about *things*. Each statement is comprised of three pieces of information: the thing we're making the statement about, a *property* of the thing, and the *value* of that property. In RDF parlance, this is called a *triple*, and the thing, property, and values are called *subject*, *predicate*, and *object*, respectively. For Example, *Firefox Hacks* (the thing) has an *author* (the property) of Nigel McFarlane (the value).

To compare RDF with SQL, here's an example of two SQL tables that have one record each. They might look like this, with data shown in plain type and schema information in bold:

```
table employee:

empid name   jobcode
----- ------ -------
2     Fred   33

table department:

depid name   manager
----- ------ -------
3     sales  2
```

RDF requires that all information be stated as facts. Look at the standard (or chrome) *.rdf* examples for a first glimpse. Here's a shorthand (one of several) for the facts covering the above two tables:

```
<- employee, empid, 2 ->
<- 2, name, Fred ->
<- 2, jobcode, 33 ->

<- department, depid, 3 ->
<- 3, name, sales ->
<- 3, manager, 2 ->
```

That's six facts, with the first one reading "employee has a property empid with value 2." Each fact must have three parts (obscurely named *subject*, *predicate*, and *object*). That provides regularity and makes it possible for processing systems to act in a general way. A set of facts are lumped together into a *fact store*. No tables are required. Here's a sample RDF document for these facts:

```
<?xml version="1.0"?>
<RDF xmlns="http://www.w3.org/1999/02/22-rdf-syntax-ns#">

  <Description about="urn:example:employee">
    <empid resource="urn:example:key:2">
  </Description>                            <!-- one fact -->

  <Description about="urn:example:key:2
    name="Fred"
    jobcode="33"/>                         <!-- two facts -->

  <Description about="urn:example:department">
    <depid resource="urn:example:key:3">
  </Description>                            <!-- one fact -->

  <Description about="urn:example:key:3
    <name>sales</name>
    <manager resource="urn:example:key:2"/>
  </Description>                            <!-- two facts -->

</RDF>
```

You can see that the RDF content is hard to digest, which is why shorthand notations are popular. If you prefer procedures, read this next bit on scripting RDF first. If you're more visual and interactive, skip down to the bit about XUL templates. If you understand database transactions, try the example in "Connect SQL to XUL" [Hack #72], although that one is more advanced.

Use of RDF facts in Firefox is restricted to secure content and to remotely delivered XUL. There are plans to make some RDF available to ordinary web pages, but that functionality is not ready as of this writing.

Manipulate Content in Firefox's Head

To load an RDF file, you need a *datasource* that can turn XML into facts. Firefox provides a one-stop shop for datasources called the *RDF Service*. You can also make your own datasource. Here's a script that loads the contents of an RDF URL into a new datasource:

```
var klass = Components.classes["@mozilla.org/rdf/rdf-service;1"];
var rs = klass.createInstance(Components.interfaces.nsIRDFService);
var ds = rs.GetDataSourceBlocking("file:///tmp/test.rdf");
```

The URL specified is a Unix one. For Windows, try *file:///C|/tmp/test.rdf*. The GetDataSourceBlocking( ) method is preferable to GetDataSource( ) if you're just starting out. It avoids strange behavior caused by asynchronous loading.

After this code runs, the ds object holds the datasource. It should be retained as a variable as long as the set of RDF facts is needed. The datasource is invisibly full of RDF facts, and you can add, delete, modify, or query it as you see fit. In RDF land, *asserting* a fact pretty much means *adding* or *inserting* one. The methods that do so are defined in the file *nsIRDFDataSource.idl*. Read that file here:

http://lxr.mozilla.org/mozilla/source/rdf/base/idl/nsIRDFDataSource.idl

Here's some code that checks whether Fred is still employed and adds Joe if that's not the case. This kind of thing is similar to transaction processing in SQL:

```
var found     = false;
var ns        = "http://www.w3.org/1999/02/22-rdf-syntax-ns#"

// RDF nodes
var pred_name  = rs.GetResource(ns + "name");
var pred_empid = rs.GetResource(ns + "empid");
var emp        = rs.GetResource("urn:example:employee");

var who        = rs.GetLiteral("Fred");
var dep        = rs.GetLiteral("sales");

// query for Fred
var empid = ds.GetSource(pred_name, who, true);
if ( empid != null ) {
  found = ds.HasAssertion(emp, pred_empid, empid, true);
}

// insert Joe
if (!found)
{
  who   = rs.GetLiteral("Joe");
  empid = rs.GetResource("urn:example:key:" + 5);
  ds.Assert(emp,   pred_empid, empid, true);
  ds.Assert(empid, pred_name,  who, true);
}
```

In this code, the variables pred_name and pred_empid are roughly equivalent to object property names: "employee 3 has a property called name with a value of Fred." pred is short for *predicate*. For RDF reasons, predicates must be URLs. The URLs are never downloaded. Each piece of a fact must be an nsIRDFNode object or a subtype of that type, so we have to construct them laboriously. The logic is simple: test for the presence of two facts and insert two more if necessary.

The test part is done with the GetSource( ) and HasAssertion( ) methods. The latter method tests for the existence of one fact. The former tests for any fact that has its second and third parts as described, and returns the unknown first part. That's how we find out Fred's employee number. Always use true as the final argument; it's almost irrelevant, but it's required. Here are the two facts we test for:

```
<- 2, name, Fred ->
<- employee, empid, 2 ->
```

If either one is missing, then Fred's not there, so Joe is added in using the Assert( ) method. You can add a fully described fact only. Here are Joe's two facts:

```
<- employee, empid, 5 ->
<- 5, name, Joe ->
```

Unlike SQL, there's no commit required, since the datasource is all in memory. The whole thing can be flushed back out to disk as RDF if required:

```
var rds = ds.QueryInterface(Components.interfaces.nsIRDFRemoteDataSource);
rds.Flush( );
```

You can also receive notification if a datasource has changed [Hack #71], either because it was refreshed from its origin or because extra facts were inserted by scripts.

Display Facts with Templates

Firefox XUL templates are one of the hardest Mozilla technologies, but a lot can be done with them once the art is learned. When starting out, *do not* experiment with tree-based templates, which are tricky, but *do* regularly check all the XUL and RDF XML that you create with an XML validation tool [Hack #59].

Here's a simple XUL page that displays the dogs and cats in an RDF datasource using two templates. This example uses the *simple template syntax* (as opposed to examples of the extended template syntax [Hack #72]). Notice here (everywhere) how the template syntax hooks into the normal XUL syntax:

```
<?xml version="1.0"?>
<?xml-stylesheet href="chrome://global/skin"?>
<window
 xmlns="http://www.mozilla.org/keymaster/gatekeeper/there.is.only.xul">
  <hbox>
    <vbox style="border:solid thin"
```

```
           datasources="pets.rdf" ref="urn:test:dogs">
           <template>
             <label uri="rdf:*"
               value="Dog: rdf:http://www.example.org/test#name"/>
           </template>
         </vbox>
         <vbox style="border:solid thin"
           datasources="pets.rdf" ref="urn:test:cats">
           <template>
             <label uri="rdf:*"
               value="Cat: rdf:http://www.example.org/test#name"/>
           </template>
         </vbox>
       </hbox>
     </window>
```

A template always starts with the datasources attribute lodged with the parent tag of the <template> tag. Figure 6-14 shows one window that might result.

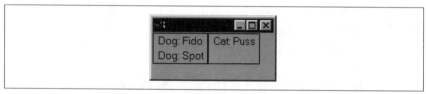

Figure 6-14. Simple XUL window showing two template queries

The contents of the window are driven by the datasource that is filled with facts from *pets.rdf*. Here's a sample file with three pets in it. The highlighted items are used by the XUL template code. Compare the two documents. This is standard RDF, but laid out in a way that templates can automatically understand:

```
     <?xml version="1.0"?>
     <RDF
       xmlns:Test="http://www.example.org/test#"
       xmlns="http://www.w3.org/1999/02/22-rdf-syntax-ns#">

       <Description about="http://www.example.org">
         <Test:Container>
           <Seq about="urn:test:dogs">
             <li resource="urn:test:dog1"/>
             <li resource="urn:test:dog2"/>
           </Seq>
           <Seq about="urn:test:cats">
             <li resource="urn:test:cat1"/>
           </Seq>
         </Test:Container>
       </Description>
       <Description about="urn:test:dog1" Test:name="Fido"/>
```

```
<Description about="urn:test:dog2" Test:name="Spot"/>
<Description about="urn:test:cat1" Test:name="Puss"/>
</RDF>
```

Even though there's just one datasource and just one RDF file, the displayed content is revealed two different ways. If the two templates were identical, the same content would be displayed in each half of the page. If the RDF file changes, the displayed XUL changes without any change to the XUL file. The user interface is thus data-driven.

Work with RSS Feeds

Suck syndicated news and blog updates into Firefox using scripts.

Really Simple Syndication (RSS) is a collection of XML-based file formats. RSS support in Firefox is in flux at the time of writing, and that heavily affects the ease with which you can get anything done. This hack provides some jumping-off points for integrating this technology with Firefox.

> Firefox and Thunderbird RSS support is ongoing, and remarks made here should be reviewed for versions that are greater than 1.0. That said, most of the comments here are general and should be accurate for some time.

Understand the RSS Mess

Here is a list of reality checks for RSS:

- There is no *feeding* of any kind. RSS does not use an event or message-forwarding architecture, unless an RSS client and RSS server pair are particularly sophisticated. In order to receive RSS information, the client must poll the server at regular intervals. This is what Mozilla technology does.

- RSS describes documents. Feed content is in the form of XML documents, usually delivered over HTTP, and has no special status beyond that.

- RSS is not based on RDF. Early versions were a mixture of alleged RDF and non-RDF XML. Modern versions have nothing to do with RDF. No version can be considered RDF.

- There are many versions of RSS. According to this URL, the number of subtle variants is quite high, although some are no longer popular:

  http://diveintomark.org/projects/feed_parser/

- Atom and CDF are not specifically RSS, unless you use RSS as an umbrella term for XML-based feed technology. Even that, however, is not an accurate use of RSS, because asynchronously delivered SOAP messages [Hack #65] can be used to implement a true feed system (which is not trivial to do in Firefox). Such SOAP messages have nothing to do with RSS.

Exploit Firefox Support for RSS

RSS documents are XML, so they can be loaded into Firefox as XML using standard web techniques. The XMLHttpRequest object can be used to download such documents from the server of origin, and from elsewhere if the right security is in place.

Loading RSS documents as plain XML is not much of a start, though, because the RSS-specific tags receive no special treatment. That raw XML must be reduced to more useful information. There are several alternate strategies for turning RSS into RDF-like content, which is a more useful format for processing purposes:

- Use W3C DOM 2 Core operations
- Use code borrowed from Thunderbird
- Deliver the content to Firefox's bookmark datasource as a set of Live Bookmarks

In the first two cases, the syndicated information ends up in JavaScript as a DOM 2 Document Fragment or Document. It can be further processed into RDF facts for use in a datasource. If that is done, XUL templates and other Mozilla RDF technology can be applied to the feed data in a simple and flexible way. In the third case, the data is automatically inserted into the bookmarks datasource, where it is automatically visible to the user.

Datasources can be used only in a secure environment, not in ordinary web pages. Firefox does not support Internet Explorer's addBookmark( ) feature for security reasons.

To see how to parse the XML content of an RSS feed, study or steal Thunderbird source code last seen at the following URL:

http://lxr.mozilla.org/aviarybranch/source/mail/extensions/newsblog/ content/Feed.js

To put that content in a datasource, just use script operations to assert the required facts [Hack #70].

Firefox does not offer any XPCOM components that directly support RSS feeds. The parsing of RSS data is buried deep in the platform and can't be accessed by JavaScript. The bookmarks datasource provides indirect access via Live Bookmarks. Here are the component details:

```
@mozilla.org/browser/bookmarks-service;1 nsIBookmarksSerivce
```

Treating RSS data as a Live Bookmark just to get automated RSS support is a major hack. Care must be taken to bury the Live Bookmark deep in the bookmarks folder hierarchy so that the user doesn't see it on the Bookmarks Toolbar, unless that is a desirable effect.

Receive Notification of New Items

If you turn RSS content into RDF facts and use a datasource, then all the facilities of datasources are laid open to scripting. This provides a flexible environment for complex handling of RSS information.

If RDF facts in a datasource change, a script can find out the changes without constantly probing the datasource by installing an observer. This tactic is similar to using the DOM 2 Events addEventListener( ) method for events like click. Here's part of an RDF datasource observer:

```
// object implementing nsIRDFObserver
var obs = {
  onAssert(ds, sub, pred, obj) {
    window.alert('New fact added to datasource ' + ds.URI +
        'with fact subject of ' + sub.Value);
  },
  onUnassert(ds, sub, pred, obj) { ... },
  onChange( ... ) { ... },
  ...
};

// lodge the observer, 'ds' is a datasource object.
ds.addObserver(obs);

// finished initialization
```

The incomplete part of the definition is much the same as the sample implementation of the onAssert( ) method. Search Mozilla Cross-Reference (*http://lxr.mozilla.org*) for the *nsIRDFObserver.idl* file for the interface details.

Once the observer has been added to the datasource, it will be notified of all datasource changes. In this particular observer, an alert will result each time a fact is added. Any processing at all can be done where the alert occurs.

Connect SQL to XUL
#72   Use Mozilla technologies to send and retrieve SQL queries.

One of the most powerful uses of the Mozilla technologies is when they are combined with other web technologies to produce a complete client/server solution. This hack combines Mozilla's XML interface language XUL with RDF, PHP, and a MySQL database. This is an advanced hack, and you need to be comfortable with extensions and packages before the whole thing will work for you. Get comfortable with those technologies first.

In a nutshell, we will enter an SQL query in a Firefox form. This will send the request to a PHP script running on a remote server. The PHP script will run a query against the MySQL database, converting the output into an RDF document. This document will be returned to Firefox, where XUL will use the RDF to display the results of the query. Figure 6-15 shows the input and output displayed when the roundtrip from user to database to user is complete.

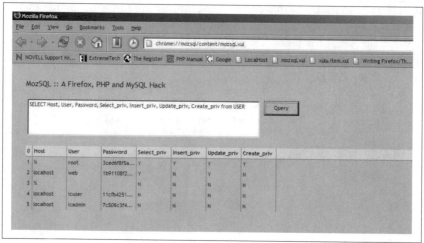

Figure 6-15. MozSQL, showing the results of an SQL query

Get Ready for Dynamic XUL

Every part of the Firefox interface is created using XUL [Hack #68]. We use it to create entire application interfaces. Whether it is bookmarks or toolbars, menus or buttons, in Firefox, XUL is ultimately responsible.

Most XUL can be created upfront and hardcoded. However, some XUL needs to be built dynamically; bookmarks are a good example of XUL that can't be hardcoded. To this end, XUL supports templates [Hack #70]: dynamic portions of a XUL document that are populated at runtime, based on some external XML data.

The XML data that Firefox is most concerned with is RDF. To recap, RDF is concerned with making statements about *things*. Each statement is comprised of three pieces of information: the thing we're making the statement about, a *property* of the thing, and the *value* of that property. In RDF parlance, this is called a *triple*, and the thing, property, and values are called *subject*, *predicate*, and *object*, respectively. For example, *Firefox Hacks* (the thing) has an *author* (the property) of Nigel McFarlane (the value). In RDF, we would write this statement roughly as follows (but this is just illustrative):

```
<rdf>
  <Description about="FirefoxHacks">
    <author>Nigel McFarlane</author>
  </Description>
</rdf>
```

This is an RDF triple, which an XUL template uses to build XUL dynamically. When the RDF changes, so does the XUL document.

Enough of concepts; start by creating a mozsql chrome package [Hack #86], including modifying *installed-chrome.txt*, and create the new package's standard *contents.rdf* file. We'll use a straightforward directory structure, not a JAR file. There's no extensions, overlays, themes, locales, or skins; we just want the chrome://mozsql URL to be working so that our XUL code can run in a fully secure environment.

Make an XUL Template

Here is the XUL document we will use to create and then render the RDF returned by our PHP script. This goes inside the mozsql chrome package that you need to create to run XUL content as chrome. Call it *mozsql.xul*, and put it in the *content* subdirectory of the package:

```
<?xml version="1.0"?>
<?xml-stylesheet href="chrome://mozsql/content/global.css" type="text/css"?>
<page id="MozSQL"
      xmlns="http://www.mozilla.org/keymaster/gatekeeper/there.is.only.xul">

  <script type="application/x-javascript" src="chrome://mozsql/content/
  mozsql.js"/>

  <description id="lblTitle" value="MozSQL :: A Firefox, PHP and MySQL
  Hack"/>
  <hbox>
    <textbox id="tbQueryString" multiline="true" value="SELECT * from USER"/>
    <vbox>
      <button id="cmdQuery" label="Query" tooltiptext="Execute SQL Query"
              oncommand="doQuery();"/>
    </vbox>
  </hbox>

  <vbox id="vbResults" datasources="rdf:null" ref="urn:mozsql">
```

The next bit of code, which immediately follows the preceding set, deals with the XUL template. Only a part of the document is dynamic; the remainder (above) can be static:

```
<template>
  <rule>
    <conditions>
      <content uri="?uri"/>
      <member container="?uri" child="?row"/>
      <triple subject="?row"
              predicate="http://www.example.com/mozsql#value"
              object="?value"/>
    </conditions>
    <action>
      <hbox col="?value" uri="?row" class="hbCell">
        <label value="?value" crop="end"/>
      </hbox>
    </action>
  </rule>
</template>
    </vbox>
  </page>
```

The conditions tag looks for the RDF statements that match the values we're interested in. The action tag is the XUL produced when our RDF statement matches the condition.

We've also created some pretty CSS style information for this document. It is decorative, not functional. Call it *global.css* and put it next to the *mozsql.xul* (it's not a theme or skin):

```
@namespace url("http://www.mozilla.org/keymaster/gatekeeper/there.is.only.
xul");

#MozSQL    {
    background-color: -moz-Dialog;
    color: -moz-DialogText;
    font: message-box;
    padding: 30px;
}
#lblTitle    {
    font-size: 150%;
    padding-bottom: 20px;
}
#tbQueryString    {
    width: 500px;
    height: 75px;
}
#cmdQuery    {
    height: 30px;
    width: 75px;
}
```

```
.hbCell > label        {
    border-right: 1px solid #999999;
    width: 75px;
    padding: 3px;
}
vbox hbox[id^="rdf"] > label    {
    max-width: 15px;
}
vbox > hbox[col="0"]    {
    margin-top: 20px;
    background-color: #E4E4E4;
    border-bottom: 1px solid #999999;
    font-weight: bold;
}
```

And finally, here's the included script that adds a datasource to the template and fills it with data from the server. Call it *mozsql.js* and put it in the same folder as the other files:

```
function doQuery( )         {
    //the template root
    var dsElem = document.getElementById( "vbResults" );

    // the HTTP GET request
    var tbQuery = document.getElementById( "tbQueryString" );
    var dsURL = "http://www.example.com/MozSQL/mozsql.php?query=" +tbQuery.
value;

    // Quick hack to prevent composites, comment out to aggregate results
    dsElem.setAttribute( "datasources", dsURL );

    // Create, Init and add a CompositeDatasource to the dsElem
    var cd = "@mozilla.org/rdf/datasource;1?name=composite-datasource";
    var dsCom = Components.classes[cd].createInstance();

    var dsItem = dsCom.QueryInterface(
        Components.interfaces.nsIRDFCompositeDataSource );
    dsElem.database.AddDataSource( dsItem );

    // Now get the RDF service
    var = rs "@mozilla.org/rdf/rdf--service;1";
    var rdfSvc = Components.classes[rs].getService();
    var rdfItem = rdfSvc.QueryInterface( Components.interfaces.nslRDFService );

    // Run the HTTP GET request and add the server-supplied response data
    var ds = rdfItem.GetDataSource( dsURL );
    dsItem.AddDataSource( ds );
}
```

When the button is clicked, the tbQueryString string is retrieved from the text box and appended to our remote URL under the HTTP GET variable query. Next, we get the element that holds the template root (the <vbox id="vbResults"> element) and add the remote URL to it.

The remainder of the code is the RDF content generated by the server. We use the following PHP script to create an instance of an RDF datasource, add it to our <vbox> element, and then call the RDF service to handle this and call GetDataSource(dsURL); to retrieve the remote document from the PHP script. This script is stored on the *www.example.com* server (change this to suit yourself) in the file *MozSQL/mozsql.php*:

```php
<?php
define( 'HOSTNAME', 'localhost' );
define( 'DATABASE', 'mysql' );

// Mozilla expects RDF to be returned as XML
header( 'Content-Type: application/xml' );

if ( !isset( $_GET ["query"] ) )
  exit;
$query = addslashes( $_GET ['query'] );
$username = 'username';
$password = 'password';

@ $conn = mysql_pconnect(HOSTNAME, $username, $password);
if ( !$conn )    {
  exit;
}
mysql_select_db( DATABASE, $conn );
$results = mysql_query( $query ) or die( mysql_error() );
if ( !$results || mysql_num_rows( $results ) < 1 )
  exit;
// Write out the RDF preamble
echo "<?xml version=\"1.0\"?>\n".
  "<rdf:RDF xmlns:rdf=\"http://www.w3.org/1999/02/22-rdf-syntax-ns#\""
  ." xmlns:sql=\"http://www.example.com/mozsql#\">\n".
  "<rdf:Seq rdf:about=\"urn:mozsql\">\n".
  "<rdf:li>\n";

$row = mysql_fetch_array( $results, MYSQL_ASSOC );
$row_keys = array_keys( $row );
$row_count = mysql_num_rows( $results );
$col_count = count( $row_keys );
mysql_data_seek( $results, 0 );            // Reset results var

for( $i = 0; $i < $row_count; $i++ )        { // Iterate over each row
  $row = mysql_fetch_array( $results );
  echo "<rdf:Seq sql:value=\"" .$i ."\">\n";
  for( $j = 0; $j < $col_count; $j++ )  { // Iterate over each column in row
    echo "<rdf:li rdf:resource=\"urn:row" .$i .":col" .$j ."\"/>\n";
  }
    echo "</rdf:Seq>\n";
}
echo "</rdf:li>\n</rdf:Seq>\n";
mysql_data_seek( $results, 0 );
// Write out Column headers (keys) first
```

```
    for( $j = 0; $j < $col_count; $j++ )           {
      echo "<rdf:Description rdf:about=\"urn:row0:col" .$j
            ."\" sql:value=\"" .$row_keys[ $j ] ."\"/>\n";
    }
    for( $i = 0; $i < $row_count; $i++ )           {      // Write remainder items out
      $row = mysql_fetch_array( $results );
      for( $j = 0; $j < $col_count; $j++ )         {
        echo "<rdf:Description rdf:about=\"urn:row"
              .$i .":col" .$j ."\" sql:value=\"" .$row[ $j ] ."\"/>\n";
      }
    }
    echo "</rdf:RDF>";         // Close root RDF element
    mysql_free_result( $results );
  ?>
```

You, of course, will need to set your own *host*, *database*, *username*, and *password*. Finally, here is an example of the RDF we expect the PHP script to produce:

```
<?xml version="1.0"?>
<rdf:RDF xmlns:rdf="http://www.w3.org/1999/02/22-rdf-syntax-ns#
         xmlns:sql="http://www.example.com/mozsql#">
    <rdf:Seq rdf:about="urn:mozsql">
       <rdf:li>
      <!-- This is called an 'anonymous resource',
                as it has no explicit rdf:uri -->
            <rdf:Seq sql:value="1">
       <!-- This ListItem points to the item with the same URI,
                    this is called an 'assertion' or 'arc' -->
                <rdf:li rdf:resource="urn:row1:col1"/>
                <rdf:li rdf:resource="urn:row1:col2"/>
            </rdf:Seq>
       <!-- Next row of data -->
            <rdf:Seq sql:value="2">
                <rdf:li rdf:resource="urn:row2:col1"/>
                <rdf:li rdf:resource="urn:row2:col2"/>
            </rdf:Seq>
        </rdf:li>
    </rdf:Seq>

    <!-- These predicates hold the actual data (rdf object) -->
    <rdf:Description rdf:about="urn:row1:col1" sql:value="Col1"/>
    <rdf:Description rdf:about="urn:row1:col2" sql:value="Col2"/>
    <rdf:Description rdf:about="urn:row2:col1" sql:value="Col1"/>
    <rdf:Description rdf:about="urn:row2:col2" sql:value="Col2"/>
</rdf:RDF>
```

Weigh It Up

This is a rough-and-ready example of what you can achieve by combining XUL and other web technologies alongside remote RDF. With the addition of other XUL elements, such as a drop-down list to select databases and other text boxes for usernames and passwords, it doesn't take much imagination to see that this isn't far off from a Mozilla-based MySQL frontend management utility.

One of the coolest things about RDF is a feature called *aggregation*, where multiple RDF sources are combined as if they were one. Comment out the bolded line in the previous JavaScript lists and see what happens; XUL templates can do operations similar to SQL's JOIN or UNION. Imagine now, instead of adding just a single remote URL, we add another, but this time to a different host, perhaps a Windows server running Microsoft SQL. Now, without that bold line, the remote data from these two hosts is aggregated, so we can effectively query and combine data from both hosts in real time! The cost of proprietary software to achieve this type of solution can leave the bank manager running for cover.

—Neil Stansbury

HACK #73   Generate XUL Using PHP Libraries

There's more than one way to create XUL content. Here's how to do so using PHP libraries.

We have already seen a number of ways to create XUL content for Mozilla [Hack #72]. The first and the simplest is just manually written, static XML. The second is to use XUL templates and XML-RDF to generate XUL based on assertions in RDF. The third is to use JavaScript in conjunction with the Mozilla Document Object Model (DOM) and create the XUL elements programmatically.

The fourth and final way is the subject of this hack: to generate XUL procedurally on a remote host and *stream* the content like a web page into Mozilla. This hack uses PHP to create the XUL content.

Finding PEAR Libraries for XUL

PEAR (*http://pear.php.net*) is a collection of reusable PHP libraries. One such PEAR library is *XML_XUL*, which allows remote generation of Mozilla's XUL using PHP's XML DOM. You can find the PHP XUL Libraries at *http://pear.php.net/package/XML_XUL*

While it is great to see XUL getting such widespread support, generating XUL in this fashion is a big design choice. In reality, all the programmer is doing is creating an extra unnecessary layer on top of XUL, which blurs the distinction between the XUL user interface (UI) and its data. If you view your network-enabled service as a data service (for example, a stock market feed), don't do this. If you view your network-enabled service as remote application delivery or as a media-oriented content-delivery solution (like Oracle's HTMLDB), this is the way to go.

XUL doesn't have the clear-cut semantic split that XML usually has of *content versus presentation* (XUL by definition is presentation!). Maintain a clear distinction between content (the RDF data) and presentation (XUL, CSS, and JavaScript) even if both are generated server-side. That will provide maximum flexibility.

Motivation for Server-Side UI Generation

Imagine a web application in which sales staff can update customer details, but other staff members can only view those details. We might use these PEAR/PHP libraries to procedurally generate <textbox> elements for our sales staff to edit the information, but create only <label> elements for everyone else.

Although we could create a one-size-fits-all XUL page, perhaps using templates, we might not want to do that. We might be worried about security. In that case, we don't want technically able end users lifting the lid on our application using their favorite tools. To get around this, we'll have to manufacture separate XUL for each type of employee on the server. Even if users are smart, they'll only be able to hack into the user interface that their security level lets them see. So let's generate code that way.

Getting Oriented with XML_XUL

Assuming PHP and XUL is your bag, let's look at some examples of using this technology. First, make sure you have downloaded and installed the *XML_XUL* libraries from *http://pear.php.net/package/XML_XUL/download*. PHP Tools (*http://www.phptools.de*) also has some good examples, showing both the PHP code and the resultant XUL. Each XUL element is described as a PHP class that inherits from the base PHP class element. Here's a brief outline of the setup required.

First, you need to include the base XUL package:

```
<?PHP
require_once 'XML/XUL.php';
```

Then, create the root XML document:

```
$doc = &XML_XUL::createDocument( );
```

Add in the base stylesheet:

```
$doc->addStylesheet('chrome://global/skin/');
```

Create a <window> element and add it into the base XML document doc:

```
$win = &$doc->createElement('Window', array('title'=>'Firefox Hacks'));
$doc->addRoot($win);
```

All elements are created by calling the createElement( ) method on the document root. This will return a new DOM node; then, with the exception of the root node, you'll need to remember to call the appendChild( ) method to add the new node into the correct location in the document tree. This is pretty standard DOM programming and will be familiar to anyone who has used the DOM before. Notice how the attributes on the XUL elements are handled as an associated PHP array.

Our special security system might extract the user's security from a bit of server data and generate code to match:

```
if ( user_is_sales() )
    $field = &$doc->createElement('label', array('value'=>$customer));
else
    $field = &$doc->createElement('label', array('value'=>$customer));
$doc->getElementById('customer-list')->appendElement($customer);
```

The final step, after creating the document node by node, is to return it to Mozilla for rendering, by calling the XML documents send( ) method:

```
$doc->send( );
?>
```

While you could end up with a lot of PHP code to accomplish something fairly trivial, the great part about working with the DOM and its nodes is that the XML tags are automatically closed—great for those of us who have poor memories!

Weighing It Up

The XUL PHP libraries are certainly neat and easy to use. If the XUL/RDF template model is too eclectic, convoluted, and overly complex for your needs, then server-generated content might be the way to go. In both cases, you can mix static XUL content with server-generated code; it's just a matter of how much.

—Neil Stansbury

Get a Taste of E4X Scripting
Learn the future of XML scripting techniques.

The JavaScript language is officially named ECMAScript. *E4X* (ECMAScript for XML) is the new ECMA-357 standard (at *http://www.ecma-international. org*) that extends Edition 3 of ECMAScript. It adds a drop of extra syntax that makes it easy to manipulate XML. This hack presents a brief tour of these features.

E4X is new, and it isn't available in Firefox 1.0. It is being implemented rapidly, though, and is likely to be present in the 1.1 release or thereabouts. It's fun to play with, and it's the future of XML scripting.

Where E4X Fits In

JavaScript code is just one way of manipulating the content of an XML document in the browser. If you want to do so, you have to embed or attach a JavaScript script to that document. That remains the case for E4X.

Once JavaScript is running inside a web document, there are four established ways to interact with that document's content. To briefly review, you can:

- Use widely supported but nonstandard DOM 0 JavaScript host objects, such as `document.images[3]`. Strengths: simple. Weaknesses: limited to HTML.
- Use W3C DOM 1, 2, or 3 interfaces, usually starting with `document. getElementById( )` or Microsoft's nonstandard `document.all( )`. Strengths: generic to all XML. Weaknesses: verbose.
- Use nonstandard `.innerHTML` features to turn a string containing XML into DOM content, or more rarely use the DOM 3 Load & Save interfaces. Strengths: simple. Weaknesses: nonstandard.
- Use XPath query patterns [Hack #63], perhaps inside XSLT [Hack #64]. Strengths: powerful. Weaknesses: limited coding features.

E4X uses syntax as simple as the first method to achieve all of the most common uses of the other three. It consists of:

- A starting point integrated with the familiar (to many) JavaScript environment
- New, simple syntax that makes HTML and XML element access easy
- Four new native JavaScript objects, if you happen to like objects
- A near-invisible connector to the non-E4X DOM objects in the XML document

Setting Up a Playpen for E4X

You can play with E4X in any old web page, with one restriction. If your script wants to take advantage of E4X, then this won't work for you:

```
<script type="text/javascript" src="test.js"></script>
```

This is the new way forward:

```
<script type="text/javascript;e4x=1" src="test.js"></script>
```

For this simple exploration, it doesn't matter too much what your test page looks like. Since E4X is intended for XML first and foremost, we're doing the right thing, using XHTML 1.0 instead of HTML 4.01. Here's a simple test document:

```
<?xml version="1.0"?>
<!DOCTYPE html PUBLIC "-//W3C//DTD XHTML 1.0 Strict//EN"
    "http://www.w3.org/TR/xhtml1/DTD/xhtml1-strict.dtd">
<html xmlns="http://www.w3.org/1999/xhtml">
  <head>
    <script type="text/javascript;e4x=1" src="test.js" />
  </head>
  <body>
    Test me! <p id="tag-with-no-content" />
  </body>
</html>
```

Notice the special value for the type attribute. Suppose we also have both the document and a specific tag available in two convenient variables. These might be set up somehow by the *test.js* script:

```
var doc = window.document;
var tag = document.getElementById("tag-with-no-content");
```

So far, this is all plain JavaScript 1.5 or ECMAScript Edition 3. Remember, you have to have an E4X-enabled version of Firefox. Check the release notes for 1.1 and later for details. At worst, you can compile the SpiderMonkey test program called simply js. But that's another story.

Experiment with E4X Features

So let's play. Let's first add two XML tags the old way. We'll add non-XHTML tags, just for fun. First, let's use dirty nonstandard tricks:

```
tag.innerHTML = '<list><item type="round">ball</item></list>';
```

Note how two types of quotes are required, but at least it's short. Next, let's use existing DOM standards:

```
var text = doc.appendChild(doc.createTextNode("ball"));
var list = doc.createElement("list");
var item = doc.createElement("item");
    item.setAttribute("type", "round");
    item.appendChild(text);
    list.appendChild(item);
tag.appendChild(list);
```

That's quite verbose, but at least it's portable. Now, use E4X standard object syntax:

```
// 'tag' is an E4X object as well as a DOM one.
tag.list.item = "ball";        // add the two tags, and innermost content.
tag.list.item.@type = "round"; // add an attribute, and give it a value.
```

The syntax on the left side is the E4X quick way of stepping down through a tag or element hierarchy. That's convenient by itself. Even better though, if the tags don't exist, they're automatically created as they're referenced (because the tag object is an XML object). Best of all, the right-hand side is automatically added as the content of the specified left-hand side. Very simple.

E4X provides an alternate, XML-based syntax. Here's the same addition as the previous bit of code:

```
var list = <list>
              <item type="round">ball</item>
           </list>;
tag += list;
```

In this example, the XML is *literally* and lexically part of the JavaScript syntax. No quotes or translation functions are required; it's all automatic. Note how the XML isn't trapped inside a string. The second assignment adds special and convenient semantics to the += operator. It's equivalent to this DOM 1 code:

```
tag.appendChild(list);
```

Suppose the data added isn't all static. E4X XML content can be also constructed using variables or expressions, as shown in this final alternative:

```
var shape = "round";
var type = 1;
var thing = "item";
var list = <list>
              <{thing} type={shape}>
                 { (type == 1) ? "ball" : "stick"; }
              </{thing}>
           </list>;
tag += list;
```

Everywhere you see braces (curly brackets), a JavaScript expression can be put in. To do the same thing using traditional notations, even .innerHTML, used to require complicated string concatenations. Not anymore.

You can also query the XML content very simply using E4X—no XPath required. This line returns any and all tags named <item> that are in the tag hierarchy held by list, no matter how deeply nested they are:

```
var items = list..items;
```

A set of objects is returned if there's more than one match. For our sample data, there's only one match. This syntax is equivalent to the use of // in XPath.

This further line returns all immediate child tags of the <list> tag, which happens to be the same result as the previous case:

```
var items = list.*;
```

This final line returns all the attributes of the <item> tag as a list:

```
var atts = list.item.@*;
```

E4X supports XML namespaces and a few other goodies as well. Unlike the ECMAScript standard, the E4X standard is easy to read. Download a copy today from *http://www.ecma-international.org/*.

## CHAPTER SEVEN

Hack the Chrome Ugly
Hacks 75–83

This chapter is for people with no time and no patience. It explains how to modify the files that make up the Firefox user interface using quick-and-dirty methods.

Why would anyone want to do that? There are lots of reasons. Perhaps you're building a prototype for a demo. Perhaps you keep pressing the wrong shortcut key and you wish it were gone. Perhaps you don't like a feature, or you want to add a feature. You might be experimenting with or testing the browser, or you might need the browser to hook into something else you're testing. Finally, fiddling with the browser is a first step on the path to learning Mozilla application development.

Part of the Firefox installation is a set of files called *the chrome*. These are the files to which you can make quick or extensive changes. They're all human-readable, human-editable files stored on the local disk. The directories they're stored in are also called the *chrome*, and they're usually named *chrome* as well. Typically, files in the chrome have all security restrictions lifted. That presents a major opportunity to step outside the limits of web pages and create something different.

Hacking the chrome, whether cleanly or ugly, bears some resemblance to web development. There are XML, JavaScript, and CSS files to manipulate, for starters. So modifications to the chrome are particularly easy for those with web development skills.

Chapter 8 describes the preparation, coding, and bundling steps required to formally deploy a Firefox enhancement. Here, we just cut to the chase and edit files in place.

Do Groundwork for Ugly Chrome Hacks

#75 Learn the first steps required to modify Firefox without using formal release
processes.

At the base of Firefox is an efficient and unchangeable runtime engine. On
top of that is a thick layer of interpreted content. That thick layer of content
is human-readable and human-changeable. This hack describes how to find,
open, and modify these files without getting burnt and without preparing an
extension.

Files centrally associated with the chrome are found in the Firefox install
area. Because these central chrome files aren't implemented as extensions,
the `-safe-mode` command-line option [Hack #10] doesn't apply. If you damage
chrome files, there is no way to successfully restart Firefox without repair or
reinstall. You've been warned.

Understanding Chrome

The chrome represents the entire user interface that Firefox has to offer.
That's a collection of XUL, CSS, JavaScript, image, RDF, plain text, and
HTML documents. RDF [Hack #70] and XUL [Hack #68] are the most important
document types. The chrome appears in several concrete ways.

First, the chrome is a little database of information held in Firefox's memory. This database is created at startup time from many separate RDF files.
Only those pieces of user interface that are known to this database are considered chrome. *RDF package registration* is required to make a package
known. You can't place a file in the Firefox install area and expect it to be
treated as chrome unless it is part of a registered package.

Second, the chrome is a set of URLs. The little chrome database in Firefox's
memory maintains a list of all valid `chrome:` URLs. Any URL with a `chrome:`
scheme gets the benefits of the chrome. Primary benefits are full security
privileges, overlays, and locale and skin switching. Each `chrome:` URL translates (maps) to a "real" URL, specified during registration. In practice,
whole directories are registered, not specific files. The chrome resource:

```
chrome://mypackage/content/mypackage.xul
```

could be mapped to this "real" URL at registration time:

```
file:///users/fred/tests/content/mypackage.xul
```

It's more normal, though, to see it mapped to this kind of URL, which refers
to the Firefox install area folders:

```
resource:/chrome/mypackage/content/mypackage.xul
```

You can load either URL into the browser and the same document will be accessed. Only when you load with a chrome: URL do the special characteristics of chrome apply.

Most of the chrome files are physically located in the install area. Rather than use the nonportable file: scheme, Firefox provides an extra scheme specifically for the install-area folder. It's called resource:, and it points at the top of the install area. So, chrome: URLs typically map to resource: URLs.

The third expression of chrome is just a set of files on disk. These are the particular XML, script, and CSS files that make up the user interface itself, plus the RDF registration files that identify that content. These files are all content and fair game for hacking.

Understanding JAR Files

Firefox keeps related chrome content together in *JAR files*. This is entirely optional; such file can also be located as plain files on disk. A JAR file is a ZIP format archive, that's all. JAR files have the benefit of being compact, fast to read from disk, fast to download, and digitally signable. Rather than splatter scores of chrome files all over the local disk, Firefox keeps them together neatly. You can use JAR files for:

- A whole window's content (such as the Firefox browser itself in *browser.jar*)
- A skin or theme (such as the standard theme in *classic.jar*)
- A locale (such as the default of U.S. English in *en-US.jar*)
- Any combination of the previous three options (such as the DOM Inspector's window, theme support, and locale information all collected in *inspector.jar*)

A JAR file can have a URL, just like any file. A special Firefox URL scheme allows you to refer to one of the files that is contained within the JAR file. If a JAR file */tmp/example.jar* contains the file *example.txt*, that *example.txt* file can be specified by this URL:

```
jar:file:///tmp/example.jar!/example.txt
```

Note the mandatory leading slash after the !. JAR files destined for the chrome usually contain one or more chrome packages. Such JAR files have restrictions on the way package content is laid out. One fairly weird rule says that the normal directory hierarchy is reversed inside the JAR file.

If a package exists unarchived on disk using the standard layout:

```
mypackage/content/...
mypackage/skin/...
mypackage/locale/...
```

then all these files must be rearranged before repackaging them into a JAR
file:

```
content/mypackage/...
skin/mypackage/...
locale/mypackage/...
```

This reordering is designed to make searching the archive faster at runtime.
A second oddity is the placement of any *contents.rdf* files at the start of the
archive. This is also for performance, but it is just a clever trick, not a
requirement.

To open a JAR file, copy it, use an unzip program like unzip -l to report the
contents (save this), and then unzip it for real into a temporary directory.
Edit any of the files normally. Zip the archive up again, change the file
extension back to *.jar*, and put the file back. It's that simple.

Locating Standard Chrome Files

The standard chrome files reside in the install area, in the *chrome* subdirectory. The topmost file is called *installed-chrome.txt*. It lists all the standard
packages currently in the chrome, so start here. This file is written at install
time, but you can add packages by hand-editing it. If this file is modified or
updated, Firefox will re-read it when it next starts up. If that happens, any
new packages created since the last run will be added to the set of known
packages.

The *installed-chrome.txt* file is sensitive to bad syntax. A line like this:

```
content,install,url,resource:/chrome/help/content/
```

means that a content package (not a skin or locale package) in the install
area (as opposed to in the rarely used profile area) is located in the *chrome/
help/content* directory. In particular, it says that those files are stored as separate files in a normal hierarchy of folders (directories).

These registration lines, however, typically refer to JAR archives, rather than
to plain folder names. Here's an example:

```
content,install,url,jar:resource:/chrome/help.jar!/content/help/
```

The default name for per-package registration files is *contents.rdf*. This is the
second file of importance. This file contains the registration details that
make the package available via chrome: URLs. For the first example, it
would be located at:

```
resource:/chrome/help/content/contents.rdf
```

The remainder of the files for the package are all those residing in the same
directory as the *contents.rdf* file or in subfolders of that directory. The most

important file usually has the same name as the package name—for example:

```
jar:resource:/chrome/help.jar!/content/help/help.xul
resource:/chrome/help/content/help.xul
```

or, after chrome registration:

```
chrome://help/content/help.xul
```

This XUL file is the one that everything else hangs off of. In this example, it's the main window of the help system. For more central changes, this is the place to start:

```
chrome://browser/content/browser.xul
```

Locating Other Chrome Files

Chrome files also appear in the install area under the *extensions* directory. There, additional packages are defined and packaged up as extensions. There is a separate registration system for extensions [Hack #84].

Finally, ordinary chrome packages and extensions can also be placed in the user profile. That's common for extensions, but rarely done for ordinary packages.

What to Hack

Nearly all supplied Firefox files can be hacked [Hack #22]. If you know what you're doing, you can usually ignore *installed-chrome.txt* and any *contents.rdf* and just hack on the chrome content help inside the JAR files. Use touch afterward to update the last-modified date on the *installed-chrome.txt* file so that Firefox notices your changes next time it starts up. Read the rest of the hacks in this chapter for examples.

HACK #76 Spy on Chrome with the DOM Inspector

Put a microscope to the XUL that makes up the browser chrome with the DOM Inspector.

If you want to hack the existing Firefox chrome, that means building on someone else's work. There's usually no time to study all that code at length, so shortcuts are required. The DOM Inspector is a fast jumping-off point that lets you detect the relationships between different chrome files. It's a good starting point for most of the hacks in this chapter. This hack explains how to get started.

Inspecting XUL

The DOM Inspector is most commonly used to examine HTML pages [Hack #53]. However, it can also be used to inspect the XUL chrome content of any Firefox, Mozilla, or extension window. A small catch is that the DOM Inspector recognizes only windows opened *after* the inspector was started, plus the initially opened browser window. If some other window is of interest to you, this simple but ungraceful solution is required:

1. Start Firefox.
2. Open the DOM Inspector using the Tools menu.
3. Go back to the initial browser window.
4. Open a new browser window, or whatever window is required for inspection. Ideally, it should have a meaningful title displayed in its titlebar.
5. Using Alt-Tab or otherwise, change focus back to the DOM Inspector. You can do this even if the window to be inspected is a modal window.
6. In the DOM Inspector, choose File → Inspect a Window and pick the window desired.

If the normal browser window is inspected using this technique, the top of the tag hierarchy covers the whole window, not just the web page displayed. Therefore, the topmost tag is a <window> tag rather than an <html> tag. Figure 7-1 shows the result for a standard browser window.

This display is very revealing. It shows all the keyboard shortcuts specific to the window (inside <keyset>), all the window's commands that can be executed (inside <commandset>), and, given enough drilling down, all the other content of the window as well.

If you do drill down through the right set of tags, you can also discover the HTML document currently displayed inside that window. This brings the point home that the whole window is nothing more than an arrangement of tags—some XUL, some HTML—as shown in Figure 7-2.

Connecting the Dots

Figures 7-1 and 7-2 show the tag hierarchy, but they also show id and class values for those tags. The names of these IDs and classes are well-known and stable values that rarely change. Many of the popular Firefox extensions rely totally on these pieces of information. You can learn about the structure of a given window by comparing these live values with the same values as stated in files provided by the chrome.

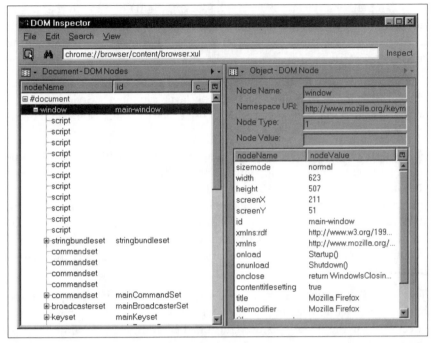

Figure 7-1. Topmost XUL tags in a Firefox browser window

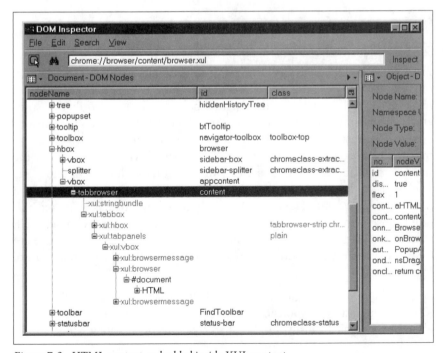

Figure 7-2. HTML content embedded inside XUL content

For example, when overlays are used [Hack #87], the ID of a tag in the master document usually matches the ID of the <overlay> tag in the overlay document. This allows you to track down where a given overlay is applied in the master document.

Alternatively, either ID or class might be used to link a given tag to a specific CSS style or to a specific piece of JavaScript logic. Stylesheets and scripts supplied in the chrome regularly use styles to hide, display, and decorate tags in order to provide user feedback.

Studying the DOM Inspector output and comparing it with the textual content of the chrome files helps you to understand how particular pieces of XUL-based user interface are operated on. As the user changes the user interface, you can use the tag breakdown and the informational panel on the right to see if the scripting logic in the window added any tag attributes or styles or not. You can use the DOM Inspector's editing capabilities to experimentally remove pieces of the examined window and see the results immediately.

This kind of matching brings you one step closer to making an ugly chrome hack. By removing, restyling, or modifying some tags, you can have a large effect on how the window is brought together from many separate files for the user's consumption.

HACK #77   Customize Firefox's Interface
Tweak and modify the browser's interface to suit your needs.

Firefox is generally hailed as having an excellent user interface (UI). The art of user-interface design is one of making compromises, where each feature must be carefully weighed and evaluated before inclusion. While this strategy of catering to the lowest common denominator leads to the greatest amount of satisfaction for the largest number of users, it generally fails to maximize utility for individual users. There will inevitably be parts of the browser that some will find useless, unpleasant, or downright intrusive. Locked-down kiosks or other specialized uses of the browser also require a more customized interface. This hack explores how to make Firefox's UI more closely match your own needs and desires. As an example, we'll remove the links to the default email client from the Tools menu. These are only available in the Windows port, so by removing them, we actually make Firefox more portable.

Since we'll be in the neighborhood, we'll also disable the key binding (Ctrl-M or Command-M) responsible for opening a new email composition; it's all too easy to hit M instead of N when trying to open a new window, and the second or two delay while the mail window opens can be disruptive. We could also do a little nip/tuck work on the context menu, but that is left as an exercise for the reader.

You can apply this hack's logic to any menu item that you care to examine. It's the process that's important here, not the details.

Identifying the Objective

The first goal of this hack is simply to figure out what it is that needs to be removed. Figure 7-3 shows the Tools menu with the target menu items highlighted.

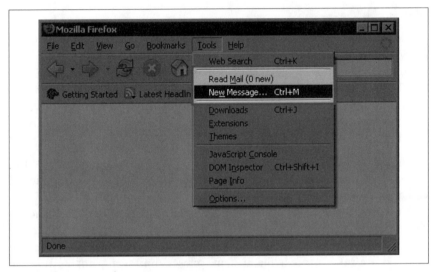

Figure 7-3. Unwanted menu items

There are actually three pieces that we want to remove: the Read Mail and New Message... menu items, plus one of the surrounding menu separators (so that we don't get two adjacent separators when we're done). In order to allow Firefox to be translated into many languages, text strings such as Read Mail and New Message are kept separate from the code that creates the menu items, so we can't simply search for them, but the keyword mail will probably lead us in the right direction.

Ready...

It is always a good idea to close Firefox before editing any files that it uses while running. Once that's done, our next task is to find the file that contains those menu items. We'll be modifying the browser code itself (this is, after all, "Hacking the Chrome Ugly"), so we'll start our search from the

Firefox executable. In Windows, this is likely to be located in *C:\Program Files\Mozilla Firefox*.

Sure enough, inside lies a promising-looking folder named *chrome*. This folder in turn contains another promising-looking item named *browser.jar*. As used by Mozilla, JAR files are simply ZIP files renamed; they can be opened with any ZIP-capable program. Use one to extract *browser.jar*'s contents into a new folder named *browser*. Later, we'll rezip this folder back to *browser.jar*, but instead of deleting the original, it's a good idea to rename it to something like *brower_original.jar* in case something should go wrong with your modified version.

Aim...

Inside the new browser folder is a content folder that contains another browser folder. Within this innermost browser folder lies the target of our search: a hefty (approximately 72 KB) file named *browser.xul*. If the Gecko rendering engine is the heart of Firefox, this file is the epidermis. It contains the XUL (XML User-interface Language) declarations that create the toolbars, menus, and context menus that surround the web pages Firefox displays.

We could manually search through the entire file to find the right lines, but it would be much easier to simply search for the relevant bits. As mentioned earlier, the word `mail` should be a good starting point for our search. The first occurrences of `mail` are on lines 93 through 97 and are commands—XUL that links GUI elements to the JavaScript code that makes them work—not what we want. The next appearances are on lines 321 through 324 and are for a context menu item—closer, but again, not what we're looking for.

The next occurrence, however, is exactly what we're looking for. The following code begins on line 844:

```
<menu label="&toolsMenu.label;" accesskey="&toolsMenu.accesskey;">
  <menupopup id="menu_ToolsPopup"
             onpopupshowing="MailIntegration.updateUnreadCount();"
  >
    <menuitem label="&search.label;" accesskey="&search.accesskey;"
              key="key_search" command="Tools:Search"/>
    <menuseparator/>
    <menuitem label="&mailButton.readMail.label;"
              accesskey="&mailButton.readMail.accesskey;"
              command="Browser:ReadMail"/>
    <menuitem label="&mailButton.newMessage.label;"
              accesskey="&mailButton.newMessage.accesskey;"
              key="key_newMessage" command="Browser:NewMessage"/>
    <menuseparator/>
```

We'll just comment out one menuseparator and the two menuitems. The onpopupshowing then becomes unnecessary, but be careful; XML does not allow attributes to be commented out, so the attribute/value string must be moved from the menupopup element to the comment, like this:

```
<menu label="&toolsMenu.label;" accesskey="&toolsMenu.accesskey;">
    <menupopup id="menu_ToolsPopup">
        <menuitem label="&search.label;" accesskey="&search.accesskey;"
                key="key_search" command="Tools:Search"/>
<!--
*** from menupopup:
            onpopupshowing="MailIntegration.updateUnreadCount();"
***
        <menuseparator/>
        <menuitem label="&mailButton.readMail.label;"
                accesskey="&mailButton.readMail.accesskey;"
                command="Browser:ReadMail"/>
        <menuitem label="&mailButton.newMessage.label;"
                accesskey="&mailButton.newMessage.accesskey;"
                key="key_newMessage" command="Browser:NewMessage"/>
-->
        <menuseparator/>
```

This is a good start, but we're not quite done. At this point, if we press the system accelerator key (Control on Windows and Linux; Command on Mac) and M, Firefox will open the default mail program and begin composing a new message. Searching *browser.xul* for other instances of command="Browser:NewMessage" shows the culprit on line 250:

```
<key id="key_newMessage"
    key="&sendMessage.commandkey;"
    command="Browser:NewMessage"
    modifiers="accel"/>
```

Simply comment out the entire element, and...

Firefox!

That's all the editing we'll be doing for this hack; now, we'll get Firefox back up and running. The process should be simple. Navigate back to the top-level *chrome* directory and then into the *browser* folder. Zip up the content folder with whatever tool you have at your disposal and rename the newly zipped folder to *browser.jar*. Then, move the new JAR file up to the *chrome* folder. You can leave the *browser* directory alone; it won't interfere with Firefox's operation. Start up Firefox, and it should now look like Figure 7-4.

—Ben Karel

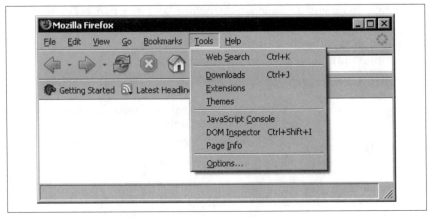

Figure 7-4. The slimmed-down Tools menu

HACK #78   Rebadge Firefox

Dig into Firefox and change some of its brand livery to something that suits you better.

This hack shows how to scratch the surface of the Firefox rebranding process. You can change many, but not all, of the obvious brand marks that Firefox displays with simple chrome hacks. For a really thorough job, you also need to rebundle the Firefox installer [Hack #28] with new brand information, and that must be done on top of a custom build [Hack #93]. It's not a trivial task to complete systematically. Here, then, are the easy bits.

Core Brand Information

Variations on the word *Firefox* appear in many places in the user interface: in menu items, in flyover help (tooltips), and even in HTML documents. Many of these places pull in the brand information from two files: *brand.dtd* and *brand.properties*. These two files are stored in the *en-US.jar* file in the install area: the default locale for a U.S. English distribution of Firefox. Pick a new brand name, modify these files in place, restart the browser, and see if the changes you need are completed or not.

Rebranding Bookmarks and Bookmark Text

The word *Firefox* also appears in the Bookmarks menu. To hack that menu, just remove the offending bookmarks:

1. Create a new Firefox profile with the -CreateProfile command-line option.
2. Start up that profile and open the Bookmark Manager.

3. Delete all Firefox bookmarks and bookmark folders.

4. Shut down Firefox.

Now, locate the *bookmarks.html* file in the new profile. Either migrate it to other profiles as required [Hack #25], or replace the standard one supplied in the Firefox installer [Hack #28].

Rebranding Icons and Images

Some brand icons are easy to remove; others are not so easy. The simplest thing to do is to override the per-window icons that appear in the top left of the titlebar. They are also displayed by process managers such as Windows Task Manager and the Alt-Tab application picker.

To do this, create the following magic directory hierarchy in the chrome area: *icons/default*. Here's the full URL of that directory:

> *resource:/chrome/icons/default*

In that directory, put icon files whose names match the id of the <window> tag for each Firefox window of interest. On Windows, these files should be *.ico* files; on Unix/Linux, they're *.xpm* files. As an example, the mail browser window, which is defined in chrome file *browser.xul*, has a <window> tag with id="main-window". The matching icon files should therefore be named either *main-window.ico* or *main-window.xpm*. To see it work, just restart the browser.

Icon files can be bundled with the installer, with extensions, or simply placed as required. There's more imagery than just icons, though.

On the easy side, there are Firefox images to change in the default theme in *classic.jar*. Look for *icon32.png*. There are several in *browser.jar* as well. There are also images to change in the standard install bundle [Hack #28]. Themes, locales, and extensions contain preview images that give away Firefox's true identity as well.

On the harder side, some copies of the Firefox desktop icons are embedded in the *firefox.exe* binary. Under Windows, you can replace these resources using a free tool such as Resource Hacker (*http://www.users.on.net/johnson/ resourcehacker/*) or the equally free, but also open source, equivalent Resource Explorer (*http://www.wilsonc.demon.co.uk/d7resourceexplorer. htm*). On the Macintosh, the BNDL resource information is embedded in the source code, and Firefox source must be edited and recompiled to change this.

If you change the entries in the StringTable section, you also prevent your rebranded browser from sharing its runtime engine with Firefox. You also change the name of the browser when viewed in the Alt-Tab list and in the Task Manager.

Rebranding the User Agent

You can change the browser User Agent string using preferences [Hack #23]. The best place to put that preference change is in the *defaults\prefs\firefox.js* file in the install area.

HACK #79 Make Firefox Match the Desktop

Take away Firefox's distinctive look, so that it appears to be just another desktop soldier.

This hack shows how to make Firefox inherit the appearance dictated by the desktop environment, whether that be Windows, Mac OS X, GNOME, or (sometime soon) KDesktop. Instead of looking like itself, Firefox can be made to look like everything else. Fundamentally, that means styling XUL content so that it looks right. There are also issues with portability [Hack #91].

There are several ways to provide desktop uniformity. The ultimate solution is to use the -moz-appearance style property, but let's dispose of the simpler alternatives first.

Building Static Skins

The simple way to make Firefox look like the desktop is to build a theme that looks exactly like the desktop. Themes are made up of *skins*, with one skin per package. The easiest way to build such a theme is to start with an existing, quality theme such as the default theme, or a popular and well-maintained theme from the Mozilla Update site (*http://update.mozilla.org*). Then:

1. Identify the JAR file that holds all the original theme's skins.
2. Replace files one at a time in the skins.
3. Restart the browser after each change to see what effect has resulted.

Static themes generally affect XUL content the most. Particularly for Firefox, a large portion of the main window is given over to HTML page display, and that display is resistant to theme changes. This is because a subset of the files in the *res* folder of the install area is always applied to HTML pages when they are displayed. *html.css* is the main file that causes these problems.

If HTML pages absolutely must look like the desktop, either hack these resource files to conform or supply a desktop theme that uses the CSS2 !important directive to override other rules.

A purely static skin is not very flexible. It applies to one and only one desktop, and can't keep up with any user changes. This is especially rigid on Unix/Linux, where a wide range of configuration options are available. If the desktop is locked down, though, it could be enough.

Building Static Skins with Smart Values

A small improvement to static skins is to use smarter values in the skin's CSS styles. The CSS 2.1 standard provides a number of font names and colors that map directly to "whatever the desktop specifies currently." This means that small changes made by the user to the desktop's appearance are also picked up by Firefox.

The fonts that act in this fashion—for example, serif—include the special -moz-fixed font [Hack #45], as well as others described in section 15.3 of CSS2.1. The colors that act like this—for example, ThreeDDarkShadow—are described in section 18.2 of CSS2.1. In addition, Firefox has some custom style properties that also apply desktop information.

Although these special values transmit desktop styles accurately, they provide a very low-level solution. A menu designed to follow the default Windows XP desktop style requires this CSS style for its right edge:

```
menupopup { -moz-border-right-colors: ThreeDShadow; }
```

By comparison, a menu designed to follow the Classic (Windows 98) desktop style requires this style for its right edge:

```
menupopup { -moz-border-right-colors: ThreeDDarkShadow ThreeDShadow; }
```

There's no clean way to support both styles at once. One simple but horrid solution is to pack all required CSS rules for all required desktop styles into a sort of Frankenstein skin and then activate portions of the style depending on some flag set in the content. For example, if an XUL <window> tag is marked with an attribute desktop set to win98 or winXP, then that attribute can selectively choose the required styles:

```
window[desktop="win98"] button { color : blue; }
window[desktop="winXP"] button { color : red; }
```

When the window starts up, a piece of JavaScript can flip the attribute, depending on the current platform. Alternatively, the script can modify the href argument of an <?xml-stylesheet?> processing instruction (PI). Both approaches are fairly desperate.

Exploiting -moz-appearance and Theme Engines

The best solution offered by Firefox is the `-moz-appearance` style. This style is based on a couple of observations:

- Windows consist of a backdrop covered with text and images, plus a set of widgets. If the backdrop, text, and images are easy to deal with, that leaves only the widgets.

- The painting of small areas on a window can be delegated to a separate display system. Such a system is usually called a *theme engine*.

The `-moz-appearance` style tells Firefox, "Delegate the painting of this CSS style target to the native theme engine."

Firefox works with Windows theme engines from Windows 98 and later, the pluggable Gtk theme engines, and Mac OS X's Carbon Appearance Manager. This technique is not used much in Firefox, although you can find some references in the *xul.css* file in the chrome. It is used extensively in the Classic style of the Mozilla Application Suite (1.x). Here is an example of the style at work. First, some XUL:

```
<?xml version="1.0"?>
<?xml-stylesheet href="chrome://global/skin"?>
<?xml-stylesheet href="mozapp.css"?>
<window xmlns="http://www.mozilla.org/keymaster/gatekeeper/there.is.only.xul">
  <hbox>
    <button id="normal"  label="No Native Theme"/>
    <button id="button"  label="Native 'button' Theme"/>
    <button id="tooltip" label="Native 'tooltip' Theme"/>
  </hbox>
</window>
```

Second, some matching CSS:

```
* { border-width :thick }
#normal  { -moz-appearance : none; }
#button  { -moz-appearance : button; }
#tooltip { -moz-appearance : tooltip; }
```

The first three styles are typical and correct. The last style mistakenly applies the Desktop theme engine's style for tooltips to the XUL <button> tag. Figure 7-5 shows the result (using Linux for a change).

Figure 7-5. Natively themed and BlueCurve-themed XUL buttons

The thick border is applied only to the first button, because that's the only button that Gecko is directly in charge of. Since the desktop theme (Blue-Curve, in this case) doesn't specify thick borders, they're not drawn. If the theme is changed to Crux, then the window is restyled, as shown in Figure 7-6, without needing to be restarted.

Figure 7-6. Natively themed and Crux-themed XUL buttons

You would expect the window decorations (the titlebar) to change when a theme changes, but Firefox also supports changes to widgets within the window.

To find all the valid values of -moz-appearance, either look in the *xul.css* file in *toolkit.jar* in the chrome, or search for kAppearanceKTable in the *nsCSSProps.cpp* file at *http://lxr.mozilla.org.*

Make a Toolbar That Can't Be Hidden

HACK #80

Decorate window pop ups with a toolbar that no web page can remove.

You might not like HTML window pop ups, but sometimes there's no choice but to put up with them. Banking sites are a common example. When a pop-up window is stripped of all browser toolbars, it takes away more user control than technical people are comfortable with. This hack shows how to put in a toolbar that can't be taken away. It's a very quick-and-dirty hack.

Adding a Permanent Toolbar

To make this change, we'll modify the *browser.jar* chrome archive in the install area.

Make a backup copy of this file first.

Copy the existing *browser.jar* file and unpack it in a temporary directory. Edit the *browser.xul* file with a text editor. Find the <toolbox> tag; that's the tag that holds the menu bars and toolbars at the top of the browser window.

That tag's first child is a `<toolbar>` tag. Ignore that tag; it holds the menu bar. After that tag's closing tag, add this content:

```
<toolbar>
  <description>My test toolbar</description>
</toolbar>
```

That's all. Zip the contents back up into a new *browser.jar*. It doesn't matter if archive size and file order within the archive change. Move the official *browser.jar* aside, and put this one in its place. If the browser starts up, then there are no syntax errors. If you can see the toolbar, as shown in Figure 7-7, then everything's working.

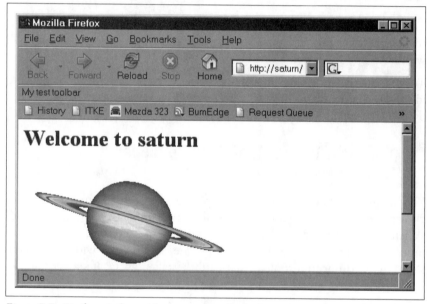

Figure 7-7. Firefox window with extra toolbar hacked in

Testing the New Toolbar

Here's a simple HTML document to test the toolbar:

```
<html>
  <body>
    <script>
      function do_it() {
        window.open("test.html", null,
          "toolbar=no,location=no,menubar=no,status=no,scrollbars=no");
      }
    </script>
    <p>Open a stripped-down window</p>
    <p><input type="button" value="Do it" onclick="do_it()" /></p>
  </body>
</html>
```

Figure 7-8 shows the results with a trivial *test.html* page.

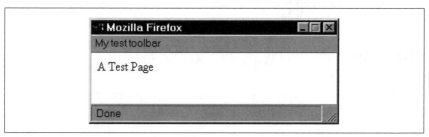

Figure 7-8. The pop-up window with toolbar and status bar enforced

The test toolbar is this hack's doing. By default, Firefox always shows the status bar. You can change that by unsetting this preference:

```
dom.disable_window_open_feature.status /* default = true */
```

Decorating the New Toolbar

You can put anything you like in the new toolbar. The following widgets open a new browser window, a window with a given URL, and a text field in which JavaScript statements can be evaluated:

```
<toolbar>
  <description>My test toolbar</description>
  <script>
    function open_it(url) { window.open(url, null, ""); }
  </script>
  <description>My test toolbar</description>
  <button label="New Window"
          onclick="open_it('chrome://browser/content/browser/xul')" />
  <text value="Location:"/>
  <textbox onchange="open_it(this.value)" />
  <text value="Eval: "/>
  <textbox onchange="eval(this.value)" />
</toolbar>
```

Figure 7-9 shows the result.

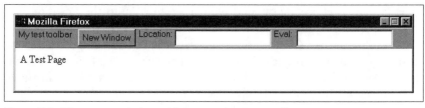

Figure 7-9. The pop-up window with improved custom toolbar

You'll need to apply extra styles to make it pretty.

What does it do? Type a URL into the Location field, and a new window will be displayed when you press Tab. Type any JavaScript expression into the Eval field, and the code will be executed when you press Tab.

HACK #81 Content Filter Without Your Smart Friend Noticing

Hide a content filter in Firefox's core to make web sites vanish like Ninjas in the dark.

Blocking access to certain web sites is a common project, whether to protect one's children from the perceived dangers of the Internet or as an April fool's joke for a coworker or friend. Unfortunately, most existing methods fall short in one of two areas.

On the one hand, they might be too blatant in their approach, as with most proxy-based solutions, serving up a honking "this page has been blocked" replacement page instead of the requested site. On the other hand, the hosts file is hard to keep secure and safe from tampering.

By injecting a few lines of code into Firefox's core, we can get a subtle, effective, and almost undetectable way of preventing the browser from visiting less-than-desirable sites. As a bonus, we can even trick the unlucky user into thinking that the problem lies on the remote server's end rather than the user's.

Starting Points

The setup for this hack will be virtually identical to disabling Firefox menus [Hack #77], except this time, we'll be editing the JavaScript code in *browser.js* instead of the frontend UI code in *browser.xul*. The first step remains the same: identify the code we'll be targeting. We want our code to run between the point where the user enters a URL into the Location bar and the point where Firefox begins actually loading the entered URL. Thus, our search begins at the Location bar.

Open a new Firefox window and type about:blank into the Location bar. Then, open the DOM Inspector from the Tools menu. Choose File → Inspect Window → Mozilla Firefox to let the DOM Inspector look at the chrome code that surrounds the browser viewport. In the DOM Inspector, the inspected location should change from about:blank to chrome://browser/content/browser.xul. Now, select Search → Select Element By Click in the DOM Inspector and click the Go button in the Firefox browser window. It should flash with a red box, and the DOM Inspector's DOM Node tree listing should have a toolbarbutton element selected. Hidden in the

DOM Node listing is the attribute/value pair we're interested in: the oncommand handler return handleURLBarCommand(event);, which is shown in Figure 7-10.

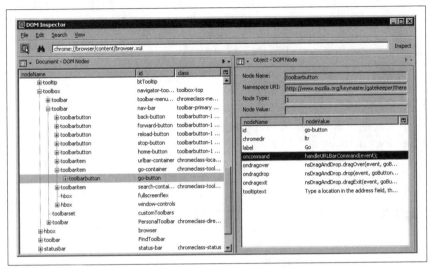

Figure 7-10. Starting point for the hack

Finding the Files to Hack

The key nugget extracted from that foray into the DOM Inspector was a single function name: handleURLBarCommand. If we had absolutely no idea where that function was actually declared, we could use LXR (*http://lxr.mozilla. org/aviarybranch/*) to search through the entire Firefox code base and find any references to that string.

One thing to note about LXR is that the paths it returns are not chrome:// URLs, but rather are reflective of the way the code is organized before compilation and packaging. LXR says that the function we're interested in is defined in */browser/base/content/browser.js*, rather than *chrome://browser/ content/browser.js*. However, we're smart enough to know that there aren't too many *browser.js* files used by Firefox. Sure enough, entering chrome:// browser/content/browser.js into the Location bar presents us with a plaintext JavaScript file, confirming our hunch. We'll be using LXR a bit more later on, so we'll keep using Firefox to gather all the pieces necessary for our hack.

The actual handleURLBarCommand function is short—containing less than 10 lines of actual code. The last line is another function call: BrowserLoadURL(aTriggeringEvent, postData.value);. This new function is declared earlier in *browser.js*. It's longer and more confusing, but again, there's one promising-looking function call: loadURI. This function is called many times in *browser.js*, so it will be easiest to go straight to the function declaration by searching for function loadURI. This function is the shortest of the bunch, but it's the end of the yellow brick road—where the magic happens. loadURI calls what looks like a JavaScript function, but it's actually linked to the C++ XPCOM code that does the real heavy lifting in Firefox, and C++ is too heavyweight for a quick chrome hack.

Coding Options

In any case, we've now found a host function for our stealth code. What should we actually do? The simplest solution is to simply return early from the function, before the XPCOM code gets a chance to run. Unfortunately, that wouldn't create a very convincing spoof of a connection error. Instead, we'll emulate Firefox's behavior for web sites that appear not to exist. Try entering does.not.exist into the Location bar; Firefox will change the cursor and the status bar text ("Looking up does.not.exist"), wait a second or so, and then pop a dialog saying "does.not.exist could not be found. Please check the name and try again," along with a change of the status bar text to "Done." For simplicity, we'll ignore the cursor change and just do the status bar and dialog.

In fact, we might not actually want to downright block the web site. For some sites, such as *http://www.whitehouse.com* or *http://www.fafsa.com*, we'd rather just automatically redirect the browser to the correct web sites (*http://www.whitehouse.gov* and *http://www.fafsa.ed.gov*, respectively.) Thus, instead of just a blacklist, we could also have a redirect list that contains mappings of "bad" sites to good sites.

Another alternative direction for the hack to take would be to make the URL bar more forgiving of typing errors in the Location bar, such as treating firefox,com as firefox.com. With that many features, though, the code is more deserving of a full extension rather than just a quick chrome hack.

All right, enough features, already. We'll keep it simple and then get down and dirty!

Quick-and-Dirty String Changes

The "correct" way to access strings from JavaScript—especially strings shipped with the browser—is to use property files and Mozilla stringbundles. However, since this hack will vanish if the browser is upgraded, we can get away with hardcoding the strings instead of fetching them from a stringbundle. This saves us from having to modify *browser.xul* in addition to *browser.js*, and it makes our end code a little clearer to read.

Speaking of which, all this talk translates in only a few measly lines of changed code. Here's the loadURI function before we hack it:

```
function loadURI(uri, referrer, postData)
{
  try {
    if (postData === undefined)
      postData = null;
    getWebNavigation().loadURI(uri, nsIWebNavigation.LOAD_FLAGS_NONE,
                               referrer, postData, null);
  } catch (e) {
  }
}
```

Here's how the function looks after we hack it:

```
function loadURI(uri, referrer, postData)
{
  try {
    if (postData === undefined)
      postData = null;
    var blacklist = /fafsa\.com|whitehouse\.com/;
    if (blacklist.test(uri)) {
      window.status = 'Looking up ' + uri;
      var s = 'The connection was refused when attempting to contact ' + uri;
      setTimeout( function(s) { window.status = 'Done'; alert(s); }, 1337, s);
    }
    else {
      getWebNavigation().loadURI(uri, nsIWebNavigation.LOAD_FLAGS_NONE,
                                 referrer, postData, null);
    }
  } catch (e) {
  }
}
```

> Note that you shouldn't be thrown off by the use of uri instead of URL. The differences are semantic only; here they're interchangeable.

In any case, our additions begin at var and end at else. The first line declares our blacklist—a regular expression with a number of web site names separated by a pipe character (|), which is the equivalent of a logical OR operator. The dots are escaped (\.) because in regular expressions, the dot is a special character that can mean any character at all.

The second line simply checks the URL to be loaded against the blacklist. *http://mozilla.org/* would be allowed to pass and load normally (test( )

returns false), whereas *http://www.whitehouse.com* would trigger the blacklist and cause our code to be executed.

The first two lines of the blocking code are straightforward, but the third deserves a closer look. The setTimeout( ) function of the window object is JavaScript's way of scheduling asynchronous code execution. It's usually passed a string of code to execute after some number of milliseconds, but it can also take a function as the first argument. This function's arguments are whatever is passed to setTimeout after the time delay; we pass the string to be displayed in an alert dialog.

Wrapping Up

It's time to wrap up this hack. Make sure Firefox isn't running, and then zip up the *content* directory into *browser.jar* and move it into the top-level *chrome* folder, making sure you back up the last version first. If necessary, refer back to "Customize Firefox's Interface" [Hack #77] for a memory jogger.

Now, when a user enters whitehouse.com in the Location bar, the three lines of code together will set the window status to "Looking up whitehouse. com,"; then, a cool second or so later, they will reset the status bar to "Done" and alert the user that "The connection was refused when attempting to contact whitehouse.com." Whatever page the browser was looking at before whitehouse.com was entered in the Location bar will remain undisturbed. To the user, it'll look just like *http://www.whitehouse.com* is down; they'll be none the wiser as to what's actually going on.

—Ben Karel

H A C K   #82   Add a New XPCOM Component

Extend Firefox's component library with a new object that's usable in the chrome.

Firefox comes preinstalled with over a thousand XPCOM objects (classes and interfaces). Most of these objects provide fundamental services, such as access to files, networks, and data. Nearly all of these objects are written in C++ and are provided in compiled libraries. This hack shows how to add new components written in JavaScript. Typically, new objects provide application-level abstractions on top of the existing libraries, but in theory, they can do anything.

We'll use as an example the creation of a simple persistence class—one that dumps a simple string of information to a disk-based file. We'll put all the required logic into a single script named *nsStringSave.js*, which we'll put in the *components* directory in the install area. We'll use limited error checking, which could easily be done more robustly.

The whole component creation process comes down to dancing to the beat of the XPIDL (Cross Platform Interface Definition Language) drum. Mozilla interfaces are specified in XPIDL. They're part of the Mozilla source code; you can also download them in convenient form from *http://www. nigelmcfarlane.com/books/radmoz_support.html*.

Naming the New Component

Components and interfaces must be defined by both names and numbers. We're creating one new component and one new interface, so that's two names and two numbers. To get the name, we make it up, using some existing conventions. To get the number (called an ID), we run uuidgen or guidgen from the command line or /msg mozbot uuid on the #mozilla channel of *irc.mozilla.org*. On Windows, you can get uuidgen with free Microsoft compiler products [Hack #93].

Interface names are defined in XPIDL files, so here's such a file named *nsIStringSave.idl*:

```
#include "nsISupports.idl"
[scriptable, uuid(A35ED730-4817-4BE3-943E-75E9124FC4D7)]
interface nsIStringSave : nsISupports
{
  void set_file(in string pathname);
  void dump(in string str);
};
```

All components should implement the *nsISupports* interface, which is the fundamental interface. We generate a type library from this file. The original IDL serves as documentation only. To make this library, you need the tool xpidl. It's available in nightly Mozilla builds [Hack #92]. Use it to generate a *nsIStringSave.xpt* file. On UNIX/Linux/Macintosh:

```
xpidl -m typelib nsIStringSave.idl
```

On Windows:

```
Xpidl.exe -m typelib nsIStringSave.idl
```

Put this *.xpt* file in the *components* directory.

Component names are defined along with the component—in this case, done as follows in JavaScript:

```
const SSComponentName = "@mozilla.org/example/string-save;1";
const SSClassID      = Components.ID('{a81d9b27-6adc-47c7-a780-
dced1e1e4cb3}');
```

Again, uuidgen is used to create a unique identifier. We'll put these statements in a script shortly. Naming of the new component is now complete.

Creating and Implementing a Module

Modules are the ultimate containers for XPCOM components. Each module holds zero or more components. Modules themselves implement the nsIModule interface. Here's our new module in JavaScript:

```
const SSComponentName = "@mozilla.org/example/string-save;1";
const SSClassID      = Components.ID('{a81d9b27-6adc-47c7-a780-
dced1e1e4cb3}');

var nsStringSaveModule = {
  getClassObject : function (mgr, cid, iid, ) {
    if ( !cid.equals(SSClassID) ) throw "unknown";
    var component = (new nsStringSave()).QueryInterface(iid);
    component._init();  // the module knows its components
    return component;
  },
  registerSelf   : function () { /* contstructor - does nothing here */ },
  unregisterSelf : function () { /* destructor - does nothing here */},
  canUnload      : function () { return false; /* can't unload */ }
};
```

The getClassObject( ) method checks its arguments and returns an instance of the only component that it knows about. The module object does nothing by itself; an equivalent of C's main( ) is required. For module definition scripts, Firefox expects to find the special hook function named NSGetModule( ), so we add that as well:

```
function NSGetModule() { return nsStringSaveModule; }
```

Creating and Implementing a Component

The getClassObject( ) method in the previous section creates an object that's an instance of the component. It uses the following custom JavaScript object constructor to do so. Append this lot to the file containing the module code:

```
var Cc = Components.classes;     // shorthand
var Ci = Components.interfaces;  // shorthand

function nsStringSave () {};

nsStringSave.prototype = {
// --- "private" data ---
  _file    : null,
  _stream  : null,
  _init    : function () {
    _file  = Cc["@mozilla.org/local/file;1"].createInstance(Ci.nsILocalFile);
```

```
    _stream = Cc["@mozilla.org/network/file-output-stream;1"];
    _stream = _stream.createInstance(Ci.nsIFileOutputStream);
  },
  // --- nsIStringSave ---
  set_file : function (path) {
    _file.initWithPath(path);
    _stream.close();
    _stream.init(_file, 0x0A, 0644, true);
  },
  dump : function (str) {
    _stream.write(str, str.length);
  },
  // --- nsISupports ---
  QueryInterface : function (iid) {
    if ( !iid.equals(Components.interfaces.nsISupports) )   throw "unknown";
    if ( !iid.equals(Components.interfaces.nsIStringSave) ) throw "unknown";
    return this;
  }
};
```

There's a bit of complexity at work here, both in the use of JavaScript proto-
types and in the opening and administering of file objects. The important bit
is that the object constructor constructs an object that implements the two
required interfaces: nsISupports and nsIStringSave.

Installing the Component

The *nsIStringSave.js* file, once complete, should be put in the *components*
directory. After that, we have to fool Firefox into thinking that the install
area's been patched with new files (in truth, it has). Once that misdirection
is achieved, Firefox will do extra work the next time it starts up. It will do a
big audit of all the stuff it has to work with, and that includes discovering all
XPCOM modules and components.

 Make a backup of the user profile's *compreg.dat* before
proceeding.

To flag that the audit should occur, move to the user profile area. Find the
file named *compatibility.ini*. Edit it with a text editor and decrement the
Build ID date by one day. Save the file in place.

When Firefox next starts up, it will do its big audit because it thinks that it
has been patched (the build date has gone up). It will find the *nsStringSave.*
xpt file and also the new NSGetModule( ) call. From those things and others, it
will write out a file called *compreg.dat*. Each time Firefox starts up subsequently, it will rely on the *compreg.dat* file for an accurate list of available

objects. When getting ready for the audit, it is therefore critical that you back up this file, in case there are programming errors in your new modules, components, or interfaces. Those errors will cause the regenerated *compreg.dat* file to be flawed, and in that case, you'll need the old one to go back to.

Running the Component

From any secure scripting environment (in the chrome, a signed web page, or using the `xpcshell` testing tool) this is all the code you need to use your new component:

```
var saver = Components.classes["@mozilla.org/example/string-saver;1"];
saver    = saver.createInstance(Components.interfaces.nsIStringSaver);

saver.set_file("C:\tmp\test.dat");
saver.dump("A test string of no particular import");
```

`xpcshell` is a small, non-GUI JavaScript interpreter available in nightly builds that can manipulate XPCOM objects.

Add a New Command-Line Option

HACK
#83
Customize the startup process and the process of starting windows by adding support for new command-line arguments.

The set of Firefox command-line arguments isn't fixed. You can add more options if you want. In the complex case, new command-line options can be compiled up into dynamic link libraries using C/C++. It's easier to use a simple JavaScript script, though. This hack shows how to implement the simple case. We'll make a --my or /my option that displays a page stored in the install area on startup.

Preparation

The straightforward thing to do is to add an option that starts up a window of your own design. In order to do that quickly, you have to sidestep the Extensions system by hacking on the install area directly. You have to create a specific set of objects to make everything hang together properly.

As in "Add a New XPCOM Component" [Hack #82], start by shutting down all Mozilla programs in preparation for new component registration. Find the file named *compatibility.ini* in your Firefox profile. Edit it and decrement the *Build ID* date by one day. Save the file. The *compreg.dat* component registry is in the same directory if you want to inspect it while you're there.

Make a backup copy of the *compreg.dat* file before proceeding.

Next, move from the profile directory to the Firefox install directory. In there, you'll find a *components* directory. Go to that directory. You'll see there's a number of DLL (or *.so*) dynamic link libraries, with their accompanying *.xpt* type libraries. Ignore those. Instead, note the existing *.js* files. You need to make one of those.

The *jsconsole-clhander.js* file is a good example of a command-line option implemented in JavaScript. Some of the other JavaScript files in that directory do things unrelated to command lines, so beware.

Making the Script Outline

Here's an outline of the script you need to create:

```
// Tell mozilla there's a new module of components

function NSGetModule( ) {}

// Make a module to hold the sole component

var myCommandModule = {

  registerSelf   : function () {},
  getClassObject : function () {},
  unregisterSelf : function () {},
  canUnload      : function () {}
};

// The module creates the component using a factory object

var myCommandComponentFactory = {
  createInstance : function () {},
  lockFactory    : function () {}
};

// The component itself is just a simple record

var myCommandComponent = {
  commandLineArgument : "",
  prefNameForStartup  : "",
  chromeUrlForTask    : "",
  helpText            : "",
  handlesArgs         : true,
  defaultArgs         : "",
  openWindowWithArgs  : true
}
```

As in "Add a New XPCOM Component" [Hack #82], the NSGetModule( ) function is included to be detected by Firefox at startup time. It's the hook that will install all the rest of the claptrap. After that, you have three objects to create:

- The myCommandModule object has an nsIModule interface. It is the topmost container that holds the components we're creating.

- The myCommandComponentFactory object has an nsIFactory interface. It will be returned by the module when Firefox detects that a new command-line object is needed.

- The myCommandComponent object has an nsICmdLineHandler interface. It represents the command-line option we're creating. Because the required interface is quite simple, the object looks like a simple collection of data, which it is.

In this skeleton code, we've been a bit naughty and specified the component as a singleton object rather than as a full JavaScript object constructor. The factory object would really like to construct a whole new handler object each time. It works as is, though, and we're unlikely to use the same command-line option twice anyway.

We won't ever call or use any of these objects from other scripts. An object embedded in the Firefox browser called the *command-line manager* will call them for us whenever that's necessary. NSGetModule( ) is called by the module registration system, as before. This hack is a good example of the extensive *delegation* programming that's common across Firefox's design. One object defers to another in a handover style of processing.

Filling in the Script

Filling in the details of this script outline can be done quickly. We haven't bothered here with all the fancy error handling; you can add that if you want. Just copy it from one of the other command handlers. Put the following completed script in *myoption.js* in the *components* directory:

```
// give the new component an identity

const HandlerPrefix   = "@mozilla.org/commandlinehandler/general-
startup;1?type=";
const MyContractID    = HandlerPrefix + "my";
const MyClassID       = Components.ID('{75034172-c6bd-4f3d-bbb0-
0c572428e3c1}');

// Tell mozilla there's a new module of components

function NSGetModule( ) { return myCommandModule; }
```

```
// Make a module to hold the sole component

var myCommandModule = {

  registerSelf   : function (compMgr, file, location, type) {
    var reg = compMgr.QueryInterface(
      Components.interfaces.nsIComponentRegistrar
    );
    reg.registerFactoryLocation(
      MyClassID, "My Service", MyContractID, file, location, type
    );
  },

  getClassObject : function (compMgr, cid, iid) {
    return myCommandComponentFactory;
  },

  unregisterSelf : function () { },
  canUnload      : function () { return false; }
};

// The module creates the component using a factory object

var myCommandComponentFactory = {
  createInstance : function (outer,iid) { return myCommandComponent;},
  lockFactory    : function () { }
}

// The component itself is just a simple record

var myCommandComponent = {
  commandLineArgument : "-my",
  prefNameForStartup  : "general.startup.my",
  chromeUrlForTask    : "resource:/res/mypage.html",
  helpText            : "My Help",
  handlesArgs         : true,
  defaultArgs         : "default",
  openWindowWithArgs  : true
}
```

Let's run through the code briefly. We're creating a -my command-line
option. --my will also work, and we get /my on Windows as an extra bonus.
The only part of the contract ID that can vary is the very last bit, as shown in
the bolded line. The rest must be stated to match what the command-line
manager expects. To get a class ID, just run uuidgen or guidgen from the
command line, and cut and paste the output.

NSGetModule( ) passes back our module object, a trivial task. The module
object is able to register the sole component type we've created. It's too
dumb to be able to unregister or do other fancy management. It can also
pass back our factory object if it's asked to. Finally, the factory object can

extrude our singleton handler instance. You can see how a request for a command-line handler is delegated first from the module level down to the factory level, and then finally down to a component instance. Who uses the final component instance? The command-line manager embedded inside Firefox does.

Here are the interesting bits—first, the handler itself. The only things worth changing in the handler record are `commandLineArgument` and `chromeUrlForTask`. The former is the option we're creating. The latter, despite the name, can be any URL. We've chosen an HTML page that we'll put inside the Firefox install area. The `resource:` URI scheme points to the top of that area, so we'll be able to put *mypage.html* into the *res* subdirectory under there. That's a safe place for a startup file to live.

The second interesting bit is debugging. The first time you run Firefox, your module is registered. Unless you have fundamental syntax problems, that much should work. You can confirm it by finding the filename in *compreg. dat* in your profile. After that, you get no feedback at all unless you've got a debug build of Firefox. In that case, you can use `dump( )`. For the normal case, you'll have to check your JavaScript very carefully. Use a syntax-highlighting editor and examine constant strings and keywords carefully for typos. To see your new option work successfully, just run:

```
firefox -my
```

If nothing appears to work, try `-jsconsole` to prove to yourself that everything is still sane. Don't forget to fully shut down Firefox if you suspect it's become confused.

This command-line stuff is really designed for XUL-based windows, not HTML ones. It will work for HTML windows if you're careful. Some weird results are possible if your HTML page isn't coded tightly, though. Start with a trivial page before you try anything fancy. Either way, the displayed document is free to do its own scripting. That code can pick up where the command-line code left off. Hack the `createInstance( )` method in the script if you really want to do extra processing before the window opens.

Hack the Chrome Cleanly

Hacks 84–90

This chapter describes how to create and deploy Firefox enhancements properly. Enhancements include skins, themes, extensions, and applications. This chapter covers the creation of JAR and XPI files, their contents, and the web site features that are used to deliver them.

Firefox browser windows (and other Firefox windows) can be compared to the command-line environment. Just as a command-line interface can be used to start many different programs, so too can Firefox windows. They are good places from which to launch other applications or enhancements. Such applications can be started through Firefox's menu system, the keyboard, or the mouse, and they can be trivial or complex. They can be highly integrated with Firefox, like extensions, or they can be mostly separate, like the DOM Inspector.

The Firefox web browser is also Internet-enabled and is therefore a kind of application portal for applications that are local, remote, or remotely installed. The concept of being able to launch your own application (or simple feature) from a widely used and free application portal like Firefox is very attractive to some service providers. Firefox provides them with an automatic deployment mechanism.

To build a quality enhancement that can be invoked from a Firefox window, the content that makes up that enhancement must be built out of *chrome technology*: XUL, CSS, JavaScript, and images. That content must then be annotated and bundled up correctly, using RDF, so that when Firefox first gets it—usually through a URL—all the right bookkeeping is done in the small text files that Firefox maintains. With that bookkeeping in place, the extension (or application or theme) can reliably be made available to the end user.

This chapter is mostly concerned with explaining how that bookkeeping is done correctly. Chapter 7 takes a more immediate look at how to build chrome content. The introductory concepts described in "Do Groundwork for Ugly Chrome Hacks" [Hack #75] also apply to this chapter. The main difference is that this chapter requires more organization and more discipline.

HACK #84 Do Groundwork for Extension Development

Understand how extensions, themes, and locales fit into the Firefox architecture.

Chapter 7 introduced the key ideas of chrome, chrome: URLs, JAR files, and packages [Hack #75]. Those concepts also apply to more formal chrome enhancement projects. Such projects also require the concepts of extensions, themes, locales, XPIs, and XPInstall. This hack describes those concepts in more detail. It's all about collecting together the jigsaw pieces in preparation for solving the puzzle.

There are some basic differences between quick hacks to the chrome and fully prepared extensions. These are the main advantages of extensions:

- They have a formal concept of version.
- They can be updated after they are installed.
- They can be updated across the Web from a web site.
- If Firefox is upgraded, installed extensions are not lost.
- Registration information exposes details of extensions to scripts.
- Extensions are, by default, stored per-profile in the profile area.
- Firefox's -safe-mode option allows extensions to be disabled easily.

Spot Extension Files

All installed extensions live in the *extensions* directory, either in the profile area or in the install area. In that directory are two important files. *Extensions.rdf* is a small database of all the currently installed extensions. The other file, usually named something like *installed-extensions.txt*, lists the extensions that were discovered the last time Firefox did a big audit of all the extensions in the *extensions* directory. This happens when the *installed-extensions.txt* file is updated, through the same approach used for the install area's *installed-chrome.txt* file [Hack #75].

Separate from these two files are the actual extensions. Directories with names like this contain one extension each:

```
{972ce4c6-7e08-4474-a285-3208198ce6fd}
```

The name exactly matches the UUID that uniquely identifies the extension. Generation of UUIDs is done the same way as for XPCOM components [Hack #82]. The contents of these directories are the unpacked contents of the *.xpi* file in which the extension was delivered. Subdirectories named *chrome*, *components*, *defaults*, and *uninstall* inside each extension directory perform the same roles as those directories in the install area. For example, the *.jar* content files for the extension can be found in the extension's *chrome* subdirectory.

Firefox must scan all of these directories at startup (although the XUL Fast-Load cache can reduce this burden to zero), so installing many extensions can affect startup performance a little. Then there is the matter of what the extensions do once they start up.

Spot Extension Installers

Extensions are delivered as *.xpi* (XPI stands for cross (*X*) platform *install*) files. They're usually delivered by clicking a link in an HTML page and require a special web server setting [Hack #27]. At the Mozilla Update web site (*http://update.mozilla.org*), you can see many of these files behind the download links, and if you context-click on one such link, you can save the *.xpi* file to disk and open it up instead of installing it. These files are ordinary ZIP files, except that they have a special directory layout that includes an optional install script named *install.js* and an install manifest named *install.rdf*. They can also be digitally signed.

Three Kinds of RDF Files

Here's a summary of the preceding remarks from a Resource Description Framework (RDF) perspective. RDF is used to provide all the management information about extensions, locales, themes, and packages.

Since extension content is typically delivered as one or more JAR files, extensions contain (inside those JAR files) one or more *contents.rdf* files. These files provide package registration and overlay registration information for the extension's chrome content. They're all about the lowest-level detail—packages and content—and they know nothing about extensions.

Extension JAR files are put into an XPI file along with an *install.rdf* file. This second RDF file contains all the registration information about the extension. The content of this file allows Firefox to manage the extension across versions, update it when required, and display its details in the Extension Manager dialog box.

Finally, the *Extensions.rdf* file in the profile area is the place where all of the information about extensions is aggregated. It contains all of the important information from all of the *install.rdf* files supplied by all of the extensions.

Compare Locales, Themes, Applications, and Extensions

Locales, themes, applications, and extensions are four types of download-able enhancements that have a great deal in common. They all use some combination of content hierarchy that combines a *package* directory with one or more *skin, locale,* or *content* directories.

They differ in the registration information that's stored in RDF. Pieces of data for each kind of enhancement are recorded with different kinds of Uniform Resource Names (URNs). A URL can be either a URL or a URN; see the IETF RFC 2396 technical note for a definition (*http://www.ietf.org*). Once you understand the basic URN naming scheme, browsing through the complex syntax of RDF files is a little easier.

These are the URN registration prefixes for themes and extensions:

```
urn:mozilla:theme:...details...
urn:mozilla:extension:...details...
```

These URNs are downloaded during extension or theme install. At the same time additional URNs that record the install bundle are also saved. Here's an example:

```
urn:mozilla:install-manifest:...details...
```

By comparison, locales are generally bundled with a localized Firefox install and are not installed via extensions. If they are delivered as extensions, they acquire the same registration prefixes as ordinary extensions do.

For install-bundled locales and install-bundled applications (like Firefox), the only registration URNs that appear are the traditional package ones:

```
urn:mozilla:locale:...
urn:mozilla:package:...
urn:mozilla:skin:...
```

This package configuration information is present in all cases, not just for bundled items.

Find the XPInstall Missing Link

When an extension is downloaded, it doesn't appear in the browser window as content and it doesn't get saved to disk (unless you choose that option). So how is it delivered to the Firefox profile area or install area?

The answer is XPInstall (Cross (*X*) Platform *Install*), a small piece of Firefox that offers a JavaScript hook in web pages and that can also recognize XPI content types. When an extension is installed, the XPI file is sucked directly into XPInstall (that is, into the Firefox executable's memory), where it is pulled apart. Each piece of the extension is then placed in the right spot. It's a system similar to InstallShield, but much less complex and entirely embedded inside the Firefox executable. XPInstall is close to fully automatic in its processing, so there's nothing much to do other than benefit from it.

HACK #85 Study Packages with the Chrome Manager
Demystify the way the chrome system is organized with this handy tool.

The XML dialect called RDF is not exactly a simple system to use, and Firefox relies on RDF files a lot. This hack shows how to use the Chrome Manager tool, an extension that provides a simple breakdown of these complex structures. Together with the InfoLister extension [Hack #38], you can get a complete picture of what's installed in the chrome.

Get the Chrome Manager

This useful extension is buried where it's hard to find. It's written by Karsten Düsterlo as part of the larger and cryptically named *Mnenhy* extension. "Mnenhy" stands for *Mail-News ENHancement-Y*. Whatever. You can install it from here:

> *http://mnenhy.mozdev.org/*

The beauty of this extension is not its mail and news features any more than it is its cryptic name. Its beauty is in the small Chrome Manager tool that's included almost as an afterthought. Mnenhy can be safely installed as an extension in Firefox, but at the time of writing (at Version 0.7), not all of its features are complete or reliable. You've been warned. It is safe to use as a view-only tool; don't make changes with it unless you are an expert.

Chrome Simplified

Figure 8-1 shows the initial window that the Chrome Manager presents.

It's strongly recommended that you *don't* push any of the buttons circled in Figure 8-1. You might regret it if you do. Avoid the temptation, or else study the online help before diving in bravely.

What's important about this window is the division of all the chrome that Firefox possesses into three simple categories: packages, skins, and locales.

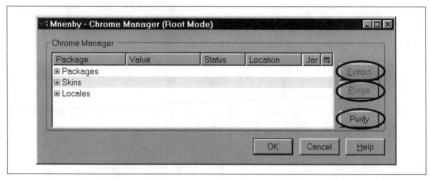

Figure 8-1. The Chrome Manager window, with highlighted danger buttons

In the end, these things are all that the chrome has to offer and all that can be accessed using the special chrome: URL. So, all the confusion about themes, skins, extensions, locales, and so on is really just matter of labels; all these things boil down to those three simple categories.

This display is derived from all the aggregated RDF information that Firefox keeps in memory [Hack #75] while it's running.

Understand Packages

Figure 8-2 shows the packages part of the chrome hierarchy opened up one level.

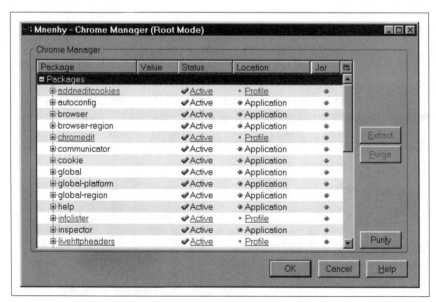

Figure 8-2. The Chrome Manager, showing packages

In Figure 8-2, underlined package names are installed in the profile area. As you can see, all underlined packages are named after an extension, and each extension adds exactly one package. That's the normal case, but not an absolute rule. If you bring up this display and scroll down, you'll see that the *Mnenhy* extension provides seven packages.

More interestingly, the package names that are marked as applications are the ones that are provided with the default install of Firefox. They reside in the install area, but they're still just packages. In Figure 8-2, you can see the browser package that is the main Firefox interface, the help system, the Cookie Manager, the DOM Inspector, and even a bit of leftover Netscape Communicator 4.x in the communicator package. It hasn't been completely deprecated yet. In short, the entire Firefox user interface, including extensions, is just a set of packages. If this window is rearranged and manipulated a little, Figure 8-3 results.

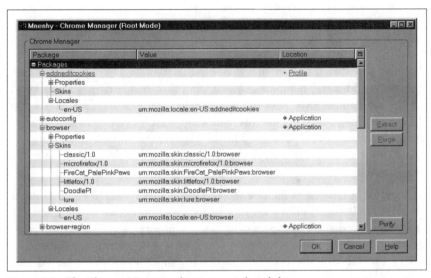

Figure 8-3. The Chrome Manager, showing contributed skins

Here, the relationship between packages, locales, and skins is made obvious. The browser package (Firefox itself, appearing at line 8) is well supported by the five or so additional themes that have been installed. There's a skin for the browser package from each of those five themes, plus the default theme's skin. The lesser-known addneditcookies package has received no special skins from those themes. That's the price of obscurity. Fortunately, there's always a global skin, and all packages can trivially benefit from that. Similarly, the only locale that contributes to the browser is the default of en-US (U.S. English). The addneditcookies package has only that locale as well, so that extension can't be installed in the German version of Firefox; if it were, it would be missing the required de-DE locale, and no text would appear in its user interface. It should be enhanced.

Packages Versus Extensions

It's revealing to compare the Chrome Manager with the report generated by the InfoLister extension [Hack #38]. The Chrome Manager reports on the low-level packages, locales, and skins that make up all the user-interface content. The InfoLister window reports the names of the products that delivered those packages: extensions, plug-ins, and themes. It's the latter information that's used to check for updates across the Web. The lower-level information is what Firefox uses when it needs to display a window or dialog box.

 HACK Create a Chrome Package
#86 Packages are the fundamental concept underlying most chrome content.
Here's how to make one.

Pieces of software installed on top of Firefox are called extensions, themes, locales, or add-ons. The name *extension* and those other names are all product bundle names. Extension product bundles, for example, are handled by the Extension Manager. Inside these product bundles is the lower-level nuts-and-bolts concept of a package. This hack covers the different package representations and the extra steps that are needed for packages to be formally recognized by Firefox in the chrome registry.

An extension's packages include the extension's user-interface (UI) content, plus some additional information. This information makes up the extra bits and pieces needed for the extension to work in Firefox. Users see an extension as something that carries out a particular task for them. This encompasses the UI and the code to implement any functionality. A package includes these files, but it also serves as the name of the extension as it is used in file paths and in RDF files. Packages underlie all themes, locales, and extensions for Firefox.

Here are the steps needed to bring a package into existence:

1. Create your files locally on disk.
2. Choose to leave them in a flat file structure or put them in a JAR.
3. Create the *contents.rdf* files necessary for Firefox chrome registration.
4. Enable special chrome:// URLs for your package.

After these steps, the package is ready for further bundling into an XPI file
[Hack #88] and final distribution.

Create a Local Folder Hierarchy

Before you begin to write your extension, the first thing you should decide
on is the folder structure on disk for development. It should closely mirror
the structure of the JAR file or packaged folders that you will create. Let's
have a look at an example.

> Examples in this chapter are drawn from a real extension out
> in the wild called chromEdit. This is a simple yet very useful
> program for customizing the appearance and preferences of
> Firefox. As its name suggests, it allows you to edit files in
> Mozilla chrome, but not the ones talked about in this chap-
> ter. You can change *userContent.css* and *userChrome.css* for a
> personalized look and use *user.js* to change preferences.
> "Play With the Preference System" [Hack #23] covers these files
> in more detail. You can download chromEdit from *http://cdn.
> mozdev.org/chromedit*, and it is also available from *http://
> update.mozilla.org*.

On disk, a typical structure looks like this:

```
chromedit
  content
    chromeedit.xul
  locale
    en-US
      chromedit.properties
    fr-FR
      chromedit.properties
  skin
    classic
      chromedit.css
    groovy
      chromedit.css
```

Each directory requires different kinds of files. As a general rule, content
contains XUL and JavaScript files, locale contains DTD and string bundles,
and skin contains CSS files and images.

Create a Package Representation

The local folder hierarchy must be converted into a formal package. You
have a choice between a flat file structure or a JAR file. A package must use
one or the other format. Firefox's standard install provides packages in JAR
format.

Flat file structure. If you choose this option, it means that files arranged on disk stay *as is* and are not compressed or reorganized. This is suitable for small packages. There is no set rule regarding how many files you need to have to prefer this approach. It is entirely up to you. However, a good rule of thumb is that if there are more than four or five files, they should be compressed in a JAR for space-saving purposes. The choice of the flat structure means that the files stay in the same folders as they are on local disk. That makes life easier if you are debugging a package. Here's that standard directory layout for the chromedit package:

```
chromedit
  content
  locale
    en-US
    fr-FR
    ...
  skin
    classic
    groovy
    ...
```

There's just one top-level directory, named after the package. This listing is the same as the previous listing.

JAR representation. At the most abstract level, the JAR representation of a package is a simple JAR filename, the same name as the extension's package name. In the case of this sample JAR file, the filename is *chromedit.jar*. The internal hierarchy in the JAR file looks like this:

```
content
  chromedit
locale
  en-US
    chromedit
  fr-FR
    chromedit
  ...
skin
  classic
    chromedit
  groovy
    chromedit
  ...
```

In this case, there are three top-level directories: *content/*, *locale/*, and *skin/*. The files are compressed in ZIP format, leaving a smaller footprint on disk and making for a smaller download. Contained within the JAR file are the subdirectories, with their hierarchy intact. In this case, though, the package name dangles underneath the other details. A JAR file can contain more than one package.

Default URL names for package files. At this point, the files, whether flat or in a JAR file, are each accessible via a resource:// URL if they are placed in the Firefox install area. However, once registered, the package gains full security privileges and file access is achieved via chrome:// URLs, as we're about to see.

Register a Package with the Chrome Registry

Having the right folders and files gets you only halfway to where you want to go. Once the package is bundled and installed [Hack #88], it will just sit in its destination directory anonymously unless it provides some information needed by Firefox to recognize it internally. This process is known as *chrome registration* and is enabled by RDF files known as *manifests*.

Make a contents.rdf manifest file. The nature of the term *manifest* is not something be dwelled upon; what is more important is the form that manifest files take and how they work. The form they take in chrome registration is one or more *contents.rdf* files placed in the folder hierarchy. They tell Firefox that, if it finds a *contents.rdf* file in a particular folder, this folder will be one of the core *content*, *skin*, or *locale* folders that matches up with special chrome:// URLs to access files internally.

Here is a standard boilerplate *contents.rdf* file to be placed in the *content/* folder of an extension or package; all *contents.rdf* files look almost identical to this one:

```
1  <?xml version="1.0"?>
2  <RDF:RDF xmlns:RDF="http://www.w3.org/1999/02/22-rdf-syntax-ns#"
3           xmlns:chrome="http://www.mozilla.org/rdf/chrome#">
4    <RDF:Seq about="urn:mozilla:package:root">
5      <RDF:li resource="urn:mozilla:package:chromedit" />
6    </RDF:Seq>
7    <!-- Extension information -->
8    <RDF:Description about="urn:mozilla:package:chromedit"
9                 chrome:description="A Simple User Profile File Editor"
10                chrome:name="chromedit">
11   </RDF:Description>
12 </RDF:RDF>
```

The bolded information is the only part that varies between packages (in the simple case). This RDF file has standard XML syntax and uses two namespaces: RDF and chrome. The most important items are the type of the manifest and the description. Lines 4 through 6 state the name of the package, which is also the folder name of the package. This information is added to the package root, which holds the full list of packages. That parent resource is called urn:mozilla:package:root.

Lines 7 through 11 tell us a little bit about the extension—here, the name and a description. These attributes are largely redundant, due to the front-end metadata contained in another file, *install.rdf* [Hack #88]. However, for completeness, Table 8-1 provides a complete list of attributes.

Table 8-1. Chrome package attributes

Attribute	Description
Author	Name of person or organization that created the extension
AuthorURL	Web site of the extension
Description	A one-liner about the extension
DisplayName	Full *pretty* name of the extension
Extension	Boolean value to enable/disable the package as an extension, a legacy of the days before the Extension Manager
Name	The internal name of the package

When Firefox starts up for the first time after you install the extension, it will read this information in and make the necessary chrome registry changes. It knows where to find these files because it is told where to look in *install.rdf* [Hack #88].

Use the new chrome: URLs. Recall that a chrome: URL is a special internal path that can be used to access files registered in the chrome. A typical chrome: URL looks like this:

   chrome://chromedit/content/filename.js

This particular URL can be used in a XUL file, for example, to pull in the JavaScript file. The extension name registered for the chrome URL is chromedit and is extracted from the package *contents.rdf*. In the sample *contents.rdf* manifest, it is included in what is known as the root-sequence section:

```
<RDF:Seq about="urn:mozilla:package:root">
  <RDF:li resource="urn:mozilla:package:chromedit" />
</RDF:Seq>
```

It is possible to distribute and register more than one extension. All you have to do is add another resource list item in the root sequence.

The URL *chrome://chromedit/content/* resolves to the directory where the *contents.rdf* file was found. So, typically, this is where you would place all your application XUL and JavaScript files. Subdirectories are fine to use, but they have to be included in the URL. So, if you have a folder called *overlays* under the folder where the *contents.rdf* lives, the URL would look like this:

chrome://chromedit/content/overlays/filename.xul

For completeness, here are the *contents.rdf* files for *skin/* and *locale/* of the extension, necessary to register chrome URLs for these portions:

chrome://chromedit/skin/
chrome://chromedit/locale/

When filenames are omitted from the URL, such as in the previous examples, the URL resolves to the package name and the default extension for each component. So, *chrome://chromedit/content/* looks for *chromedit.xul* in that folder. The default extension for *skin/* is *.css*, and *.dtd* is the default for *locale/*.

This example shows how the skin part of a chrome: URL is registered:

```
<?xml version="1.0"?>
<RDF:RDF xmlns:RDF="http://www.w3.org/1999/02/22-rdf-syntax-ns#"
         xmlns:chrome="http://www.mozilla.org/rdf/chrome#">
  <RDF:Seq about="urn:mozilla:skin:root">
    <RDF:li resource="urn:mozilla:skin:classic/1.0" />
  </RDF:Seq>
  <RDF:Description about="urn:mozilla:skin:classic/1.0">
    <chrome:packages>
      <RDF:Seq about="urn:mozilla:skin:classic/1.0:packages">
        <RDF:li resource="urn:mozilla:skin:classic/1.0:chromedit"/>
      </RDF:Seq>
    </chrome:packages>
  </RDF:Description>
</RDF:RDF>
```

This example shows how the locale part of a chrome: URL is registered:

```
<?xml version="1.0"?>
<RDF:RDF xmlns:RDF="http://www.w3.org/1999/02/22-rdf-syntax-ns#"
         xmlns:chrome="http://www.mozilla.org/rdf/chrome#">
  <RDF:Seq about="urn:mozilla:locale:root">
    <RDF:li resource="urn:mozilla:locale:en-US"/>
  </RDF:Seq>
  <RDF:Description about="urn:mozilla:locale:en-US"
                  chrome:displayName="English(US)"
                  chrome:name="en-US">
    <chrome:packages>
      <RDF:Seq about="urn:mozilla:locale:en-US:packages">
        <RDF:li resource="urn:mozilla:locale:en-US:chromedit"/>
      </RDF:Seq>
    </chrome:packages>
  </RDF:Description>
</RDF:RDF>
```

—*Brian King*

Make a Bottom-Up Overlay
#87   Bottom-up (RDF-driven) overlays allow existing Firefox GUIs to be enhanced.

In the context of Mozilla, an *overlay* is a hunk of user-interface (UI) data, most commonly XUL, that is extracted to separate files and pulled in at runtime to parts of the UI that include it. Think of it as a reusable widget or set of widgets.

In general, there are two types of overlays. One is a directly specified overlay that you put in your extension. These are used to keep your code modular or to reuse in multiple places in the extension. The second type is something that you want to appear in the Firefox default application, perhaps to carry out a particular function of your extension. For example, you might want to add a menu item to the Tools menu to launch your extension. In a sense, in that case, you are adding to the default UI for Firefox.

This hack focuses on the latter approach, with instructions on which type of overlays you can have, how to make them, and some general insight into how Firefox handles the overlays.

Adding an Item

For the overlay puzzle to fall into place, you need three parts of the puzzle:

- Entries in *contents.rdf* to register the overlay
- The name of file that is the target of the overlay
- The code that will be pulled in from the overlay to its destination

The best way to understand each piece is by walking through an example. Here, we are going to add a menu item to the Firefox Tools menu to launch the chromeEdit application.

Register the overlay. "Create a Chrome Package" [Hack #86] explained *contents. rdf* files for the purpose of registering extensions. Lets add to the sample *contents.rdf* file in that hack to show how to register overlays:

```
<?xml version="1.0"?>
<RDF:RDF xmlns:RDF="http://www.w3.org/1999/02/22-rdf-syntax-ns#"
         xmlns:chrome="http://www.mozilla.org/rdf/chrome#">
...<!-- extension information omitted -->

<!-- overlay information -->
<RDF:Seq about="urn:mozilla:overlays">
  <RDF:li resource="chrome://browser/content/browser.xul"/>
</RDF:Seq>
<RDF:Seq about="chrome://browser/content/browser.xul">
```

```
    <RDF:li>chrome://chromedit/content/chromeditBrowserOverlay.xul</RDF:li>
  </RDF:Seq>
</RDF:RDF>
```

This time, we skip over the extension information and move on to overlay information. This information tells Firefox to take some extra chrome from the *chromeditBrowserOverlay.xul* file. The first bolded sequence says that this extension has overlays that it wants registered and lists the files in Firefox that will be overlaid. In this instance, it is the main browser window file, *browser.xul*.

The second highlighted sequence lists all the extension overlay files that will be pulled into the overlaid Firefox file. So, at this point, all we have is a correlation between Firefox files and an extension file, defining their connection from a high level. The low-level detail of what widget goes where is done in the overlay file.

The overlay file. Now that we've registered the *chromeditBrowserOverlay.xul*, let's look inside the overlay file to create the menu item and place it in the Tools menu. The structure of an overlay file is the same as any XUL file, with the main difference being that the root element is <overlay>. This tag needs a namespace attribute only, though an ID is also recommended:

```
<?xml version="1.0"?>
<!DOCTYPE overlay SYSTEM "chrome://chromedit/locale/chromeditMenuOverlay.
dtd">
<?xml-stylesheet href="chrome://chromedit/skin/chromedit.css" type="text/
css"?>
<overlay id="ceTasksOverlay"
       xmlns="http://www.mozilla.org/keymaster/gatekeeper/there.is.only.xul">
  <script type="application/x-javascript">
  <![CDATA[
    // functions go here
  ]]>
  </script>

  <menupopup id="taskPopup">
    <menuitem oncommand="showChromEdit()"
            label="Edit User Files"
            id="chromedit-aviary"
            insertbefore="menu_preferences"
            class="menuitem-iconic menu-iconic icon-chromedit16"/>
  </menupopup>
</overlay>
```

The overlay has a name: ceTasksOverlay. The chunk to be placed in the browser UI is a menu-item widget. It is to be placed in an existing, identified container tag. In this case, this is the Tools <menupopup>, which has an id of taskPopup. The id is the bit of the overlay that is matched up with an identical id in the Firefox target file, so this must not be left out. Everything contained within that id tag in the overlay will be placed in the <menupopup> in the target file. The new <menuitem> has a label, and a command to call a function to launch the extension. Separate from the detail that coordinates the overlay fragment with the rest of Firefox, the class attribute is used by the chromedit package to apply icon-laden styles to the menu item, for a pleasing effect.

At runtime, Firefox looks up the list of overlay files, scans then, find matches for widget IDs, and merges the new XUL into the UI. Figure 8-4 shows how the new Edit User Files menu item looks for chromEdit. Note the styled-in icon.

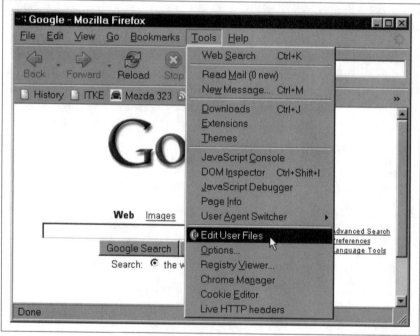

Figure 8-4. Overlaid Tools menu in Firefox

Other Places to Overlay

So far, our example has concerned adding a menu item to the Firefox Tools menu, but there are other areas of the Firefox UI into which you can overlay. It's possible to overlay into any area of the visible UI, once you know the id of the widget to which you want to add. For example, the Download Manager Tweak extension (*http://dmextension.mozdev.org*) adds a button to the Downloads panel in Firefox's Options window.

The ForecastFox extension (*http://forecastfox.mozdev.org*) **[Hack #37]** gives the option of showing temperatures and conditions in either the menu bar, the main toolbar, or the status bar. Here is a list of the most-used areas where extensions put overlays, but it is by no means definitive:

- Menu bar
- Main toolbar
- Personal toolbar
- Status bar
- Options

Adding a Sidebar

Firefox has a sidebar that can be accessed via the View → Sidebar menu item. The default features that are available as sidebar panels are Bookmarks, History, and Downloads. You can add a sidebar panel for your extension. Here's an example of how to do so with chromEdit:

```
<menupopup id="viewSidebarMenu">
  <menuitem observes="viewChromEditSidebar" class="icon-chromedit16"/>
</menupopup>

<broadcasterset id="mainBroadcasterSet">
  <broadcaster id="viewChromEditSidebar"
    autoCheck="false"
    label="ChromEdit"
    type="checkbox" group="sidebar"
    sidebarurl="chrome://chromedit/content/"
    sidebartitle="ChromEdit"
    oncommand="toggleSidebar('viewChromEditSidebar');"/>
</broadcasterset>
```

The first thing to note in this example is that a sidebar needs two XUL blocks. Similar to the Tools menu overlay, we have a menu item. In this case, it is attached to the View → Sidebar menu using the viewSidebarMenu id, which opens or closes chromEdit in the sidebar when activated. The menu item is then hooked up to a broadcaster via the observes attribute. The new broadcaster for the sidebar is overlaid into Firefox's main broadcaster set. The menu-item attributes are abstracted to the overlay simply to allow it to be used in more than one place.

The sidebar holds the information on what file to open in the sidebar (sidebarurl), and the name it will have there (sidebartitle).

Under the Covers

Just for debugging purposes, there is a place to look to see if your overlays are being pulled into Firefox—a section of chrome called *overlayinfo*. You will find it in two places on disk. The first is in the install area under *chrome/overlayinfo*, and the second is in the profile area under *chrome/overlayinfo*. Because Firefox extensions are installed in the user profile directory, you will find your overlay information in the latter.

Under the *overlayinfo* folder you will find multiple subfolders, but the relevant one for Firefox is *browser*. Enter the content folder and locate the file *overlays.rdf*. If the completed chromedit *contents.rdf* file registered correctly when Firefox was restarted, you should see the following entry in that overlay file:

```
<?xml version="1.0"?>
<RDF:RDF xmlns:c="http://www.mozilla.org/rdf/chrome#"
         xmlns:NC="http://home.netscape.com/NC-rdf#"
         xmlns:RDF="http://www.w3.org/1999/02/22-rdf-syntax-ns#">
  <RDF:Seq RDF:about="chrome://browser/content/browser.xul">
    <RDF:li>chrome://chromedit/content/chromeditBrowserOverlay.xul</RDF:li>
  </RDF:Seq>
</RDF:RDF>
```

If your overlay file is not listed here, there was a problem with registration and you should go back and double-check your *contents.rdf* file. You should not manually add entries to this file.

Skin Overlays

When you overlay the browser, the widgets you add are now in that scope. You might also want to add styles to those widgets. For example, you might want to add an icon to the menu item via a class attribute. The best way to do this is via a skin overlay.

The first step is to add entries to the skin *contents.rdf* manifest with target and stylesheet information. Start with the standard skin registration *contents.rdf* manifest [Hack #86]. Then, add the following entries:

```
<RDF:Seq about="urn:mozilla:stylesheets">
  <RDF:li resource="chrome://global/content/customizeToolbar.xul"/>
  <RDF:li resource="chrome://browser/content/browser.xul"/>
</RDF:Seq>

<RDF:Seq about="chrome://global/content/customizeToolbar.xul">
  <RDF:li>chrome://chromedit/skin/chromedit.css</RDF:li>
</RDF:Seq>

<RDF:Seq about="chrome://browser/content/browser.xul">
  <RDF:li>chrome://chromedit/skin/chromedit.css</RDF:li>
</RDF:Seq>
```

The stylesheet sequence (urn:mozilla:stylesheets) lists the Firefox files to be overlaid. The *chromedit.css* file is added to each one. This is the same system that is used to develop a theme **[Hack #89]**.

Inside *overlayinfo*, the location to search for the stylesheet overlay listing is in a file called *stylesheets.rdf* in the profile area under *chrome/overlayinfo/ browser/skin*.

—Brian King

Make, Bundle, and Publish an XPI
Create an XPI installer for your extension and publish it for others to discover and use.

If you've stepped through the hacks in this chapter in order, or done any serious XUL experimentation, then you're ready to consider releasing that XML as an extension. You have your content, locale, and skin files in place as a package, written and tested. All that is left is to bundle it up and release it. The best method to bundle it up is to use Mozilla's Cross-Platform Install (XPI) technology. XPI files are compressed files that can be put together using standard zip tools. Firefox can load and install XPI files.

This hack explores the structure of the XPI format—in particular, which files go where in the compressed archive. We'll also dissect the *install.rdf* install file to ensure that installation is successful. Finally, to ensure your extension is not hidden away, we'll discuss the best ways to distribute it for people to use.

Making a Firefox XPI File

Once created, the XPI file has a rigid structure for Firefox extensions, more so than it does for a Mozilla Application Suite extension. Most extensions just install chrome (i.e., a JAR file or directory with XUL, JavaScript, CSS, and locale files). However, there are optional folders for distributing other files, including XPCOM components **[Hack #82]**, command-line handlers, preference files, and icons. Here's an XPI directory breakdown:

```
chromedit.xpi
  chrome
    chromedit.jar
  components
  defaults
    ce-main.xpm
    ce-main.ico
    userChrome-example.css
    userContent-example.css
  install.rdf
```

Each of the folders—*chrome/*, *components/*, and *defaults/*—is optional. The *install.rdf* file, however, is compulsory. chromEdit does not have any XPCOM components. To view this example on your computer, save the *chromedit.xpi* file locally (by right-clicking the download link) from *http:// cdn.mozdev.org/chromedit/* and unzip it.

To compress the JAR and XPI files, you can use any standard ZIP program, such as WinZip on Windows. This is something you will be doing frequently during the development cycle, especially if you are using a JAR file. Instead of constantly dealing with GUI ZIP programs or manually working with ZIP files, your best bet is to automate the process.

Here is a simple shell script for compressing the JAR file and the XPI file:

```
#!/bin/sh
echo "building chromedit ...";          # cleanup any old stuff
rm chromedit.xpi;
rm chrome/chromedit.jar;
echo "JAR file ...";                     # make and move the JAR
zip -r0 chromedit.jar content locale skin
mv chromedit.jar chrome;
echo "XPI file ...";                     # make the XPI
zip -r9 chromedit.xpi install.rdf defaults chrome
echo "Extension build finished.";
```

This script uses the standard Info-ZIP zip program, which can also be found on Windows as part of the Cygwin package. The ZIP flags used here are -r to recurse into subfolders, -0 to store only (no compression), and -9 for maximum compression.

Understanding install.rdf

The core install file for a Firefox extension is called *install.rdf*. This file lives at the root of the XPI file. During install, if Firefox detects this file, it reads in the metadata to add the extension. Here's a sample install file for the chromEdit extension:

```
<?xml version="1.0"?>

<RDF xmlns="http://www.w3.org/1999/02/22-rdf-syntax-ns#"
     xmlns:em="http://www.mozilla.org/2004/em-rdf#">

  <Description about="urn:mozilla:install-manifest">
    <em:id>{2cf89d59-8610-4053-b207-85c6a128f65d}</em:id>
    <em:version>0.1.1.1</em:version>

    <!-- Firefox -->
    <em:targetApplication>
      <Description>
        <em:id>{ec8030f7-c20a-464f-9b0e-13a3a9e97384}</em:id>
```

```
    <em:minVersion>0.9</em:minVersion>
    <em:maxVersion>1.0+</em:maxVersion>
  </Description>
</em:targetApplication>

<!-- Front End MetaData -->
<em:name>ChromEdit</em:name>
<em:description>A Simple User Profile File Editor</em:description>
<em:creator>Chris Neale</em:creator>
<em:contributor>Andrew Wooldridge</em:contributor>
<em:contributor>Brian King</em:contributor>
<!-- more ... -->

<em:homepageURL>http://cdn.mozdev.org/chromedit/</em:homepageURL>
<em:updateURL>http://cdn.mozdev.org/chromedit/update.rdf</em:updateURL>

<em:iconURL>chrome://chromedit/skin/images/ce.x32.png</em:iconURL>

<em:file>
  <Description about="urn:mozilla:extension:file:chromedit.jar">
    <em:package>content/</em:package>
    <em:skin>skin/classic/</em:skin>
    <em:locale>locale/en-US/</em:locale>
    <em:locale>locale/de-DE/</em:locale>
    <em:locale>locale/it-IT/</em:locale>
    <em:locale>locale/nl-NL/</em:locale>
    <em:locale>locale/pl-PL/</em:locale>
  </Description>
</em:file>
</Description>
</RDF>
```

Every extension needs its own unique ID in Firefox, and the format this takes is a UUID. A UUID is a registration code that can be generated in a number of ways, including on Windows using *guidgen.exe*, on Unix using *uuidgen*, or using IRC by connecting to *irc.mozilla.org* and typing the following commands:

```
/join #mozilla
/msg mozbot uuid
```

This ID is used throughout the deployment of the extension and should stay with it for its lifetime.

Let's break up the sample *install.rdf* file into its most important parts for further explanation. Entries don't have to be in any particular order, but for clarity, the first entries in the install-manifest description should be for the extension. The em:id tag holds the unique UUID, and em:version holds the version of any given release.

The <em:targetApplication> tag contains information about the program you are targeting, such as Mozilla, Thunderbird, or in this case, Firefox. Like extensions, each program has its own UUID. Firefox's unique ID is {ec8030f7-c20a-464f-9b0e-13a3a9e97384}. You specify the versions that your extension works with in minVersion and maxVersion. It's tempting to pick these version numbers out of the air, especially for the older releases for minVersion, but it is wise to test first!

What follows is some more information about your extension. Table 8-2 shows all possible tags. Each needs to be prefixed with the Extension Manager namespace (em:).

Table 8-2. Extension manifest elements

Tag	Description
Name	UI friendly name
Description	One-liner about the extension
Creator	Individual or company's name that wrote the extension
Contributor	Other authors (can be more than one)
HomepageURL	URL of extension homepage
UpdateURL	URL of update file
AboutURL	URL (usually chrome:) to about dialog for the extension
IconURL	URL to image shown in the Extension Manager
File	Pointers to packages, skins, and locales that this extension registers

Finally, the file states the ordinary packages, skins, and locales that this extension registers. Relative JAR file paths are used to point to the locations of the package, skin and locale *contents.rdf* files.

The First Big Release

So, now you have reached the point where you have the XPI installer file or files, and all that's left is for people to find out about it and download/install it. This section covers the two ways you can do this: either hosting it on Mozilla's update service or hosting it on your own servers with helper scripts to get you going.

Using Mozilla Update. At the time of writing, the process of getting your extension listed is not mature and can be frustrating. This is because all requests for listings and updates must be done through Mozilla's bug tracking system (*http://bugzilla.mozilla.org*). The admin interface, which will eventually be part of the site and easily accessible, is not up and running yet. The plan is that extension authors, once logged in, will have complete control over their distributions: the uploading of new versions, editing of the description, and moderation of user comments. The download counter is a good measure of how popular your extension is.

DIY publishing. There is an alternative to using Mozilla Update, and that is to host the XPI on the server of your choice. The most straightforward approach is to just upload the file and link directly to it from an HTML page. However, there are some helper JavaScript install scripts that you can use to assist installation. Here is a very basic one:

```
function install(aXpi) {
    if (!InstallTrigger || !InstallTrigger.updateEnabled())
        return false;
    else
        return InstallTrigger.install(aXpi);
}
```

It can be called like this in the HTML:

```
<a href="#" onclick="install('http://myhost.com/extension/extension.xpi')">
```

The `install` function checks that software installation is enabled (Tools → Options... → Web Features → "Allow web sites to install software") and, if so, proceeds with the installation. Note the use of the global `InstallTrigger` object. You can find more information about it at *http://www.xulplanet.com/references/elemref/ref_InstallTrigger.html*. Make sure the web server is set up correctly [Hack #27].

> Once installed, the extension will not become active until Firefox is restarted. The extension on local disk is located here:
>
> ```
> <user profile dir>/extensions/<UUID of extension>/
> ```
>
> Try Right-clicking on the extension when it appears in Extension Manager to see the operations you can perform on it.

Distribute Software Updates

This section covers extension updates. Firefox has a built-in update mechanism [Hack #13]. Earlier in this hack, in "Understanding install.rdf," you might have noticed this entry in that file:

```
<em:updateURL>http://cdn.mozdev.org/chromedit/update.rdf</em:updateURL>
```

This entry tells Firefox where to look for the update file that will contain version information and links to updates for the extension. The following example shows the file for the jsLib extension (*http://jslib.mozdev.org/updateLite.rdf*):

```
<?xml version="1.0"?>
<RDF:RDF xmlns:RDF="http://www.w3.org/1999/02/22-rdf-syntax-ns#"
        xmlns:em="http://www.mozilla.org/2004/em-rdf#">

    <RDF:Description about="urn:mozilla:extension:{DF8E5247-8E0A-4de6-B393-
0735A39DFD80}">
```

```
<em:updates>
  <RDF:Seq>
    <RDF:li resource="urn:mozilla:extension:{DF8E5247-8E0A-4de6-B393-
0735A39DFD80}:0.1.214"/>
  </RDF:Seq>
</em:updates>
<em:version>0.1.214</em:version>

<em:updateLink>http://download.mozdev.org/jslib/xpi/jslib_current_lite.
xpi</em:updateLink>
    </RDF:Description>

    <RDF:Description about="urn:mozilla:extension:{DF8E5247-8E0A-4de6-B393-
0735A39DFD80}:0.1.214">
      <em:version>0.1.214</em:version>
      <em:targetApplication>
        <Description>
          <em:id>{ec8030f7-c20a-464f-9b0e-13a3a9e97384}</em:id>
          <em:minVersion>0.9</em:minVersion>
          <em:maxVersion>1.0</em:maxVersion>

          <em:updateLink>http://download.mozdev.org/jslib/xpi/jslib_current_
lite.xpi</em:updateLink>
        </Description>
      </em:targetApplication>
    </RDF:Description>
</RDF:RDF>
```

> Unlike *install.rdf*, this update manifest can have any name;
> it's delivered by a web server. *update.rdf* is the convention
> for static versions.

Again, the server must be set up with the right types [Hack #27]. This example
shows two necessary description blocks. The first one covers the extension
itself, telling Firefox that an update is available for an extension of a given
ID. The new version number of that extension is also listed, along with the
location of the new extension.

The second description block details the target application that the extension applies to. In this case, it is Firefox; so the Firefox em:id is given, plus
the minimum and maximum version of Firefox that this update applies to.
When Firefox checks for updates, it compares the version already installed
with the version in the update file. If a later version is found, the user is
given the option to install the newer version.

—*Brian King*

Build an Installable Theme

#89 Build an installable theme that changes the way Firefox windows look.

This hack describes how to make, bundle, and offer a new theme for installation. Firefox's theming system is not as comprehensive as some generic GUI skin engines. For example, it can't completely reorganize the Firefox user interface as flexibly as WinAMP's themes can. Firefox themes are restricted to effects that are possible within CSS. However, those effects are expanding in number as CSS becomes more popular.

Getting the Content Together

Before building the theme's bundle, make sure you have the content ready.

Do the creative bit. No one can give you a formula for creativity, and this hack isn't going to try. Before you can assemble the theme, you have to have a creative starting point, a plan, and a design. That should lead to a set of prepared images and some color scheme information.

Do the systematic bit. Your images and colors must be tied to CSS styles before they will have any effect. That means studying the CSS selector sites (tag names, attribute names, IDs, and classes) and structures (tag hierarchies) implicit in the XUL content to which your theme will apply. That, in turn, means studying the browser package as a bare minimum. Once that's done, you build the stylesheets that tie the images and colors to the content. Those stylesheets generally match the names of the sheets used in the windows to be styled. So, if this reference appears in an XUL document, you have the opportunity of supplying a stylesheet named *special/decorations.css* that will affect that window:

```
<?xml-stylesheet href="chrome://browser/skin/special/decorations.css"?>
```

This one-to-one match between theme sheets and referenced sheets can be distorted by two mechanisms. One mechanism is to use the *contents.rdf* file ["Building the Theme JAR File," later in this hack]. The other way is to use the @import CSS directive. For example, most theme sheets start by importing the global theme:

```
@import url("chrome://global/skin/");
```

You can import whatever other sheets you see fit. You can, for example, leave the stylesheet empty except for an @import statement that includes some completely foreign sheet. In general terms, though, it makes sense to follow the pattern of sheet names implied by the XUL you're seeking to theme up.

Collect together skins. The stylesheets and images must be collected together into *skins*. Each theme provides one skin per supported package. A skin is just a group of files in a common directory, possibly with some subdirectories. At a minimum, you should create skins for the browser, global, and mozapps packages. In an ideal world, you would also create skins for every package ever developed—past, present, and future. Since that's not feasible, there is a fallback mechanism.

Nearly all XUL windows include the special global package's skin. The global skin is important, because it is the fallback resource for all packages that you don't explicitly write skins for. All well-written XUL documents know that the global skin is the first thing they should include. It's up to the theme designer to ensure that the global skin contains enough resources to support fallback. You should put all your generic images here and refer to these images from the other, more specialized skins that you create.

Building the Theme JAR File

There are three different ways to deliver a theme:

- As a JAR file bundled with the Firefox installer and put in the install area
- As skin content that is part of a downloadable extension
- As a complete and separate downloadable theme

Each approach requires different packaging of the skin information.

Build an install-bundled theme. This approach requires that the JAR file contain the skin information in the standard, inverted hierarchy [Hack #86]:

    skin/theme-name/package-name/skin-file

The JAR file must also include a *contents.rdf* file for each skin:

    skin/theme-name/package-name/contents.rdf

This *contents.rdf* file should match this example exactly, also covered in "Create a Chrome Package" [Hack #86]. We've just spaced it out a little more for discussion and included is a skin overlay [Hack #87].

```
<RDF:RDF xmlns:RDF="http://www.w3.org/1999/02/22-rdf-syntax-ns#"
         xmlns:chrome="http://www.mozilla.org/rdf/chrome#">

  <RDF:Seq about="urn:mozilla:skin:root">
    <RDF:li resource="urn:mozilla:skin:theme-name/1.0" />
  </RDF:Seq>

  <RDF:Description about="urn:mozilla:skin:theme-name/1.0">
    <chrome:packages>
```

```
<RDF:Seq about="urn:mozilla:skin:theme-name/1.0:packages">
  <RDF:li resource="urn:mozilla:skin:theme-name/1.0:package-name"/>
 </RDF:Seq>
 </chrome:packages>
</RDF:Description>

<RDF:Description about="urn:mozilla:skin:theme-name/1.0:package-name"
        chrome:skinVersion="1.5"/>

<!-- optional forced inclusion of one skin stylesheet into one page -->
<RDF:Seq about="urn:mozilla:stylesheets">
  <RDF:li resource="chrome://package-name/content/some-file.xul"/>
</RDF:Seq>

<RDF:Seq about="chrome://package-name/content/some-file.xul">
  <RDF:li>chrome://package-name/skin/extra-styles.css</RDF:li>
</RDF:Seq>

</RDF:RDF>
```

The skin overlay is the last chunk of code. Since this is package registration, not extension registration, only attributes that describe packages are understood. Almost identical copies of this file can be drawn from most skins, with just the names changed. Since the theme is bundled with the install, the *install.js* script at the top of the install bundle must also be updated so that it knows to register the additional skins.

Build skins into downloadable extensions. This case is the same as the install-bundled case, except that the skin content is combined with locale and extension content in the one JAR file, which is then made into an extension XPI file [Hack #88].

To use this approach is to make a skin masquerade as a full extension. That's entirely possible, but the price is that Firefox expects that the extension's package will have content. Even if there are no content files, the package must still be registered using:

```
<RDF:Seq about="urn:mozilla:package:root">
  <RDF:li resource="urn:mozilla:package:package-name" />
</RDF:Seq>
```

Build skins into complete and separately downloadable themes. The format of the required JAR file in this case is different than in the previous two cases. It is a simplified format, and there is no need for an XPI file at any stage. The word skin and the theme name is redundant, since the theme bundle holds exactly one theme, so paths to skin files inside the JAR need only be constructed like this:

```
package-name/skin-file
```

At the top level, the JAR file must contain these additional files:

```
contents.rdf
install.rdf
preview.png
icon.png
```

The two *.png* files and some information in the *contents.rdf* file are used in the Theme Manager dialog box to preview and describe the theme. See any downloadable theme for an example. The files can be any raster image format the Firefox understands. There is only one *contents.rdf* file in the JAR archive; it aggregates all the content of the various *contents.rdf* files that would otherwise appear one-per-skin in these locations:

```
package-name/contents.rdf
```

Finally, the *install.rdf* file contains the product registration information [Hack #88] for the theme. Some of this is also visible in the Theme Manager.

Installation Support

To install a downloadable theme, use the same web page scripts that extensions require [Hack #88]. Because themes have a very regular and predictable format, there is no special *install.js* file required—just make sure the XPI file is delivered with the right content type. Firefox reads the downloaded theme, unpacks the JAR, and automatically deploys all of the pieces into the right spots. Alternatively, you can trigger XPInstall the old-fashioned way with a script and a raw JAR file:

```
<script>
function get_theme( ) {
  InstallTrigger.installChrome(
    InstallTrigger.SKIN,
    'http://mydomain.com/themes/mytheme.jar',
    'myTheme v0.1');
}
</script>
<a title="Install my cool theme" href="javascript:get_theme( )">
  Install myTheme v0.1 now!
</a>
```

HACK #90   Identify Reusable Toolkits

Don't code everything from scratch: reuse bits and pieces of Firefox.

The chrome files supplied with Firefox—XUL, CSS, JavaScript, and others—can be reused by your extension or chrome application project. If you're familiar with these pieces, you can possibly save yourself a lot of time. At least you'll save yourself a lot of confusion.

Poking Around Inside toolkit.jar

In the install area, inside the *chrome* directory, lies the *toolkit.jar* archive. This is the starting point for all XUL pages and therefore for all extensions and chrome applications. It consists of a number of pieces.

This *toolkit.jar* file changed a small amount when it was updated from the Mozilla Application Suite (1.x) to Firefox. Because that change involved renaming and was advertised in a number of influential places, some people assumed that there would be significant compatibility issues. This is not the case. The most important files in *toolkit.jar* have changed very little, so there is substantial and extensive compatibility with other Mozilla-based products. There is 100 percent compatibility with Thunderbird and Nvu, at least. Furthermore, the *toolkit.jar* file is just a file, and it is easy for extensions to specialize or override portions of it with their own tailored files. There is therefore no reason to consider this file an immovable requirement. It is just a well-tested and convenient starting point.

The global package. The global package has special status in the chrome. It provides default functionality that XUL pages can pick up, regardless of which theme or locale is the current one. Each new theme that is created must implement a *skin* for the special global package.

The global package also holds *locale* and *content* information. The locale information is delivered in the default locale JAR file, such as *en-US.jar*, but the content information is in *toolkit.jar*. This content information includes all the ultra-generic XUL dialog boxes that an XUL application might want. Examples include print dialog boxes, file pickers and savers, and the XUL content that's displayed when the JavaScript alert( ) method is called.

 These dialogs can also be called from XPCOM components [Hack #82].

The xul.css master XBL stylesheet. A special part of *toolkit.jar* is the *xul.css* file. This is the place to look for any and all details about the definition and behavior of XUL tags. This stylesheet is applied to every XUL document that Firefox displays. It uses the -moz-binding style property [Hack #69] to define every XUL tag (and therefore the whole XUL vocabulary).

This file is therefore used in place of a DTD, an XML Schema definition, or a hardcoded solution (there is also a little bit of XUL hardcoding). It is therefore the ultimate authority and reference on XUL. All of the XBL bindings attached to tags using this stylesheet are also located in *toolkit.jar*.

Modifying *xul.css* modifies the look and/or behavior of all XUL-based extensions and applications. Don't modify this file directly; extend or override it with your own if you need to make changes.

The mozapps package. Another source of common dialog boxes appears in the mozapps package, which is also located in *toolkit.jar*. Rather than contain generic dialog boxes, this package contains functionality that represents "The Mozilla Way." If your chrome application wants to offer an extension interface, a themes interface, an update manager, or XPInstall functionality, then you'll find some generic pieces you can reuse.

Scavenging Application Pieces

The *toolkit.jar* archive is not the only place to find useful application pieces. Firefox's *browser.jar* chrome archive also contains some reusable bits. These include the Bookmark Manager and the Cookie Viewer. There's also the Help system, which is stored separately in *help.jar*. In general, any and all chrome content can contain gems that you can reuse, but as your application becomes more specific and more specialized, reusable pieces are harder to find.

Finding Embedded Components

Separate from the chrome proper are the XPCOM components that are used extensively in chrome scripts. It's not so easy to determine from scratch which components support which interfaces.

The *cview* extension (*http://www.hacksrus.com/~rginda/*) goes a little way toward listing all these components and their interfaces. For a complete set of reports, try the downloadable files from the book *Rapid Application Development with Mozilla* (Prentice Hall PTR). You can find them at the author's web site, *http://www.nigelmcfarlane.com/books/radmoz_support.html*.

Reusing Script Libraries

In addition to user-interface pieces, you can speed up your application by using existing JavaScript libraries. Here are two examples.

nsDragAndDrop.js
> This is a script library supplied with *toolkit.jar* that eases the development of mouse-driven drag-and-drop functionality. Instead of having to housekeep complex state systems, this script provides a predefined manager object that you can climb on top of. This particular example is of medium difficulty to learn, but it's easy to use.

The jsLib library
The jsLib library (*http://jslib.mozdev.org*) provides wrapper objects that seek to make common tasks like file handling and RDF datasources easier to use. Although some simplicity is achieved, the library presents a number of separate objects, and fitting them all together might not be what you had in mind as a time-saver. Nevertheless, it provides a medium-level abstraction that several extensions have deemed worthy of use.

## CHAPTER NINE

Work More Closely with Firefox

Hacks 91–100

This chapter describes all the other Firefox browsers that are out there. The standard installation of Firefox is based on something called the *default build*, which is the safest thing for most people to use. It's a version for users who don't care about programming or software design.

If you do care about programming or design, there are many other Firefox variants that you can play with. Large corporations, hobbyists, volunteers, and entrepreneurs are the main kinds of people who might want to do so. This kind of hacking is intensive and time-consuming, though, so it's a matter of continual gratification rather than instant gratification.

Building and improving Firefox is a big job. There's a horde of people all hammering away on it. They're ensuring that the development, distribution and promotion processes get as much attention as possible. You too can be one of those people, and if you're technically minded or promotionally minded, it can be a satisfying, enjoyable, and social experience. It's nice to develop a special bit of expertise that you can own for yourself. Here's how to proceed.

HACK #91 Handle Cross-Platform Differences

Manage the differences among standard Firefox installs on different platforms.

Firefox works hard to provide the same user interface and web page displays on all platforms: Windows, Unix/Linux, and Macintosh. A great deal of effort has gone into this, especially with respect to the Gecko layout engine. Where the underlying operating systems are different, or where specific installations are different, differences can sometimes show through. This hack points out the most obvious cases and shows how to manage them.

At first, such differences might be irritating or awkward for users, but the consequences are felt mostly in XUL-based user-interface development, where a little care in constructing XUL documents is required.

Fundamentally, a single, compiled Firefox program cannot run on all platforms. Therefore, the standard Firefox install is created and customized separately for each platform. Although there is only one source code base, some small parts of it are operating-system-specific.

Handling Obvious Big-Ticket Differences

Human Interface Guidelines (HIGs) are standards that encourage all applications in a given desktop environment to provide similar idioms of use. Since HIGs for Apple, Microsoft, and Linux (e.g., GNOME) all differ, a tool that hopes to get a standards tick on every platform must look different on each platform. These are the big-ticket differences and how Firefox handles them:

The hidden window menu bar
The menu bar on the Macintosh is lifted to the desktop's system menu bar and doesn't appear on each window.

The Firefox Macintosh menu bar is automatically boosted to the system menu bar. This is the source of the *hidden window* feature sometimes remarked upon in Mozilla's Bugzilla. No action is required, unless your XUL application has no menu bar at all, in which case the system menu bar will be blank.

File and Print dialog boxes are different on each platform
Firefox wraps up the operating-system-supplied File and Print dialog boxes in XPCOM objects that present one interface on all platforms; use that. The XUL <dialog> tag contains buttons designed to support HIG dialogs on every platform, but in general, it must be carefully coded if it is to work portably and look right.

Accelerator keys sometimes differ
Macintosh has a Command key, Windows a Windows key, and Unix/Linux might make use of a Meta key. In general, keyboard shortcuts differ.

The XUL and XBL <key> tag accepts the generic term accel. This refers to the accelerator key native to the current platform: Alt on Windows, Command on Macintosh, and Alt or Meta on Unix/Linux. Firefox is also accompanied by a different set of keyboard shortcuts on each platform, with common keystrokes for most but not all popular commands. See the *resource:/builtin/platformHTMLBindings.xml* file for more details.

Different locations for user configuration system
The main user configuration system is under Edit → Preferences on Unix/Linux, under Tools → Options on Windows, and under Firefox → Preferences on the Macintosh.

At the time of writing, there's no extension yet to make the menu location of the Options dialog box uniform across operating systems.

Unix/Linux Window managers tend to lack support for modal dialog boxes
Although it might be possible to make an application modal, it's usually not possible to force the focus to stay on the dialog window.

In addition to `window.open( )`, secure web pages and chrome content can also call `window.openDialog( )`. Both support the special keyword `modal` in their feature string argument; that keyword locks the parent window of the dialog box on all operating systems, so that it (at least) cannot get the focus back while the dialog box is open.

Command-line options differ
Differing command-line options is just part of life [Hack #10], unfortunately.

Desktop integration differs
Windows has a Windows Registry, Unix/Linux has a *.gtkrc* file, and desktop application icons (shortcuts/launchers) work differently.

The XPInstall system, which runs the *install.js* file bundled with the standard install and *install.js* scripts bundled with extensions, includes operating-system-specific features that such scripts can exploit. In particular it allows reading and writing to the Windows Registry, and knows the operating-system-specific locations of many important folders. Any secure script can exploit that information nonportably if it wishes. Examine these scripts for examples of `nsIDirectory`-style names at work.

Firefox obeys all window-management hints or instructions that it receives. Under X11/Gtk, a window cannot be 0×0 pixels in size (it can on Windows). There are no perfectly portable solutions for desktop theme integration [Hack #79], unfortunately, but with a lot of work you can come close.

Handling Widget Differences

Each operating system provides or supports a GUI library that can be used to draw interactive widgets. Firefox does *not* draw widgets using these libraries. Firefox uses its own widget-drawing code to draw widgets on a blank canvas supplied by those libraries. So, for example, Firefox for

Windows does not depend on *COMCTL32.DLL* (or *.OCX*), and replacing that library is therefore of no use.

There are two areas of the desktop GUI that Firefox widgets depend upon. One is the theme engine for natively styled widgets [Hack #79]. Not all platforms support all -moz-appearance values, so applying such a style property can do nothing in some instances, but at least that's harmless.

The second area is the operating-system accessibility API. This is wrapped up in a portable XPCOM object with the nsIAccessible interface. It is used in the XBL definitions for XUL widgets [Hack #90]. You can't see the equivalent use for HTML tags unless you turn on XHTML tag support.

Where there is accessibility support, follow the guidelines at *http://www. mozilla.org/access/xul-guidelines* for best results in XUL.

In general, don't try to lay out XUL or HTML widgets in pixel-perfect style. What looks good on one operating system will be up for debate on another. It is better to pack widgets *loosely*, using the naturally flowing layout of the page: line boxes and blocks for HTML, boxes for XUL.

Handling Font Differences

Firefox must source, choose, analyze, resize and lay out font information [Hack #30] before it can ultimately be displayed. On Windows, Firefox uses some low-level features of GDI such as GetTextExtentPoint32 or ExtTextOutW, but ultimately it uses its own layout and font selection algorithms.

Get a Custom, Prebuilt Version
#92   Find versions of Firefox that are different than the standard installation.

Firefox, and Mozilla technology in general, are under constant development by the Mozilla Foundation. The Firefox source code is also freely available for anyone to compile, so executable or installable versions of Firefox could come from anywhere. Most such distributions aren't widely known, though. This hack explains what's out there, where to find it, and what makes sense to try out.

Rebundled Firefox Versions

Some people take standard Firefox installers and rebundle the same product up into a form that provides an alternate install process. It's the same old Firefox, just packaged slightly differently. Such things aren't full rebuilds.

Windows versions. Here are some examples of alternate versions for Windows:

- PortableFirefox [Hack #31] rebundles Firefox for USB use.
- The MozOO distribution (*http://www.mozoo.org*) includes Firefox.
- The U3 project (no URL at the time of this writing) is a consortia inter-ested in bundling applications on Flash USB devices. Firefox is to be one such application.
- Microsoft Installer (MSI) bundles. This rebundling of Firefox 1.1 and Mozilla 1.8 betas is described in Mozilla bug 231062

Linux versions. Here are some versions for Linux (there are numerous others):

- The BeatrIX Bootable CD distribution (*www.watsky.net*).
- Sun's Java Desktop System provides Firefox RPMs.
- RedHat and Fedore Core provide downloadable Firefox RPMs.
- Linspire (*http://www.linspire.com*) provides Firefox via its CNR Ware-house.

Alternate Builds of Standard Firefox

There's an unending stream of changes being made to the source code that Firefox derives from, and experimental builds are being made constantly and automatically for several platforms. There are many different Firefox builds, but they can be divided into three rough categories:

Developer builds
These are based on Firefox source code of no particular significance. Typically, these builds are experimental and unstable. Examples include *nightly builds*, *trunk builds*, and *debug builds*.

Branch point builds
These are builds of special significance and are marked in the source code repository with a CVS tag and a CVS branch tag. Such builds are given a name. Examples include *alphas* (1.8alpha2), *betas* (1.8beta3), *release candidates* (Firefox 1.0 RC3), *minor versions* (Firefox 1.1), and *major version* (Firefox 2.0). Such builds are usually built optimized.

Branch patch builds
Once a branch point is made, no more features are added to the branch, only bug fixes. Those few fixes will be lost to all other builds unless extra steps are taken to copy them from the branch. Often a branch has none of these fixes at all, as the developers are already moving on to more impor-tant changes. Examples include minor *security releases* (Mozilla 1.7.3).

In this system, CVS branches are rarely used for innovative development of Firefox or Mozilla. The branches are used just to quash bugs. Nearly all new work is done on the CVS *trunk*, which is not a *branch*. There is some confusion about this. While Firefox was in early development, development was done on a special branch (a *long-lived branch*) called aviary. Now that Firefox has reached 1.0, that long-lived branch is no longer required, and the trunk is being used for most things again, including all new Firefox development.

Generally speaking, the developer builds carry small risks of strange bugs and strange side effects that might confuse your desktop. Don't use them on an important computer, unless you know what you're doing. If they're debug builds, as many are, they will generally run more slowly than standard Firefox.

Developer builds don't always have full installers. To proceed on Windows, first install standard Firefox. Next, rename the folder that holds the Firefox install area. Unarchive the downloaded build into a temporary folder. Rename the temporary folder to the original install area folder's name. Start the Firefox executable in that replacement folder. On Unix/Linux and Macintosh, just unarchive the build into any folder and run.

To get any or all of these builds, visit the Mozilla download site at *http://ftp.mozilla.org/pub/mozilla.org/firefox/*.

Mozilla developers sometimes make experimental builds with special features in place. They're examples of *custom builds*.

Treasure-Hunting Custom Builds

To build Firefox from source code, an enthusiast needs four things in place: a baseline, a target, a *.mozconfig* file [Hack #93], and source code. The *baseline* is the set of tools used to build Firefox; the *target* is the platform the new Firefox is meant for; a *.mozconfig* file specifies all the options that will apply to the build; and the *source code* is some set of Firefox source files from somewhere in CVS. Amidst all these factors, any number of subtly different builds might be created.

The main motivation for such custom builds is to add back features that are available in the source code but that aren't in the standard install. Popular examples iclude MNG image support; SVG support (with or without Cairo); Pango, Xft, or Qt support on Linux; optimizations; and experiments with alternate compilers.

For gossip on builds, try the MozillaZine "Third Party/Unofficial Builds" Forum (*http://forums.mozillazine.org*). There's a Sticky Thread near the top that lists the more organized custom builders. The Moox builds are noteworthy for their speed improvements on modern Windows hardware. An orderly list of some custom builds is located at *http://www.pryan.org/ mozilla/firefox/*. For a glimpse of the possibilities of the *.mozconfig* file, have a look at *http://webtools.mozilla.org/build/config.cgi*.

All of these build alternatives are fairly harmless, but finding someone willing to commit to fully maintaining their special build is almost impossible. Such builds should be seen as wonderful experiments, not as mainstream products—at least not until the builders become more organized.

Some semi-official examples of custom builds can also be found at *http://ftp. mozilla.org/pub/mozilla.org/firefox/nightly/contrib/*.

HACK   Make Firefox Software
#93   Turn Firefox source code into an executable program.

The Firefox product is open source, so you can make it yourself from the original code. This hack provides one pathway that gets you through this task on Linux. It provides a few pointers only for Windows and Macintosh. If you step off the narrow path described here, then you're on your own. Compiling a large product such as Firefox with custom code can be heinously complex.

Pointers for Windows and Macintosh

Here's a brief overview for Windows and Macintosh.

Getting oriented under Windows. The standard install is compiled with Microsoft Visual C++ (msvc); that's recommended as a starting point. The compile is not driven by a project definition file, and it does not use .NET (the /CLR option). The compilation process drives msvc entirely from the command line. You can get a free and fully functional command-line version of the compiler at *http://msdn.microsoft.com/visualc/vctoolkit2003/*.

The Firefox compilation system also requires free Cygwin tools (*http://www. cygwin.com*). This set of tools provides a rich, Unix-like environment, somewhat similar to Microsoft's free Microsoft Windows Services for Unix. Cygwin is ideal for the large, automated task that is Firefox compilation. Because this toolset is used as a starting point, automated compilation is not done in a traditional Microsoft-oriented way. For more details, try the official page at *http://www.mozilla.org/build/win32.html*. For one person's Firefox-on-Windows compile steps (using the free MinGW compiler), look to *http://gemal.dk/mozilla/build.html*.

Although it isn't officially supported, Firefox will compile and run under Windows 95, as well as more recent versions. Firefox does not deliver any of Windows's own DLLs in its install.

Getting oriented under Macintosh. Even more briefly, Firefox is supported only on Mac OS X. For best results, Mac OS X 10.3 or higher is recommended. The Firefox compile is a Mach-O compile, so your Mac OS X development box requires that Unix Services be present. Read all the gory details at *http://www.mozilla.org/build/mac.html*.

Getting Ready for Linux Compilation

These steps assume you have 2 GB of free disk space. That's a safe amount for one compilation of Firefox. For several separate experiments, have 10 GB free.

Checking your compile baseline. If you are going to compile Firefox, you don't want your development environment to be a moving target. Turn off all automated product/patch/package update mechanisms so that tool versions on your box are stable. Next, check that your box meets the build requirements documented at *http://www.mozilla.org/build/unix.html*. These commands will yield the version information you need:

```
ls /lib/libc*
gcc --version
perl --version
gmake --version
cvs --version
gtk-config --version gtk
ls /usr/lib/libIDL*
zip -v
```

These are the equivalent RPM packages for rpm -q *package-name*:

```
glibc gcc perl make cvs gtk+ gtk2 libIDL zip
```

Don't radically update gcc just because it's possible. You can make a mess out of your box's standard headers and libraries if you're not careful. Work with what you have to start with.

Checking your runtime baseline. You also need to match the runtime requirements once the compile is finished. Minimum requirements are documented at *http://www.mozilla.org/products/firefox/system-requirements.html*. To test for the required versions, try these commands:

```
dmesg | grep -i 'linux version'
xdpyinfo | grep -i version
fc-cache -V
ls /usr/lib/libstdc*
```

Grabbing a source baseline. The Firefox source is hosted in a CVS source code repository on the Internet at *http://cvs.mozilla.org*. Large portions of the repository are available via anonymous CVS login, including all source required for Firefox. To pull all the source files from the repository one by one is bandwidth-intensive, so the usual way to start is to pull a source code bundle (about 40 MB compressed) and then update that baseline to include the latest changes as a separate step. If you have lots of bandwidth, you can pull everything directly from the CVS server, as described next.

Of the required source, 90% is generic to Mozilla; only a small amount is Firefox-specific. Make a directory for each test compilation:

```
mkdir /local/myfirefox
```

All source code tarballs are located at *http://ftp.mozilla.org/pub/mozilla.org/*. The most recent source code tarball is in this subdirectory:

mozilla/nightly/latest-trunk/mozilla-source.tar.bz2

The tarball for the official 1.0 release (from the defunct AVIARY_1_0_20040515 branch) is in this subdirectory:

firefox/releases/1.0/source/firefox-1.0-source.tar.bz2

Either way, once you've acquired the tarball, unpack it. Assuming you download to /tmp/source-archive.tar.bz2 and want to maintain the source in /local, run these commands:

```
mkdir -p /local/myfirefox
cd /local/myfirefox
tar --bzip -xvf /tmp/source-archive.tar.bz2
```

This creates a *mozilla* directory inside your *myfirefox* directory. Keep the top-level directory for your logs, notes, and other junk. Don't put junk inside the *mozilla* directory. Don't rename the *mozilla* directory either. You can use this setup to configure and compile one product at a time. You can't compile everything in one big hit without adding extra scripts. You can, however, compile Firefox, Thunderbird and other products in turn from the same *mozilla* directory. To do so, modify your *mozconfig* file after each product compiles ["Compiling Firefox," later in this hack].

Updating the source. Update the tarball source from CVS to the latest version using the following shell script:

```
#!/bin/bash
# interactively login with password 'anonymous'
export CVSROOT=:pserver:anonymous@cvs-mirror.mozilla.org:/cvsroot
cvs login

# Get the Makefile that drives everything, including 'cvs'
cvs co mozilla/client.mk

# We're building Firefox specifically, get its app config file.
cvs co mozilla/browser/config
```

```
# Update to the latest source by asking 'make' to call 'cvs update'
cd mozilla
make -f client.mk checkout
```

If you're working with the old aviary branch, add -r AVIARY_1_0_20040515 to all cvs co commands. Don't ever use cvs update directly or by hand; always use make to call cvs indirectly via *client.mk*.

Compiling Firefox

The following instructions are accurate at the time of writing (February 2005). Compare CVS changes between then and now if you think the build process might have been modified or updated.

To build Firefox, create one file called *.mozconfig* with your options in it and then set the compile running. Here's a script to automate that the process:

```
#!/bin/bash
cd /local/myfirefox/mozilla

# provide multi-build support for the ~/.mozilla/firefox profile.
export MOZILLA_OFFICIAL=1

# build options for .mozconfig
cat <<-'EOF' > .mozconfig
 . $topsrcdir/browser/config/mozconfig
 ac_add_options --enable-optimize
 ac_add_options --disable-debug
 mk_add_options MOZ_OBJDIR=/mnt/disk2/firefox
EOF

# set the compile running.
make -f client.mk build
```

The magic MOZILLA_OFFICIAL variable allows Firefox to share existing profiles, without triggering complaints about versions and patches. The first line of the sample *.mozconfig* points the make system at the default options for Firefox. The next two lines are illustrative only and match the defaults. The last option tells Firefox to put all compiled stuff in */mnt/disk2/firefox*. That last line keeps the source code tree free of compiled junk. If you ever compile directly in the source code tree (which works fine), this option won't work afterward. In that case, delete */local/myfirefox/mozilla* and start again. Here's what you can put in *.mozconfig*:

- Common environment flags noted in *mozilla/config/config.mk*
- Common command-line switches reported by running mozilla/ configure --help

To compile Thunderbird after the Firefox compile is finished, you must modify the *.mozconfig* file so that the compile is driven by Thunderbird's requirements, not Firefox's. Instead of this config line:

```
. $topsrcdir/browser/config/mozconfig
```

use this one:

```
. $topsrcdir/mail/config/mozconfig
```

To put the generated files somewhere separate from Firefox's, also change this line:

```
mk_add_options MOZ_OBJDIR=/mnt/disk2/thunderbird
```

You can then run the compilation as before:

```
make -f client.mk build
```

Running Your Own Firefox

If the compile finishes without error, look for goodies in */mnt/disk2/firefox/ dist/bin* (in this example). Move to that directory and run `./firefox`. Or set the `MOZILLA_FIVE_HOME` variable to that directory, update and export `$PATH`, and run Firefox from anywhere.

Creating a New Installer

Following from the previous steps, here's how to make the install bundles that the Mozilla Foundation makes:

```
#!/bin/bash
cd /mnt/disk2/firefox/xpinstall/packager/unix
make installer
cd ../../../installer
ls -l sea
```

If you want to install Firefox, rather than make an installer, then run these commands instead:

```
cd /local/myfirefox/mozilla
su root
make install
```

 # HACK Run Multiple Mozilla Browsers
#94   Run as many Mozilla browsers as you want on your single desktop.

Unless you're extremely technical, Internet Explorer 6 is a one-shot affair: either you install it once or you don't install it at all. Firefox is not like that; you can install many versions and related products and pick between them as you see fit. There remain one or two combinations to avoid, as we'll point out in this hack.

Running Different Browsers Simultaneously

To run the Mozilla Application Suite, Camino, Galeon, Compuserve, Netscape, or Epiphany on the same computer as Firefox, just install both products in separate directories. You can run both products at once. You can do that with Firefox and Thunderbird as well, or with Firefox and Nvu, or with Firefox and Komodo. However, there is one combination to avoid.

Mozilla-based browsers do not yet fully support profile sharing between products. Firefox and Thunderbird are a partial exception, since they overlap only in a few profile files, such as the certificate database. If you run two Mozilla products that use the standard profile system and the same profile, it's possible, but not likely, that you will corrupt the profile if you make extensive configuration changes. You could lose your bookmarks and other content.

To solve this problem, use the -CreateProfile command-line option to create a separate profile for each product. Change shortcuts and menu items so that they call each product with the -Profile *profilename* option.

Some of the information stored by Firefox is not used by the Mozilla Application Suite, and vice versa. Bookmark detail and some RDF information are two examples. In general, starting the wrong product against a given profile is fairly harmless; the extra, unknown information will simply be ignored. For Firefox 1.0, there have been few changes or no changes in the file formats of common profile files. Read the release notes for future versions to see if planned changes to the profile system have taken place yet.

Running Two Separate Versions of Firefox

As in the previous case, you can install two separate versions of Firefox and alternate between them. By default, you can't run them in parallel on Windows. However, there's no problem doing so on Unix/Linux. Here are two sources of unwanted behavior:

- On Windows, if you start Firefox version A while Firefox version B is already running, all you get is another version B browser window.

- Running a nightly or debug version of Firefox **[Hack #92]** always carries a small risk. Think carefully before running such a version with a profile or desktop that contains important long-term information.

Nightlies and debug versions are mostly used for testing, and it's possible to construct tests that destroy the only displayed browser window without also shutting down Firefox. That leaves the browser running invisibly in memory as though it were a server. It then has to be found and killed by hand. If you're running several versions of Firefox, this behavior can be a major source of confusion. It's another good reason to treat nightlies with care.

Running Two Instances of Firefox Simultaneously on Windows

The problem of two simultaneous versions of Firefox on Windows can be solved with simple hacks. Once one (or more) installation of Firefox is hacked, you can run two (or more) separate instances. You can do so even if the two instances are the same version.

Temporary solution. Window users who use one instance of Firefox as their main browser and wish to debug another instance can do so with an environment variable. Simply set the environment variable MOZ_NO_REMOTE=true to run the two Firefoxes simultaneously (see bug 131805). Put this variable in *c:\autoexec.bat* or equivalent.

Permanent solution. To put this hack in place, first grab a free Windows executable editor, such as Resource Hacker (*http://www.users.on.net/johnson/resourcehacker/*) or Resource Explorer (*http://www.wilsonc.demon.co.uk/d7resourceexplorer.htm*).

Next, locate the Firefox binary *firefox.exe* in the install area. Open it with your editor and drill down to the 102 and 103 entries in the StringTable section. Change these values to an alternate value, such as Myfirefox. Figure 9-1 shows this section of the resource fork of the binary.

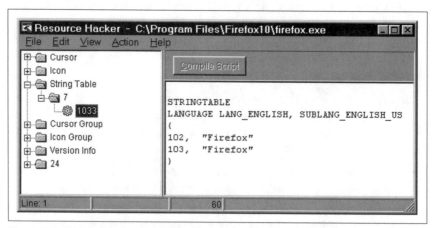

Figure 9-1. Unique instance names inside the Windows Firefox binary

Save the changes: choose Compile Script and select File → Save. Now you're ready to start up the modified Firefox. Just run it as normal.

Running Only One Instance of Firefox on Unix/Linux

On these platforms, the problem is rather the reverse of Windows: by default, any command-line invocation of Firefox will start a whole new browser instance. You can get around that, too.

Quite often, nonbrowser programs have to open web pages. An example is when the user clicks a Help link. Those programs would rather that such pages display in the user's currently opened browser than start a whole new browser instance.

On Unix/Linux, Firefox supports an xremote feature to make this possible. It allows you to configure these other programs to drive Firefox in a programmatic way. This can have an effect different from defaults offered in the preferences. For example, another program can instruct Firefox to use a new tab for the required page if there is a current Firefox instance already running, or else launch Firefox and open the required page if it's not running. The following script does so:

```
#!/bin/sh
mozilla-xremote-client -a firefox "openURL($1,new-tab)" || firefox "$1"
```

The mozilla-xremote-client binary (provided on Unix/Linux by default) is a small tool provided with the standard Unix/Linux Firefox install.

If, for example, you save the preceding script as a file named *openlink* and give it executable permissions, you can then configure other programs to run it as required:

```
openlink "http://www.mozilla.org"
```

Other options possible with this script are noted here: *http://www.mozilla.org/unix/remote.html*. Beware that this page is slightly out of date; mozilla-xremote-client is the correct tool to use.

Make Extensions Work Outside Firefox

HACK #95

Extensions are designed for Firefox, but sometimes you can use them elsewhere.

Individuals might move nimbly to Firefox, but organizations can take far longer. Some folks out there are still trying to escape Netscape 4.0 or Internet Explorer 5.0. A typical slow upgrade path is Netscape 4.x → Mozilla Application Suite 1.x (classic theme) → Firefox. You don't have to wait for Firefox to start benefiting from extensions, though. A significant number of extensions also work with the Mozilla Application Suite (MAS) and possibly in other tools as well.

In principle, you can design an extension [Hack #84] to install on all Mozilla-based applications. In practice, the extra development effort required to provide portability discourages most extension creators.

Porting Extensions to Thunderbird and NVu

Thunderbird and NVu use the same extension-management system as Firefox. Because they are not browser products and because extensions typically integrate closely with Firefox's XUL interface, most extensions are unlikely to be portable. Extensions that hang off the Firefox Tools menu and extensions that act as independent mini-applications (such as calculators, games, and accessories) have some chance of successful integration. They might possibly hang off the Thunderbird Tasks menu.

Changing the target application. The first step required for that integration is to hack the *install.rdf* file that's supplied in the extensions installable *.xpi* file. In particular, Firefox extensions contain this RDF:

```
<em:targetApplication>
  <Description>
    <em:id>{ec8030f7-c20a-464f-9b0e-13a3a9e97384}</em:id>
    <em:minVersion>0.7</em:minVersion>
    <em:maxVersion>1.2</em:maxVersion>
  </Description>
</em:targetApplication>
```

To modify this RDF for Thunderbird, change the targetApplication to this ID:

```
<em:id>{3550f703-e582-4d05-9a08-453d09bdfdc6}</em:id>
```

Changing overlay destinations. The XUL content that the extension adds to the application has to fit with the application's DOM structure. Usually, such extensions are bottom-up overlays [Hack #87], so finding the right integration point is critical.

For Thunderbird, the Tasks menu overlay target is ultimately located in the main window, which is called *messageWindow.xul*. The ID of the <menupopup> used for the Tasks menu is taskPopup. It's defined in *mailWindowOverlay.xul*.

To make this change, rip the *contents.rdf* file out of the extensions JAR archive that's inside the *.xpi* bundle. Add something like this:

```
<!-- overlay information -->
  <RDF:Seq about="urn:mozilla:overlays">
    <RDF:li resource="chrome://messenger/content/messenger.xul"/>
  </RDF:Seq>
```

```
<!-- messenger items for Messenger -->
<RDF:Seq about="chrome://messenger/content/messenger.xul">
  <RDF:li>chrome://myexample/content/toolsOverlay.xul</RDF:li>
</RDF:Seq>
```

In this case, the `myexample` package is the basis of the extension.

Changing overlay content. Finally, edit the *toolsOverlay.xul* file and hack the `<menupopup>` ID to read `taskPopup` instead of `menu_ToolsPopup` (the Firefox alternative). Rebundle, install, and see what happens.

Back-Porting Extensions to the MAS

Back-porting extensions to the MAS is a far easier task than moving extensions between applications. The browser in the MAS and the Firefox browser have a degree of similarity in their internal structures. Furthermore, MAS has no extension registration mechanism (at least it has none in Versions 1.7 and earlier). That means it totally ignores the *install.rdf* file supplied inside an extension's *.xpi*. So, that part can be ignored, but there are other steps to which you must attend.

Making multiple-application overlays. Here's an example of the overlay information for the Diggler extension. This extension supports both MAS and Firefox, at least as recently as its 0.9 version (despite the creator's protestations). It works by duplicating overlay information, but relies on the fact that the overlay target (a tag id) is the same for both products:

```
<RDF:Seq about="urn:mozilla:overlays">
  <!-- Firefox -->
  <RDF:li resource="chrome://browser/content/browser.xul"/>
  <!-- Mozilla Application Suite -->
  <RDF:li resource="chrome://navigator/content/navigator.xul"/>
</RDF:Seq>

<!-- Firefox -->
<RDF:Seq about="chrome://browser/content/browser.xul">
  <RDF:li>chrome://diggler/content/digglerOverlay.xul</RDF:li>
</RDF:Seq>

<!-- Mozilla Application Suite -->
<RDF:Seq about="chrome://navigator/content/navigator.xul">
  <RDF:li>chrome://diggler/content/digglerOverlay.xul</RDF:li>
</RDF:Seq>
```

There are support files inside the extension for both MAS-style preference menus and for Firefox-style Options menus. Unzip the Diggler *.xpi* file and poke around inside to see how it's done.

Delivering backward compatibility for extensions. This piece of web page JavaScript is standard for recent versions of MAS and Firefox:

```
onclick="triggerURL('url');"
```

This special function, available only in recent Mozilla-based browsers, causes the XPInstall subsystem to fire up. It downloads the provided URL, expecting that it will be an installable *.xpi* file. Older versions of MAS (such as the stable 1.4 release) don't have this functionality. They use this instead:

```
onclick="InstallTrigger.install( { "myextension" : "url" } );
```

The most general solution is to get the server settings right [Hack #27] and to serve up the extension as a raw file:

```
<a href="http://www.example.com/myextension/myextension.xpi">Get it here</a>
```

If that's not possible, the web page must sniff the browser's exact version and use an XPInstall trigger call that matches it.

HACK #96 Turn on Firefox Diagnostics
Make Firefox spew out every last detail that it knows.

Firefox and its extensions are good for several different debugging or diagnostic activities, including diagnosis of web pages and debugging of chrome applications. This hack shows how to diagnose Firefox itself—at least, just a little bit. It's an outsider's view of the tools that the core Mozilla programmers have left in place, hidden for discovery and experimentation by those that are curious.

Diagnostics are a last resort when Firefox is not providing any other useful information—for example, during the reading of proxy or preference files. The main limitation of this extra diagnostic material is that a full understanding of the output can be obtained only if you also study the Firefox source code. Nevertheless, some of the information produced is revealing in its own right.

Turning On Diagnostics with NSPR Logging

At the base of the Mozilla technology stack is a C library of cross-platform features called Netscape Portable Runtime (NSPR). This library includes a logging feature that allows code to be instrumented so that it reports diagnostic strings. Mozilla programmers have divided the Firefox code up into named logging modules. Strings output sent from the code using PR_LOG( ) can be selected for display at runtime.

The standard install of Firefox supports this logging. Up to 75 KB of output can be generated just by starting up Firefox. If the version of Firefox used is compiled with --enable-debug, over 50 times that amount can be generated. Diagnostic output is therefore quite verbose.

Turning on logging. The NSPR_LOG_MODULES environment variable controls what is logged. Set it to a comma-separated set of module specifiers. Each module specifier has the format:

```
name:number
```

where *name* is a known module name and *number* is usually a digit in the range of 0 to 4. Here's an example (for Unix shell):

```
NSPR_LOG_MODULES="nsHttp:4,cooke:1"
export NSPR_LOG_MODULES
```

On Windows, you can set such variables by going through Control Panel → System → Advanced → Environment Variables. Some of the module names that are useful for non-programmers are:

```
cache cookie JSDiagnostics ldap MCD negotiateauth nsHttp nsSharedPrefHandler
NTLM proxy syspref
```

These names are magic strings buried in the code. Table 9-1 shows the meaning of the numeric digit.

Table 9-1. Logging values and their meanings

Value	Meaning
0	Don't log anything
1	Log informational messages
2	Same as 1, plus error messages
3	Same as 2, plus warning messages
4	Same as 3, plus debug and notice messages
99	Any number bigger than 4 acts the same as 4

There are several special module names:

all
 Turn on logging to the specified level for all known modules.

sync
 A special flag. Log strings straight away. Don't buffer them inside Firefox memory; flush them out right away. This does not cause a sync-to-disk operation and is useful if you think Firefox is going to crash or become confused.

bufsize
 A special flag. Change the amount of space available for buffered-up strings. The default is 16384 bytes; make it huge if you want to reduce the effect of disk-based logging or of scrolling screen output on Firefox performance.

Viewing logged output. Two forms of output are produced: informal diagnostic messages that are controlled by the log level and delivered via printf( ), and formal diagnostic strings that are controlled by the log level and delivered by the PR_LOG( ) logging system. These are sent to stdout and stderr, respectively. To see the output on Windows, start Firefox with the -console option:

```
set NSPR_LOG_MODULES=all:5
"C:\Program Files\Firefox\firefox.exe" -console
```

The informal strings can be captured to a file by simply redirecting the standard output:

```
"C:\Program Files\Firefox\firefox.exe" > stdout.log
```

On Unix/Linux, the formal strings can be sent to a file by redirecting standard error:

```
/local/install/firefox/firefox 2> stderr.log
```

On all platforms, setting the NSPR_LOG_FILE environment variable to a file's full pathname causes the formal strings to be written to that file.

On Windows, if NSPR_LOG_FILE is set to the special value WinDebug, the formal strings go to the Windows OutputDebugString( ) API. Any debug tool that knows how to register itself with Windows can capture these strings. One useful, free, and simple tool is DebugView. Get it here:

http://www.sysinternals.com/ntw2k/freeware/debugview.shtml

What you make of the diagnostic output is up to you!

Finding Talkback Crash Records

If you choose to install the Quality Feedback Agent when Firefox is first installed, extra diagnostics are produced in rare cases. These errors are produced only if Firefox crashes or otherwise catastrophically fails. They can be submitted (on your approval) over the Internet to the Mozilla Foundation, where a server stores and analyzes them. The primary thing they contain is a stack dump of the state of the Firefox program at the moment of crisis. You can see and query the database of crash incidents at *http://talkback-public. mozilla.org*.

Hooking Up Firefox to a Debugger

As for any compiled program, if there's enough information in the executable, you can apply a runtime debugger to the code. For Firefox, you really need a build that's compiled for debug, such as a nightly build [Hack #92].

Here's an example of setting up a debugging session on Linux, using gdb and bash. Run Firefox and then hook gdb up to it as follows:

```
cd `type -P firefox`
./firefox &
gdb firefox-bin pid
```

The *pid* used should be that of the Firefox binary, not the Firefox wrapper script. Find it with ps -ef. Once inside gdb, stop Firefox and orient yourself as for any interactive debugging session:

```
gdb> break
gdb> continue
gdb> backtrace
```

You can then step through the code for as long as your interest is sustained.

Tips on how to debug Firefox on Windows can be found at *http://www.mozilla.org/build/win32-debugging-faq.html*

 H A C K **Find the Right Forum for Your Issues**

#97 Find the right people to discuss the outcomes of your Firefox investigations with.

There are lots of places in the Mozilla community where you can participate. If you walk in blindly, you can accidentally spoil the ambience of the forum you've chosen and raise the ire of the other participants. This hack explains the range of places to go.

Overall, finding a spot to participate depends on several dimensions. One thing to consider is whether you want to acquire information (*pull*), deliver information (*push*), or swap information (*converse*). Another is whether you want to be objective and analytical or subjective and expressive.

Picking Forums for Pulling Information

You can look for information that's feather-light and simple or that's deeper and more technical. Starting with the lightest, here are some suggestions. Overall, there are numerous web pages on the topics of Mozilla and Firefox. Search engines such as Google are your friends. Seek and you will find:

- For marketing hype, the evangelism zoo, and the sound of drums, try *http://www.spreadfirefox.com/*.

- For an informed, independent overview, search for Firefox at *http://www.wikipedia.org*.

- For more sedate news, public issues, and progress updates on the product release cycle, try *http://www.mozillazine.org* or *http://www. mozillanews.org.*

- The bulletin board forums at *http://forums.mozillazine.org* are packed with useful conversations, common issues, and problem-solving discussions from the fan base.

- The Mozilla Foundation's own web site (*http://www.mozilla.org*) contains a huge and eclectic mass of information. You'll never discover it all by following the homepage links; use the search feature. There are also numerous mailing lists, some closed and some public, scattered throughout the web site.

- The Mozilla Foundation newsgroups are archived at *http://www.gmane. org.* and at *http://groups.google.com/groups?q=netscape.public.mozilla.**.

- The Mozilla Foundation newsgroups at *news.mozilla.org* are also archived at *http://www.gmane.org.* They contain deeper technical discussion of the finer points, speculative thinking, and the occasional technical summary from the core developers.

- The W3C (*http://www.w3.org*), ECMA (*http://www.ecma.ch*), and IETF (*http://www.ietf.org*) web sites contain the authoritative documents on web-related standards.

- Mozilla's Bugzilla database **[Hack #98]** at *http://bugzilla.mozilla.org* is the final decision-making place for technical features and fixes. A great deal of history is captured there.

- The ultimate source of information on Firefox is, well, the source. Read it at *http://lxr.mozilla.org/mozilla* or download a copy **[Hack #93]**. Use the *CVS Log* link when a specific file is displayed to see its gory history.

Picking Forums for Pushing Information

Not everyone wants your information. Put it where it counts and where it will be appreciated. From mostly subjective to mostly factual, here's a range of options.

Current trends in Firefox self-promotion require that you build a web site with an actively maintained blog and an RSS feed. Cover your site with Firefox branding. Next, you must form good relationships with other well-known self-promoters in order to cross-market and expand your audience. Having done so, find people less organized or newer than yourself. Demonstrate your expertise to them so that others can observe your power. That consolidates your position. At some point, you must produce content worth reading or using, but that is increasingly less relevant. In short, it's all rather medieval.

I'm a bad example to follow, since I mostly leave the work I do to speak for itself. I'm a lousy self-promoter. Any attempt to dazzle, dominate, or curry favor happens more by accident than by design.

There are Mozilla- or Firefox-specific news submission opportunities everywhere. The ones with the greatest focus or greatest exposure for technical Firefox audiences are at *http://www.slashdot.org*, *http://www.spreadfirefox.com*, *http://www.mozillazine.org*, and *http://www.mozillanews.org*.

Since Firefox is a web browser, web pages that demonstrate feature use, abuse, or failure have a great deal of merit. Construct your demonstration page, and then ask someone else in the community to review it. Perhaps post its location in a forum.

Providing critiques of Firefox is a tricky business. If you are negative about the product, you are unlikely to persuade any useful person of anything. Just as all major software vendors are *solution providers*, so too must you be. Provide solutions, explanations, or ways forward if possible. If you need to vent frustration, the USENET newsgroup *alt.mozilla* is safely away from most judgments. Despite the requirement to be positive, there is overall a shortage of quality critiques of Firefox.

If you are still sure that you have discovered a shortcoming or bug in Firefox, do your homework. You should be able to state the problem in a single sentence, followed by a short, accurate description. Log a bug with Mozilla's Bugzilla **[Hack #98]**. If your issue causes Firefox to crash, submit a talkback dump through the automated dialog boxes that appear on those occasions.

If you are frustrated with the Web, the ultimate recourse is to debate the standards. There are mailing lists at *http://www.w3.org* and at the newer and more speculative *http://www.whatwg.org* where public feedback can be left. Do extra homework for these forums.

Picking Forums for Conversations

If you want a conversation, there are also several places to go.

The forums at *http://forums.mozillazine.org* are a great place to spend idle time. Some members there have consistently posted 10 messages a day for over a year. Choose the most general *after dark* forums for such purposes. Some of these forums are of more specific use, too.

The *irc.mozilla.org* chat network (try the Chatzilla extension at *http://update.mozilla.org*) is a place of mixed fortunes for conversation. Some channels are highly technical, and idle banter, or even insightful end-user remarks, are not welcome. Look for a Firefox channel served by another network if you want small chit-chat.

The *news.mozilla.org* newsgroup hierarchy is a place to meet Mozilla developers rather than end users. Insightful comments and intellectualized issues are mostly welcome here, but cross-posting is not. These forums are irregularly monitored for spam.

If intellectual rigor excites you, Mozilla's Bugzilla [Hack #98] is the penultimate test of accuracy. Log your bug or enhancement, or buy into an existing debate. It's easy to get burned, so go in with your eyes wide open.

The ultimate conversation about Firefox is a bug fix. Having mastered Bugzilla, CVS, the end-user experience, and numerous other Firefox constraints, submit your first attempt at a bug fix in full expectation that it will be ripped apart by the review process. You can lose your Bugzilla privileges if you spam or otherwise culture-jam the conversations.

HACK #98 Survive Bugzilla

Survive and thrive in the scary world of Mozilla's Bugzilla database.

Bugzilla, like Firefox, is a product of the efforts of the Mozilla Foundation and, before that, of Netscape Communications. Its home page is *http://www.bugzilla.org*. Within the Mozilla community, the Bugzilla installation at *http://bugzilla.mozilla.org* contains a great deal of the workflow, history, current status, and collective memory associated with Mozilla technology. This hack provides a brief introduction.

Landing on Planet Bugzilla

Anyone can contribute to Mozilla's Bugzilla database, but it is a place of work, not a place of play. Marc Prensky's *Digital Game-Based Learning* (McGraw Hill) describes a related concept called "hard fun." Bugzilla requires systematic rather than spontaneous participation, so any hard fun only comes through hard preparation. Spontaneous participation is poorly received in Bugzilla.

Differences between labor and work. In a normal workplace, such as an office, you might be accustomed to a workflow that involves several people. When you hand tasks to those after you, you expect them to be done. When people before you hand tasks to you, they expect you to take them on. This is all based on an obligation that you incurred. You agreed to supply labor in return for money from the workplace. You can't meet your obligation without assistance from your coworkers.

Bugzilla does not operate like that. Most participants are volunteers or have solved the money problem. None, or very few, of the Bugzilla participants have a labor contract. They work only because they want to. As a result, most participants can *do* or *not do* whatever they want. There is no point making rules, because there is no labor obligation. Even those with labor contracts are employed for what they *might* do, rather than what they *must* do.

Regardless of how you judge Mozilla culture, it is this freedom of individuals to wander about without any formal arrangement that makes Mozilla a community.

Gift culture. If you put a piece of work into Bugzilla that someone else has cause to appreciate, that's good for them. Eventually, someone will put something into Bugzilla that you will have cause to appreciate. That is all there is to it: nonspecific gift giving.

The gifts offered, however, are not entirely nonspecific. Software development is an intensive activity that requires concentration. People don't like their concentration being broken, especially by irrelevancies. Gifts that fit with the narrow topics a recipient works on are welcome. All other gifts are not. Precision and accuracy in gift giving is very important—let's say *critical*—in Bugzilla.

Furthermore, new gift givers represent a risk. The risk is that their gifts might not be appropriate. The new gift giver could be a burden on the whole community, which is trying hard to concentrate. It takes existing participants a long time to let their guard down and accept that a new participant is contributing in a way that's reliable and not merely disruptive.

Typically, a gift offered in Bugzilla might just be a few sentences. Said out loud, a few sentences carry little weight. In Bugzilla, they carry a great deal of weight.

Dissecting Bug Reports

Each Bugzilla bug report contains several kinds of information, all mixed together.

This figures in this hack show the different sets of fields present in a bug report. These screenshots are from the URL *https://bugzilla.mozilla.org/show_bug.cgi?id=193068*, which you can examine at any time. The pages diplayed here have been slightly hacked so that all important fields fit in a single window. There's no effect on the way the form works.

Figure 9-2 highlights the fields that contain the essential information about the bug.

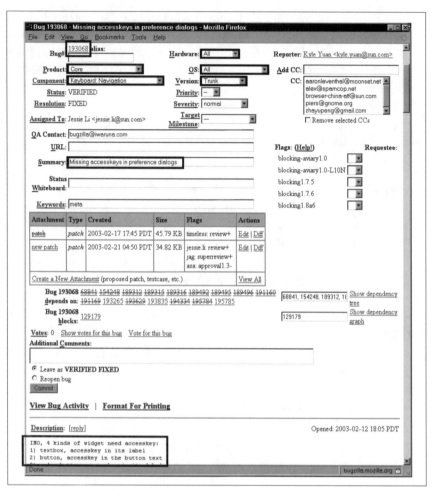

Figure 9-2. Essential fields for a bug report

These few fields are all that's really required to start a bug report. The bug number is generated automatically. These fields are also just about all you need when doing a free text search for bugs. It is not trivially obvious where the description information is stored. It can be searched from Bugzilla's query page using the comments field. That's where it resides.

As shown in Figure 9-3, the bug report is burdened with lots of helpful information for beginners. Many of the links lead nowhere, except to an explanatory Help screen. This is a little confusing, because other controls on the page do form submission or query requests. Perhaps one day, there'll be a separate Help system for Bugzilla.

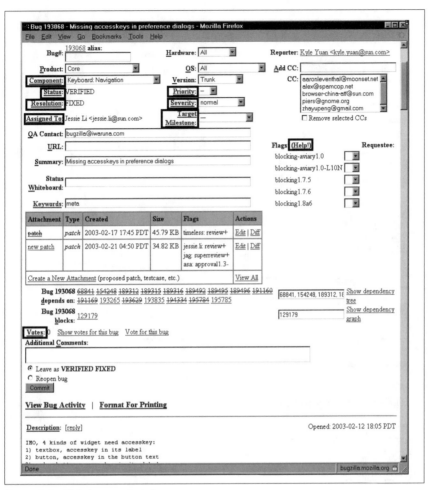

Figure 9-3. Help hotspots in a bug report

After the bug is entered, it starts its journey through a set of states (the combination of Status and Resolution) until it reaches its end. That end could be the garbage bin, an accepted new feature of Mozilla or Firefox, or a number of other options. This is a complex process, and the best way to learn it is to CC yourself on a new bug or bugs and watch the email reports come in as work on the bug progresses. During this journey, more information is added to the bug that describes the problem or issue at hand, such as test cases and patch fixes.

The particular bug being reported in Figure 9-4 has no test-case attachments; instead, it has two candidate patch fixes. Figure 9-4 shows all this in-process bug data and the things to click or type into that add data to the bug.

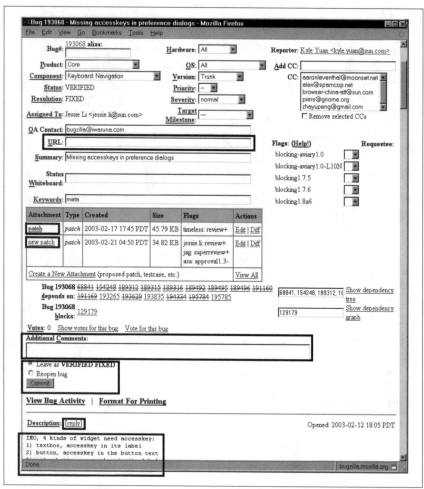

Figure 9-4. Data entry and data for a bug report

While the bug report is underway, lots of people are interested in it. They show their interest by adding their email addresses and by marking the bug in many different ways. This marking behavior supports each interested person's own work practices; they can then recall the bug using special or standard queries.

Release Managers, module owners, and QA people need these marks to get their jobs done, so there are some standard and agreed-upon marks that shouldn't be used for other purposes. If a mark includes a +, that means "looking good for a given release" (good news). If a mark includes a -, that means "this bug is to be stalled or slipped past a given release" (bad news). A + used on a version number has a different meaning than a + as described above; when used on a version it means "this is a trunk version that includes experimental changes on top of the noted release." Figure 9-5 points out examples of many marks.

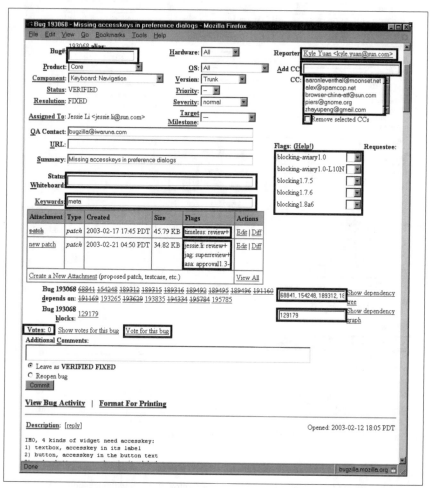

Figure 9-5. Marks and observers placed in a bug report

Finally, the bug report contains more information than can possibly fit on one page. A number of bug-report features just replace the current page with special reports and ancillary information about the bug, as shown in Figure 9-6.

Try loading up this page and running through the screenshots in Figures 9-2 through 9-6. There's no substitute for experience with Bugzilla, but some early orientation can help.

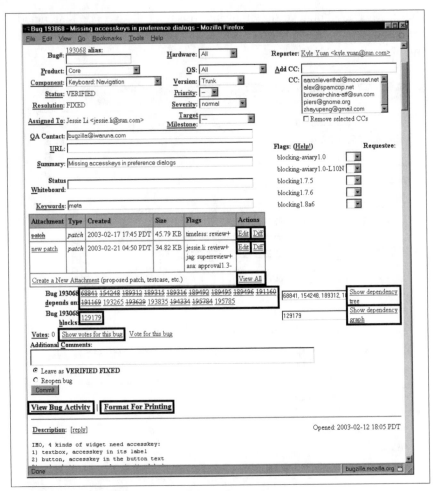

Figure 9-6. Ancillary information for a given bug report

Find Out What Has Been Fixed

HACK
#99

Work out the differences between minor Firefox versions without reading the code.

Every day brings more bug fixes. Every day brings several nightly builds to play with. This hack shows how to find out what's in a given Firefox version, whether it's new features or fixes for known problems. You can get lightweight or detailed reports on the changes that have been made, so let's start with the lightweight ones.

Release Notes

Every major Firefox release, whether it be 1.0 or 1.1, comes with a brief overview of the features that it contains. Go to *http://www.getfirefox.com* to find out the major items made available or new in such releases.

A more systematic breakdown of feature changes is provided by the highly organized Burning Edge web site (*http://www.squarefree.com/burningedge/releases/*), which reports on the code changes made by the Mozilla community. Look here for a stack of release summaries, including one that forecasts the contents of the next minor release.

The FAQ at the Burning Edge site (*http://www.squarefree.com/burningedge/faq.html*) also lists a number of other resources that provide release information.

Change Logs

More detailed and more up to date than release notes are change logs listing bug fixes. There are two excellent resources to turn to. The first is Asa Dotzler's release change logs, which are single HTML pages. These logs are poorly advertised and rarely linked to, but they provide the most authoritative list of bug fixes available. Under the current arrangements, the change logs are located here:

> *http://www.mozilla.org/releases/version/changelog.html*

where *version* is a Mozilla version's flag name. So, the `mozilla1.8a5` release has a change log here:

> *http://www.mozilla.org/releases/mozilla1.8a5/changelog.html*

The other source of change logs is the front page of the Burning Edge web site:

> *http://www.squarefree.com/burningedge/*

Tree Status

At the absolute bleeding edge of Mozilla and Firefox, you can find individual changes that have made their way into the Mozilla CVS source repository and the automated compilation system. To do so, have a play with the Bonsai query interface: *http://bonsai.mozilla.org*. It provides reports on changes to the source code. As a starting point try this set of values:

`Module:`
    All files in the repository

`Branch:`
    HEAD (exact match)

Directory:
    mozilla/browser
File:
    Leave this blank (exact match)
Sort By:
    Date
Date:
    In the last week

Finally, beyond the bleeding edge lies Tinderbox (*http://tinderbox.mozilla.org*). Choose SeaMonkey when you're directed to the list of source code trees. This interface adds CVS change records to compilation outcomes and concludes whether the changes were good ideas or not. The tabular output is green when all's well, yellow when the jury's still out, and red when code changes are stopping nightly (or more frequent) builds from completing properly.

HACK #100 Help with the Future of Firefox

Much of the work done to make Firefox successful is volunteer effort. You too can help.

The Firefox browser is the end result of thousands of people's contributions. People contribute because they think that it's a good idea, a worthy cause, or perhaps just an enjoyable activity. If you care to participate as well, this hack explains how.

Deciding

In *Giving It Away: In Praise of Philanthropy* (Scribe Publications), Denis Tracy says that happy volunteers and successful philanthropists take many different paths when contributing to their favorite causes. Applying his ideas, any contribution to Firefox or Mozilla will be a blend of the following elements:

Money
    The Mozilla Foundation and its regional affiliates are grateful for any subsidization of their electricity bills and salary costs. Make a donation or buy their stuff.

Time
    Life is meant to be lived, not lost. Spend your time on things that matter to you. If Firefox and the Web happen to be on your list, then tinker with them.

Energy
If you have buckets of energy and nowhere to put it, you might care to direct it Firefox's way or toward the upholding of a free and public standards-based Web. You may not need a crusade, but you may enjoy having a cause.

Skill and knowledge
If your own time is limited but your expertise is not, a drop of advice or guidance can turn a poorly organized or poorly informed participant into a productive Firefox contributor.

Passion
Enthusiasm is a catalyst for action, and it's also infectious. Ignite other people with your passion if you care about Firefox.

Contributing Engineering Effort

Here are some more concrete strategies for making a contribution. The good news is that you don't have to be a hardcore C++ programmer to participate. There are plenty of other ways to contribute. These are the big four areas where you can help turn Firefox into better code:

Triage
When Bugzilla bugs are first logged, they are sorted by the triage team to see if they are duplicates of existing bugs or indicate other problems. Some are closed right away, while others are demoted in priority or severity. All you need to do is log onto Bugzilla, query all bugs logged in the last week or day, and go to work.

You must apply for extra Bugzilla privileges (log a bug to get them) in order to be able to dispose of other people's bugs.

Quality assurance
Part of this work is the testing of fixed bugs and running regression tests for new releases. In general, there's a lot of product reality testing that developers don't get around to. Read the QA pages at *http://www. mozilla.org*, and start testing.

Test-case reduction
Logged bugs often produce poorly defined or overly complicated test cases. If you enjoy seeing software fail, a useful contribution is to take triaged bugs and boil down any supplied test cases to the essential minimum. That makes it a lot easier for the final bug fixer to locate the problem lines in the source code.

Writing code

If you happen to be hot on programming, feel free to fix things. Note, however, that all you can do is propose fixes; it's up to the peer review process to decide whether your fixes are suitable. You don't have to fix Firefox code specifically; you can also fix Bugzilla code or any of the other small systems that run the Mozilla web sites.

All these tasks have review functions as well; you can provide review of anything that goes on in the Mozilla community.

Contributing Organizational Effort

Outside the code, there's also lots to do.

Documentation and web page writing and editing is one large area for contribution. The Mozilla web site's documentation is a massive archive in constant need of updating and redesign. Once you have access, you can pull it from CVS. Third-party web sites that don't work properly with Firefox, because they're too old or too poorly made, need to be politely asked for an update. Inaccurate and ancient fan documents exist all over the Web, and their owners should be helped with updates. The same goes for the Firefox Help system.

Another form of web activity is to propagate the Firefox brand. If you're network-oriented or evangelical, you can spend your time persuading others to put Firefox iconography on their web sites. See *http://www.spreadfirefox.com/* for details.

The MozillaZine forums are bursting with people, new and old alike, and it's a simple matter to sit in those forums and contribute answers to questions. That's an easy way of spreading Firefox education.

In summary, anywhere that Firefox activity occurs helps the browser. If you can't find a place to contribute, make such a place yourself, with a web site or a local special interest group—whatever you see fit to do. Give a copy to your family and friends.

Contributing Creative Effort

Some of the best Firefox innovations come from unguessed-at quarters. The popular Tabbed Browsing feature was originally an enthusiastic experiment by programmers not associated with the main Mozilla project. If you have lots of creative energy, set up your own project and do something unexpected. Your output contributes to the diversity of the Mozilla community.

Contributing Professional Effort

Firefox is an emerging global brand, and astute professionals outside the programming industry would do well to take notice. There are cross-promotion opportunities to be had by contributing to the Firefox brand. It's a matter of history that professionals from public relations, marketing, design, illustration, and law have all benefited in public profile and business from their association with Firefox and Mozilla. It's only a matter of time before other professionals seize a Firefox-related niche as well.

Being a Fan

The simplest contribution you can make to the Firefox browser is merely to use it. Sit back (or forward) and enjoy. After all, Firefox is there to make your life easier, not harder.

Index

A

about:config, 117
  Modify, 5
  Reset, 5
  setting preferences, 4, 81
  Toggle, 5
access rules, 72
accessibility, 176
  navigating with, 13
  screen readers, 179
Acrobat PDFWriter, using to save
  HTML web page, 150
ActiveX, enabling, 41
ad blockers, 112
Adblock extension, 123
Add & Edit Cookies extension, 183
addEventListener( ) method, 253
adKiller, 112
ads
  blocking, 122
  controlling display of, 121
AdSubtract ad blocker, 112
Advanced Search Button extension, 2
aggregation, 260
Almost Standards mode, 202
alpha blending, 164
AniDisable extension, 124
Anonymizer web site, 74
anonymous browsing, 74
Apache, 52
  configuring Firefox content types, 92
  rewriter for IE, 94

appearance, changing, 23
Assert( ) method, 249
asynchronous
  GET request, 173
  listener, creating, 235
  POST request, 173
atGuard ad blocker, 112
Atom and RSS, 251
AutoConfig, 102
  handling failover scenarios, 103

B

Back (keyboard shortcut), 21
BeatrIX Bootable CD distribution, 334
Bookmark Manager, 17
bookmarklets, 25
bookmarks
  adding (keyboard shortcut), 21
  importing, from other browsers, 25
  keyword, 115
  live, 116
  navigating with, 11
  rebranding, 278
  RSS feeds and, 116
  searching, 17
  sidebar, 115
  sidebar (keyboard shortcut), 21
  tab group, 114
border crossings, 27
Bottom of page (keyboard shortcut), 21
<browser> tag, 129
browser window, standard, 5

We'd like to hear your suggestions for improving our indexes. Send email to *index@oreilly.com*.

browser.jar chrome archive, 328
browsers
  CSS incompatible, 166
  default, 26
  detecting by the Document Object
    Model (DOM), 169
  detecting by UserAgent, 168
  detecting JavaScript version
    support, 170
  detection scripts, updating, 168
  disabling caching, 188
  display contracts, 167
  importing from other, 25
  Quirks mode versus Standards
    mode, 167
  running different browsers
    simultaneously, 341
  speeding up, 31–35
  strict mode display contract, 168
  tabs
    links from other applications, 118
    modifying, 117–121
    setting preferences, 117
  user agent (UA) string, 168
  viewport, 168
browsing
  without images, 122
bug reports, 353
Bugzilla, 198, 352–357

C

cache
  directory, 79
  disabling, 188
  increasing memory for
    performance, 34
capabilities, signed scripts, 74
capability and security, 72
Card Games extension, 153
caret
  browsing (keyboard shortcut), 22
  navigating with, 12
Cascading Style Sheets (see CSS)
Certificate Authorities (CAs), 62
Certificate Rejection Lists (CRLs), 65
change logs, 359
character entity reference, 107
Chatzilla extension, integrating with
  Firefox, 145

chrome, 23
  determining what to remove, 275
  directory, 9, 77, 79
  DOM Inspector and, 271
  editing and repackaging, 277
  file locations, 271
  global package, 327
  hacking cleanly, 299–329
  hacking quick-and-dirty, 267–298
  overlayinfo, 316
  overview, 267
  package attributes, 310
  packages, locales, and skins, 305
  simplified, 303
  standard files, 270
  technology, 299
Chrome Manager tool, 303
chrome: URL, 310
chrome-free windows, 7
chrome/overlayinfo directory, 77, 79
clearing, flushing, and resetting, 29
code validation, 176
command-line options, 35–38
  creating new, 294–298
  DumpHelp( ) function, 38
  X11 options and, 36
compilers, upgrading for
  performance, 35
compiling Firefox code, 336
components directory, 77
computed values, 160
configuration files
  editing, 76–80
  special, 100
Conquery search extension, 126
console games, 153
content versus presentation, 261
contents.rdf, 324
Convert( ) function, 236
convertFtoC( ) function, 236
cookies, 40, 182
  Cookie Manager, 182
  extensions, 183
  managing, 182–184
  scripting, 183
  security concerns, 182
copy and paste, navigating with, 12
Crap Cleaner helper application, 86
createElement( ) method, 262
createProxy function (JavaScript), 234

Cross Platform Interface Definition
    Language (XPIDL), 291
cross-platform differences in
    Firefox, 330–333
Cross-Platform Install (XPI), 317
CSpider JavaScript library, 152
CSS, 9
    border styles, 162
    color styles, 163
    compatibility, 165
    editing, 161
    fonts, 164
    Gecko display engine, 162
    Internet Explorer 5.x and, 166
    Internet Explorer on the Mac
        and, 166
    Netscape 4.x and, 166
    see-through content support, 164
    styling across all modern
        browsers, 167
    userChrome.css, 9
    userContent.css, 9
    XSL versus, 219
customized builds of Firefox, 335
customized versions of Firefox, 333
customizing, 9
cview extension, 328

D

daemons, 111
datasources and RDF Service, 247
debugging
    Bugzilla, 198
    recovering, 198
    tricks, 191, 192
    using alert( ), 191
    Venkman, 193
    watch points, 192
deconstructing pages with DOM
        Inspector tool, 187
default browser, 26
default installation directories, 1
defaults directory, 78
defaults/autoconfig directory, 78
defaults/pref directory, 82
deleting (keyboard shortcut), 21
deploying (see installation)
detection scripts, updating, 168
developer builds of Firefox, 335

diagnostics, 346–349
dial up automatically on startup
    Linux/Unix, 91
    Mac OS X, 91
    Windows 95/98/98SE/ME, 90
    Windows NT/2000/XP, 90
dialog boxes, once-only,
        stopping, 25–28
dial-up modem
    fixing bottlenecks, 31
Dict extension, 126
digital certificates, 62
digitally signed content, 65–69
display contracts, 167, 200
display modes for HTML and
        XML, 200
DOM 0 web page object model, 42
DOM hierarchy, 9
DOM Inspector, 10
    chrome and, 271
    finding inherited values, 160
    tool, 185
Down Them All extension, 150
Download Manager, 49, 112
    helper application, 86
    window (keyboard shortcut), 22
drag and drop, navigating with, 12
DTD entity definitions, 78
DumpHelp( ) function, 38

E

E4X
    features, 264
    playpen setup, 263
    scripting, 262
    standard download web site, 266
    syntax, 263
    XML namespaces support, 266
easyGestures extension, 154
ECMAScript, 184
    for XML (see E4X)
EditCSS extension, 158
email
    integrating with Firefox, 143
    Thunderbird, 143
enablePrivilege( ) method, 69
examples.getStateList function, 229
expando icon, 17

eXtensible Stylesheet Language (see XSL)
Extension Manager, namespace, 320
extensions, 23
  Adblock, 123
  Add & Edit Cookies, 183
  adding a sidebar panel, 315
  Advanced Search Button, 2
  alternatives to master certificates, 72
  AniDisable, 124
  back-porting to the MAS, 345
  Card Games, 153
  Chatzilla, 86
  Conquery, 126
  creating, 237
  creating a chrome package, 306
  cview, 328
  deleting folder, 30
  Dict, 126
  directory, 78, 80, 271, 300
  DIY publishing, 321
  DOM Inspector, 10
  Down Them All, 150
  easyGestures, 154
  EditCSS, 158
  feature managers, 141
  ForecastFox, 131
  gesture, 156
  Gmail Notifier, 138
  icons, 19
  Image Toolbar, 124
  Image Zoom, 124
  ImageShowHide, 124
  InfoLister, 135
  installers, 301
  installing, 2–3
  installing, from other than the Mozilla Update site, 3
  install.rdf, 318
  JAR files, 301
  JavaScript Debugger, 10, 85
  Launchy, 145
  Live HTTP Headers, 180
  Magpie, 120, 124, 150
  Mnenhy, 303
  Mycroft web site, 125
  Nuke Anything, 124
  Open Java Console, 85
  overlays, 315
  overview, 300

  packages versus, 306
  porting to Thunderbird and NVu, 344
  Quick Tab Pref Toggle, 119
  releasing on Mozilla Update, 320
  running outside of Firefox, 343
  Sage, 129
  Show Image, 124
  Slogger, 152
  Tabbrowser, 120
    Preferences, 119
  tabs, 119
  unsigned, 3
  updates, 47
    distributing, 321
  user interface icons and related extensions, 141
  View Cookies, 183
  Web Developer, 158
  .xpi, 24

F

failover scenarios, handling with AutoConfig, 103
favelets, 25
feature manager extensions, 141
files, using the operating system to lock, 99
filesystem, clearing, flushing, and resetting with the, 30
filetypes, associating, 42
filtering content subtly, 286–290
filtering tools, 112
  ad blockers, 112
  download tools, 112
  securitymonitors, 112
Find As You Type, 15
Find Links As You Type, 15
Find toolbar, 14
Firefox Launcher (USB launcher), 110
Firefox variations, 330–363
firewalls, 111
flexible HTML parser, 200
flushing, clearing, and resetting, 29
fonts and character support, 104–107
  character entity reference, 107
  installing good fonts, 104
  numeric character reference (NRC) and, 107

overriding web page fonts, 105
overview, 106
selecting good language fonts, 105
userContent.css, 106
XML and, 107
fonts, widgets, cross-platform
differences, 333
ForecastFox extension, 131
form information, 18
Formal Public Identifier (FPI), 209
forms, submitting background form
data, 171–174
forums, 349–352
Forward (keyboard shortcut), 21
frame, move to next (keyboard
shortcut), 22
Free Download Manager, 148

G

games
card games, 153
console, 153
text adventures, 153
toys and, 153
Gecko
display engine, 162
display modes, 201
Runtime Engine (GRE), 78
gesture extensions, 156
getClassObject( ) method, 292
GetDataSource( ) method, 248
GetDataSourceBlocking( ) method, 248
GetSource( ) method, 249
global history, 17
global package, 327
global skin, 23
Gmail Notifier extension, 138
Gmail tips, 140
GNOME desktop versus KDE
desktop, 35
Go to the nth tab (keyboard
shortcut), 22
greprefs directory, 78
Gtk configuration system, 36

H

hacking, connotations, xiii
handleURLBarCommand function, 287
HasAssertion( ) method, 249

History
global, 17
importing, from other browsers, 25
navigating with, 12
searching, 15
History sidebar (keyboard shortcut), 21
Home (keyboard shortcut), 21
HTTP caching, disabling, 189
HTTP headers, 180
Human Interface Guidelines
(HIGs), 331
hyperlinks, clicking, 11
hypertext rendering mode, 211

I

icons
directory, 78
identifying, 19
IE
CSS and, 166
keyboard shortcuts, Firefox
versus, 21
native Apache rewriter, 94
Perl CGI content rewriter, 94
PHP content rewriter, 94
XHTML and, 93
IETF draft-brezak-spnego-http-04.txt
SPNEGO over HTTP, 51
Image Toolbar extension, 124
Image Zoom extension, 124
images
blocking, for faster browsing, 122
controlling display of, 121
extensions to control, 124
resizing, 124
turning off, 31
ImageShowHide extension, 124
ImapMail directory, 80
importing, from other browsers, 25
InfoLister extension, 135
inherited values, finding, 160
init( ) function, 214
<input> tag, 128
installation, 76–112
application area, 1
changing the install bundle, 97
configuring content types in
Apache, 92
customizing user profile creation, 98

installation (*continued*)
default locations, 1
files not to hack, 79
finding files after, 1
fonts and character
support, 104–107
helper applications, 86
install area, 1
Java JVM, adding, 84
Knoppix-like CD distribution, 111
list of subdirectories, 77
locking preferences with
ReadConfig, 101
mobile devices, 108–111
Mozilla Application Suite (MAS)
features, adding, 85
on a laptop, 109
on a USB drive, 110
on memory-rich consumer
devices, 109
overwriting files on login, 98
plug-ins, adding, 84
preparing for wide
deployment, 95–98
customizing, 97
standard install, 97
via disk image, 97
profile area, 1
RAM drive, 111
roaming VPN, 109
server-based VPN, 109
USB launcher, 110
USB-aware, 110
installer, creating new, 340
install.rdf, 318
integrating with other applications, 143
Internet Explorer (see IE)
<interpret> tag, 128
IRC Chat extension, 86
IRC, integrating with Firefox, 145

J

JAR files, 301
overview, 269
reversed hierarchy, 269
themes, 324
JAR package representation, 308

Java
applets, 48
Console extension, 85
JVM, adding, 84
JavaScript
Console, 193
Debugger extension, 10, 85
disabling, 48
preferences, 43
version support, 170
javascript: URLs, 191
jsLib library, 329

K

KDE desktop versus GNOME
desktop, 35
Kerberos, 53
security, 51
key binding, disabling, 274
keyboard shortcuts, 20
Firefox versus IE, 21
Help system, 22
unique to Firefox, 22
web resources, 22
keyword bookmarks, 115
kiosk mode (full-screen), 7
keyboard shortcut, 21
Knoppix-like CD distribution, 111

L

LAN Manager security, 51
Launchy extension, integrating Firefox
with, 145
link validation, 178
Linspire, 334
Linux compilation of Firefox, 337
live bookmarks, 116
Live HTTP Headers extension, 180
loadURI function, 289
local folder hierarchy, 307
Location bar
keyboard shortcut, 21
navigating with, 11
locking files, 99
lockPref( ) function, 84
login forms, 28
login information, searching, 17
LXR tool, 287

M

Magpie extension, 120, 124, 150
Mail directory, 80
manifests, 309
master certificate, 69
  alternatives, 72
  delegating trust to others, 71
  deploying, 70
  in a conservative environment, 70
  in a liberal environment, 70
  versus master password, 69
  versus Update Manager, 70
math rendering mode, 211
mathematical equations, 208
MathML content, 207–212
  block expression, 210
  fonts, 208
  inline expression, 210
  reports in, 206
  Universal MathML StyleSheet
    (UMSS), 211
  viewing source, 212
memory
  buffer, resetting, 34
  increasing cache for performance, 34
Menu bar, navigating with, 13
menu navigation (keyboard
    shortcut), 21
<META> tag, 190
<mfrac> tag (MathML), 211
<mi> tag (MathML), 211
<mn> tag (MathML), 211
Mnenhy extension, 303
<mo> tag (MathML), 211
mobile devices
  installing on, 108–111
modems, fixing bottlenecks, 31
modes
  Almost Standards, 202
  Quirks, 201
  Standards, 201
mouse gestures, 156
-moz appearance style, 282
mozapps package, 328
MozBackup backup tool, 87
Mozilla browsers, running
    multiple, 340–343
Mozilla Client Customization Kit
    (CCK), 95
Mozilla Project, xiv

Mozilla Update web site, 3
  stopping secret updates, 46
MOZILLA_OFFICIAL variable, 339
MozOO distribution, 334
<mrow> tag (MathML), 210
<msqrt> tag (MathML), 211
<msup> tag (MathML), 211
myCommandComponent object, 296
myCommandComponentFactory
    object, 296
myCommandModule object, 296

N

navigation, 11–13
Navigation toolbar, 18
Netscape Portable Runtime
    (NSPR), 346
Netscape Security Services (NSS), 66
network access
  preferences, 60
  speeding up, 32
network activity, stopping, 46
news, 129–134
  integrating with Firefox, 143
News directory, 80
nontechnical users, security
    configuration, 44
nsDragAndDrop.js script library, 328
NSGetModule( ) function, 293, 296,
    297
NTLM security, 51
NTLMSSP security, 51
Nuke Anything extension, 124
numeric character reference (NRC), 107

O

object signing, 66
Online Certificate Status Protocol
    (OCSP), 65
opacity, 164
Open a file (keyboard shortcut), 21
Open a new window (keyboard
    shortcut), 21
open source software, xiii
overclocking, 32
overlay
  overview, 312
  skin, 316
<overlay> tag, 274

P

package representation, creating, 307
page display, speeding up, 33
parsers, 201
Password Manager, 40
passwords, 28
   importing, from other browsers, 25
   setting automatically, 40
Paste (keyboard shortcut), 21
PC-Anywhere, 34
PDF, saving web page as, 150
PEAR, overview, 260
performance
   hangs, 196
   speeding up, 31–35
Perl CGI content rewriter for IE, 94
permanent toolbar, creating, 283
PHP content rewriter for IE, 94
PHP libraries and XUL, 260
PHP Tools web site, 261
PHP XUL Libraries web site, 260
pie menus, 154
pipelining, 32
plug-in IDs (PLIDs), 85
plug-ins
   adding, 84
   anatomy of a search plug-in, 126
   <browser> tag, 129
   common, 45
   creating a search plug-in, 146
   deleting folder, 30
   directory, 78
   increasing access, 41
   <input> tag, 128
   <interpret> tag, 128
   Mycroft web site, 125
   script, 174–176
   <search> tag, 127
policies, 73
   signed scripts, 74
pop-up blocking icon, 19
Popup Manager, 44
PortableFirefox, 334
   USB installation, 110
ports, disallowing, 60
pref( ) function, 83
preference system, 80–84
   about:config, 81
   database table, 80
   modifying files, 83

preferences, 4
   clearing, 30
   controlling configurations
      remotely, 99–104
   JavaScript, 43
   links from other applications, 118
   network access, 60
   network settings, 32
   searching, 18
   sockets, 62
   special configuration rules and
      files, 100
   tab settings, 49
   tabbed browsing, 117
   Tabbrowser extension, 120
   tabs, 49
      loading foreground or
         background, 118
   tweaking, 193
   update settings, 46
   using AutoConfig to update, 102
   using ReadConfig to lock, 101
prefs.js script, 83
Print (keyboard shortcut), 21
Print Preview, 8
printouts, 5–11
privacy settings, 29
profile, 1
profiles
   default locations, 1
   directory, 30
   migrating, 86–89
      between different operating
         system users, 89
      between different operating
         systems versions, 88
      between identical platforms, 87
      between versions of Mozilla, 87
      from Windows to Linux, 89
   salting, 43
   subdirectories, 79
propositional calculus and RDF, 246
proxies, 54–60
   configuring options, 55
   direct connection, 56
   fully qualified domain name
      (FQDN), 60
   PAC, scripted, 57
   proxy.pac file, 57
   special functions, 58

static, 56
WPAD, automatic proxy
configuration, 59
proxy, creating with JavaScript, 234
push content, 129–134

Q

quality assurance
accessibility, 176
downloads, 179
images, 177
links, 178
screen readers, 179
valid code, 176
Quality Feedback Agent, 348
Quick Launch, speeding up startup, 34
Quick Tab Pref Toggle (QTPT)
extension, 119
Quirks mode, 201
versus Standards mode, 167

R

RAM drive installation, 111
Raptor, 204
RDF, 205, 254
aggregation, 260
datasources, 247
files, 77
manifests and, 309
overview, 245, 246
package registration, 268
RSS and, 251
Service, 247
shorthand notation, 247
SQL versus, 246
triple, 254
ReadConfig, 101
Really Simple Syndication (see RSS)
rebranding Firefox, 278
bookmarks, 278
browser User Agent, 280
icons and images, 279
-moz appearance style, 282
to match desktop environment, 280
Redo (keyboard shortcut), 21
registry file, 78
release notes, 359

Reload
current page from origin (keyboard
shortcut), 21
Remote Access Services (RAS), 90
reports in XHTML, MathML, and
SVG, 206
res directory, 78
resetting, flushing, and clearing, 29
Resource Description Framework (see
RDF)
Resource Explorer tool, 279
Resource Hacker tool, 279
RFC 2478: The Simple and Protected
GSS-API Negotiation
Mechanism, 51
RFC 2616: Hypertext Transfer protocol
-- HTTP/1.1, 50
RFC 2617: HTTP Authentication: Basic
and Digest Access
Authentication, 50
RFC 2743: Generic Security Service
Application Programming
Interface, Version 2, 51
RFC 822: Standard for the format of
ARPA Internet text
messages, 50
roaming VPN, 109
RSS, 252
Atom and, 251
bookmarks and, 116
CDF and, 251
feeds, 129–134
icons, 19
Live Bookmark and, 253
overview, 251
parsing XML content of a feed, 252
RDF and, 251
receiving notification of new
items, 253
support in Firefox, 252
running two separate versions of
Firefox, 341
RXP tool, 204

S

Sage sidebar extension, 129
salted
directories, 99
directory names, 79

salting, 97
   profiles, 43
Samba, 52
Same Origin policy, 48
Scalable Vector Graphics (see SVG)
Schematron Validator, 204
screen readers, 179
script libraries, 328
script plug-ins, 174–176
scripts, 195
SeaMonkey, 360
search status icons, 20
<search> tag, 127
search tools, 125–129
   adding search engines, 125
   creating a search plug-in, 146
   searching without search box, 126
search-bar search engines, 78
searching, 14–19
   bookmarks, 17
   by search string (keyboard
      shortcut), 22
   Find As You Type, 15
   Find Links As You Type, 15
   for login information, 17
   form information, 18
   Go menu, 17
   History, 15
   keyboard shortcuts, 15
   link by search term (keyboard
      shortcut), 22
   preferences, 18
   repeat last Find operation backward
      (keyboard shortcut), 22
   repeat last Find operation forward
      (keyboard shortcut), 22
   select next search engine in location
      bar (keyboard shortcut), 22
   source code of a web page, 15
   using the current search engine and
      keyword (keyboard
      shortcut), 22
   web, using Navigation toolbar, 18
   within a displayed web page, 14
searchplugins directory, 78
Secure Sockets Layer (SSL), 27
   single sign-on versus, 49
security, 27, 39–75
   access rules, 72
   anonymous browsing, 74

blacklisting local networks, 57
capabilities, 72
certificates, 63
configuring for nontechnical
   users, 44
cookies and, 182
default settings, 39
digitally signed content, 66
icons, 20
Kerberos, 51
LAN Manager, 51
loosening restrictions, 42
master certificate, 69
monitors, 112
Netscape Security Services (NSS), 66
NTLM, 51
NTLMSSP, 51
policies, 73
ports, disallowing, 60
regime, 50
resetting and clearing data, 28
setting socket limits, 61
trust and identity, 65
whitelists, 53
Security Support Provider Interface
   (SSPI), 52
see-through content support, 164
Select all content (keyboard
   shortcut), 21
selections
   copying (keyboard shortcut), 21
   cutting (keyboard shortcut), 21
semantic markup, 165
send( ) method, 262
server-based VPN, 109
session history, 17
Show Image extension, 124
sidebar bookmarks, 115
sidebar panel, adding, 315
sidebars, creating HTML element, 242
Simple Object Access Protocol (see
   SOAP)
simple template syntax, 249
single sign-on servers, 49–54
single-window mode, 118
skin
   overlays, 316
skins, 9, 23, 280
   overview, 324
   static, 280

static, with smart values, 281
themes and, 324
Slogger extension, 152
SOAP, 222
    CGI versus, 223
    Lite, 224
    locating in Firefox, 223
    making web page with, 226
    scripts, 224
    security and, 224
    synchronous and asynchronous
        messaging, 224
    XML-RPC versus, 228
SOAPCall method, 232
source code, 336–340
    baseline, 337
    compiling, 339
    updating, 338
    window, 6
speeding up performance, 31–35
spidering, 148
splash screens, 10
SPNEGO, 53
    standard, 51
SQL query in Firefox, 254
Squid, 52
standard Firefox, alternate builds, 334
    branch patch, 334
    branch point, 334
    developer, 334
Standards mode, 201
    Quirks mode versus, 167
startup, speeding up with Quick
        Launch, 34
Stop current operation (keyboard
        shortcut), 21
strict mode display contract, 168
strict XML parser, 200
style rules, locating, 158
<style> tag (JavaScript), 214
SVG
    content, 212–215
    making interactive diagram, 213
SVG, reports in, 206
synchronous and asynchronous
        messaging with SOAP
        server, 224
synchronous GET request, 172
synchronous POST request, 172

T

tabbed browsing, 48, 117–121
Tabbrowser
    Extension, 120
    Preferences (TBP) extension, 119
tabs, 48, 49
    closing current (keyboard
        shortcut), 21
    loading foreground or
        background, 118
    move to next (keyboard
        shortcut), 22
    move to previous (keyboard
        shortcut), 22
    multiple displayed at startup, 114
    navigating, 13
    open new (keyboard shortcut), 22
    open URL in new (keyboard
        shortcut), 22
    preferences, 117
    single-window mode, 118
tag hierarchy, 272
talkback crash records, 348
text adventure games, 153
text size
    decrease (keyboard shortcut), 22
    increase (keyboard shortcut), 22
    restore (keyboard shortcut), 22
themes, 23
    building, 323–326
    installing, 326
    JAR files, 324
    skins and, 324
Thunderbird, 143
Tinderbox, 360
Toolbar icons, 19
toolbars, 134–140
    adding icons, 134
    creating one that can't be
        hidden, 283
    Gmail Notifier, 138
    InfoLister, 135
toolkit.jar archive, 327
Top of page (keyboard shortcut), 21
translucency, 164
transparency, 164
trust credentials, 3

U

U3 project, 334
UNC pathnames versus file paths, 96
Undo (keyboard shortcut), 21
Unicode, 105
Uniform Resource Names (URNs), 302
uninstall directory, 78
Universal MathML StyleSheet
    (UMSS), 211
unlockPref( ) function, 84
unsigned extensions, 3
update icon, 20
Update Manager, versus master
    certificates, 70
updates
    automatic, 43
    configuration, 47
    extensions, 47
    stopping, 46
USB drive, installing onto, 110
USB launcher, 110
USB-aware installation, 110
user agent (UA) string, 168
user interface
    customizing, 274
    icons and related extensions, 141
userChrome.css, 9
userContent.css, 9, 106, 192
userContent.css stylesheet, 122
user.js script, 83
user_pref( ) function, 83
UUID
    overview, 319

V

various builds of Firefox, 330–363
Venkman, 193
    tutorial, 196
vertical bar character, separating URLs
    with, 114
View Cookies extension, 183
viewport, 168, 219
VNC, 34
volunteer efforts, 360–363
VPN
    roaming, 109
    server-based, 109

W

wallpaper styles, 23
watch points, 192
WeatherFox (see ForecastFox extension)
Web Accessibility Initiative (WAI)
    guidelines, 177
Web Developer extension, 158
    locating style rules, 158
web developer tools, 157–198
web pages
    displaying, 5–11
    navigating, 11–13
    save as file (keyboard shortcut), 22
    saving, 149
    source, viewing (keyboard
        shortcut), 22
web proxies, 54–60
web remote service calls, 236
Web Services Description Language (see
    WSDL)
web spider, defined, 148
web surfing enhancements, 113–156
web trail, 16
WebServiceProxyFactory
    documentation web site, 235
whitelists, 53
wide deployment, preparing for, 95–98
widgets, cross-platform differences, 332
window.open( ) scripting, 6
windows
    chrome-free, 7
    closing (keyboard shortcut), 21
    navigating, 13
Windows Remote Desktop, 34
WPAD, 59
WSDL, 232

X

X.509 certificate standards, 64
XBL, 242
    creating a custom widget, 243
    overview, 241
    XHTML and, 242
XHTML
    and XBL, 242
    IE and, 93
    reports in, 206
XMethods SOAP web site, 225

XML
  attaching XSL to document, 221
  display modes, 200
  feature creep, 199
  fonts and character support, 107
  mixing with XHTML, 206
  namespaces, 199
  Namespaces specification, 205
  parsers, 200
  parsing an RSS feed, 252
  Raptor, 204
  RSS and, 252
  RXP tool, 204
  schema, 223
  Schema Primer, 224
  Schematron Validator, 204
  selecting a nodeset, 215
  standards support, 199
  SVG content and, 213
  validating, 203
  validation, 202
  viewport and, 219
  well-formed, 202, 218
  WSDL and, 232
  XLink, 199
  XML Spy, 204
  XMLStarlet, 204
  XSL and, 218
XML Binding Language (see XBL)
XML User-interface Language (see XUL)
XMLHttpRequest object, Firefox versus
      IE, 171
XML-RPC, 228
  local, 228
  scripting with JavaScript, 230
  versus SOAP, 228
XML_XUL libraries, 261
XPath
  client-side, 215
  exposing expression axes, 216
  standard, 218

XPCOM
  adding new component, 290–294
  components, 77
  RSS feeds and, 252
xpcshell testing tool, 294
.xpi extension, 24
XPI files, 317
  creating, 317
  signing, 68
XPInstall, 24, 303
XPM icons, 78
X-servers and X-clients, 34
XSL, 216
  client-side, 218
  stylesheet, creating, 220
  versus CSS, 219
XUL, 6, 230
  applications, 237
  caching, disabling, 190
  creating a template, 255
  dynamic, 254
  extension, creating, 229
  Firefox templates, 249
  generating with PHP libraries, 260
  overlays, 312
  sending application data to a
      server, 239
  simple template syntax, 249
  Spider application, 152
  SQL and, 254
XUL Planet, 223
xul.css master XBL stylesheet, 327
XUL/RDF template model, 262

Z

ZoneAlarm security monitor, 112

Colophon

Our look is the result of reader comments, our own experimentation, and feedback from distribution channels. Distinctive covers complement our distinctive approach to technical topics, breathing personality and life into potentially dry subjects.

The tool on the cover of *Firefox Hacks* is a flashlight. The flashlight is a portable illumination device that is typically fashioned from a miniature electric lightbulb and a parabolic reflector, which are mounted in a cylindrical casing containing an electric circuit, batteries, and a power switch. Invented in the late nineteenth century, the flashlight received its name because the batteries originally used to power the device had so little juice in them that people commonly switched the object on for just a brief instant at a time, emitting a quick "flash" of light to brighten their surroundings.

Sanders Kleinfeld was the production editor and copyeditor for *Firefox Hacks*. Jamie Peppard was the proofreader. Philip Dangler and Claire Cloutier provided quality control. Reg Aubry wrote the index.

Hanna Dyer designed the cover of this book, based on a series design by Edie Freedman. The cover image is an original photograph by Kevin Thomas. Emma Colby produced the cover layout with Adobe InDesign CS using Adobe's Helvetica Neue and ITC Garamond fonts.

David Futato designed the interior layout. This book was converted by Keith Fahlgren to FrameMaker 5.5.6 with a format conversion tool created by Erik Ray, Jason McIntosh, Neil Walls, and Mike Sierra that uses Perl and XML technologies. The text font is Linotype Birka; the heading font is Adobe Helvetica Neue Condensed; and the code font is LucasFont's TheSans Mono Condensed. The illustrations that appear in the book were produced by Robert Romano and Jessamyn Read using Macromedia FreeHand MX and Adobe Photoshop CS. This colophon was written by Sanders Kleinfeld.

Keep in touch with O'Reilly

1. Download examples from our books

To find example files for a book, go to:
www.oreilly.com/catalog
select the book, and follow the "Examples" link.

2. Register your O'Reilly books

Register your book at *register.oreilly.com*

Why register your books? Once you've registered your O'Reilly books you can:

- Win O'Reilly books, T-shirts or discount coupons in our monthly drawing.
- Get special offers available only to registered O'Reilly customers.
- Get catalogs announcing new books (US and UK only).
- Get email notification of new editions of the O'Reilly books you own.

3. Join our email lists

Sign up to get topic-specific email announcements of new books and conferences, special offers, and O'Reilly Network technology newsletters at:

elists.oreilly.com

It's easy to customize your free elists subscription so you'll get exactly the O'Reilly news you want.

4. Get the latest news, tips, and tools

http://www.oreilly.com

- "Top 100 Sites on the Web"—PC Magazine
- CIO Magazine's Web Business 50 Awards

Our web site contains a library of comprehensive product information (including book excerpts and tables of contents), downloadable software, background articles, interviews with technology leaders, links to relevant sites, book cover art, and more.

5. Work for O'Reilly

Check out our web site for current employment opportunities:

jobs.oreilly.com

6. Contact us

O'Reilly & Associates
1005 Gravenstein Hwy North
Sebastopol, CA 95472 USA
TEL: 707-827-7000 or 800-998-9938
(6am to 5pm PST)
FAX: 707-829-0104

order@oreilly.com
For answers to problems regarding your order or our products.
To place a book order online, visit:
www.oreilly.com/order_new

catalog@oreilly.com
To request a copy of our latest catalog.

booktech@oreilly.com
For book content technical questions or corrections.

corporate@oreilly.com
For educational, library, government, and corporate sales.

proposals@oreilly.com
To submit new book proposals to our editors and product managers.

international@oreilly.com
For information about our international distributors or translation queries. For a list of our distributors outside of North America check out:
international.oreilly.com/distributors.html

adoption@oreilly.com
For information about academic use of O'Reilly books, visit:
academic.oreilly.com